NAPOLEON
AND
WELLINGTON

NAPOLEON
AND
WELLINGTON

Andrew Roberts

Weidenfeld & Nicolson
LONDON

o 46810822

First published in Great Britain in 2001
by Weidenfeld & Nicolson

A CIP catalogue record for this book
is available from the British Library.

ISBN 0 29764607 9

Typeset by Selwood Systems, Midsomer Norton

Printed in Great Britain by
Butler & Tanner Ltd, Frome and London

Weidenfeld & Nicolson

The Orion Publishing Group Ltd
Orion House
5 Upper Saint Martin's Lane
London, WC2H 9EA

For Henry
Vive l'Empereur!

CONTENTS

ILLUSTRATIONS

ACKNOWLEDGMENTS

'It has become customary', wrote an author forty years ago in his introduction to a book about Napoleon's literary culture, 'for each new book or article on Napoleon to be prefaced by the author's apologies for adding yet more to the already enormous bibliography of this apparently overworked subject.' Pieter Geyl, in his great work *Napoleon: For and Against*, said that to qualify as a Napoleonic expert 'one must have devoted a lifetime to the study of the man and his period'. Even the Oxford historian J. Holland Rose, who did actually devote a lifetime to them, and produced perhaps the best single-volume biography ever written on the emperor, also prefaced his work with an apology for 'giving to the world a new life of Napoleon I'.

This book does not pretend to be a biography of either Napoleon or Wellington, but is instead a study of the personal relationship between the two men, and of the way that it evolved through their careers. It is therefore not a history of the Peninsular or Napoleonic Wars, nor a 'joint' biography, but I believe that it does have the merit of being an original idea. Others have written about the two men's military interaction, but this book concentrates on what each man thought, wrote and said about the other. Of course it is true that they never met, yet neither did Elizabeth I and Mary, Queen of Scots, but that did not preclude Schiller from writing a play about them.

To find a new angle on Napoleon has not been easy. On the shelves of the London Library alone there are books on his boyhood, his military education, his racial background (Arabian, according to one work), his libraries, his parents, his exiles and his religious beliefs. There are works covering his activities as a journalist, lover, revolutionary, gaoler, ruler of Elba, diplomat, family man, 'bisexual emperor', martyr, Corsican, patron of the arts, legend, tyrant and murder victim. There is a whole book devoted to his Coronation, and another to a single bequest in his will.

Then there are the books about Napoleon's relations with Louis XVIII, Marshal Bernadotte, the Jews, the Vendée, Jean-Jacques

Rousseau, the Empress Marie Louise, Poland, Persia, Palestine, Pope Pius VII, Talleyrand, the Archduke Charles, Egypt, the Spanish Court, Germany, the Bourbons, Queen Hortense, Europe, his parliaments and America.

There are books about the books about Napoleon, books likening him to Adolf Hitler, so-called 'autobiographies' of him, books about his iconography and many collections of his military maxims and *bons mots*. Archbishop Whately and J. B. Pérès even devoted clever little volumes to the proposition that Napoleon never existed. One day a book will be written about the books written about the books written about him. As a consequence, I feel little trepidation in adding this snowball to the avalanche of published Napoleana.

I should like to thank the Duke of Wellington for his gracious permission in allowing me full access to his private libraries at Apsley House and Stratfield Saye. Alicia Robinson, director of the Wellington Museum at Apsley House, was tremendously kind with her time and expertise, as were Hon. Georgina Stonor and Victoria Crake at both Apsley House and Stratfield Saye.

I should also like to thank Professor Jeremy Black, Brooks's Club for allowing me to quote from its Betting Book, Dr David Chandler, Stephen Duffy of the Wallace Collection, the late Col. John Elting, Roman Golicz, Paddy Griffith, John Gross for explaining literary allusions, Robin Harcourt Williams, Peter Hofschröer, Alistair Horne, Martin Howe QC for advice on the Code Napoléon, Dr James Le Fanu for his views on Napoleon's real and supposed illnesses, Lionel Leventhal of Greenhill Books, the unfailingly courteous and efficient staff at the London Library, the Marquess of Londonderry, Lady Longford, Grania Lyster, Philip Mansel, David Marks of Napoleonic Wargamers, Frank and Pauline McLynn, Rodney Melville, Gilbert Menne for showing me around Le Caillou, Dr Rory Muir, the staff of the National Army Museum, especially Julian Humphrys, Lord Powell of Bayswater, Dr Frank Prochaska, Dr Stuart Semmel, the staff at Southampton University Archives, Jonathan Terris of the Napoleonic Wars Re-enactment Society for explaining the complexities of musketry, Jean Tulard and Andrew Uffindell.

Several friends and specialists have done me the honour of reading my manuscript, and I should like to thank Claus von Bulow, Ian Fletcher, Leo Groth, C. W. Haigh, Col. John Hughes-Wilson, Julian Humphrys, David McAlpine, John Ogden, Richard Old, Stephen Parker and my father Simon Roberts for their enormously helpful advice.

I would like in particular to thank Ian Fletcher of the incomparable Ian Fletcher Battlefield Tours for showing me around the battlefields of Talavera, Albuera, Badajoz, Campo Mayor, El Bodon, Fuenteguinaldo, Almeida, the Coa, Fuentes d'Oñoro, Ciudad Rodrigo, Salamanca, Garcia Hernandez and Waterloo, which has been one of the greatest pleasures in writing this book. Philip Haythornthwaite's encyclopædic knowledge of the Napoleonic period and generosity with his time has also been invaluable.

For their great help in translating documents, I should like to thank Leone von Groot, Julietta Longcroft and Santa Sebag Montefiore. For their tremendously professional work, as well as their personal help and encouragement, I would like to thank my editor at Weidenfeld and Nicolson, Ion Trewin, my agent Georgina Capel of Capel & Land, and my copy-editor Peter James.

Camilla Roberts typed up the first eight chapters for me, for which I am, as for so much else, hugely in her debt. This book is dedicated to our three-year-old son Henry, in the hope that he will gain as much pleasure from the study of history in his life as I have in mine.

Andrew Roberts
andrew@roberts-london.com
May 2001

COMPARATIVE CHRONOLOGY

NAPOLEON

(compiled with grateful acknowledgments
to Felix Markham)

1769	AUG 15	Born
1779	JAN 1	Attends religious school at Autun
	MAY 15	Attends cadet school at Brienne
1784	OCT 30	Enters École Militaire, Paris, as *cadet-gentilhomme*
1785	FEB 24	Father dies of stomach cancer
	SEP 1	Leaves École Militaire as *sous-lieutenant* of artillery
1786	SEP 1	Goes to Corsica on leave (until June 1788)
1789	JUL 14	The storming of the Bastille
	SEP 15	Returns to Corsica
1790	JUL 14	On Paoli's return to Corsica, N. initially adhered to him
1791	FEB 10	Returns to regimental duty at Auxonne
	APR 1	Promoted *premier lieutenant*
	JUL 6	Takes oath of allegiance to National Assembly
1792	APR 1	Elected *lieutenant-colonel*, 2nd Battalion of Corsican Volunteers
	AUG 10	Witness to massacre of the Swiss Guards at the Tuileries
	AUG 19	Prussians invade France (defeated at Valmy on Sep 20)
1793	JAN 21	Execution of King Louis XVI
	FEB 1	Convention declares war on Britain and Holland
	MAR 3	Breaks with Paoli
	MAY 31	Reign of Terror starts in Paris under the Committee of Public Safety

WELLINGTON

(compiled with grateful acknowledgments
to Elizabeth Longford)

1769	MAY 1 *circa*	Born
1781	MAY	Father dies
	OCT	Enters Eton
1784		Leaves Eton and goes to Brighton for tutoring
1785		Goes to Brussels with his mother
1786	JAN 16	Enters School of Equitation, Angers, Anjou (until the end of the year)
1787	MAR 17	Gazetted ensign in the 73rd Highland Regiment
	DEC 25	Promoted lieutenant
1788	FEB	Arrives in Dublin as aide-de-camp to the viceroy
1790	APR	Elected MP for Trim in Ireland
1791	JUN 30	Promoted captain
1793	APR 30	Promoted major
	SEP 30	Promoted lieutenant-colonel

	JUN 13	Arrives with family in Toulon from Corsica
	AUG 27	Toulon handed over to British by Royalists
	SEP 16	Given command of artillery besieging Toulon
	OCT 18	Promoted *chef de battailon*
	DEC 17–19	Toulon recaptured
	DEC 22	Promoted *général de brigade*
1794	FEB 6	Given command of the artillery of the Army of Italy
	JUL 27	*Coup d'état* of 9 Thermidor, Year II
	JUL 28	Execution of Robespierre ends the Terror
	AUG 9–20	Imprisoned at Antibes on treachery charges
1795	MAY 2	Leaves Italy for Paris
	OCT 5	Day of the Sections insurrection put down by 'whiff of grapeshot'
	OCT 16	Promoted *général de division*
	OCT 26	Appointed to command the Army of the Interior
	OCT 30	Directory replaces the Convention as government of France
1796	MAR 2	Appointed to command the Army of Italy
	MAR 9	Marries Josephine de Beauharnais
	MAR 26	Assumes command of the Army of Italy
	APR 12	Defeats Austrians at Montenotte
	APR 13	Defeats Sardinians at Millésimo
	APR 14–15	Defeats Austrians at Dego
	MAY 10	Defeats Austrians at Lodi
	MAY 15	Enters Milan
	AUG 2–3	Defeats Austrians at Lonato
	AUG 5	Defeats Austrians at Castiglione
	NOV 15–17	Defeats Austrians at Arcole
1797	JAN 14	Defeats Austrians at Rivoli
	FEB 19	Signs the treaty of Tolentino with the pope
	MAY 16	Occupies Venice
	SEP 14	*Coup d'état* of 18 Fructidor, Year V
	OCT 17	Peace treaty of Campo Formio between France and Austria
	OCT 27	Appointed to command the Army of England
1798	FEB 23	Advises Directory against invading England
	APR 12	Appointed to command the Army of the Orient
	JUN 12	Annexes Malta
	JUL 1	Disembarks at Alexandria
	JUL 21	Defeats Mamelukes at the battle of the Pyramids

1794 JUNE   Commands a brigade in Flanders
     SEP 15   Fights first engagement at Boxtel

1795 MAR   Returns home

1796 MAY 3   Promoted colonel
     JUN   Sails to India in command of the 33rd Regiment of Foot

1797 FEB   Arrives in Calcutta

	AUG 1	French naval squadron destroyed by Nelson at the battle of the Nile
	DEC 2	Second Coalition formed against France
1799	FEB 20	Advances into Palestine
	MAR 7	Captures Jaffa and massacres Turkish prisoners
	MAR 18	Besieges Acre
	MAY 17	Abandons the siege of Acre, returns to Cairo (on Jun 14)
	AUG 23	Leaves Egypt for France (landing, Oct 9)
	NOV 9–10	Becomes consul after the 18th Brumaire Year VIII *coup d'état*
	DEC 12	Constitution of the Year VIII; first consul for ten years
1800	FEB 19	Takes up residence in the Tuileries Palace
	MAR 14	Pius VII elected pope
	MAY 15–20	Crosses the Great St Bernard Pass
	JUN 14	Defeats the Austrians at Marengo
	DEC 24	Survives assassination attempt in Paris
1801	FEB 9	Peace of Lunéville between France and Austria
	APR	Establishes invasion camp at Boulogne
	APR 2	Nelson destroys the Danish fleet at Copenhagen
	OCT 1	Preliminary Anglo-French peace treaty
1802	JAN 26	Becomes president of the Italian Republic
	MAR 25	Peace of Amiens between France and Britain
	MAY 19	Institutes the *légion d'honneur*
	AUG 2	Proclaimed first consul for life Annexes Elba
	SEP 2	Annexes Piedmont
	OCT 15	France invades Switzerland
1803	MAR 11	Orders two flotillas for invasion of Britain
	MAY 16	Britain declares war on France
	AUG 23	Invasion camps and flotillas assembled
1804	FEB	Generals Moreau and Pichegru arrested
	MAR 21	Duc d'Enghien kidnapped and executed
	MAR 24	Promulgation of the Code Civil (also known as the Code Napoléon)
	MAY 18	Proclaimed emperor of the French
	MAY 19	Eighteen marshals of the Empire created

1799 MAY 4   Seringapatam stormed and Tippoo Sultan killed.
               Becomes governor of Mysore

1800 SEP 10   Defeats Dhoondiah Waugh

1802 APR 29   Promoted major-general

1803 AUG 3   Second Mahratta War against Scindia of Gwalior
               and allies
      SEP 23   Victory at Assaye
      NOV 29   Victory at Argaum
      DEC 15   Surrender of Gawilghur
1804 SEP   Knighted

	DEC 2	Crowned emperor at Notre Dame in presence of Pope Pius VII
1805	MAY 26	Crowns himself King of Italy in Milan Cathedral
	AUG 3	At Boulogne, waiting to invade Britain
	AUG 9	Austria joins Britain and Russia in the War of the Third Coalition
	AUG 23	Breaks camp at Boulogne to march east
	OCT 20	Defeats the Austrians at Ulm
	OCT 21	Battle of Trafalgar
	NOV 14	Enters Vienna
	DEC 2	Defeats the Austrians and Russians at Austerlitz
	DEC 15	Convention of Schönbrunn between France and Prussia
	DEC 27	Treaty of Pressburg between France and Austria
1806	JAN 23	Death of William Pitt the Younger
	JUL 12	Becomes 'Protector' of the newly created Confederation of the Rhine
	AUG 6	Dissolution of the Holy Roman Empire
	OCT 7	Invades Saxony and Prussia
	OCT 14	Defeats Prussians and Saxons at Jena
	OCT 27	Enters Berlin
	NOV 21	Berlin Decrees create the Continental System
	DEC 18	Enters Warsaw
1807	FEB 8	Indecisive battle against the Russians and Prussians at Eylau
	JUN 14	Defeats Russians and Prussians at Friedland
	JUN 24	Confers with Alexander I and Frederick William II on a raft on the River Niemen
	JULY 7-9	Treaty of Tilsit between France, Russia and Prussia
	NOV 19	France invades Portugal
	NOV 30	Junot occupies Lisbon
1808	FEB 16	France invades Spain
	MAR 18	Charles IV of Spain forced to abdicate; Ferdinand VII declared king
	MAY 2-5	Anti-French revolt in Madrid, put down by Murat
	JUN 6	Joseph Bonaparte proclaimed King of Spain
	OCT 6	Alliance between France and Russia at Erfurt
	NOV 5	Assumes command of the Army of Spain
	NOV 23	Defeats Spaniards at Tudela
	DEC 4	Enters Madrid

1805	MAR 10	Returns home, calling at St Helena on the way
	SEP 10	Reaches England
	DEC	Takes a brigade to the Elbe

1806	JAN 30	Succeeds Lord Cornwallis as colonel of the 33rd Regiment
	FEB	Returns from the continent. Posted to Hastings
	APR 1	Elected MP for Rye
	APR 10	Marries Kitty Pakenham in Dublin

1807	FEB 3	A son, Richard Arthur Wellesley, born
	APR 3	Joins the Duke of Portland's ministry as Chief Secretary for Ireland
	JUL 31	Danish Expedition (until Sep 30)

1808	APR 25	Promoted lieutenant-general
	JUL 12	Placed in temporary command of expeditionary force to Portugal
	AUG 1	Lands in Mondego Bay, Portugal
	AUG 17	Defeats General Delaborde at Roliça
	AUG 21	Defeats General Junot at Vimeiro and is afterwards superseded
	AUG 31	Convention of Cintra; W. recalled to face an inquiry

	DEC 21	Crosses the Guadarrama in pursuit of Sir John Moore
1809	JAN 16	Moore dies at the battle of Corunna, but British evacuate
	JAN 24	Leaves Valladolid for France
	MAY 13	Enters Vienna
	MAY 17	Annexes the Papal States
	MAY 20–23	Defeated by Austrians at Aspern-Essling
	JUL 5–6	Defeats Austrians at Wagram
	OCT 14	Treaty of Schönbrunn between France and Austria
	DEC	Divorces Josephine by act of Senate
1810	APR 2	Marries Archduchess Marie Louise of Austria
	APR 17	Marshal Masséna appointed to command the Army of Portugal
	JUL 9	Annexes Holland
	AUG	Annexes Westphalia
	DEC	Annexes north-west Germany
1811	JAN	Annexes Oldenburg
	MAR 20	Birth of François-Charles-Joseph, King of Rome
1812	JAN 10	Occupies Swedish Pomerania
	JUN 24	Crosses the River Niemen into Russia
	AUG 18	Captures Smolensk
	SEP 7	Battle of Borodino
	SEP 14	Enters Moscow, which burns until 19th
	OCT 19	Evacuation of Moscow; the retreat begins
	NOV 14–18	Defeated by Russians at Krasnoi
	NOV 26–28	Disaster crossing the River Beresina
	DEC 5	Leaves the Grande Armée
	DEC 18	Arrives in Paris
1813	MAR 16	Prussia declares war on France
	MAY 2	Defeats Russians at Lützen
	MAY 20–21	Defeats Russians and Prussians at Bautzen
	JUN 4	Armistice of Pleischwitz brokered by Metternich
	AUG 12	Austria declares war on France
	AUG 26–27	Defeats Russians and Austrians at Dresden

1809	APR 26	Lands at Lisbon with a new British army
	MAY 12	Crosses the Douro and defeats Soult at Oporto
	JUN 27	Enters Spain
	JUL 6	Appointed marshal-general of the Portuguese army
	JUL 27–28	Defeats King Joseph and Marshal Jourdan at Talavera
	SEP 4	Created Viscount Wellington of Talavera
		Secret construction of the Lines of Torres Vedras
1810	SEP 27	Defeats Marshal Masséna at Busaco
	OCT 8	Enters the Lines of Torres Vedras
1811	MAR 5	Masséna begins retreat from Portugal to Spain
	MAY 3–5	Defeats Masséna at Fuentes d'Oñoro
	MAY 10	Marshal Marmont takes over Army of Portugal
	MAY 11	Almeida fortress surrenders
	MAY 16	Marshal Beresford defeats Marshal Soult at Albuera
1812	JAN 8–19	Captures Ciudad Rodrigo
	FEB	Created Earl of Wellington and Duque de Ciudad Rodrigo
	APR 6	Storms Badajoz (besieged since Mar 16)
	MAY 11	Spencer Perceval assassinated; Lord Liverpool becomes first lord of the Treasury
	JUL 22	Defeats Marmont at Salamanca
	AUG 12	Enters Madrid
	AUG 18	Created Marquess of Wellington
	SEP 19	Unsuccessful siege of Burgos (until Oct 21)
	SEP 22	Appointed generalissimo of Spanish Armies
	OCT 22	Retreat from Burgos (until Nov 19)
1813	MAR 4	Awarded the Order of the Garter
	JUN 21	Defeats King Joseph at Vitoria; becomes field marshal
	JUL 25	First assault on San Sebastián abandoned; city besieged
	JUL 28–30	Defeats Soult at Sorauren

	OCT 16–19	Defeated by Austrians, Russians, Prussians and Swedes at Leipzig
	OCT 18	Bavaria and Saxony join the Allies
1814	FEB 10	Defeats Russians at Champaubert
	FEB 11	Defeats Russians and Prussians at Montmirail
	FEB 12	Defeats Russians and Prussians at Château-Thierry
	FEB 14	Defeats Russians and Prussians at Vauchamps
	FEB 18	Defeats Westphalians and Austrians at Montereau
	MAR 1	Treaty of Chaumont between the Allies
	MAR 30–31	Allies enter Paris
	APR 2	Deposed by French Senate
	APR 6	Abdicates
	APR 26	Louis XVIII proclaimed King of France
	APR 27	Sails to Elba
	NOV 1	Congress of Vienna opens
1815	FEB 26	Sails from Elba
	MAR 1	Lands at Golfe Juan near Cannes
	MAR 18	Defection of Marshal Ney
	MAR 19	Louis XVIII flees Paris
	MAR 20	Enters Tuileries
	JUN 1	Ceremony of the Champ de Mai
	JUN 12	Leaves Paris and heads for the Army of the North
	JUN 15	Crosses Belgian frontier; captures Charleroi
	JUN 16	Defeats Prussians at Ligny
	JUN 18	Defeated by Anglo-Allied and Prussian armies at Waterloo
	JUN 22	Abdicates again
	JUL 7	Allies enter Paris
	JUL 15	Surrenders to Captain Maitland of HMS *Bellerophon* at Rochefort
	AUG 7	Leaves Plymouth on HMS *Northumberland* for St Helena
	OCT 17	Lands at St Helena
	DEC 7	Marshal Ney shot
1821	MAY 5	Dies
1840	DEC 15	Buried at Les Invalides

	AUG 31	Fall of San Sebastián
	OCT 7	Crosses Bidassoa river into France
	NOV 10	Defeats Soult at the Nivelle
	DEC 12	Defeats Soult at the Nive
1814	FEB	Crosses the Ardour and invests Bayonne
	FEB 27	Defeats Soult at Orthez
	MAR 12	Captures Bordeaux
	APR 10	Defeats Soult at Toulouse
	MAY 3	Created Duke of Wellington
	MAY 4	Reviews troops in Paris with Louis XVIII
	JUN 14	Bids farewell to troops at Bordeaux
	JUN 23	Returns to England for peace celebrations
	JUL 5	Appointed ambassador to France
	NOV 1	Congress of Vienna formally opens

1815	FEB 3	Arrives in Vienna as British plenipotentiary
	MAR 7	Congress hears of Napoleon's escape from Elba
	MAR 13	Congress 'outlaws' Napoleon
	MAR 28	Leaves Vienna
	APR 4	Arrives at Anglo-Allied army headquarters at Brussels
	JUN 15	Hears of French invasion of Belgium; Duchess of Richmond's ball
	JUN 16	Battle of Quatre Bras
	JUN 17	Withdraws to Mont St Jean
	JUN 18	Defeats Napoleon at Waterloo
	JUN 22	Crosses Belgian border into France
	JUL 3	France capitulates by treaty of St Cloud
	JUL 7	Allies enter Paris
	JUL 8	Louis XVIII restored to French throne
	OCT 22	Appointed commander-in-chief of the Allied army of occupation
	DEC 7	Marshal Ney shot

1828	JAN 9	Becomes prime minister
1830	NOV 16	Resigns premiership

1852	SEP 14	Dies
	NOV 18	Buried at St Paul's Cathedral

INTRODUCTION

It was not the Roman army which conquered Gaul, but Cæsar;
it was not the Carthaginian army which, before the gates of Rome,
made the Eternal City tremble, but Hannibal.

NAPOLEON

The Emperor Napoleon seemed confident of victory when he break-fasted with his senior generals at Le Caillou farmhouse on the Charleroi–Brussels road at eight o'clock on the morning of Sunday, 18 June 1815. He had feared that the Anglo-Allied army under the Duke of Wellington might have withdrawn from its defensive positions on the ridge of Mont St Jean during the night, but dawn had revealed it still in place. The meal was served on silver plate bearing the imperial arms, and once it was cleared away maps of the area were spread across the table and the council of war began.

'The army of the enemy is superior to ours by one-fourth,' Napoleon announced (incorrectly, as in fact the 72,000 French outnumbered the 68,000 Anglo-Allied troops). 'We have nevertheless ninety chances in our favour, and not ten against us.' At this, Marshal Ney – 'the bravest of the brave' – who had only just arrived, having reconnoitred the Anglo-Allied lines, warned: 'Without doubt, Sire, provided Wellington be simple enough to wait for you. But I must inform you that his retreat is decided, and that if you do not hasten to attack, the enemy is about to escape from you.' 'You have seen wrong,' the emperor confidently told him, 'and it is too late now. Wellington would expose himself to certain defeat. He has thrown the dice and they are in our favour.'

Marshal Soult, Napoleon's chief of staff, was not so sanguine. The previous evening he had urged the emperor to recall Marshal Grouchy, who had been sent off that morning with a very substantial force to chase the Prussian army after its defeat at Napoleon's hands at the battle of Ligny. As Soult had told a member of his staff, it was 'a great mistake to separate so large a force of some thirty thousand men from the main army which is facing the English', and he reiterated this view at the pre-battle conference.[1]

Soult had fought against Wellington in the Iberian Peninsula, always coming off worst, and consequently held the British army and its commander in high regard. Napoleon now used that fact against him, retorting that 'Because you have been beaten by Wellington, you consider him a great general. And now I tell you that Wellington is a bad general, that the English are bad troops, and *ce sera l'affaire d'un déjeuner.*' (A modern colloquial translation might be: 'We'll settle this matter by lunchtime,' or even 'This'll be a picnic.') It was a brutal put-down, and an unconvinced Soult merely answered: 'I earnestly hope so.'[2]

Soult's views were then supported by General Honoré Reille, the commander of II Corps, who entered the farmhouse in the company of his subordinate commander, Jérôme Bonaparte, Napoleon's youngest brother. When Napoleon asked Reille, who had also seen much service in the Peninsula, for his views on the British army, he was told:

> Well posted, and Wellington knows how to post it, and attacked from the front, I consider the English infantry to be impregnable, owing to its calm tenacity, and its superior aim in firing. Before attacking it with the bayonet, one may expect half the assailants to be brought to the ground. But the English army is less agile, less supple, less expert in manoeuvring than ours. If we cannot beat it by a direct attack, we may do so by manoeuvring.

According to those present, Napoleon had no verbal answer to this, merely rejecting Reille's warning with a dismissive shrug. General Maximilien Foy, yet another Peninsular veteran, then also interposed to say: 'Wellington never shows his troops, but if he is yonder, I must warn Your Majesty that the English infantry in close combat is the very devil!' Foy had been on the losing side in no fewer than eight major engagements against Wellington, with whom he had personally discussed 'la guerre' at dinner only the previous October.

Jérôme Bonaparte, meanwhile, warned his brother of a conversation overheard by a Belgian waiter at the King of Spain Inn in nearby Genappe, in which one of Wellington's staff officers had spoken of the Prussians linking up with the Anglo-Allied army. 'After such a battle as Fleurus', Napoleon said of the engagement now called Ligny, 'the junction between the English and Prussians is impossible for at least two days; besides, the Prussians have Grouchy on their heels.'[3] It seems not to have occurred to any except Jérôme, not even to the pessimistic Soult, that the Prussians might start to appear on the French right flank a mere five hours later.

Napoleon then laid down his plan of attack, which was far removed from the tactical manoeuvring called for by Generals Reille, Foy, d'Erlon and others. The Prussian field marshal Prince Blücher had been defeated at Ligny by a direct frontal assault, and now Napoleon wanted to repeat the tactic against Wellington. There would be a brief diversionary attack designed to draw the Anglo-Allied reserves away from the target area on their centre-left. Then, after a massive artillery bombardment, Napoleon's heavy cavalry, Imperial Guard and reserves would break Wellington's line and simply roll it up.[4] 'Gentlemen,' the emperor announced as he rose from the table to summon his mare Marie, the first of several horses he was to ride that day, 'if my orders are carried out well, tonight we shall sleep in Brussels.'[5]

Napoleon certainly seems implicitly to have believed it; he had even ordered his robes of state to be brought along for his address to the people of Belgium after his victory. Furthermore, the Old Guard had been ordered to carry their parade dress in their knapsacks for a triumphant entry into Brussels, and the emperor even ordered a well-done shoulder of mutton for his dinner that evening.[6]

With such seemingly overwhelming evidence of Napoleon's hubristic behaviour on the morning of the battle, it is hardly surprising that historians have accused him of gross over-confidence, of 'self-delusion', even of incipient lunacy. His underestimation of Wellington's capabilities is regularly held up as a factor to explain his subsequent defeat.[7]

The duke, meanwhile, was no less confident of success. He was pleased with the fields at Mont St Jean that he had reconnoitred the previous year for just such a defence. They had fine topography and access roads, and, most importantly, the Prussian army was within a few hours' hard march.[8] Early that morning Wellington had received word via his Prussian liaison officer, Baron Philipp von Müffling, that Blücher had 'put himself at the head of [his] troops, for the purpose of immediately attacking the enemy's right flank, should Napoleon undertake anything against the Duke'. Referring to a rude remark Napoleon had once made about him, Wellington told Müffling: 'Now Bonaparte will see how a general of sepoys can defend a position.' He afterwards stated that he had never taken so much trouble over his troop dispositions, as he knew he could never afford to make the slightest slip in the presence of a general as impressive as Napoleon.

It is understandable that almost all the historians of Waterloo have concluded that, in the words of one of them: 'Whereas Napoleon consistently misunderstood and underrated Wellington, Wellington was never in doubt about the genius of Napoleon.'[9] Yet the reality is not nearly so simple. History might not repeat itself, but historians repeat one another, and the myth has grown up of ludicrous Napoleonic over-confidence. This in turn, almost for the sake of contrast, has spawned a mirror myth of Wellington's modesty and near-perfect gentlemanliness, always ready to accord Napoleon the first place in the hierarchy of generalship. It is these two myths that the present work sets out to dispel, for the truth is far less straightforward and much more interesting.

Although Napoleon and Wellington never met or corresponded, and fought only one battle against each other, they spoke about one another a great deal both before Waterloo and afterwards. This study of their constantly evolving relationship will show that the received wisdom about Napoleon's disdain for Wellington's generalship and Wellington's respect for Napoleon's is, despite what was said at Le Caillou, entirely wrong.

We shall see how both Napoleon and Wellington regarded each other's military ability highly by the time they met at Waterloo. Thereafter both changed their minds and slowly began to damn each other's martial prowess to the point where – in part through a series of misunderstandings – Napoleon came to loathe Wellington, and rant about his ineptitude. Meanwhile, while maintaining a public stance of great respect for his opponent, Wellington came privately to despise Napoleon both as a general and as a man. This is not a joint biography, but rather a study in beliefs and rivalry, propaganda and rancour.

Napoleon and Wellington were not equals in any sense until they faced each other across the fields of Waterloo. In 1804, when Napoleon was proclaimed Emperor of France, Wellington was merely a knight of the Bath. From 1808 until 1814, when Napoleon was master of Europe, Wellington was only the commander of an expeditionary force in the Iberian Peninsula. Nor was Wellington in any sense the author of Napoleon's nemesis; that honour must go to the emperor himself when he conceived his plan to invade Russia in 1812. If the relationship between two men were reflected in a fable it would be that of the hare and the tortoise.

Napoleon's ambitions were monumental, incorporating Europe, Russia and even the Orient, while Wellington's were those of the rest of his class and profession, entirely circumscribed by parliamentary government. Yet although their characters are usually described as mirror opposites – romantic Napoleonic genius versus prosaic Wellingtonian practicality – there was a single-minded determination for victory and a tendency to ruthlessness that united them. Napoleon had won sixty of his seventy battles; Wellington had fought far fewer, but had won them all. For both men Waterloo was to be their last.

PART I

The Road to Waterloo

ONE

'A Fine Time for an Enterprising Young Man'
1769–1799

The Revolution is over. I am the Revolution.

NAPOLEON

The similarities between Napoleon and Wellington are, at first sight, extraordinary. They were born in the same year – 1769 – although controversy exists in both cases as to the precise day. Wellington is generally thought to have been born on 1 May, although the accounts of his nursemaid, the local newspapers and the baptismal record in the parish church differ. Similarly the exact date of Napoleon's birth is contested, but he himself chose 15 August, so it is likely that Wellington was around three months older. Wellington was born in Ireland, the son of a nobleman of English ancestry, part of the Protestant Ascendancy caste that ruled the island for the nearby larger power. Napoleon's father was one of the *noblesse* of Corsica who helped administer that island for France. Napoleon was educated away from his birthplace, at a French military academy; so too was Wellington. French was their second language. The Earl of Mornington, Wellington's father, died when he was twelve. Carlo Buonaparte died when his son Napoleon was fifteen. Both boys had four brothers and three sisters, and were brought up in straitened circumstances by formidable mothers.

In May 1798 Wellington changed his surname from Wesley to Wellesley (it had only a century before been Colley). Two years earlier, Napoléone Buonaparte (formerly Buona Parte) had become Napoléon Bonaparte, although 'it was one of the little meannesses of English and Royalist writers to insist upon the "u" in order to emphasise his alien origin'.[1] Both men chose Hannibal as their ultimate military hero. Both were autodidacts as young officers, setting aside a certain number of

3

hours each day for intellectual self-improvement; they both took Cæsar's *Commentaries* on campaign.

They saw their first action within a year of one another: Napoleon in Toulon on 16 September 1793 and Wellington in Holland on 15 September 1794.[2] Their greatest big breaks in life came through the good offices of their brothers: Lucien Bonaparte organised the Brumaire coup to make Napoleon first consul in 1799; and Richard Wellesley, the governor-general of British India, gave Wellington independent command in the Second Mahratta War in 1803. Attractive to women and voraciously sexual, neither man enjoyed a happy marriage. They did share two mistresses, however, or more precisely Wellington picked up two of the emperor's cast-offs. Also, Wellington's brother married Napoleon's brother's ex-wife's sister-in-law. George Bernard Shaw appreciated the paradoxes, quipping that: 'An English army led by an Irish general; that might be a match for a French army led by an Italian general.'

As soldiers, both men gave particular regard to topography and the study of maps, and were at ease with mathematics. (Trigonometry had a crucial practical function in enabling them to calculate the height of an escarpment for the benefit of artillery.) Both came to national prominence fighting in peninsulas. But there the similarities cease. For by the time Wellington – as I shall call him throughout – gained his first European command of any great note, in Portugal in 1808, Napoleon was already master of the continent. Yet, in the very meteoric nature of his rise, the seeds of Napoleon's nemesis were sown.

⌣

Since Wellington's refusal to be overawed by Napoleon primarily stems from his invincible self-assurance, which in turn came largely from the nature of his schooling, it is worth while examining his psychology up to the time, in the summer of 1793, when he, in an action pregnant with symbolism, burned his violin and embarked on a serious professional military career.

Wellington's remark about the battle of Waterloo having been won on the playing fields of Eton might well not have been a reference to the cricket pitches. An Eton historian, Lionel Cust, believes he was more probably alluding to 'the mills at Sixpenny Corner', which was where the boys went to fight one another. It was there, where the Wall Game is now played, that Wellington had a fight with Robert Percy 'Bobus' Smith, although sources differ on the outcome.[3]

4

In the three years that he was at Eton before being withdrawn, probably but not certainly for financial reasons, Wellington entirely failed to
distinguish himself in any capacity. 'A good-humoured, insignificant
youth' was all a contemporary, the 3rd Lord Holland (admittedly later
a political opponent), could remember about him there. Although it
might be too hard to call him 'the fool of the family', as the Eton beak
George Lyttelton did in one of his letters to the author Rupert Hart-
Davis, he was intellectually far behind his eldest brother Richard, who
had so shone at the school that he chose to be buried there.[4]

A glance at the Eton College register for the three years that
Wellington was a pupil there, from 1781 to 1784, shows how many of his
contemporaries were drawn from the aristocracy. Although Winchester
and Westminster had rivalled her socially in the past, by the late eight-
eenth century Eton was pulling away to become, as she unquestionably
was by the early nineteenth century, the grandest school in the country.
Wellington was educated with the offspring of three dukes, a marquess,
thirteen earls, five viscounts, seven barons and a countess whose title
was so ancient that it also went through the female line.

His Etonian contemporaries were a colourful lot, and provided a
number of his senior officers later on. Robert Meade, son of the 1st Earl
Clanwilliam, was a lieutenant-general by 1814, as was William Lumley,
son of the 4th Earl of Scarborough. Hugh Craven, son of the 6th Lord
Craven, was a colonel in 1814, a major-general in 1825, and shot himself
in his house in Connaught Place in 1836 owing to his losses on the race-
course at Epsom. At least his exit was intentional; Lord Barrymore, son
of the 6th Earl of Barrymore, died in an accidental explosion of his
musket while conveying French prisoners from Folkestone to Dover in
1793. George Evans, son of the 3rd Baron Carbery, died at Reddish's
Hotel in London from a burst blood vessel on New Year's Eve 1804,
and George de Grey, son of the 2nd Baron Walsingham, was burned to
death in bed at his home in Upper Harley Street. Robert King, son of
the 6th Baron Kingston, was tried at Cork assizes in 1798 for the
murder of Henry Fitzgerald, who had eloped with his sister. It was a
pretty clear-cut case but, astonishingly even for eighteenth-century
justice, he was unanimously acquitted by the House of Lords.

One of Wellington's school contemporaries, Henry Fitzroy, son of
Lord Southampton, married Anne, Wellington's sister, but he was less
fortunate in two others. Lord Holland, son of the 2nd Baron Holland,
and Charles Grey, son of Earl Grey, became leading Whigs and political opponents of his. Holland was later a bitter personal critic, describing Wellington in his memoirs as 'destitute of taste, wit, grace or

imagination', and a man whose vanity even 'exceeds his ambition' and who, 'little care[s] what troops he leads or what cause he serves, so that he, richly caparisoned in the front, be the chief pageant of the show and reap the benefit of the victory and the grace of the triumph'.[5] (The Whig hostess Lady Holland, an heiress of forceful personality, great beauty and ten thousand pounds a year, had heard Robespierre speak to the National Assembly during her five-year Grand Tour and had been most impressed.) The exaggerated loathing of the Whigs for the man who threatened and finally defeated their idol Napoleon was to be a constant feature throughout Wellington's career. They emerge from this story not as witty, brilliant, big-hearted Olympians of politico-social mythology, but as quotidian, nit-picking, mean-minded quasi-traitors.

Napoleon went to Brienne Military Academy speaking a Corsican patois and returned speaking French, but there is no suggestion that Wellington had even a smattering of an Irish brogue before attending Eton. Indeed throughout his life Wellington felt himself to be markedly superior to the Irish, once saying, albeit perhaps apocryphally, that they required 'only one thing to make them the world's best soldiers. White officers.'[6] He is also believed to have quipped that his own Irish birth no more made him an Irishman than being born in a barn made one a horse.

Eton gave Wellington a belief in himself and his capabilities that his ten subsequent years of doing very little indeed entirely failed to dent. There are suggestions that he was taken away from school not because the Wellesleys were too poor after the death of his father the 1st Earl of Mornington in 1781, but because his academic prospects were so unpromising.[7] This is somewhat discounted by the fact that Lady Mornington took him to Brussels, where the cost of living was noticeably lower, and where Wellington was taught by a local lawyer.

In 1786 Wellington was sent with an English tutor to the Royal Academy of Equitation at Angers in Anjou in western France, which was almost as much a finishing school as a military academy. He was thus able, in the dying days of the aristocracy-dominated, pre-Revolutionary *ancien régime* of the Bourbons, to catch a whiff of its splendour, while seemingly not noticing the stench of putrefaction below. 'How strange it would have been, Sir,' said a friend sixty years later, 'if instead of Angers you had been sent to Brienne and brought up with Napoleon!' Unfortunately Wellington's severely practical mind failed to speculate on the inherent possibilities, and he merely replied: 'Yes; but it could hardly have been. Brienne was reserved for Royal Military pupils.'[8]

Angers Academy left Wellington a lifelong francophile. Not for him the personalised dislike of the French exhibited by Nelson and Blücher, and reminiscent of Sir Francis Drake's fanatical loathing of the Spanish. Almost the only description we have of Wellington at Angers is of him 'lying on a sofa playing with a white terrier', although we know that he came away fluent in written and spoken French and, having met several of Anjou's nobility, a firm believer in the benefits of aristocratic government, something he upheld for the rest of his life.[9] His year in Angers aged seventeen was under the tuition of an unreconstructed admirer of the *ancien régime*, Marcel de Pignerolle, who brought him into contact with French nobility such as the Ducs de Brissac and de Praslin and the Duchesse de Sabran. (Brissac was later guillotined.)[10]

'There is a time of life', wrote a wise thinker and Tory statesman, 'when preferences and antipathies are easily implanted, and grow to be ineradicable moral sentiments of maturer years.'[11] Such a time was the late adolescence and early adulthood of Wellington. De Pignerolle helped mould his prejudice in favour of Bourbon Legitimism, the ancient government of France, which never left him. The death of de Pignerolle, shot for his opposition to the Revolution, only confirmed Wellington in his opinion. Political views are often formed as a reaction to external events that take place when in adolescence. Pitt the Younger was deeply affected by the American Revolution, which broke out when he was seventeen; Lord Salisbury was infuriated by the repeal of the Corn Laws when he was sixteen; Lenin was radicalised aged seventeen when his elder brother was hanged for attempted regicide; and Margaret Thatcher's views on Germany could not fail to have been influenced by the events of 1940, which took place when she was sixteen. Wellington was no different.

After Angers, despite his mother's admonition that 'anyone can see he has not the cut of a soldier', Wellington was gazetted a lieutenant in the 73rd Highland Regiment on Christmas Day 1787, but shortly afterwards left for the 76th Regiment, then for the 41st, then for the 33rd, largely for social reasons and to avoid service in the West Indies, which offered few opportunities for promotion or glory but many for illness and an early death. As an aide-de-camp to the lord-lieutenant of Ireland at Dublin Castle, a family-arranged appointment, and as an Irish MP representing his family borough in County Meath after his twenty-first birthday, Wellington simply trod water, showing little capacity for anything very worthwhile. A 438-page book has been written about Napoleon's 'genesis', his intellectual and moral development up to the age of twenty-four. Nothing of the kind could be possible for Wellington. We know that he was musical, taking after his father who, as well as an aristocrat, had been a professor of music at Trinity College, Dublin. He was 5 foot 9 inches tall, slim, with penetrating blue eyes and short curly hair, but by 1793 he was essentially a wallflower-cum-courtier going nowhere in particular in life. Then a Damascene conversion seems to have taken place.

Wellington could simply have sold his violin; he could have given it to a friend or relegated it to a cupboard, but instead he chose deliberately to burn it. We do not know the exact date in the summer of 1793 that it happened, but its message is obvious. The days of organising viceregal picnics were over. He was twenty-four and getting too old for fripperies. France had executed King Louis XVI that January and declared her egalitarian principles to be universal, something the rest of Europe, still largely ruled by their aristocracies, could not accept. In February, Britain formed the First Coalition against Revolutionary France, comprising Austria, Prussia, Holland, Spain and Sardinia. If Wellington was to become a professional soldier, rather than an uninspired amateur, he needed to forswear gambling and hard drinking – which he also did soon afterwards – and take his commission in the 33rd Foot seriously.[12] He would soon be sent on active service abroad, in the Low Countries, India, Spain, Portugal and eventually France itself. Did he resolve to roam while his fiddle burned?

In September 1794, Wellington came under fire for the first time during the ill-fated British expedition to the Low Countries in the War of the First Coalition against Revolutionary France. He was under the overall command of the Duke of York, who was grand but at thirty-one not particularly old, and who was as impressive a military administrator as he was unimpressive a battlefield commander. Wellington distinguished himself in the Low Countries, and came away having learned crucial lessons about how not to fight a campaign.[13] Learning much the same lessons at much the same time was Napoleon, who had also been learning many more besides.

⌐⌐

If his sense of class superiority was central to Wellington's psychological make-up, Napoleon was, at least initially, driven by a no lesser sense of racial insecurity, and by the suspicion that his father might have been a traitor to Corsica. 'I have a presentiment that one day this small island will astonish Europe,' wrote Jean-Jacques Rousseau in *The Social Contract* in 1762, and seven years later Napoleon was born.[14] Unlike Wellington, who hailed from the upper class, Napoleon was, at least in Corsican terms, upper-middle class. His mother Marie-Letizia

Ramolino was the daughter of a military engineer and the half-sister of Joseph Fesch, the archdeacon of Ajaccio Cathedral and a future cardinal. Fesch boasted how 'never had the Bonaparte family bought oil, wine or bread', because they owned the land on which it was produced.[15] (Fesch later became Napoleon's ambassador to the Holy See.)

Wellington considered Napoleon not to be a gentleman, but this was not on account of low birth. 'There are genealogists who would date my family from the Flood and there are people who pretend that I am of plebeian birth,' said Napoleon about his own social background; 'the truth lies between these two. The Buonapartes are a good Corsican family, little known for we have hardly ever left our island but much better than the coxcombs who take upon themselves to vilify us.'[16] When Wellington spotted this quotation in a book about Napoleon he made a pencil mark in the margin.

Although Napoleon was named after an uncle who had been killed fighting for Corsican independence, he was the first of his parents' children to be born a French subject. In 1761 the romantic Corsican patriot General Pasquale Paoli had expelled the Genoese, who had hitherto exercised sovereignty over the island. Then in 1768 France bought Corsica from Genoa and invaded. In 1769, the year of Napoleon's birth, the French defeated Paoli, who fled Corsica for London, where the British Government was considering its own invasion of the island. Had Carlo Buonaparte, a lieutenant and former secretary of Paoli's, gone over with him, Napoleon would have been brought up in England, with unimaginable historical consequences. Instead, however, in 1770 Carlo made his peace with the French and returned to Ajaccio.

His parents' friendship with the French governor, M. de Marbeuf, won Napoleon a place at Brienne, one of the twelve new cadet schools set up for sons of the *noblesse*. He attended Brienne, in the Champagne region, from 1779 to 1784, when he entered the École Militaire as *cadet-gentilhomme* to study artillery. As a defence against the teasing he had to endure at school as a Corsican whose claims to nobility were at best rather flimsy, Napoleon became a committed Paolist patriot.[17]

This did not throw him against his father, who died in February 1785 of stomach cancer, and whose accommodation with French rule was probably, like much of Corsica's, at best short term and opportunist. Paoli seems to have admired the young Napoleon, saying, perhaps apocryphally, that 'This young man is formed on the ancient model. He is one of Plutarch's men.'[18] However in 1791, when Napoleon asked Paoli to recommend documents from which he could write a history of the Corsican struggle for liberty, Paoli refused on the altogether laudable grounds that history-writing was no occupation for young men. Instead of writing history Napoleon decided to make it, and stood for election for the lieutenant-colonelcy of the 2nd Battalion of Corsican Volunteers, a more powerful post in the island than it sounds. In a contest violent and corrupt even by eighteenth-century small-town Corsican standards – featuring kidnapping, bribery, intimidation and thuggery – Napoleon was elected and his family's political friends in Paris blocked all investigation into the means.

Paoli, however, was horrified by what he called the 'corruption and intrigue' that the Bonaparte family had employed, and within a year Napoleon had broken with him altogether. The Bonapartes were eventually forced by the Paolists to leave Corsica for Toulon, where they arrived on 13 June 1793.[19] Within two months the French Royalists – who opposed the regicidal Revolution more than they did the idea of British troops on French soil – handed over Toulon to the Royal Navy. In helping to recapture the vital naval port, Napoleon embarked on the political and military odyssey that ultimately led to Waterloo.

The final break with Paoli, which took place on 3 March 1793, was not just another political event in a life full of such splits. Paoli had introduced Napoleon's parents to one another, had engaged his schoolboy and adolescent dreams for Corsican liberty, and had fired his early ambitions. Corsican independence was the great international liberal cause of the day; even James Boswell wrote an impassioned book on the subject. His schooling had nonetheless taught Napoleon that France, rather than an island of only three thousand square miles, was the proper stage for someone of his talents. To serve France precluded serving Paoli. On St Helena, Napoleon reminisced how at one stage 'Paoli urged me to enter the English service, he then had the power of procuring me a commission in as high a rank as I could expect; but I preferred the French because I spoke the language, was of their religion, understood and liked their manners, and I thought the beginning of a revolution a fine time for an enterprising young man.'[20] Conspicuously absent from this list was any reference to political principle or Gallic patriotism. Napoleon had been deracinated by his schooling; he was no longer fully Corsican, but he was not yet really wholly French. (Napoleon's opponent the writer François René de Chateaubriand later accused him of being 'so lavish with French blood because he does not have a drop of it in his veins'.)

Whether or not Napoleon had a country, he certainly had ambition and phenomenal intelligence. Well read, knowledgeable and keen to discuss literature, he 'studied books like a judge studying evidence in a lawsuit' (Goethe). An historian of his literary culture regards Napoleon as 'the young disciple of Rousseau, the young follower of the *philosophes*, the lover of French classical theatre, the admirer of Ossian'. The odd man out here is definitely Ossian, the ancient Gaelic martial poet 'discovered' in the 1760s by the impoverished Scottish writer James Macpherson. Ossian's poems had supposedly been written 1,500 years previously. Goethe admired Ossian, Boswell thought he 'excelled Homer', and Thomas Jefferson thought him 'the greatest poet that has ever existed'. So Napoleon, who took an Italian translation of Ossian's poems with him on campaign and had a series of paintings of the scenes from them made for his palace at Malmaison, was in good company in being taken in by Macpherson's elaborate literary hoax. Only Dr Samuel Johnson denounced the poems as forgeries, and, when asked whether he thought any modern man could have written them, answered: 'Yes, sir, many men, many women, and many children.'[21]

We know the books from which Napoleon made notes during his schooldays, including Machiavelli's *Histoire de Florence*, Voltaire's *Essai sur les moeurs*, Mirabeau's *Sur les lettres de cachet* and Barrow's *Histoire nouvelle et impartiale d'Angleterre*, and it is clear from these, from his recorded table-talk and from many of his actions that he possessed a fantastically powerful brain and cultured sensibility. Here is a man who attended the tragic play *Iphigénie en Aulide* no fewer than ten times, *Cinna* twelve times, *Andromaque* nine times, *Phèdre* ten times, *Hector* six times, *Mort de César* and *Mort de Pompée* five times each. Small wonder therefore that he saw himself in the classical military tradition.[22]

Napoleon made sure he had a front-row place at the most terrible event of the era, the French Revolution. He was a spectator at the storming of the Tuileries royal palace on 10 August 1792, where the King's Swiss Guard was massacred and after which the royal family was imprisoned. He later said that Louis XVI could have ended the Revolution there and then, 'if only he had got on his horse'. But the virility of earlier days had been replaced by sterility or even lunacy in almost all the courts of Europe. No amount of genius could have permitted Napoleon to impose his will on the Europe of Frederick the Great of Prussia (*reg* 1740–86), Louis XV (*reg* 1715–74), Catherine the Great of Russia (*reg* 1762–96), Maria Theresa of Austria (*reg* 1740–80) and George III of England (*reg* 1760–1820), who had together controlled the continent in the 1760s and 1770s. Yet, a mere sixteen years after 1780, Frederick had been replaced by the weak Frederick William, Catherine by the foolish Tsar Paul, and King George III had gone insane. (Austria took another generation to produce a near-imbecilic ruler, in Emperor Ferdinand, who was described by Lord Palmerston as 'the next thing to an idiot', and whose best-known announcement was 'I am the Emperor and I want dumplings!') By the 1790s, therefore, its leadership ensured that Europe was ripe for anarchy and war. The age made Napoleon quite as much as Napoleon made it.

One of the reasons why France succeeded in dominating Europe militarily is that she had a vast population relative to her neighbours. In 1780 the figures were roughly as follows (in millions): France 25.1, Great Britain 9.5, Prussia 5.4, Austria 20.2, Italy 12.8, Spain 9.9 and Russia 26.8. With national conscription of a substantially larger population than other racially cohesive western European countries, France would have found herself in a strong position militarily even without Napoleon. For all the logistical problems of the Russian campaign of 1812, for example, the difference in the two countries' populations was not so marked.

Napoleon's rise to power could hardly have been more meteoric. In December 1793, a supporter of the Revolution and aged only twenty-four, he was instrumental in recapturing Toulon from the Royalists and the British navy, and he was promoted *général de brigade*. Only three months later he was given command of the artillery of the Army of Italy, an important theatre of war as France tried to export her revolutionary principles to a rich peninsula the northern part of which was keen to throw off the yoke of Austria. France had been at war with Austria since April 1792, and with Sardinia since the following July, and it was felt that the heaviest blows could be dealt against them in Italy. After a brief but presumably terrifying period in prison at Antibes on suspicion of treason, he was back with the army. By 16 October 1795 he was a *général de division*, and ten days later he was promoted to command the Army of the Interior. Only five months after that, still aged just twenty-six, Napoleon was appointed to command the Army of Italy.

There were many reasons to explain his rise, relating to the military situation, other generals and French domestic politics, which had little or nothing to do with Napoleon, but the fact remains that he was the right man at the right time, as his brilliant series of victories in April 1796 over the Austrians and Sardinians at Montenotte, Millésimo, Dego and Mondovi all immediately bore witness. Yet just as Shakespearean tragic heroes have a fatal flaw, almost unnoticeable at the time of their greatness, the speed of Napoleon's promotion from *chef de bataillon* (major), achieved in October 1793, to commander-in-chief of the Army of Italy in March 1796 left him with an Achilles heel. He never handled infantry in combat at regimental level.

'I do not believe in the proverb that in order to be able to command one must know how to obey,' said Napoleon, and from 1796, and certainly after the *coup d'état* of 18th Brumaire, Year VIII (9 November 1799) which installed him as a consul, and soon afterwards as first consul, he only ever had to obey his own instincts, or (much more occasionally) his conscience. His successes on the field of battle had marked him out for political advancement in a France sick of the Terror and desperate for stability, yet his lack of experience at the regimental level was to cost him dear at Waterloo. Whereas Wellington could, and did, enter into the thick of the fighting and take over the command of individual regiments, such as Maitland's Foot Guards, understanding precisely how such troops could be handled to best effect, Napoleon had spent too long with grand strategy and with maintaining overall morale to know what he could realistically expect even from the Imperial Guard, which he all but wasted during the battle. When on the morning of Waterloo Napoleon's generals begged for manoeuvrability rather than a massed assault, they were demonstrating their experience of warfare at the regimental and company level. Yet Napoleon, who had almost none, overruled them. His experience of company-level action was virtually confined to the suppression of riots, in Lyon in August 1786, Seurre in April 1789, Auxonne in July 1789, Ajaccio in June 1793 and, most famously, the 'whiff of grapeshot' he administered to the Parisian Royalists in putting down the 'Day of the Sections' attempted coup in October 1795.[23]

For twenty years none of this would matter, as Napoleon imposed his genius upon Europe as army commander, then consul, then first consul for life. In one of those superb coincidences in which history abounds, in the same week in May 1804 that Napoleon was proclaimed emperor of the French by the Senate and Tribunate, his greatest British political opponent William Pitt the Younger returned to office as prime minister. Wellington, meanwhile, had to content himself that September with a mere knighthood.

Already by 1804 the scene was therefore set for the next decade. Napoleon, the meteor, was master of France, yet for all his great genius the seeds of his future destruction were being sown. He had never learned how to handle infantry at regimental level and all that he had learned about supply lines and not relying on living off the land on campaign he was starting to forget as victory piled upon victory and his ambitions stretched further and further afield. Meanwhile Wellington's campaigns in India had taught him lessons that were to prove invaluable a decade hence.

TWO

Apprenticeship at Arms
1799–1805

At twenty-nine years of age I have exhausted everything.
It only remains for me to become a complete egoist.
NAPOLEON

The remark Wellington made to Müffling on the morning of
Waterloo – that he would show Napoleon what a 'sepoy
general' was capable of – demonstrates that the emperor's dismissive description must have hit home. It was a common enough
assumption made by soldiers who had never served in India that campaigning there did not quite constitute real soldiering. Even in the
British Empire those soldiers whose primary experience had been in
India were often, very unfairly, deemed second rate. As one of
Wellington's military textbooks plaintively put it: 'An English general,
who returns from India, is like an admiral who has been navigating
the Lake of Geneva.' Yet the British army had been fighting in
defence of the East India Company's interests in the sub-continent for
over half a century, and very successfully.

In a tale told by Sir William Fraser, a collector of Wellingtonian
anecdotes, when Napoleon heard about Wellington's victory over the
Mahrattas at the battle of Assaye in September 1803, he exclaimed:
'That is the man with whom I shall have to deal.' When the 2nd Duke
of Wellington tried to ascertain the story's provenance from Fraser
while out riding in Hyde Park years later, all Fraser could say was that
he 'was quite sure that I heard it on some very good authority'.[1] In
fact it sounds like a typical example of the 'destiny-anecdote' of a type
well known to historians. The story is most probably as apocryphal as
another one in which Paoli was supposed to have told Napoleon to
'Go forth and be the successor of Alexander.' One should always view
with caution stories in which two antagonists 'destined' to meet years

later are reported to have made fateful predictions about one another.

Assaye was, however, a brilliantly fought engagement – indeed, along with the battle of Nivelle in 1813, Wellington himself rated it his best. He attacked an enemy force of forty thousand across a river with only seven thousand men, and had one horse bayoneted and another shot from under him. 'I never saw a man so cool and collected,' recollected a staff officer afterwards. For all his coolness at the time, that night he seems to have suffered from what today might be termed a form of post-traumatic stress disorder. 'I slept in a farmyard,' he later recalled, 'and whenever I awakened, it struck me that I had lost all my friends, so many had I lost in that battle. Again and again, as often as I awakened, did it disturb me. In the morning I enquired anxiously after one and another; nor was I convinced that they were living till I saw them.'[2]

Wellington deserved far better than to be dismissed by Napoleon as a 'sepoy general', not least because sepoys – the Indian private soldiers serving under the British – were in the main excellent fighting men, something Napoleon never really appreciated. Moreover, as a result of campaigns such as the Mahratta Wars, Wellington and his brother Richard Wellesley, the governor-general of India and later 1st Marquess Wellesley, were able to annex a larger territory than the whole of Napoleon's conquests in Europe to an empire that was to last much longer.[3] His soldiering in India taught Wellington, as he put it, that 'Articles of provision are not to be trifled with, or left to chance.' Indian armies that did not properly organise supply simply starved, and Wellington – who had commanded a sepoy army of over fifty thousand by the time of his thirty-fifth birthday – put the lessons he learned there to invaluable use in the Iberian Peninsula from 1808.

Napoleon's dismissal of Wellington's Indian service came from his automatic assumption of the inferiority of non-white troops in general, which his expedition to Egypt in order to threaten British India in 1798 had done nothing to dispel. At the battle of the Pyramids that July, when he was trying to subdue Egypt, Napoleon lost only thirty men against two thousand of the Mameluke enemy killed, and captured four hundred camels and fifty cannon. He told his troops before the battle that forty centuries were contemplating their efforts in the shadow of the Pyramids, and he took it entirely for granted that a white army would defeat a black one. He was deeply unimpressed in 1801 when he sent his brother-in-law General Victor Emmanuel Leclerc to San Domingo (modern-day Haiti) to oust the black dictator Toussaint l'Ouverture, and Leclerc failed, dying in the attempt.

In a conversation on St Helena with Captain Basil Hall, RN, who was returning from China and India in 1817, Napoleon 'adverted in a careless way to our news from India, and spoke of the Mahratta War as a circumstance of no importance'.[4] He had long assumed that he needed only to have presented himself on the borders of India with a relatively small army for the whole sub-continent to fall to him. 'The time is not far distant when we shall feel that, in order truly to destroy England, we must occupy Egypt,' Napoleon informed the French government, the Directory, in August 1797, long before he was appointed to command the Army of the Orient. As early as 1788 he had annotated a book on Turkish warfare with the words: 'Through Egypt we shall invade India, we shall re-establish the old route through Suez, and cause the route by the Cape of Good Hope to be abandoned.' Meanwhile Wellington had the previous year recognised the French threat, writing that 'As long as France have an establishment in Mauritius, Great Britain cannot call herself safe in India. They will come here to seek service in the armies of the native princes, and all Frenchmen in such a situation are equally dangerous.'[5]

It was Napoleon's plan, after taking Egypt, to join forces with the anglophobic Tipu Sultan of Mysore in south-west India, in order to attack the British. Packing James Rennell's *Bengal Atlas containing maps of the Theatre of War and Commerce on that side of Hindoostan* (1781), Napoleon sailed for Egypt on 19 May 1798. By mid-September Wellington's brother Richard Wellesley had received orders from London to require 'a satisfactory explanation' of Tipu's conduct, and if Tipu mobilised his army he was authorised to 'carry our arms into our enemy's country'.

If Napoleon had not heard of Wellington at this early stage in their careers, he would undoubtedly have known of his eldest brother, Richard Wellesley the 2nd Earl of Mornington. A committed empire-builder and foe of France, Wellesley was keen to invade Mysore. The secretary for war, Henry Dundas, had been warned by his spy the Abbé de Lisle, via a source in Frankfurt, that Tipu and Zeman Shah, the ruler of Afghanistan, had both been promised troops by Napoleon to use against Britain.[6]

On 1 August 1798 Admiral Nelson, having missed Napoleon's original disembarkation at Aboukir Bay near Alexandria in Egypt by only a matter of days, had caught up with and destroyed the French fleet there at the battle of the Nile. Only two of the thirteen French ships-of-the-line escaped. Diving research on the fleet has confirmed that Admiral Brueys had left far too large a gap between his fleet and the shore, through which Nelson manoeuvred his ships. The sarcasm dripped from Richard Wellesley's pen as he informed Tipu of the victory: 'Confident from the union and attachment subsisting between us that this intelligence will afford you sincere satisfaction, I could not deny myself the pleasure of communicating it.'[7] A letter from Napoleon written ten weeks later told Tipu that he had 'arrived on the coasts of the Red Sea with an innumerable and invincible army, filled with the desire to deliver you from the iron yoke of England'. In fact Napoleon only had thirteen thousand men and was about to be halted by the British admiral Sir Sidney Smith at the walls of the crusader city of Acre. By the time the letter arrived at Seringapatam four months later, Tipu was dead and Wellington was its governor.

It is not hard to guess how long Tipu might have fared as an independent sovereign had Napoleon triumphed at Acre. 'France, being mistress of Egypt, would also regain mastery of Hindoostan', Napoleon later opined when in exile on the island of St Helena. At the time he wrote of sixty thousand men and fifty thousand camels reaching the Euphrates in forty days and joining forces with the Sikhs and Mahrattas to destroy the British in India, in what he portrayed as a relatively straightforward campaign.[8] He often returned to the subject. In 1808 he instructed his ambassador in Moscow, General Armand de Caulaincourt, to tell the tsar 'that I am seriously considering an expedition to India and a partition of the [Turkish] Ottoman Empire. To carry out this project, I would march an army of twenty to twenty-five thousand Russians, eight to ten thousand Austrians, and thirty-five to forty thousand French into Asia and thence to India. Nothing is easier than this operation.'[9]

Even when he was about to embark on the road to Moscow in 1812 Napoleon told his war minister, the Comte de Narbonne, that:

> this long road is the road to India. Alexander left from as far away as Moscow to reach the Ganges. . . . I imagine Moscow taken, Russia overthrown, the Tsar reconciled or murdered by a palace plot, a new or dependent throne perhaps; and tell me if it is not possible for a large army of Frenchmen and auxiliaries to leave Tiflis and gain access to the Ganges, and that the touch of a French sword is all that is needed for the framework of mercantile grandeur to collapse.[10]

That is all that British India was to Napoleon – 'mercantile grandeur' – and men like Wellington who were busy defending and extending it were mere 'sepoy generals' whose armies would collapse at 'the touch of a French sword'. There is no real reason why Napoleon, now first consul, should have particularly concerned himself with the activities of the Indian governor-general's younger brother in 1800, while he was occupied smashing the Austrians thousands of miles away in Italy, but if he had he would have noticed a ruthlessness and willingness to scorch earth that was a decade later to turn his forces back from the heavily fortified Lines of Torres Vedras in Portugal.

Although he was later renowned for his clemency and dislike of war, in May 1800 Wellington ordered the commander of a punitive expedition to Malabar in India to burn the Mapilla tribes' villages and carry off their property and livestock. He explained this policy of near-extermination in the following chilling, if compelling, terms: 'The confidence of our native troops will be increased and that of their opponents diminished.'[11] He even explicitly advocated the employment of 'Terror'. Later that year his brother appointed him to command the expedition to attack those French whom Napoleon had left stranded in Egypt, via the Red Sea. First the plans changed, and then so did the commanders, and finally, while still in Bombay, Wellington was brought down by a particularly unpleasant form of ringworm called the 'Malabar Itch'. Were the Mapillas exacting their revenge?

One of his twentieth-century biographers, Richard Aldington, employed full poetic licence in drawing a word-picture of Wellington's situation towards the end of 1802:

> Even the news received in the late autumn, that he was gazetted major-general, failed to move him to any expression of excitement or gratitude...for over in Paris was another general officer, three months his junior, and not only Commander-in-Chief of the greatest army in the world but First Consul and Consul for Life – dictator of France. Ten thousand sepoys and Mysore were small beer in comparison; and campaigns against Tipu, Phoondiah, and minor Rajahs and Polygars trifling when compared with Lodi, Rivoli, the Pyramids, and Marengo. The whole world was ringing with the name of Napoleon Bonaparte; outside the services and a circle of friends who had heard of Major-General the Honourable A. Wellesley? Was he destined to return home with a modest competence, and to end his days as a General on half-pay, entertaining the ladies with oft-told stories of Seringapatam and the Bullum Polygar?[12]

To make matters worse, a month later Wellington discovered that

Britain had signed a peace treaty with France at Amiens back on 25 March 1802, ending the War of the First Coalition. His brother was livid, writing to the former foreign secretary and leader of the 'war' party in the House of Lords, William Grenville: 'I believe I should have expired of grief, shame and indignation if I had been on the spot.' Despite being instructed to return captured French territories under the terms of the peace treaty, Wellesley held on to them, hoping that the peace would collapse, as it eventually did when Britain declared war on France on 16 May 1803.

‹~›

Napoleon had every excuse for not being cognisant of Wellington by the time of the battle of Assaye, although the man who had destroyed his would-be ally Tipu Sultan might have been expected to have excited a modicum of interest. He seems to have read a book in or about 1809 which greatly praised his future opponent's military exploits, and which ought to have opened his eyes to the realities of campaigning in India. Two months after landing on St Helena in 1815, Napoleon had a conversation with Colonel Mark Wilks, the governor of the island, who had served with Wellington in Mysore and Deccan. It went as follows:

> Napoleon: But how does it happen that the Indians are so *lache* [cowardly] as to allow you to remain: are they in intellect and physical powers no better than Africans?
> Wilks: I know of the Hindus to be equal to our own; the physical powers are certainly inferior to those of Europeans; but the courage of the military classes is of a high order.
> Napoleon: Then you reckon your sepoy troops equal to Europeans?
> Wilks: The best of them are, at least, equal.

Napoleon then asked whether Wilks had read Lord Valentia's work, a three-volume book entitled *Voyages and Travels in India, Ceylon, the Red Sea, Abyssinia, and Egypt in the Years 1802–1806*, which had been published in 1809. Wilks wrote that Napoleon was 'intimating that he had himself seen it, and enquiring my opinion regarding its merits'. Wilks discounted Valentia's work, which surprised Napoleon: 'How? Are not his facts correct!'[13] Wilks had known Viscount Valentia in India and disliked him for breaking the convention whereby presents received from the local princes were subsequently handed over to the East India Company's representatives. He also complained that Valentia travelled 'full speed through a country' and therefore misapprehended the places he visited, which considering the viscount spent four and a half years compiling his information in them seems not to have been his best argument.

In the second volume of his work, which was republished in 1811 with a dedication to Wellington's brother Richard, Valentia went into pæons of praise about 'the military and civil talents of General Wellesley' during the Mahratta Wars. In particular he instanced Wellington's brilliant mastery of supply and provisioning: 'Of this branch of the military art, General Wellesley has shown himself a perfect master; and had added to it a decision in council, a spirit in action, which has rarely appeared in India...Uniform success attended him in the Mahratta War.'[14]

It might of course be that Napoleon read Valentia's book in the period between the battle of Waterloo in June 1815 and the conversation with Wilks in January 1816, by which time its information about Wellington's talents would have been galling but useless. Far more probable, however, is that with his interest in an eventual recrudescence of his Oriental ambitions Napoleon read *Voyages and Travels* some time after 1809, when its references to Wellington's abilities could have been a useful pointer to explain what was then going on in the Iberian Peninsula.

⤳

Napoleon appears to have no had racial prejudice against Wellington on the grounds that he came from Ireland. In the *Moniteur*, France's official newspaper, he or one of his propagandists regularly tried to encourage the Irish to rise against English 'tyranny' there, but otherwise Napoleon's views on Ireland seem to have been confined to thinking the French General Humbert's 1799 invasion attempt of Ireland 'une opération aussi ridicule'. His later castigation of Wellington as representative of the 'English oligarchy' implies that he almost certainly appreciated that Wellington was part of the Protestant Ascendancy of Ireland – racially entirely Anglo-Saxon with not so much as a hint of Celtic blood.

Napoleon's views on the English are usually summed up in his infamous phrase 'The English are nothing but shopkeepers, and their glory consists in their wealth,' popularly recalled as 'The English are a nation of shopkeepers.' It is however doubtful that the phrase was even originally his. It has been attributed to General Paoli – rather ungrateful of him if so, considering the refuge they afforded him for years – and also to the politician Barère who told the National Assembly about Admiral Howe's great naval victory in the English Channel on the Glorious First of June 1794: 'Let Pitt then boast of his victory to his *nation boutiquière*.' Nonetheless the phrase is taken to be Napoleon's last word on his most consistent and committed enemy.

Yet here is a selection of other remarks Napoleon made about the English, which show that he had a much more complicated view of his opponents than is generally appreciated:

In England the aristocracy are absolute masters, and the moment any reform threatens their power or privileges they raise the habitual cry: 'The foundations of the constitution are being destroyed.'

England, which the economists who preach freedom of trade constantly quote as a model, is in reality the country of prohibitions.

There is a greater number of honourable men, proportionately, in England than in any other country; and yet they have some very bad men there – they are in extremes.

All the evils, all the scourges that can afflict humanity, come from London.

England is said to traffic in everything. I should advise her to sell liberty, for which she could get a high price, and without any fear of exhausting her stock.

Shakespeare had been forgotten in England for two centuries: Voltaire, who lived in Geneva, and who wished to flatter Englishmen of his acquaintance, praised him, and everybody began to repeat that Shakespeare was the greatest poet in the world.

What might not be hoped from the English army, if each who behaved well had the chance of becoming a general some day?

The English seem to prefer the bottle to the society of their women; after dinner they dismiss the ladies from the table and remain for hours drinking and intoxicating themselves.

The English are in everything more practical than the French; they emigrate, marry, kill themselves, with less indecision than the French display in going to the opera.

You must never mention insurrection to an Englishman; it frightens people in his country, where the people's party has been suppressed.

Napoleon, as with so many people of the day, was much given to ascribing stereotyped characteristics to entire nations. The Spanish, he told Caulaincourt, were 'lazy', 'half savage', superstitious, unpatriotic smugglers who 'only go into danger where there was hope of booty'. They were at an even lower stage of civilisation than the Russians, and the Spanish peasant 'hates anything that tends to bring him out of his condition of barbarism'.[15] The Italians, though certainly civilised, were little better, as Napoleon complained to the diplomat Prince Charles-Maurice de Talleyrand in October 1797: 'You do not know the Italian people. They are not worth the lives of forty thousand Frenchmen. Since I came to Italy I have received no help from this nation's love of liberty or equality, or at least such help has been negligible. Here are the facts: whatever is good to say in proclamations and printed speeches is romantic fiction.' (And thus not unlike the propaganda Napoleon himself put out. The French had a simile for it: 'to lie like a bulletin'.)

Wellington was not far different in his views, especially when it came to the Spanish, whom he also described in extremely unflattering terms. His letters home were full of complaints about 'the inactivity of the [Spanish] magistrates and the people: to their disinclination to take any trouble, excepting that of picking up their property and running away when they hear the approach of a French patrol; and to their habits of insubordination, and disobedience of, and the want of power in, the Government and their officers.' Spanish quarter-masters and especially vendors of victuals for the troops aroused his special ire. He made it his business not to take any risks trusting the assurances of Spaniards, from Don Martin de Garay, the war minister, via the commander-in-chief, General de la Cuesta, right down to the lowliest supplier. Wellington ensured that British quartermasters controlled every step of the re-supply route from the place the Royal Navy brought stores ashore all the way up to the front line.

As for Spanish troops in action, Wellington wrote of 'the frequent – I ought to say, constant and shameful misbehaviour of the Spanish troops before the enemy... In the battle of Talavera [in 1809] whole corps threw away their arms, and ran off in my presence when they were neither attacked nor threatened, but frightened, I believe, by their own fire.' Later on he wrote of the 'lamentable' Spanish infantry: 'I have never seen them behave otherwise than ill.' The Portuguese initially fared little better. Writing to Lord Castlereagh's half-brother, Sir Charles Stewart, the British minister to Prussia, in July 1813, Wellington complained that the British army had 'met with nothing but ingratitude from the Government and authorities of Portugal for their services... I hope... that we have seen the last of Portugal.'[16]

Individual Spaniards could be absolved; one of the members of Wellington's staff at Waterloo was his friend General the Marquess of

Alava. When Miguel Alava was forced out of Spain by reactionaries long after the Peninsular War, he was put up in a house on Wellington's Hampshire estate and introduced to Coutts' Bank with the noble words: 'This is my friend, and as long as I have any money at your house, let him have it to any amount that he thinks proper to draw for.' Overall, however, Wellington's view was that 'Nothing can ever be done with the Spaniards, except by coming to extremities with them,' and he did not allow the Spanish army to enter southern France in 1814 because he knew the plundering would destroy his hopes of bringing Frenchmen over to the Allies.[17]

Britain's greatest military hero was thus advanced by unashamed nepotism, purchase and jobbery, helped in his campaigning by racial assumptions which led him never to rely too much on the word of local suppliers, and was above all sustained in his belief in ultimate victory by his snobbery and consciousness of class superiority over his rival, whom he considered to be not a real gentleman. A combination, therefore, of nepotism, racism and snobbishness – all anathema to twenty-first-century liberal society – saved Europe from despotism.

Wellington's castigation of Napoleon as not a gentleman was made explicit in 1826 when he told a friend, the Tory politician John Wilson Croker, that 'Buonaparte's mind was, in its details, low and ungentlemanlike. I suppose the narrowness of his early prospects and habits stuck to him; what <u>we</u> understand by <u>gentlemanlike</u> feelings he knew nothing about.' As an instance of Napoleon's ungentlemanly behaviour, Wellington told Croker of a watch made by Breguet in Paris that had been given him by his former second-in-command in the Peninsula, Sir Edward Paget. It had a map of Spain 'most admirably enamelled' on the case. Napoleon had ordered it as a present for his brother Joseph, the King of Spain, but when he heard about Wellington's victory at the battle of Vitoria in June 1813 he wrote to forbid its being presented. 'The best apology one can make for the strange littleness is that he was offended by Joseph; but even in that case, a <u>gentleman</u> would not have taken the moment when the poor devil had lost his *châteaux en Espagne*, to take away his watch also.'[18] A more charitable explanation might be that Napoleon appreciated how a watch with a map of Spain would not be the most tactful present for a monarch so recently deposed from his throne, but that does not seem to have occurred to Wellington.

Wellington's view of Napoleon as ungentlemanly was implicit in all that he said and wrote about the emperor from far earlier than 1826. There are several grounds on which he could have based this unflattering assessment of Napoleon's character, not all of them wholly fair. The foremost historian of the British army, Sir John Fortescue, wrote that Wellington was prouder of being an 'English gentleman' than of anything else (clearly agreeing with the duke himself about the lack of any Irish dimension to him). Wellington has also been described by a present-day historian as 'perhaps the most perfect embodiment of the gentlemanly ideal England has ever produced'.[19] It certainly infused Wellington's sense of moral, social and personal superiority over Napoleon, and helped instil that self-assurance which presaged victory. For, from the moment he landed in Portugal in 1808 at the start of the Peninsular War, probably bringing himself to Napoleon's attention for the first time, Wellington seems never to have considered the possibilities of defeat.

His social rank as son of a peer and his Eton schooling were epicentral to his conception of himself as a gentleman, but what made Wellington so sure that Napoleon was not also one? The phrase 'narrowness of his early prospects and habits' used in the conversation with Croker does not entirely explain it. Napoleon's 'early prospects' were not particularly narrow, especially once he had attended a French military academy not unlike Wellington's own. His 'habits' were of continual study and intellectual self-improvement, rather like Wellington's after the immolation of his violin. Nor would it have necessarily been his Corsican background to which Wellington was referring. Wellington was perfectly ready to accept that non-Britons could be gentlemen; he accorded that status to the aristocratic French marshal the Marquis de Grouchy, just as he denied it to his own General Picton, a bluff Welshman whom he called 'a rough foul-mouthed devil as ever lived'.

The criteria by which Wellington refused Napoleon the status of gentleman seem to have been that he believed Napoleon was an ill-mannered 'bully' and show-off, who furthermore 'harangued' his troops. In this he was echoing, unsurprisingly, the view of Napoleon held by much of the British press, especially such papers as *The Times*, the *Courier*, the *Quarterly Review* and the *Morning Post*, the last of which described Napoleon as 'a vulgar upstart, devoid of any gentlemanly breeding'.[20]

Wellington seems to have taken some interest in Napoleon's ancestry. In the only book on Napoleon in his library at Apsley House that he annotated, Dr Barry O'Meara's *Napoleon in Exile*, he put pencil marks down the margin adjacent to the report of a conversation the former emperor had held with his surgeon at St Helena. Napoleon had appointed Marshal Henri Clarke ambassador to Florence, where the snobbish Clarke, who boasted descent from the Plantagenets, made great efforts in the Florence state archives to try to establish an aristocratic background for the Buona Parte family. 'He plagued me with letters upon this subject,' Napoleon recalled to O'Meara, 'which caused me to write to him to attend to the business for which he had been sent to Florence, and not to trouble his head or mine with his nonsense about nobility; that I was the <u>first</u> of my family.'[21] That Wellington considered such remarks of Napoleon worthy of annotation shows the interest he took in Napoleon's natal, if not personal, claims to gentility.

There is no doubt that on one level Napoleon was no personification of the 'gentil parfait knight'. He once seized his friend Marshal Berthier's head and hit it against a wall. A set of bad economic figures merited his finance minister Louis Molé a sudden kick in the crotch. He even shot his wife Josephine's swans at her country home near Paris, Malmaison. He would hit servants with his riding crop and was master of the gross personal insult. 'Madam,' he told one woman, 'they told me you were ugly; they certainly did not exaggerate.'[22] Although Wellington was probably not aware of all these – and very many more – instances of Napoleon's cruelty and ungentlemanly conduct, he clearly instinctively guessed the truth.

Yet Wellington himself, despite being consistently held up as the *beau idéal* of gentlemanliness, particularly in later life by Victorian hagiographers, also possessed a rasping tongue. Although he would never kick a servant or shoot the Duchess of Wellington's pets, and although he always made a point of greeting his guests on arrival and bidding them farewell on departure, he could be direct to the point of rudeness as well as staggeringly insensitive. When General Craufurd died after storming the Spanish town of Ciudad Rodrigo in 1812, Wellington later told Croker that the dying man had talked 'in the way one has read of in romances'.[23] Asked if he minded being caricatured in the press he cruelly told a lady friend: 'Not a bit! Not a bit! There's only one caricature that has ever caused me annoyance: Douro!'[24] The Marquess of Douro was his eldest son.

Wellington treated his subordinates harshly during the Pensinsular War, ruthlessness being an integral part of his character. Charles Stewart was reduced to tears by his hectoring over the interviewing of deserters; Dr James McGrigor, a distinguished physician and later the director-general of the Medical Board, was berated in front of Goya; Captain Norman Ramsay, the army's heroic artilleryman, was even placed under arrest for three weeks over a trifle. On two occasions the recipients of his scorn − Lieutenant-Colonel Charles Bevan after the siege of Almeida in 1811 and Colonel Henry Sturgeon after the battle of Orthez in 1814 − actually committed suicide, one by shooting himself and the other by taking an unnecessary risk in order to redeem himself.[25] As the historian Sir William Napier noted, Wellington had a policy never to admit that he was wrong.

After the retreat from Burgos in 1812, which had been forced upon him after he failed to capture the great Spanish town, Wellington wrote a 1,200-word memorandum condemning his officers − largely unfairly − for the reverse. Nor was he as modest as his Victorian worshippers, including Disraeli, made out. 'They really are heroes when I am on the spot to direct them,' he said of his Peninsular army, 'but when I am obliged to quit them they are children.' In fact several corps commanders won fine reputations in the Peninsula, including Generals Craufurd, Hill and Picton, but Wellington was notoriously partial in his despatches home about the relative worth of infantry, allies, cavalry and artillery − the latter two regularly failing to get the praise they deserved. Examples of his selective blindness include the King's German Legion at Bayonne in 1814, the artillery at Fuentes d'Oñoro in 1811, the Royal Engineers generally and the 52nd Regiment at Waterloo. After the battle of Campo Mayor in 1811 he let his unfair and damning criticism of the 13th Dragoons stand in the record even after being personally acquainted with the truth of their meritorious conduct.[26]

Wellington was very conscious of his social position and its obligations. He was nicknamed the 'Peer' by his officers in the Peninsula. In defending his remarks about Napoleon not being a gentleman, his great-grandniece Muriel Wellesley wrote that it was 'said in excuse and not in condemnation. It excused the little gaucheries and vulgarities that so often accompany the rise to great position of a man who has no hereditary training for that position.'[27] Several other of Wellington's opponents had also risen from the ranks, including Marshals Soult (the son of a small-town notary), Ney (the son of a barrel-cooper), Victor (the son of a bailiff) and Masséna (the son of a small shopkeeper), but, although at least one historian believes Wellington may well have seen them as social upstarts, in his many recorded comments about them he tended not to question their claims to gentility.[28]

Napoleon was different, and it seems that Wellington despised his display and in particular his uplifting pre-battle proclamations. Whereas Napoleon famously issued morale-boosting messages to his troops before battles – in Egypt telling them that forty centuries looked down upon them from the Pyramids, or in the Italian campaign declaring, 'Soldiers! You are destitute: I am leading you into the richest plains in the world' – Wellington merely penned accounts afterwards. As Wellington told his friend Lord Mahon in 1831: 'The proclamations you read of in the French army were much more seen in the papers than by the soldiers – they were meant for Paris...As to speeches – what effect on the whole army can be made by a speech, since you cannot conveniently make it heard by more than a thousand men standing about you?'[29] Napoleon's conscious exploitation of his own undoubted charisma seems to have struck Wellington as ostentatious, a far cry from the Etonian gentlemanly ideal.[30]

(Lord Mahon – later 5th Earl Stanhope – was the nephew of the traveller Lady Hester Stanhope and a great-nephew of William Pitt. Born in 1805, he came to Wellington's attention when he made a speech opposing the extension of the parliamentary franchise in 1831 as MP for Wootton Bassett. 'His duty to the Muse of History was clear,' wrote Wellington's biographer Philip Guedalla, 'and after a few meetings with the Duke his interlocutor began to take careful notes of his conversation, continuing the practice over a period of twenty years.' Stanhope's celebrated *Notes of Conversations with the Duke of Wellington* were published by his son in 1888, and are invaluable for biographers not least because Wellington had no idea he was being Boswellised in such a fashion.)

It was probably the kidnap and execution of the Bourbon Duc d'Enghien and the mysterious death in his prison cell of the Royalist General Charles Pichegru that most marked Napoleon as being outside Wellington's gentlemanly ethic. They were held at the time to represent his greatest crimes, along with the massacre of around 4,400 Turkish prisoners at Jaffa during the Syrian campaign in March 1799, something Napoleon would never have considered visiting upon European soldiers. (Soon afterwards, following a plague outbreak in Jaffa which afflicted many French soldiers, Napoleon suggested killing off the sick with lethal doses of opium, which was also subsequently held against him.)[31] Certainly it is the references to the deaths of d'Enghien, the nephew of Louis XVIII who had been kidnapped in 1804 and was executed by firing squad, and of the presumed Royalist plotter Pichegru who was found hanged in his cell, which Wellington marked in his heavily annotated copy of O'Meara's *Napoleon in Exile*. The execution of d'Enghien was considered particularly Corsican of Napoleon; a vicious act of dynastic vengeance in return for an assassination attempt that had been made against him, supposedly but not definitely on Bourbon orders.

As a result of Wellington's education, his prejudices and his political opinions – he was a High Tory and supporter of the Bourbons, Napoleon initially a supporter of the Revolution – he was always likely to despise Napoleon, quite apart from whatever admiration he might have expressed for him as a soldier. The dichotomy was best expressed by the duke to his friend Lord Ellesmere, who years after Waterloo mentioned an author's low opinion of Napoleon's military talents and exploits. Wellington said of the writer, Mitchell, author of a biography of Prince Wallenstein: 'He is certainly wrong. Napoleon was the first man of his day on a field of battle, and with French troops. I confine myself to that. His policy was mere bullying, and, military matters apart, he was a Jonathan Wild.'[32]

This analogy with the notorious head of London's criminal fraternity who had been hanged at Tyburn in 1725 was one that Wellington further pursued with John Croker in 1826. When continuing the discussion he had had about Napoleon's behaviour towards King Joseph over the Breguet watch, Wellington said of his great rival:

> I never was a believer in him, and I always thought that in the long-run we should overturn him. He never seemed himself at his ease, and even in the boldest things he did there was always a mixture of apprehension and meanness. I used to call him Jonathan Wild the Great, and at each new coup he made I used to cry out 'Well done Jonathan', to the great scandal of some of my hearers. But, the truth was, he had no more care about what was right or wrong, just or unjust, honourable or dishonourable, than Jonathan, though his great abilities, and the great stakes he played for, threw the knavery into the shade.[33]

This dichotomy, of admiring Napoleon as a soldier while despising him for everything else and particularly his moral character, was the central feature of Wellington's public attitude towards Napoleon.

THREE

A Near Miss
1805–1808

In War <u>men</u> are nothing: it is a <u>man</u> who is everything.
NAPOLEON

On his return from India in 1805 on board HMS *Trident*, Wellington stopped for a month on the island of St Helena, a rocky Atlantic outcrop of forty-seven square miles that has been described as 'further away from anywhere else in all the world'. Eighteen hundred miles from Brazil and twelve hundred from Angola, its nearest neighbour is the tiny Ascension Island, itself seven hundred miles away.[1] Wellington, who stayed at a house called The Briars, found the climate 'the most healthy I have ever lived in', although he did arrive there during the summer. When Napoleon first saw it ten years later in mid-October the weather was very different.[2] While staying with the Balcombe family for five nights at a house called The Pavilion, Wellington used the simple blue china and placed his papers upon the same round teak table that in 1815 was to be used by Napoleon, although Betsy Balcombe tactfully did not say as much to her later guest.[3]

Having landed in England, Wellington was given the command of an infantry brigade stationed at Hastings to repulse Napoleon's latest threat of invasion, his earlier ones of 1797–8 and 1801 having been successfully thwarted. It was something of a demotion for the Hero of Assaye, but he did the job conscientiously and well. Thirty years later, recovering from an illness at Walmer Castle in Kent, his official residence as the lord warden of the Cinque Ports, he told his friend Lord Ellesmere 'that if Buonaparte had landed, he would have got to London, our force at that time was so ill organised and commanded'.[4] He knew that Napoleon agreed, as he had made annotations of his remarks on the subject as vouchsafed to Dr O'Meara in *Napoleon in Exile*. Napoleon's intention in 1804 had been to land near Chatham and to capture London with two hundred thousand men in four days. 'What resistance could an undisciplined army make against mine in a country like England, abounding in plains?' he asked rhetorically. Wellington also noted Napoleon's intentions had he been successful: 'I would have proclaimed a republic...the abolition of the nobility and house of peers, the distribution of property of such of the latter as opposed me amongst my partizans, liberty, equality and the sovereignty of the people...a democracy.'

It was partly to oppose such possible future 'partizans' that Wellington became the Tory MP for Rye in April 1806. (He later sat for Mitchell in Cornwall and Newport on the Isle of Wight.) He had been present on the immortal occasion at the Lord Mayor's Banquet at the Guildhall on 9 November 1805, shortly after Nelson's victory at the battle of Trafalgar, when Pitt had stated that 'England has saved herself by her exertions and will, as I trust, save Europe by her example.' Of this two-sentence speech, Wellington years later told Lord Mahon: 'Nothing could be more perfect.'[5] Shortly before his death on 23 January 1806, Pitt further predicted to Wellington that Spain would be the place where Napoleon would attempt to kindle 'the sort of war which will not cease till he is destroyed'. Wellington had also very briefly met Nelson, in the anteroom to Lord Castlereagh's offices in Whitehall. Some have even seen these meetings with both Pitt and Nelson shortly before their deaths in terms of a semi-mystical handing-on to Wellington of 'their great task' of defeating Napoleon.[6] It is not an idea that would have detained Wellington for long; when once Lord Mahon tried to interest him in a philosophical discussion over whether men created their environments or were created by them, Wellington told him: 'It would take a volume to answer your question. I must go and take off my muddy boots.'

In the two years after Wellington returned to England in September 1805, Napoleon had been triumphant as the precarious European peace had disintegrated. He defeated the Austrian General Mack at the battle of Ulm and then smashed the Austro-Russian armies at Austerlitz. He had made his brother Louis King of Holland and had dissolved the ancient, vast but now obsolete Holy Roman Empire. In October 1806 he had defeated the Prussians at Jena, on the same day as Marshal Davout defeated them at Auerstädt, and then he entered Berlin. Soon afterwards he entered Warsaw and defeated the Russians at Pultusk, following it up with another victory over them at the battle of Friedland. In July 1807, after a conference with Tsar Alexander I of Russia and King Frederick William II of Prussia on board a raft on the River Niemen, he signed the treaty of Tilsit, by which those powers recognised Napoleon's changes to the map of Germany and promised to close their ports to British ships. Wellington years later described this moment as the highest point Napoleon ever reached. 'To me he seems to have been at his acme at the Peace of Tilsit,' he told his friend the banker, poet and host Samuel Rogers, 'and gradually to have declined afterwards.'[7]

The abolition of the Holy Roman Empire and its replacement by Napoleon's Confederation of the Rhine brought to an end a thousand years of European history, but, as Goethe recorded, the Empire was by then so moribund that the announcement of its demise inspired less comment among his travelling party than a row which had broken out between their coachman and the innkeeper. (Napoleon was an admirer of Goethe, and met him at Erfurt and Weimar in 1808 to discuss the theatre of tragedy, something it is quite impossible to imagine Wellington wanting to do.) When Napoleon offered Louis-Engelbert, sovereign Duke d'Aremberg of the Holy Roman Empire, the title of count of the French Empire, perhaps out of sympathy with the duke's blinding at sixteen by the British ambassador out hunting, the duke accepted, and had visiting cards engraved to announce him as 'Le Comte d'Aremberg, né Duc d'Aremberg'.

Throughout the period, European coalitions against France largely financed by Britain were formed and dissolved – there were no fewer than seven in all by 1815. As the Third Coalition expired at Tilsit, and Napoleon established his mastery over the continent, Wellington could do little more than watch in dismay. He became chief secretary for Ireland and fought in a brief and successful campaign in Denmark designed to weaken the French hold on that country, but it was a frustrating time for him. His first authenticated remark about Napoleon, made in May 1808, was entirely neutral in character. Writing to the lawyer James Traill, Wellington took issue with the idea that 'Buonaparte's ill-treatment of the Pope would induce the Roman Catholics of Ireland to detest the name of Buonaparte'. As the man who was to risk his premiership for Catholic emancipation twenty years later, his reasons were interesting. He argued that Roman Catholics in Ireland were 'indifferent upon the fate of their religion', and 'it will be found that they will laugh at the Pope, his guards, and Cardinal Caponi, and only increase their admiration of Buonaparte.' Wellington nonetheless recommended that Napoleon's orders that the

Papal Guard 'shall in future be commanded by officers not priests' should be widely circulated in Ireland, as 'this is another instance effecting a revolution in an ancient and respectable state by a mere order to his troops'. The magistrates should circulate it, ordered Wellington, as the Irish priesthood could not be relied upon to help.[8]

⤿

The victory at the battle of Friedland followed by the diplomatic coup at Tilsit lured Napoleon on to make what he later came to regard as a cardinal error, involving France in a war in the Iberian Peninsula which she ultimately could not win. Having been thwarted over the invasion of Britain in 1804–5, he hoped to destroy his long-standing enemy commercially with his Berlin Decrees of November 1806, by which Europe was forbidden to trade with Britain. This attempted economic blockade came to be known as the 'Continental System', and was initially supported by Russia and Prussia at Tilsit. Portugal, half of whose business was done with Britain, defied the Decrees, so a year later General Junot invaded that country on Napoleon's orders, occupying Lisbon on 30 November 1807, only twenty-four hours before the Royal Navy evacuated the Portuguese royal family to Brazil.

The following February the French also invaded Spain, entirely opportunistically and in the belief that Spain was ripe for Bonapartist social and economic reforms, and Marshal Murat occupied Madrid on 23 March 1808. A fortnight later, Napoleon forced King Charles IV of Spain to abdicate, and, although his son Ferdinand VII was initially proclaimed his successor, in June Napoleon declared his eldest brother Joseph King of Spain, with Murat taking Joseph's vacant throne of Naples. Charles IV and Ferdinand VII were meanwhile both confined in France. In early May the Spanish people rose in open revolt against this hucksterism and usurpation, and Britain saw her opportunity to open up a major front against Napoleonic Europe.

If Napoleon had an initially low opinion of Wellington's expeditionary force that landed at Mondego Bay in French-occupied Portugal on 1 August 1808, he had every excuse. His previous experience of fighting the British, at Toulon in 1793, was unlikely to enhance his impression of their military prowess.[9] Since then, Britain's contributions to the Low Countries campaign of 1793–5 had been unimpressive, after which she failed, despite repeated promises, to commit any considerable force to any continental campaign. An attack on Holland in 1799 was incompetently organised. In 1800 Britain failed to fulfil her promise to help the Austrians in Italy with fifteen to twenty thousand men just as in 1797, when Austria had fought Napoleon, Britain had refused her a loan. In 1801 an Anglo-Turkish army did defeat the French in Egypt, but the French army was allowed home and the campaign cost the life of Sir Ralph Abercromby, one of Britain's very few good generals.

British troops were disembarked in Hanover in 1805, but when they learned about the Austro-Russian defeat at the battle of Austerlitz they hastily re-embarked without a shot being fired in anger.[10] A small but significant victory had been won at the battle of Maida in Calabria in 1806, but the following year the British army suffered a humiliating defeat at El Hamed in Egypt, and Admiral Duckworth's squadron was forced to retire from Constantinople and took a mauling as it passed and repassed the Dardanelles. Meanwhile in Buenos Aires a British army under General Whitelocke was forced to surrender. The same year a British expeditionary force sent to help the Russians arrived the day after Alexander I signed the treaty of Tilsit, and even then it landed at the wrong port. Aside from Britain's naval successes, it was a fifteen-year-long catalogue of disgrace and ignominy, and Napoleon had every reason to assume that the landing of only nine thousand British troops in Portugal would pose no great threat to his Empire. He likened France's war with Britain to that between a whale and an elephant, each equally incapable of challenging the other outside its natural environment.

The fact that Napoleon knew nothing of Wellington before the landings at Mondego Bay is proven by his letter from Nantes of 9 August 1808 to his brother Joseph, King of Spain, who was greatly alarmed by the invasion.[11] The emperor told Joseph that, when the Grande Armée was ready to march in the autumn, Spain would be inundated with French troops but in the meantime he was to hold the line of the River Douro in order to maintain communications with Portugal. 'Les Anglais sont peu de chose,' he wrote, stating that they did not have a quarter of the men they claimed. 'Lord Wellesley n'a pas 4,000 hommes.' In fact Wellington was then called Sir Arthur Wellesley and was over a year away from a peerage, when he anyhow took the title Wellington. Napoleon could hardly have been mistaking him for his elder brother, now the Marquess Wellesley, who was in Britain throughout 1808. In his first recorded mention of Wellington, therefore, Napoleon got his name wrong.[12]

Wellington's confidence in ultimate victory in Spain was total; as he told his friend Lady Salisbury thirty years later when working on the tenth volume of his despatches: 'Oh! As to the victory, I had never any difficulty about that. That was always a matter of course. There never was the slightest doubt about the result of any action when we were engaged upon it. But it was the daily detail that was the weight upon me. I never walked out, or rode out, or took a moment's recreation without having some affair or other occupying my thoughts.'[13] Nor was this bravado or *ex post facto* rationalisation. Contemporary correspondence records Wellington writing to the secretary for war Lord Castlereagh from Corunna a week before landing at Mondego saying that 'it is obvious that Bonaparte cannot carry on his operations in Spain, excepting by the means of large armies; and I doubt very much whether the country will afford subsistence for a large army', and a few days before landing he told Major-General Spencer from HMS *Crocodile* 'off the Tagus' that 'Bonaparte is not now very strong in Spain.'[14]

It is, however, his remarks to John Croker made just before he set sail which best illustrate his calm and confident state of mind. At a dinner in Harley Street on 14 June 1808, Wellington said of the French army:

> I have not seen them since the campaign in Flanders, when they were capital soldiers, and a dozen years of victory under Bonaparte must have made them better still. They have, besides, it seems, a new system of strategy which has out-manoeuvred and overwhelmed all the armies of Europe. 'Tis enough to make one thoughtful; but no matter; my die is cast, they may overwhelm me but I don't think they will out-manoeuvre me. First, because I am not afraid of them, as everybody else seems to be; and secondly, because if what I hear of the system of manoeuvre is true, I think it a false one as against steady troops. I suspect all the continental armies were more than half-beaten before the battle was begun – I, at least, will not be frightened beforehand.[15]

Colonel John Elting, a highly respected Napoleonic scholar, believed that Wellington's remarks to Croker suggest that he had studied Napoleonic strategy carefully, although nothing in his despatches implies that he made any systematic study of it up to that point.[16]

It was crucial to Wellington's success that he should exude such self-confidence, if not simply for domestic political consumption as many Whigs opposed the expedition outright. By 1809 there were 190,000

French troops in Spain and by 1811 no fewer than 360,000, so he needed all the self-confidence he could display. Just before he landed he was aided by the Spanish victory over General Pierre-Antoine Dupont at the battle of Baylen on 22 July 1808, where 17,600 Frenchmen had been forced to capitulate to a smaller army under General Castanos, with a further 2,000 casualties. The humiliation was all the worse because Napoleon had only recently appointed Dupont a count in recognition of his Spanish services. 'There has never been anything so stupid, so foolish and so cowardly since the world began,' fulminated the emperor.[17]

Wellington's initial successes against General Delaborde at the battle of Roliça on 17 August and against General Junot at the battle of Vimeiro four days later were, along with Baylen, serious blows against the myth of the invincibility of Napoleonic France, as well as a fine encouragement to other nations to renew hostilities against her.[18] The Peninsular War had important repercussions for the rest of Europe, increasing the willingness of European countries to stand up to Napoleon's blandishments. As French troops were withdrawn from other European theatres in order to serve in Spain, the war parties in Berlin, Vienna and Moscow, smarting under the humiliating terms Napoleon had pressed upon them at Tilsit, were correspondingly enboldened.[19] Napoleon was always acutely conscious of this, and complained to Joseph in August 1808: 'The army seems to be commanded not by experienced generals but by postal inspectors.' Later on that month, the same one in which Wellington had landed and begun his march on Lisbon, Napoleon told his brother, from his palace at St Cloud, that: 'In war men are nothing: it is a man who is everything.'[20] He could not have known it at the time, but that man had arrived.

∽

Within three weeks of Wellington's landing in Portugal, General Junot's army of 26,000 men had surrendered to him after the battle of Vimeiro on 21 August. Yet the British army somehow contrived to ensure that Napoleon did not need to accord Wellington any credit for his great victory. For, ten days afterwards, senior British officers – including Wellington – signed a convention with the French at their headquarters at Cintra. Napoleon believed, with some justification, that this made the man he still usually called in despatches 'the English general' into a European laughing stock.

By the terms of the Convention of Cintra, principally negotiated by Generals Sir Hew Dalrymple and Sir Harry Burrard, who were senior to Wellington but had only arrived in Portugal after Vimeiro, Junot's army was transported by forty-five Royal Navy vessels back to France. Defeated armies had been allowed to return home in the past; after Saratoga and Yorktown in the American Revolutionary War some thirty years before the British army had been allowed back; and the British had repatriated the French army in Egypt. Yet the Convention of Cintra was held to be especially humiliating for Britain because Junot's troops were allowed to escape along with their stores and weapons, and even with the Portuguese bullion and art treasures they had looted. Neither the Lisbon nor the Westminster Governments were consulted over the agreement and when the details were received in London there was an immediate, furious outcry.[21]

Napoleon was delighted by the news, especially when he heard that a Board of Inquiry had been set up in London effectively to try the three British generals who had signed it. He quipped that he 'was most grateful to the British for putting their generals on trial, since it saved him from having to bring his old friend Junot to a court-martial'.[22] Jean-Andoche Junot was a law student from Dijon when he joined the French army in 1792. Nicknamed the 'Tempest' he had a foul temper, and on one occasion Napoleon had to rebuke him for smashing up a casino in which he had been losing, beating up the dealers in the process.[23] Wellington thought little of him, recalling in 1843 how at Cintra Junot had 'received me with a vulgar, swaggering manner, trying to imitate Napoleon, which he could not do, and at the same time never losing an opportunity of throwing out some sly insinuation against him'.[24] Perhaps Junot foresaw the way Napoleon would punish him by stripping him of his honorary positions, although eventually allowing him the opportunity to command men once more (and to lose once again).[25]

In the course of the Cintra negotiations, Wellington had officially to recognise Napoleon as emperor of the French, a dignity Britain had hitherto steadfastly refused to accord him. The wording of the ceasefire document, 'resolved between Sir Arthur Wellesley, Lieutenant-General and Knight of the Order of the Bath, and Lieutenant-General Kellermann, Grand Officer of the Légion d'Honneur', made specific reference in Article One to 'Sa Majesté Imperiale et Royale, Napoleon Ier'. In his private letters Wellington referred to 'Buonaparte', sometimes as 'Bonaparte', but the exigencies of the Cintra situation seemed to require that he go along with the official French nomenclature.

Wellington afterwards denounced the Convention as 'a very extra-ordinary paper' and complained to his junior officers about its 'tone', but he nonetheless did sign it, blaming his superior officer Dalrymple for its actual contents.[26] The Inquiry, convened in the Great Hall at the Royal Hospital in Chelsea, could have ended Wellington's active career there and then. Wordsworth wrote a long political pamphlet denouncing the Convention as 'shameful', an estimation with which most of the press and public agreed. Wellington found some of his political supporters in the Government distancing themselves from him. Even Lord Castlereagh avoided sharing a carriage with him at this time. The former prime minister Lord Sidmouth denounced Cintra as 'one of the greatest misfortunes that ever befell us', and spoke of Wellington in approving terms only once the Inquiry had fully acquitted him of wrongdoing.[27]

It should be recalled that poor Admiral Byng had been shot for also allowing an enemy to escape destruction only half a century earlier, and even so much as a mildly critical report would probably have destroyed Wellington's chances of returning to the Peninsula.[28] Instead of attempting to defend the Convention on its merits – that it was essential to remove the large French presence from the region – Wellington gave evidence that 'I never considered myself in any manner responsible for its contents, or for the manner in which it was drawn up.' He could not deny that he approved in principle of the evacuation, or that he had signed the 'extraordinary paper', but he made out that it was done under protest and on Dalrymple's insis-tence. Dalrymple and Burrard were not in the end censured by the Board either, but their active service careers were over.

Napoleon was delighted with the developments, and from his palace at St Cloud he wrote to Junot, who had arrived back at La Rochelle: 'You have done nothing dishonourable; you have brought back my troops, my eagles and my artillery... You won the Convention by your courage, not by your dispositions, and the English are right to com-plain that the English general signed it.'[29] Almost all the troops evacu-ated under the terms of the Convention were then sent straight back to the Peninsular theatre.

It is one of the great coincidences of this period that at the very time that Wellington was in Chelsea defending himself, and hoping to be given another Peninsular command, Napoleon entered Spain, and it was not until Napoleon had left, in January 1809, that Wellington returned to Portugal on 26 April with a new British army. The fact that their time in the Peninsula never overlapped meant that it took far longer for Napoleon to appreciate Wellington's qualities as a military commander. If anything, Napoleon's experiences in Spain in the two months after November 1808 actually contributed to his contempt for the British army as well as to his misunderstanding of the complexities of campaigning in the Peninsula.

Advocates of free trade will take solace from the knowledge that the fall of Napoleon came about largely as a result of his commitment to protectionism and the restraint of trade. Had it not been for their flouting of his Continental System – Napoleon's economic blockade designed to deprive Britain of her export markets – Portugal and Russia would probably not have been invaded, and the King of Rome might well have succeeded his father as Emperor Napoleon II.

When Wellington landed in Portugal, the whole of continental Europe from Brest to the Urals was either occupied by or in alliance with Napoleon, all except Portugal itself, Sicily – a Royal Navy base – and Sweden, which was then fighting off the Danes, French and Russians. The Continental System, especially if exported to South America via the Spanish Empire there, presented a very genuine threat to Britain's commercial survival.[30] If the System was to bring Britain to her knees, Portugal could not be allowed to trade with her. Smuggling continued throughout Europe, even in France despite draconian penalties, but for the Continental System to work Napoleon knew it had to be truly continental. He was thus inexorably drawn into the Iberian Peninsula, because the only alternative means of defeating Britain was through a direct engagement with the Royal Navy, the dangers of which policy the battle of Trafalgar had earlier demonstrated. Napoleon suspected, probably correctly, that if a European trading blockade started to bankrupt British merchants, a Whig government intent on peace might well replace the hawkish Tories.

Napoleon lived to regret publicly his incursion into the Peninsula, blaming his harsh reception there on Marshal Murat's vigorous suppression of the anti-French rising that broke out in Madrid on 2 May 1808, the brutality of which was later to be so vividly recorded by Goya.[31] Some historians have dated the beginning of the end for Napoleon from the time of the Madrid Uprising, because it inaugurated a new form of warfare against him, one against which he could not win. It is certainly true that from that day onwards the Grande

Armée was never allowed to rest. It did not seem so at the time, but from May 1808 there would be no chance of peace or breathing space for France until Napoleon abdicated at Fontainebleau six years later.[32]

What was it about the new system of warfare in the Peninsula that Wellington spotted, but the undoubted military genius of Napoleon missed? Once Wellington was reinforced he had fourteen thousand men against an almost united continent, yet he felt himself to be opening up a front that could eventually help to drain the resources of the French Empire. His tiny force was to be the knife's edge that opened up the oyster. Of course it took the retreat from Moscow truly to break down Napoleon's mastery of Europe, but something allowed Wellington to spot that warfare in the Peninsula would be fundamentally different from the set-piece grand campaigns that Napoleon had always hitherto won.

Although he was one of the few to see Napoleon's essential weakness in Spain, Wellington was not the first.[33] According to his friend and official biographer the Reverend George Robert Gleig, Wellington had been a guest of William Pitt's at Walmer Castle when the news arrived of General Mack's capitulation at Ulm on 20 October 1805, with thirty thousand men and sixty guns, and Napoleon's subsequent march on Vienna. Gleig, who most probably had the story recounted directly by Wellington himself, recorded how the news:

> was received with the utmost consternation, insomuch that one of the gentlemen present exclaimed 'Our last hope of resistance to Buonaparte is gone!' 'Not at all,' replied Mr Pitt; 'we shall have another European coalition against him ere long and Spain will take the lead in it.' Observing that his remark was treated with apparent incredulity, Mr Pitt went on to say: 'I tell you that Spain is the first Continental nation which will involve him in a war of partisans. Though her nobles are debased and her government wretched, the people still retain their sense of honour and their sobriety, and they hate the French. Buonaparte will endeavour to tread out all those feelings, because they are incompatible with his designs; and I look to that attempt on his part for kindling the sort of war which will not cease till he is destroyed.'[34]

Within three months Pitt was dead. The story might have been inflated, but it is not too much to speculate that Wellington, whom we know Pitt admired and saw something of during this period, did indeed catch the prime minister's enthusiasm for Spain as the place where Britain could make a real contribution to the defeat of

Napoleon. If so, Wellington's confidence could only have been increased by the battle of Vimeiro, where, in essence, what in the Crimean War became known as the 'thin red line' held firm against an oncoming column of French infantry.[35]

Put crudely, Wellington discovered at Vimeiro that a well-led and disciplined line of British infantry firing accurately by company or half-company could hold back a French column advancing upon it. The usual French intention was for a column, once it had reached the enemy lines, to fan out and deploy into line, but very often in the Peninsula and also at Waterloo the accuracy of the British fire prevented them from achieving this, hemming the column in on itself until morale broke and it turned and fled.[36] Napoleon never personally witnessed British infantry performing in this way, and, although his generals attempted to warn him of it on the morning of Waterloo, he put his trust in General d'Erlon's huge formation of fifteen thousand men smashing through the Anglo-Allied line. Although there are indications that d'Erlon's column might have been a more sophisticated formation than the ones used so often to such ill effect in Spain, French tactics remained essentially the same. The advantage of the two-man-deep British line over the French column was simply that it permitted more muskets to be employed, thus maximising the firepower that could be brought to bear upon the enemy.

Because Napoleon had not seen British infantry in action since Toulon, he entirely failed to appreciate their superiority to many of the continental foes his Grande Armée had so often vanquished in the past. For reasons of cost, neither the French nor any of the other continental armies even used to fire live ammunition in training. Practising with live ammunition gave the British an immediate advantage in terms of accuracy and efficiency. Furthermore, the British muskets fired higher-calibre balls than the French, giving them more stopping-power per shot.[37]

The discipline in the British ranks was partly ensured by the liberal use of flogging, a barbaric but effective (and surprisingly popular) practice, which had been abolished in France during the Revolution. With accurate, rapid firing by men who feared their non-commissioned officers as much as they did the enemy, Wellington could hold off the best that the French could mobilise against him. Only at the battle of Sorauren in the Pyrenees in 1813 did a French column actually breach the British lines.

Wellington was not particularly innovative tactically, depending on great attention to detail, linear dispositions and discipline in a manner that Frederick the Great would easily have recognised.[38] A master of topography, he once told Croker: 'All the business of war, and indeed all the business of life, is to endeavour to find out what you don't know by what you do; that's what I called "guessing what was at the other side of the hill",' and for that he had almost a sixth sense. It helped that, as a keen rider to hounds, Wellington became a fine horseman who would criss-cross the battlefield to ensure that he was always in the most important area. The sport of hunting served him and his country well.

The basic equipment used in the Napoleonic Wars differed very little from that used a century before in the War of the Spanish Succession, and the British musket used at Waterloo was almost identical to that carried at the battle of Blenheim in 1704. In France too, a private in Louis XIV's army, 'if transported a century in time, could have picked up the weapons of a *grognard* of the Old Guard and employed them without a moment's instruction'. It was therefore in the field of tactical and strategic innovation that an edge could be gained on the enemy, but Napoleon made little attempt to alter what had for many years been a winning formula for him. 'I have fought sixty battles,' he said on St Helena, 'and I have learnt nothing which I did not know at the beginning.' It was intended as a boast, but by Waterloo it also amounted to a terrible admission.

As well as not updating his battlefield tactics to take into account what had happened in Spain, Napoleon failed to encourage the development of various inventions that were to revolutionise warfare in the future. Submarines, rockets, steamships, observation balloons and what later became known as shrapnel were all in their infancy in his time, but their potential military applications were more or less ignored by the emperor. He did construct a semaphore telegraph system across France, but although Ampère invented the electric telegraph in 1810 it did not supplant the semaphore until 1838, long after it could have been of any use to him. All this mattered greatly; as the military historian Major-General J. F. C. Fuller wrote in his memoirs in 1936:

> Though Napoleon was an infinitely greater general than Lord Raglan, the Minié rifle of 1854 would have enabled Lord Raglan to annihilate him in 1815, and had Napoleon, in 1805, placed down a challenge to the mechanical intellect of France to produce a weapon 100% more efficient than the [British] Brown Bess, it is almost a certainty that, in 1815, he would have got it; that he would have won Waterloo, and that the whole course of history would have been changed.

Several French historians have suggested that while Wellington was fine at logistics he possessed little tactical flair, whereas Napoleon was a genius let down by his support operations. In fact Wellington was perfectly capable of lightning attacks – as at the Peninsular battles of Oporto, Salamanca and Vitoria – and Napoleon, especially in the early part of his career, was an organisational genius who likened planning for a campaign to a woman's labour pains. Any attempt to compare Napoleon and Wellington's military strategies invites gross generalisations, but as with certain sports and games like chess, victory in eighteenth-century warfare often went to the protagonist who made the fewest mistakes, and Wellington rarely made any at all.

One area in which they did differ was over artillery, which, as an artilleryman, Napoleon believed could be almost a battle-winning arm. Wellington never had very many cannon in the Peninsula and so never had an opportunity to mass his batteries, as Napoleon did at Wagram in 1809, Borodino in 1812 and Ligny in 1815, and which he hoped might also deliver victory at Waterloo. Wellington instead sited his guns to support his line, not believing in counter-battery fire but preferring instead to direct his guns against the more immediate threat posed by advancing infantry. The artillery duel at the battle of Vitoria in Spain in 1813 was almost unique.[39]

Napoleon and Wellington both concentrated all major decision-making into their own hands, and made their headquarters the undoubted centres of the war effort. Whereas in Russia Tsar Alexander and General Kutuzov confusingly shared authority, in Austria General Mack, Archduke Charles and the Hofkriegsrat (Royal War Council) split theirs, and in Prussia King Frederick William imposed himself on the Duke of Brunswick, both Napoleon and Wellington left no room for doubt about who took the ultimate decisions in their armies.[40] Wellington even despised the idea of a second-in-command, and rarely confided his plans to lieutenants. When Lord Uxbridge, the commander of the cavalry and *de facto* second-in-command at Waterloo, politely asked Wellington his plans on the eve of the battle he received only a sarcastic answer, that since Napoleon was going to attack first it depended on the enemy. Although the Dutch Prince of Orange had a *de jure* independent command in the Waterloo campaign he ultimately took his orders from Wellington, and as Wellington and the Prussian field marshal Blücher were on close and friendly terms Napoleon found for almost the first time that he was up against a unified command.

One tactic that Wellington employed regularly, and about which

Napoleon should have been properly informed by the time of Waterloo, was that of the 'reverse-slope position'. This consisted of placing his men on the far side of a hill from the attacker, in the 'dead ground' below the crest. Wellington allowed his troops to lie down during bombardments, so that 'most of the balls skimmed their heads'.[41] It had the second advantage of hiding battalions from the enemy until the attackers were almost on top of them, and thus added to the surprise when the British troops suddenly appeared, fresh and ready, on the crest of the hill. This was a tactic used to devastating effect in several of Wellington's Peninsular battles, and Napoleon had no excuse not to be ready for it at Waterloo, although as Marshal Ney and d'Erlon had tactical responsibility they must bear the greater part of the blame. (In the conference at Le Caillou before Waterloo, General Foy did warn that, 'Wellington never shows his troops.')

In the early part of his career there was no aspect of the life and welfare of his troops in which Napoleon was not interested. In his 1805 campaign against Austria, for instance, his troops largely lived off the land with the unthreshed harvest still stacked in the fields, but he nonetheless built up huge magazines of biscuit rations at Göttingen, Würzburg and Strasbourg, with a million rations of biscuits, 300,000 bales of hay, flour for two million more rations and 100,000 pints of *eau de vie* also stored at Augsburg. Yet, as victory succeeded victory, Napoleon's attention to detail and supply arrangements waned. This was most notable during the Russian campaign of 1812, but even in the winter of 1806 in Poland supplies were so short that 'the emperor's pet pig, reserved for a Christmas banquet, disappeared mysteriously from its sty'.[42]

By contrast, Wellington's attention to detail was legendary right to the end of the Waterloo campaign. Here are some of his General Orders taken at random from from July and October 1809:

> General Staff, and other officers, are requested to put their names on the doors of the houses in which they are quartered.
>
> The Commander of the Forces requests that olive and other fruit trees may not be used by the troops in hutting, except in case of evident emergency.
>
> No man of the Brigades in huts must be allowed to quit the lines of his Regiment without being dressed with his side arms.
>
> In future all Officers, moving from one place to another in Portugal or Spain are to have a Route from the Quarter Master General's Department, which is to specify where the officer is to halt each day.

Every accommodation and comfort, beyond houses and stable-room, must be the result of the good will of the inhabitants, and nothing like compulsion must be used.

In the Hundred Days after escaping from the island of Elba in 1815, Napoleon had simply not the time to devote to that level of microscopic control, any more than he had as master of Europe from the time of the treaty of Tilsit onwards. Proportionately more and more men were sacrificed in his battles as his career progressed, and in his dispositions at Waterloo he adopted the vast, broad-brush strokes reminiscent of the battle of Borodino in Russia. Wellington was obliged to take a far more pointillist approach to his troop dispositions all the time. As he was later to complain, Napoleon might be able to lose whole army corps yet stay on the throne, but if he lost so much as five hundred men unnecessarily he would have been hauled up before the bar of the House of Commons to explain himself. His unaccountability to any representative institutions meant that Napoleon was able to expend the lives of perhaps as many as one and a half million of his and his allies' soldiers over the eleven years of his reign.[43] His dictatorship was thus both his making and his undoing.

FOUR

To Lie Like a Bulletin
1808–1809

The most difficult thing is to discern the enemy's plans,
and to detect the truth in all reports one receives;
the remainder requires only common sense.
NAPOLEON

Although circumstances conspired to ensure that Napoleon and Wellington were never present in the Peninsula at the same time, in one sense they did fight one another there because Napoleon tried to direct strategy by proxy, sending out instructions to his marshals from wherever he happened to be in Europe. This insistence on overall control was one of the many factors that contributed to the eventual French defeat there. In the opinion of the Napoleophile historian J. M. Thompson: 'Had Napoleon chosen to stay in Spain, he might have found an answer to [his] problems. He would at least have gained first-hand experience of Wellington's skilful and tenacious strategy that had defeated his generals and was to win the day at Waterloo.'[1]

While it is very unlikely that Napoleon avoided returning to Spain because he was reluctant to risk a contest with Wellington, as some of the duke's hagiographers and indeed Wellington himself have suggested, nor is it the case that he was always too busy campaigning abroad to have found the time to return there. Instead of inundating his marshals with orders about how to defeat Wellington, instructions which were often several weeks out of date by the time they had arrived from Vienna, Berlin, Warsaw or even, on occasion, from Moscow, he could quite easily have taken control himself. He was in France for five months in 1809–10, thirteen months in 1810–11 and six months in 1811–12, a total of two years between 27 October 1809 and his leaving for the Russian campaign on 8 May 1812.[2] Had he fully appreciated how much what he later called the 'Spanish ulcer' would suppurate, he would surely have acted sooner.

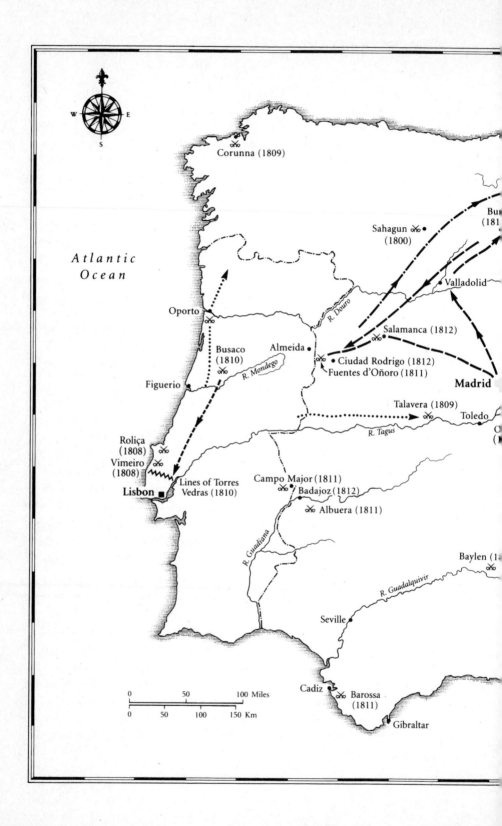

Corunna (1809)

Sahagun ⚔ •
(1800)

Bu
(181

Valladolid •

Atlantic
Ocean

Oporto ⚔

R. Douro

Salamanca (1812) ⚔

Busaco
(1810) ⚔

Almeida •

Ciudad Rodrigo (1812)
Fuentes d'Oñoro (1811)

R. Mondego

Figuerio •

Madrid ■

Roliça
(1808) ⚔

Vimeiro
(1808)

Talavera (1809) ⚔

Toledo
•

R. Tagus

O
(1

Lisbon ■ Lines of Torres
Vedras (1810)

Campo Major (1811) ⚔
Badajoz (1812) •

Albuera (1811) ⚔

R. Guadiana

Baylen (1
⚔

R. Guadalquivir

Seville •

0		50		100 Miles
0	50	100	150 Km	

Cadiz • ⚔ Barossa
(1811)

Gibraltar •

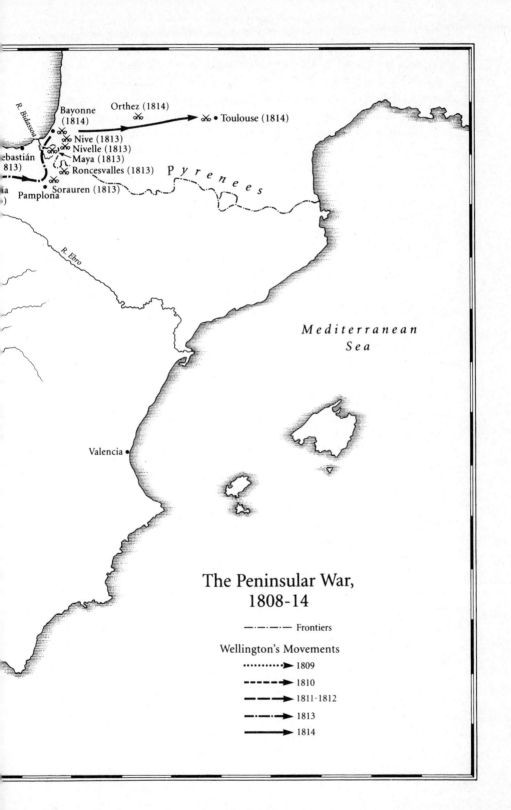

Bayonne
(1814)

Orthez (1814)
⚔

⚔ • Toulouse (1814)

R. Bidassoa

⚔
⚔ Nive (1813)
⚔ Nivelle (1813)
Maya (1813)
⚔ Roncesvalles (1813)

P y r e n e e s

ebastián
813)

⚔

• Sorauren (1813)

Pamplona

R. Ebro

Mediterranean
Sea

Valencia •

The Peninsular War,
1808-14

—·—·—·— Frontiers

Wellington's Movements

••••••••••► 1809

------► 1810

— — —► 1811-1812

—·—·—► 1813

———► 1814

Unfortunately for him in the long term, Napoleon's every effort in Spain met with success for the only two and a half months he spent there. On 5 November 1808, a week after the British general Sir John Moore had left Lisbon to invade Spain, Napoleon assumed personal command of the Army of Spain. 'I see that all have lost their heads since the infamous capitulation of Baylen,' he said, ordering the corps of Marshals Victor, Mortier and Ney from the Elbe to the Pyrenees. 'I realise that I must go there myself to get the machine working again.'[3] Assuring his close friend General Christophe Duroc and his senior secretary the Baron de Méneval that he would personally destroy the English, Napoleon defeated the Spanish at Tudela on 23 November and entered Madrid in triumph on 4 December.

On hearing the news, Moore had no option but to withdraw from the Peninsula, despite defeating Marshal Soult's cavalry at the battle of Sahagun on 21 December. He had to retreat towards Corunna on the Spanish coast as Napoleon gave chase, the French crossing the Guadarrama mountain range the following day. Napoleon then suddenly deputed Soult to conduct the pursuit of Moore to Corunna, march on Lisbon, avenge Vimeiro, pacify the southern Spanish provinces and generally disperse the continued opposition to French rule. He was therefore not present when, at the culmination of his rearguard action, Moore fought the battle of Corunna on 16 January 1809 as his troops embarked for home. Moore learned the lesson of Wolfe, Abercromby and Nelson, and secured his reputation by dying at the moment of victory, but otherwise it was a humiliation for Britain with yet another expeditionary force coming to grief. The fact that Moore had been forced, through lack of maps, to advance into Spain with no information about which roads could convey artillery had not helped.[4]

'My business in Spain is finished,' Napoleon wrote to his youngest brother Jérôme on the day of the battle of Corunna, and so it must genuinely have seemed.[5] In fact it had only just begun, because, three months after Napoleon left Spain, Wellington arrived in Lisbon with another army. William Warre, an officer serving under Wellington, wrote to his father in March 1809 to say that 'the French after they entered Corunna...spoke highly of the bravery of our men'.[6] Yet bravery had not been enough, and Napoleon took away the impression from his very brief period of campaigning there – 5 November 1808 to 24 January 1809 – that the British army would always retreat to wherever the Royal Navy could safely evacuate them. It was a view that would profoundly but disastrously influence his strategy in the Waterloo campaign six years later.

Napoleon's decision to leave Spain in January 1809 always per-plexed Wellington. He heard about it soon after he had been cleared by the Cintra Board of Inquiry. In 1826 he told John Wilson Croker:

There was something in Buonaparte's hasty return out of Spain that I have never understood. When Moore retreated, he followed him closely as far as Benevento and Astorga. He had a greatly superior force, two to one he gave out; and I should have thought, as he was afterwards so anxious *de se frotter* [to rub up] against me, he would at that time have been still more anxious to have personally performed his threat of driving the leopards into the sea; but he stopped, all of a sudden, com-mitted the command of the armies to Soult, who pushed Moore as hard as he could, while Buonaparte returned to Valladolid, where he remained a week or ten days, doing nothing that we know of while Soult was following Moore; and I think it was about the very day that the battle of Corunna was fought that Buonaparte set out from Valladolid for France, riding post through Spain, and making a wonderfully rapid journey to Paris.[7]

Napoleon actually left Valladolid on 17 January and was back in Paris by 8 a.m. on the 23rd. At the start of the journey, from Valladolid to Burgos, he was credited with covering the seventy-five miles in a five-hour gallop. Wellington had a number of possible explanations for this sudden journey, undertaken just when the emperor really ought to have been overseeing the expulsion of Moore's expeditionary force from Corunna. He was prepared to accept in part the official reason – that Napoleon had received intelli-gence reports that Austria was preparing to mobilise against France – but even that, in Wellington's opinion, could not explain his leaving his army:

at the moment that it had come in contact with Moore, and it was clear they must soon fight a regular battle; and his returning to waste, as far as I can see, ten days or a fortnight before he set out for Paris. Was he disinclined *de se frotter* against Moore? Did he wish that Soult should try what stuff our people were made of before he risked his own great reputation against us? Or did he despair of driving us out of Corunna? And was the bad news from Vienna (he generally kept bad news a profound secret) now invented or promulgated to excuse his evident reluctance to follow us up? I cannot account for his not having subtracted from the three weeks he spent in Spain after his return from

Astorga, and the three months that, I think, he spent at Paris, half-a-dozen days for so great an object as a victory over the English won by himself in person. My own notion is that he was not sure of the victory. He was certainly at that time greatly displeased with Talleyrand, and made him a *scène* on his arrival in Paris; and it is possible and even probable, that the extreme haste of his return may have had some political cause, foreign or internal; but even this does not explain my difficulty of why he did not in person attack Moore, or at all events, why he was not rather with the army the ten days that he lingered at Valladolid.[8]

Sixteen years later, Wellington still doubted that the threat that Austria would attack France had been the true reason for Napoleon's sudden and mysterious return to Paris. He told Lord Ellesmere in January 1839 that this was not the real 'cause of his haste'. By then Wellington believed that Napoleon had caught wind of 'a conspiracy between [the Chief of Police Joseph] Fouché and Talleyrand for placing Murat, the King of Naples, on the French throne, on the supposition that Napoleon would perish in Spain'.[9]

Considering that Napoleon was victorious in Spain at the time, it is unlikely that the plot involving Fouché, Talleyrand and Murat was really only contingent on his death there. It is true that he made a habit of suddenly dropping everything to get back to Paris – for example during the Egyptian campaign, during the retreat from Moscow in 1812, after escaping from Elba and after Waterloo – but in January 1809 it seems that he had good reason to break off the personal pursuit of Moore to scotch the plot which he suspected was gathering pace in Paris. Wellington's conspiracy theory seems to have been the correct one in explaining Napoleon's actions. Although Napoleon later said 'I never counted the applause of the Parisians,' and 'Frenchmen do not know how to conspire,' his actions in 1809 belie both of those transparently false statements.

It is perfectly possible, of course, that Napoleon left Valladolid both because of intelligence reports from Austria and because of the reports of the Paris plot.[10] The postmaster-general, Napoleon's loyal lieutenant the Comte de Lavalette, had intercepted a cipher letter from Talleyrand to Marshal Murat in Italy. Furthermore Talleyrand and Fouché, once deep in enmity, had been seen talking together at public receptions. When Fouché was invited to Talleyrand's private house, the Hôtel de Monaco in the rue de Varenne, it was clear to Napoleon's spies that something serious was afoot.[11] Although

Napoleon had arrived in Paris on 23 January it took five days for him to summon Talleyrand to the Tuileries for one of the most dramatic interviews of the history of the First Empire.

When Talleyrand arrived he found Napoleon surrounded by his closest cronies – Arch-Chancellor Jean-Jacques Cambacérès, Arch-Treasurer Charles-François Lebrun, the minister of marine Admiral Denis Decrès, and his secretary Méneval. In 1798 Decrès had fought a famous sea-battle in which, heavily outnumbered, he defended himself for three hours as his vessel was shot to pieces. Talleyrand was about to have to endure the social equivalent of that engagement.

Although the version Talleyrand later told Wellington of the interview was very different, it seems from the testimony of others present that Napoleon began by denouncing the diplomat's 'treason' in not supporting his war in Spain, and quickly worked himself up into a towering fury over his ingratitude and treachery. Although it is true that, as Talleyrand's most elegant biographer Duff Cooper wrote of him, 'every change of allegiance that he made was made by France', he usually anticipated rather than followed his country's political tergiversations.

'Finally the dyke burst,' recalled Méneval. 'Napoleon, whose indignation and anger grew as he spoke, reached such a pitch that it was inevitable that his scarcely contained fury would burst in a moment.'[12] Napoleon ranted at Talleyrand that he was 'a thief, a coward, and disloyal', didn't believe in God, failed to fulfil his responsibilities, deceived and betrayed everyone, and held nothing sacred. 'You would sell out your own father if you found it profitable,' he yelled, and went on to complain how he had 'heaped benefits, veritable fortunes on you', yet for the past ten months Talleyrand had been systematically betraying him. 'Why, I could break you like a glass! I have the power to do so. But I scorn you too much for that. Why didn't I have you hanged in public on the gates of the Carrousel! But there is still time for that. You are just common shit in silk stockings.'

Those who like to portray Napoleon as an earlier version of Adolf Hitler must explain why he did not imprison or execute either Talleyrand or Fouché, as the Führer undoubtedly would have done in similar circumstances. Napoleon once said that 'Cæsar, knowing the men who wanted to get rid of him, ought to have got rid of them first.' Yet, as it was, Talleyrand was not even dismissed from his post as vice-grand elector, although he did lose his place as grand chamberlain.

Not content with the 'silk stockings' remark at the interview,

Napoleon decided to indulge in pure malice: 'You did not tell me that the Duke de San Carlos was your wife's lover,' he said of Ferdinand VII's younger brother, whom Napoleon had ordered Talleyrand to imprison at his château at Valençay. 'Sire,' answered Talleyrand, 'I did not think that such matters as that could possibly enhance the glory of Your Majesty or of myself.' One suspects that, had Talleyrand made even the most elliptical mention of Josephine's own lover Hippolyte Charles, he would indeed have made an appearance on the gates of the Carrousel arch at the Tuileries.

On this occasion, however, Talleyrand's instinct for self-preservation took precedence over his love of the *bon mot*. Once he had safely left the interview, he merely observed: 'C'est dommage qu'un si grand homme soit si mal élevé!' (What a pity that such a great man should be so ill-bred!). That evening, reclining on a sofa in the drawing room of his old friend Madame de Laval, Talleyrand recounted the whole scene. When the aristocratic old lady asked why he had not 'snatched up a chair, the tongs, the poker, or anything' to attack the emperor, he languidly answered: 'Oh, I did think of doing so, but I was too lazy.' (He was also club-footed and far from robust, and would doubtless not have made much of a fist of it.) Very soon afterwards he went to the Austrian ambassador, Count Clemens von Metternich, and sold his espionage services for what is believed to have been around one million francs.

Talleyrand's own version of the interview to Wellington naturally made out his own performance to have been more impressive than in fact it was. In it, Napoleon is supposed to have said that Talleyrand obviously thought the war in Spain 'une faute' (a mistake), only for the wit to reply that it was more than a mistake, it was 'une folie'. Talleyrand claimed he had said that before the invasion of Spain the other European sovereigns had to admit that for all that they disliked Napoleon's ambition they were forced to regard him as a 'roi parmi des rois' (a king among kings). After the invasion they regarded him 'comme un joueur qui chicane sa place vis-à-vis tous les autres joueurs' (like a player who tricked his way into the game).

Wellington told this story to his friends Charles and Harriet Arbuthnot in August 1823 as 'an anecdote he had from Talleyrand himself'. Mrs Arbuthnot believed it to be genuine as 'it is so exactly in Talleyrand's epigrammatic style', adding, 'the Duke did not say how Bonaparte took this lesson, which, it must be allowed, was *un peu rude*'.[13] Indeed, so brutal was it that we are entitled to doubt whether, his life hanging in the balance, Talleyrand ever really said it at all.

Talleyrand, of whom Wellington saw a great deal in the negotiations of 1814 and 1815 and afterwards, also told him about the 'shit in silk stockings' remark. Towards the very end of his life, in December 1851, Wellington wrote to his friend Lady Salisbury to say that Lord Mahon had brought along his young daughter who had sat quietly upon his knee when the duke conversed with Mahon and the diarist Charles Greville about the passage in Adolphe Thiers' biography of Napoleon 'respecting Buonaparte's treatment of Talleyrand'. Wellington recalled Talleyrand's account of the interview and 'told them in French what had been said... They were very much amused. But I found my young lady on my knee absolutely in convulsions with laughter. I cried out "Hullo! It appears to me that you understand French!" It turned out that she did as well as English; and had been infinitely amused by my recital of what had passed.'[14] Charles Cavendish Fulke Greville, a grandson of the former prime minister the Duke of Portland, had been Lord Bathurst's private secretary in 1812 and was clerk of the Privy Council between 1821 and 1859, and was thus in a perfect position to record Wellington's remarks, which, along with Lady Salisbury, Thomas Creevey, John Croker, Lord Mahon, Harriet Arbuthnot, Samuel Rogers, Lord Ellesmere and George Chad, he faithfully did.

⌒

Although admirers of the emperor suggest that he might have been able to catch and then defeat Sir John Moore before he reached the sea, by April 1809 he was out of the Peninsula and Wellington was back there.[15] Whatever the reason for Napoleon's sudden departure, lack of confidence in victory is very unlikely to have been the correct one, he never set foot there again, and the 'ulcer' suppurated further.[16]

On 12 May 1809, only three weeks after landing in Portugal, Wellington defeated Marshal Soult at the battle of Oporto. In a surprise attack across the River Douro, he drove the French from the town. In 1835 he told Ellesmere that Soult had mistaken the British crossing the river for his own red-coated Swiss soldiers bathing in it, and so had failed to raise the alarm.[17] It was a classically bold manoeuvre, and when writing of it the French historian Pierre Lanfrey took his colleagues to task for almost always failing to give Wellington full credit for superb generalship. In view of Wellington's orders at Oporto, 'inspired by so striking a mixture of audacity and calculation', Lanfrey considered it absurd for French military writers such as

Jomini, Pelet and Marmont to write about the Englishman's 'good fortune' and 'lucky star' rather than his genuine military genius. (One could also add Foy, Marbot, Thiébault, Le Noble and Lemonnier Delafosse to the list.)[18] Lanfrey, who died in 1877, despised the French historians' practice of belittling Wellington, but it went on regardless. Witness Jean Lemoinne: 'It will not be said that Wellington was of the true race of heroes'; Victor Hugo: 'Wellington was the technician of war, Napoleon its Michelangelo'; or Jules Maurel: 'The Duke was almost unknown in France by [the time of his death in] 1852.'[19]

In the same month that Wellington defeated Soult, Napoleon suffered a serious military setback, at the hands of Archduke Charles' Austrian troops at Aspern-Essling, the news of which 'was particularly cheering for Wellesley and his embattled men in Portugal, and for the shaky Government in London'.[20] Conversely, on hearing that Soult had been driven out of Portugal by Wellington after Oporto, Napoleon wrote to his war minister, Marshal Henri Clarke, on 12 June ordering another expedition with a new army with three corps under Marshals Soult, Ney and Mortier which were to 'manoeuvre together, march upon the English... and drive them into the sea'.[21]

Napoleon could scarcely have chosen two marshals who loathed one another more than Soult and Ney; there was even talk later about swords being drawn and satisfaction being demanded between them. The French constantly found that, thanks not only to inter-marshalate jealousy but also to the breakdown of information on the partisan-infested Spanish roads, sophisticated combined operations became well nigh impossible. Yet even before Soult could act on Napoleon's orders for a new invasion of Portugal he had to try to save King Joseph, whose capital was threatened by Wellington's drive towards Talavera, sixty miles south-west of Madrid, where Wellington was advancing before Marshal Victor's retreating army.

If the French found combined operations difficult to arrange, so too did Wellington at that time. Writing to Castlereagh only five days after Napoleon had written to Clarke, Wellington complained that the Spanish commander-in-chief, General de la Cuesta, was 'as obstinate as any gentleman at the head of an army need be. He would not alter his position even to insure the safety of his army, because he supposed that this measure might be injurious to himself, notwithstanding that this alteration might have been part of an operation which must have ended in the annihilation of [the French] army.'

At the battle of Talavera on 27 and 28 July 1809, Wellington fought one of his toughest engagements. He lost 5,365 men, a quarter of the

British total force, but was left undisputed master of the field as dawn broke on the 29th, the French having retreated eastwards to Toledo with the loss of over 7,000 men. The sturdiness of the British line had again been proved when three thousand men had turned back ten thousand oncoming French, waiting until they were within fifty yards before crashing their volleys into the advancing column, 'one every fifteen seconds from each of eighty half-companies'.[22] Wellington himself was, as he put it to his brother William Wellesley-Pole, then chief secretary for Ireland, 'hit but not hurt and my coat shot through. Almost all the Staff are wounded or have had their horses shot. Never was there such a murderous battle!'

Walking the battlefield today, it is not difficult to imagine the horror of the moment when, as the engagement ended, the dry grass caught fire and the wounded were burned alive. 'I never saw a field of battle that struck me with so much horror,' wrote the Peninsular War historian General Sir William Napier. It must have been one of the engagements that led Wellington genuinely to hate war, but it also made his name. Assaye had not caught the public imagination because it had taken place in India, and the glory of Vimeiro had been, in the perceptive words of one of Wellington's descendants, 'dimmed by Cintra'.[23] It was the victory of Talavera which won Wellington his peerage, his first experience of nationwide hero-worship, and the start of the phenomenal demand for his likeness on prints, pottery, enamels, snuffboxes, medals, fans, paperweights, bells, boxes, jugs, mugs, plates, brooches, letter-openers, busts and statuettes. More and more after Talevera, 'He gallantly charged on the dials of clocks; his profile decorated the escapements of watches; the handles of knives and razors were embossed with his portrait; cast in iron he propped open doors.'[24]

Napoleon's comment on hearing of the battle was: 'I really ought to be everywhere!'[25] He sacked the chief of staff, Marshal Jourdan, and replaced Marshal Laurent Gouvion Saint-Cyr as commander of the Army of Catalonia with Marshal Pierre Augereau, the first in a long series of promotions and demotions which gave the impression that Napoleon blamed his own officers' incompetence rather than Wellington's genius for the defeats his forces suffered in the Peninsula.

It is important not to assume that, on their own, victories like Talavera could fundamentally have altered the European military or geopolitical scene. Wellington commanded only twenty thousand British troops at Talavera, while in the same month at the battle of Wagram Napoleon commanded nearly two hundred thousand. David was incapable even of threatening, let alone of felling, Goliath, and both knew it. 'As for Wellington's victories at the Douro and Talavera,' writes an historian of the Peninsular campaign, 'they were too remote from the Danube, as well as too late, to have any diversionary value at all' in the campaigns by which Napoleon smashed the latest Coalition and forced Austria to sign the treaty of Schönbrunn on 16 October 1809.[26] By its terms Austria agreed to recognise all of Napoleon's alterations to the map of Europe and to join the Continental System against Britain.

Before Napoleon even received the news of Talavera he had ordered Clarke to put off the August offensive in Spain on the grounds that the country was 'too hot'.[27] Two days later, on 31 July, he received the first news about Talavera from King Joseph. In an outrageous misinterpretation of what had really happened, his brother wrote: 'If I regret anything it is that I did not take the whole English army prisoner.'[28] The lack of objective reporting by subordinates was to bedevil Napoleon, where no marshal wished to send the unvarnished truth about defeats at the hands of Wellington. In his turn, Napoleon wanted to ensure that the domestic readership of the Government gazette the *Moniteur* read about French victories.

Napoleon therefore decided, especially once Wellington was forced by the sheer weight of numbers against him to retreat back into Portugal, to portray Talavera as a French victory. In this he was greatly aided by the fact that, owing to the Spanish general Don Gregorio de la Cuesta evacuating the town of Talavera, around 1,500 British wounded were captured by the French on 4 August. Napoleon, who admitted to Clarke that he was 'anxious for news from that country' on 18 August, nevertheless told his foreign minister Jean-Baptiste de Champagny that 'As for Spain, things are going on well; Soult is on the rear of the English, who are retreating. The King of Spain is at Toledo. At the battle of Talavera the English had a third of their army put *hors de combat*. They lost 10,000 men.'[29]

In fact Joseph was in Toledo only because the French army had retreated there after their defeat, and he spent his time there writing oleaginous despatches to Napoleon, including such sentiments as 'I sincerely think that had you been in my place, not a single Englishman would have escaped, and the war in Spain would have been finished.'[30] (Of course in his own Italian campaigns Napoleon had also regularly misinformed the government in Paris about the true nature of the military situation. In April 1796, for example, he had told the Directory that his Austrian and Piedmontese enemies numbered 72,000, whereas the true figure was closer to 42,000.)

Despite the brave face, and his keenness to talk up Talavera, it is clear from his correspondence that Napoleon soon knew that he was being lied to:

Inform Marshal Jourdan that I am extremely displeased with the inaccuracies and falsehoods contained in his reports of the 26, 27, 28 and 29 July, and that this is the first time in which the government has been so trifled with. He said on the 28th that he had seized the field of battle at Talavera, while subsequent reports show that we were repulsed the whole day long. Tell him that this infidelity towards the government is a straightforward crime, and that this crime might have fatal results, as the news that the English had been beaten was about to influence my determinations...He may say what he likes in the journal of Madrid, but he has no right to disguise the truth from the Government.[31]

Nonetheless, writing to Fouché the very next day, Napoleon claimed that:

in Spain Lord Wellesley [*sic*] has been beaten, surrounded and utterly routed. He is trying to save himself by headlong flight in the middle of the hot season. When he retired from Talavera, he surrendered to the Duke of Belluno [Marshal Victor] 5,000 sick and wounded English, whom he was forced to leave behind him. At last English blood is being shed! It is the best omen that peace is at length approaching. Undoubtedly if matters had been better managed in Spain, not a single Englishman would have escaped. But anyhow they have been beaten – 6,000 killed, 8,000 taken prisoner. Make these ideas the subject of articles in the papers; point out the folly of ministers who expose 30,000 English, in the heart of Spain, to the attacks of 120,000 French – the finest troops in the world.[32]

On the same day that he wrote to Fouché, Napoleon wrote to Champagny to say that 'Wellesley had been saved by crossing the Tagus; he had left 4,000 wounded, recommending them to the generosity of the French.'[33] Then, two days later, on 24 August, he wrote that 'Lord Wellesley' had abandoned six or seven thousand wounded or ill. He told Champagny to tell Caulaincourt, his ambassador in St Petersburg, to put it about 'that the English have been beaten in Spain, although they claim the victory; the proof is that Lord Wellesley has returned to Portugal'.

That day, 24 August, on reading Wellington's report of the battle in the British newspapers, which accurately stated that twenty guns and three flags had been captured, Napoleon decided to believe Wellington rather than his own brother. He told Clarke to 'express my astonishment to the King that they send me *carmagnoles* [revolutionary rhetoric] instead of telling me the truth. Who are the gunners who abandoned their pieces, the infantry divisions who allowed themselves to be captured?'[34] Two days after that he wrote to Joachim Murat, since August 1808 the King of Naples, to say that 'General Arthur Wellesley has fought in Spain and was forced to retreat to Lisbon leaving us all his wounded,' implying once again that Talavera had been a British defeat.[35] At least Napoleon had finally got the name of 'the English general' right, although it was not for long, as on 4 September he was created Viscount Wellington in recognition of the victory at Talavera.

Negotiating at Schönbrunn outside Vienna, Napoleon needed to portray Talavera as a victory, but it is clear from his letters to Clarke that he was under no illusions: 'What a fine opportunity has been lost! Thirty thousand English at 150 leagues from the coast in front of one hundred thousand of the best troops in the world! My God! What it is to have any army without a chief.'[36]

FIVE

First Recognition
1809–1810

Nobody has conceived anything great in our century:
it falls to my lot to give the example.
NAPOLEON

O n the same day that Napoleon was attempting to turn
Talavera into a victory, despite having read and believed
Wellington's own account of the battle, Wellington wrote an
important letter to the secretary for war Lord Castlereagh, making it
clear that he had fully understood the reason for Napoleon's successes
hitherto, and how to halt them in the future:

> People are very apt to believe that enthusiasm carried the French
> through their Revolution, and was the parent of those exertions which
> have nearly conquered the world; but if the subject is nicely examined, it
> will be found that enthusiasm was the name only, but that force was the
> instrument which brought forward those great resources under the
> system of terror which first stopped the Allies; and that a perseverance in
> the same system of applying every individual and every description of
> property to the service of the army by force has since conquered Europe.

These two great Tory men of action now had the measure of
Napoleon and his state's method of nationalised warfare, but at that
period, after the emperor had knocked Austria out of the war after the
battle of Wagram, it was almost impossible to see how he could be
beaten, however much Spain might slowly sap his power. Wellington's
and Castlereagh's political opponents in Britain, the Whigs and
Radicals, several leading members of whom, such as Lords Grenville,
Grey and Lauderdale had even opposed the parliamentary vote of
thanks to Wellington after Talavera, broadly agreed with Napoleon's

own analysis that Britain could not now prevent France from fulfilling her European hegemonic destiny, and that therefore her best answer was to appease her or make peace.

Part of the problem lay in the fact that many Whigs had originally welcomed the French Revolution and its ideals, and saw in Napoleon the man who would tame the Revolution's darker excesses while retaining its political radicalism, an ideology that many frankly wished to import to Britain. Charles James Fox, the Whig leader, had welcomed the fall of the Bastille thus: 'How much the greatest event since the beginning of the world and how much the best.' Once Napoleon's civic, legal and administrative reforms began to drag France into the nineteenth century, and his commitment to 'a career open to talent', religious liberty and the abolition of slavery was promulgated, progressively minded people in Britain began to pour adulation upon this supposed personification of republican energy and virtue, and simultaneously close their eyes to the danger his hegemony might pose to Britain's independence in the future. He was to them both everyman and an authentic foreign hero whom they could admire and hold up as a model in contrast to the supposedly reactionary Tories at home.

Napoleonism became a form of political religion for many Whigs and Radicals, which explains why they stayed faithful to the creed long after Napoleon reneged on so much of his early political promise.[1] The careers of his brothers and sisters, whom he placed on thrones in the old manner, were not opened up by their talents; he crowned himself emperor and introduced an ersatz aristocracy to reward his lieutenants and cronies; slavery was covertly reintroduced, and a concordat was signed with the pope confirming Roman Catholicism as France's premier religion. Some Whigs slipped away during this steady retreat from the principles of 1789; all too many stayed faithful. Inevitably this took forms that sailed close to outright treachery. On St Helena Napoleon spoke of his expectation in 1804 of finding 'partizans enough in England to effect a disunion sufficient to paralyse the rest of the nation' in the event of a successful invasion.[2] His military strategy in 1815 certainly seems to have been influenced by the belief that a quick victory in Belgium might topple the hawkish Tory Government and replace it with a pro-peace Whig Government. On Elba a succession of visiting Whig MPs might have encouraged him in these hopes; if so, they had blood on their hands.

The undergraduate letters of William Lamb, later Viscount Melbourne and a Whig prime minister, 'record joy at French successes and sadness at Allied triumphs'. Lamb wrote an ode to Bonaparte some months before his hero became consul, and was outraged when Pitt refused peace in 1800, accusing England of being 'fixed in bigotry and prejudice'.[3] Lord Holland described Napoleon as 'the greatest statesman and the ablest general of ancient or modern times'. The Radical journalist William Hazlitt openly mourned the result of Waterloo, to the point that it made him 'prostrated in mind and body', walking about unshaven and unwashed and almost constantly drunk.[4] Even George Canning, who was to sit in several Tory Cabinets which opposed Napoleon, said in 1803, 'I am not a panegyrist of Bonaparte, but I cannot close my eyes to the superiority of his talent, to the dazzling ascendancy of his genius,' which rather makes one wonder what he might have said had he indeed been a panegyrist.

That Wellington remained resolutely aloof from all such hero-worship, readily acknowledging Napoleon's capacities as a military commander but despising everything else about the man he insisted on calling 'Buonaparte', allowed him to keep the psychological upper hand so vital in warfare. Unlike the Whigs, Wellington admired existing and evolving British institutions and thought them inherently superior to revolutionary French ones. Moreover, as he told Lady Salisbury at his Hampshire home Stratfield Saye in 1838, he was confident that although the Whigs had disliked him they would not have replaced him once he started being victorious in the Peninsula. When Lady Salisbury told him that, had the Whigs taken office after the assassination of the prime minister Spencer Perceval on 11 May 1812, Lord Hastings would have been sent out to 'examine' him on the war, Wellington replied: 'And I should have received him very well, and he would soon have found out that I knew all about it and he knew nothing.'[5]

The doubters, whom Wellington nicknamed 'croakers', continued to criticise his handling of the war right up to 1813. They were greatly helped at the beginning of the campaign by his own officers who sent critical reports home of their commander-in-chief's capabilities. A typical example appeared in an auction house's catalogue in 1999, composed by James Ormonde, later 19th Earl and 1st Marquess Ormonde, in September 1809, who, writing to a friend about the disastrous British attack in Holland known as the Walcheren Expedition, said that 'Lord Wellington's campaign will not I fear terminate much more favourably...Some people are of opinion that he should not have been made a Peer so soon,' as Talavera was 'certainly gallant' but 'nothing more than a repulse'.

That same month Napoleon was writing to the Comte de Champagny: 'You will see in the English newspapers that General Wellesley tries to justify his Spanish expedition.'[6] Napoleon was an avid reader of British newspapers, to whose reports he generally gave far more credence than those of his commanders. 'I am angry that you have not sent me the English newspapers', he wrote to Champagny in December 1808, 'because they give us information about their positions.'[7] As Tolstoy wrote in *War and Peace* about a report of Marshal Berthier's to Napoleon, 'We know commanding officers feel it permissible to depart rather widely from the truth in describing the condition of their armies,' and as Napoleon had himself indulged in the practice he presumably knew the score. Wellington greatly resented the way in which Napoleon discovered so much about his operations in the Peninsula from the British press, which at times seems to have behaved no more patriotically than the Whig Opposition.

It is thought that some newspapers might have been smuggled across to France from Britain along with other contraband. Others were passed over during the fraternisation between the armies that took place to a surprising degree in the Peninsula. (On one occasion, General Maximilien Foy borrowed some newspapers from a British outpost outside the Lines of Torres Vedras in Portugal. Wellington was told that he had wanted to know the price of the British 3 per cent Treasury consols in which he had been speculating.)

The most effective use of newspapers was, however, made against Napoleon, by Sir Sidney Smith during the siege of Acre in May 1799. By sending him batches of British newspapers, many of them several weeks old, he made sure that Napoleon learned of the turmoil in which France had been placed after the Second Coalition declared war against her that March. Napoleon promptly raised the siege, returned to Cairo, and sailed home from Alexandria on 23 August.

Wellington was equally a keen reader of the *Moniteur*, and he might have suspected that Napoleon had a hand in falsifying its reports. On 23 December 1808, for example, Napoleon told King Joseph about Sir John Moore's expedition: 'Publish in the Madrid journals that twenty thousand English have been surprised, and are destroyed,' which was altogether untrue. In reference to just such a report, Wellington wrote: 'It is impossible that [Marshal] Marmont or [General] Dorsenne could have written such absurdities as these, to which their names are appended.'[8]

When the treaty of Schönbrunn was announced, Wellington wrote to the British minister in Portugal, John Villiers, on 20 November 1809: 'Upon seeing the paper in question, I do not think there is more reason to doubt of any of the transactions mentioned in the *Moniteur*.'[9] Wellington was not above using newspapers for his own propaganda purposes. His reports in them were generally upbeat, though never actually mendacious, and on one occasion, after reading a gloomy draft by Marshal William Carr Beresford – whose rank was Portuguese, though he was a lieutenant-general in the British army – about the battle of Albuera in May 1811, Wellington insisted: 'This won't do. It will drive the people in England mad. Write me down a victory.'[10] As the French had retired from the field, it was not an unreasonable demand.

Whereas Napoleon complained about the British press's abuse of himself, perhaps understandably in light of the *Morning Post*'s description of him as 'an indefinable being, half-African, half-European, a Mediterranean mulatto', Wellington maintained a studied public aloofness, although he did buy caricatures of himself, something that Napoleon would never have done. In private, however, Wellington was often furious at the way he believed British newspapers aided the enemy, complaining to the secretary for war and colonies, Lord Liverpool, in November 1809 about the way they printed 'paragraphs describing the position, the numbers, the objects and means of attacking possessed by the armies in Spain and Portugal', which he believed 'will increase materially the difficulty of all operations'.

Liverpool, who had declined the premiership on Pitt's death in 1806 and served as home secretary under the Duke of Portland, had followed Castlereagh as secretary for war and the colonies in October 1809. He succeeded Perceval as prime minister after the assassination, a post he then held for a record fifteen years. He naturally shrank from censoring the press, suggesting that Wellington instead censor those of his own officers who provided it with its information, but even in January 1811 *The Times* was still reporting the numbers of Peninsular troops who were *hors de combat*, something that Napoleon subsequently read with great interest.[11]

Publicly contemptuous, Wellington remained privately very concerned about the effect such 'rascally' and 'licentious' reports produced, and he vigorously protested against the freedom allowed to Henry Crabb Robinson, *The Times*' first war correspondent. He never sued for libel, despite hundreds of gross falsehoods printed about him and his generalship over the years, telling his brother Henry that nothing 'can be done with such libels and such people, excepting to despise them, and continuing one's road without noticing them'.[12] It was not the attitude adopted by Napoleon, whose closely controlled domestic press allowed no hint of criticism of the emperor. Wellington does seem to have envied Napoleon his invulnerability to domestic criticism, and mentioned it as one of the many advantages Napoleon enjoyed over him on campaign.

After the treaty of Schönbrunn, Napoleon seems to have made up his mind to go back to Spain to take on Wellington himself. As early as 29 August 1809 his personal campaign equipage, including sixty-three carriage-horses and sixty-nine saddle-horses, left Paris for Bayonne, near the Spanish border, where a mule train was already being assembled. Jardin, the emperor's personal groom, took charge of the move a month later.[13] Meanwhile Napoleon informed Soult that he intended to conduct the march on Lisbon himself.

Wellington was confident, but he fully appreciated the implications of Napoleon arriving with the Grande Armée of two hundred thousand men to attack his thirty thousand troops and thirty thousand Portuguese allies. 'I think I can already tell you that there is no occasion for taking further precautions for the safety of this army,' he told Castlereagh from Badajoz on 6 October, 'at least till affairs shall be settled in Germany, and it shall be seen whether Buonaparte can turn his whole attention to the Peninsula, than to send to Lisbon that part of the coppered tonnage of the country which can be spared from service elsewhere.' Wellington wanted the British ships to be kept in the mouth of the River Tagus at Lisbon to give confidence to his own troops and so as not to alarm the Portuguese population 'whenever it does become necessary seriously to think of embarking'.[14]

(The continued use of 'Buonaparte', as opposed to 'Bonaparte', let alone 'Napoleon', was mocked by the witty Russian diplomat Bilibin, in conversation with Prince Andrei in *War and Peace*:

> 'Buonaparte?' said Bilibin, knitting his brow to indicate that he was about to say something witty. 'Buonaparte?' he repeated, accentuating the 'u'. 'I certainly think now that he is laying down laws for Austria from Schönbrunn we must relieve him of that "u". I am firmly resolved on an innovation, and call him simply Bonaparte!'[15]

Wellington nonetheless stuck to the spelling and pronunciation which most emphasised Napoleon's Italian lineage.)

Wellington's elliptical reference to embarking, or at least the need 'seriously to think of embarking', showed that although he was confident that he could hold Portugal he was not absolutely sure, nor blind to the possibility of Napoleon bringing an overwhelming force to bear against him. It was certainly Napoleon's intention in October 1809 to do exactly that, telling Clarke that he wanted 'to bring together, for the beginning of December, 80,000 infantry and 15,000 to 16,000 cavalry to enter Spain', and this was simply to be the initial reinforcement. On 15 October, King Joseph sent his first chamberlain, senior equerry and an aide-de-camp to meet his brother at the frontier.[16]

On 28 October Marshal Berthier was officially appointed chief of staff for the French army in Spain, a sure sign that the emperor intended to fight there in person. Berthier was Napoleon's senior staff officer who had served with him in many of the greatest campaigns since Italy. On 23 November the Imperial Guard was allotted for duty in the Peninsula, with Napoleon ordering Clarke to bring its strength up to 25,000 with the necessary medical officers and field transports to be ready to start for Spain on 15 January, further evidence that he would be personally present for the campaign.[17] On 12 January 1810 Berthier's own equipage arrived in Bayonne, and a fortnight later Napoleon's was forwarded to the French stronghold of Burgos in Spain. With further reinforcements being arranged elsewhere, it was clear that Prometheus was girding his strength.

Yet even up to 20 November Wellington still viewed the future with equanimity. 'Buonaparte may be sick', he told Villiers, 'and it will certainly take some time before he can reinforce his armies in Spain to any large extent.'[18] He used the remaining time to construct the Lines of Torres Vedras, a twenty-nine-mile-long series of 165 fortified redoubts with five-foot parapets and fifteen-foot-wide ditches, most of them ten feet deep. The mountainous terrain was used to enhance the defences to the best effect, nature being employed wherever possible to help the 628 guns and 39,475 troops who guarded them. Inside the Lines a Royal Navy telegraph system relayed messages back to headquarters, and once the thousands of Portuguese labourers had finished building them Wellington considered Lisbon near impregnable.[19]

Napoleon, who had not yet heard of the existence of the Lines and never saw them in person, was utterly confident of victory. On 3 December 1809 he made a vainglorious speech to the opening session of the Corps Législatif in Paris, in which he promised:

When I show myself beyond the Pyrenees, the terrified leopard will seek the ocean in order to avoid the shame, defeat, and death. The triumph of my armies will be the triumph of the spirit of good over that of evil…I hope my friendship and protection will render peace and happiness to the people of Spain.[20]

Elizabeth Longford, in her celebrated biography of Wellington, states that Napoleon 'hit upon a particularly offensive name for his opponent – not a British lion, king of beasts, but an emaciated leopard, hideous and heraldic'.[21] The phrase Napoleon employed was 'le léopard épouvanté' (the terror-stricken leopard) which certainly evokes a big cat on the run.

For all his boasting to his pet legislators, Napoleon never went to Spain. Just as the reasons for his sudden exit in January 1809 are open to debate, so are the reasons for his non-reappearance twelve months later. Different historians have given different hypotheses, yet almost all agree that it was disastrous in the long term that he failed to expel the British there and then. Some argue that having recently survived assassination at the hands of a young Saxon, Napoleon had started to think about his own legacy, which in turn required his divorcing Josephine, who had not provided him with an heir, and making a marital alliance that would ensure his dynasty's future. It is true that on 15 December 1809 the arch-chancellor Cambacérès issued a senatorial decree in which Josephine was declared divorced, with a state pension of two million francs, but the negotiations with Russia over Napoleon's marriage with one of the tsar's sisters, or with the Emperor of Austria's nineteen-year-old daughter Princess Marie Louise could just as easily have been conducted on an Iberian campaign.

Other historians argue that since the French had defeated an army of Spanish regulars at the battle of Ocaña on 19 November, which restored Andalusia to Joseph, and were also victorious at the battle of Alba de Tormès on the 28th, and the British were back in Portugal, there was no pressing need for Napoleon to cross the Pyrenees in person. Yet this, too, seems an insufficient reason; the very presence of the British was a standing rebuke to Napoleon's European hegemony, however much he might later have claimed that he preferred them to be there than making a series of lightning attacks on his extended coastline. For all their defeats on the battlefield, the Spanish regular army never surrendered, and their irregular guerrillas were making more and more trouble.[22]

Some historians have also suggested, though with little evidence, that Napoleon 'would not risk his life in a country seething with fanaticism', and that he still feared the intrigues of Talleyrand, Fouché, Murat and now also Marshal Jean-Baptiste Bernadotte.[23] (The latter had had 'Death to Tyrants!' tattooed on his arm during the Revolution, but after Napoleon deprived him of all his appointments in September 1809 after a series of blunders at Auerstädt and Wagram it was feared that Bernadotte might now think Napoleon himself qualified for that soubriquet. His was a betrayal that was waiting to happen.)

In the course of editing his mother's memoirs, Charles de Rémusat, the son of the Comtesse Claire de Rémusat, Josephine's lady-in-waiting, recorded his belief (based on what she had written) that:

It is likely that, if the Emperor had concentrated all the resources of his genius and his Empire on the reduction of the Peninsula, he would have achieved it... Such an opportunity was well worth some risk, even should Napoleon be obliged to enter in person into the lists with Arthur Wellesley. What glory and what good fortune were reserved for the latter, as well as for his nation, by constantly adjourning the struggle, and confronting the great enemy at last only upon the field of Waterloo! The Emperor, however, did not care for the Spanish matter. It annoyed him; it had never given him a thoroughly satisfactory or glorious moment. He perceived that he had begun this business ill, conducted it with weakness, and singularly under-estimated its difficulty and importance. He tried hard to shirk it, that he might not be humiliated by it: he tried hard to neglect it, in order to escape from it. He had a repugnance, which was puerile, if indeed it was not something worse, to risk the chances of a war which did not appeal to his imagination. I venture to think that he was not perfectly sure of succeeding in that war, and that the risks of a reverse and perhaps the personal dangers to which he might be exposed, combined to disgust him with an enterprise which, even if he had resolved upon it, would have been too slow and too difficult for him. Always and above all things an *improvisatore*, it was more to his taste, and according to his customary method of action, to throw all that displeased him into the background, and to trust his fame and fortune to fresh innovations.[24]

Unreliable as the Comtesse de Rémusat's journals are, having probably been rewritten with hindsight, if her son's analysis were stripped of its personal malice against Napoleon and the imputations of fear of defeat, it serves as a good enough explanation of the emperor's unwillingness to return to Spain in the winter of 1809/10. As one biographer has put it, there was little possibility of an Austerlitz-style victory for Napoleon in Spain: 'Seeing all this clearly, yet unable to withdraw for reasons of pride and prestige, Napoleon simply distanced himself from the campaign, as he had with [the suppression of the revolt in] the Vendée in 1795 and Egypt in 1798; reasons of credibility ensured that the marshals would take the blame for a war that was in principle unwinnable.'[25]

Napoleon simply ducked the Spanish issue, sometimes even refusing to open or read despatches from Spain, and having abstracts made from them instead.[26] He nonetheless reserved the right incessantly to interfere and to complain when his marshals were defeated, by the terrain, by their own in-fighting and by adverse campaigning conditions as well as by the British, Portuguese and Spanish. He preferred vacillation to action, and as an autocrat he could get away with eternal hesitation in a way that would not have been permitted to a decision-maker responsible to representative institutions. Wellington complained of the way he had to fight with constant parliamentary supervision, but the very lack of any higher authority allowed Napoleon to avoid the one campaign he most needed to fight.

Napoleon gave out that the reason for his non-appearance 'beyond the Pyrenees' was the matrimonial one, leading to inevitable accusations that his ambition to wed a Romanov or a Hapsburg princess had contributed to his downfall. In fact it is far more likely that he did not wish to be personally associated with a difficult and costly campaign that, even if he did manage to drive the 'terrified leopard' from the Peninsula, would probably not even then end the guerrilla war. Instead, Napoleon chose one of his finest marshals, André Masséna, to defeat Wellington, with extravagant promises that as well as the hundred thousand troops under his own command he would be given whatever reinforcements and supplies were necessary to take Lisbon and expel the British from the Peninsula.

⤙

'I have always been of opinion that Portugal might be defended,' Wellington wrote to Castlereagh, nor did he change his mind when faced with the prospect of the arrival of Napoleon with two hundred thousand men. Properly supplied from the sea and always able to retreat behind the Lines of Torres Vedras, Wellington showed confidence in the face of an increasingly sceptical Government and a hostile Opposition back at Westminster. He also assumed that, as he told the Marquess Alava on 2 January 1810, 'it is Buonaparte's intention to come to Spain himself'.[27]

Marshal Beresford's quartermaster-general, Sir Benjamin D'Urban, wrote in his journal that Wellington believed 'it is possible that the inveteracy of Napoleon may prompt him to lay aside all other objects, and risk everything to fulfil his promise to the Senate of driving the "leopards" into the sea, especially as he cuts out by the root the opposition of the Peninsula. Be that as it may, His Lordship is looking forward to the expected attack, [and] wishes the militia to be immediately assembled.'[28] The question of whether Napoleon would come to Portugal was constantly posed throughout the winter and early spring of 1810, and Wellington busily perfected his Lines with the help of ten thousand Portuguese labourers. D'Urban worried that the Portuguese militias' 'mouths will embarrass more than their hands assist us', blaming the 'half-starved' condition of the Portuguese troops on the Portuguese Government.

Meanwhile, Napoleon, in a ludicrous understatement, told Berthier in late January that 'the English are the only danger in Spain'. On 8 February, hugely overconfident of success in the Peninsula, he undertook a major administrative restructuring of Spain's provincial government, effectively annexing four of Joseph's provinces – Biscay, Navarre, Aragon and Catalonia – as four French departments to be run by Marshal Augereau, General Reille, General Thouvenot and General (later Marshal) Suchet. This wrecked any hope of Joseph presenting himself as an independent monarch reigning in Spain's best interests, and simply meant that the four provinces north of the Ebro henceforth flew the tricolour, took direct orders from the French and carried the cost of the French armies stationed there.[29] Some historians suggest that Napoleon would not have much minded if his brother had abdicated over the humiliation.[30]

From letters intercepted between Berthier and Soult, Wellington discovered that the Imperial Guard had been ordered from Bordeaux to Bayonne and assumed that Napoleon was still on his way.[31] 'I truly believe that if we are able to continue the war in the Portuguese and Spanish Peninsula, Europe will not be lost,' he wrote to Dom Miguel Pereira Forjas, the Portuguese minister of war, 'and I believe also that if we are able to maintain ourselves in Portugal the war will not end in the Peninsula.'[32] Brave words, but ones supported by events.

Yet back at home there was little but vacillation and disbelief in his abilities to withstand the coming invasion. The diary of Thomas

Creevey MP for 17 February records the Radical politician meeting Samuel Whitbread MP, the Earl of Derby, Mrs Grey and Lord Downshire. Their view was that 'Wellington has very little time to effect his escape from these two armies that are approaching him in different directions. His career approaches very rapidly to a conclusion.'[33] Wellington had already written to Lord Liverpool about the demands of the Common Council of the City of London for an inquiry into his conduct, but on 10 March Liverpool himself wrote Wellington a frankly defeatist letter, telling him: 'Your chances of successful defence are considered here by all persons, military as well as civil, so improbable, that I could not recommend any attempt at what might be called desperate resistance.'

Wellington, faced with this lack of faith in him by the Whigs, the press, the City, many of his own officers and now also seemingly the Government, did not despair. In many ways this was the moment when his moral courage was shown at its best, equal even to that of his physical. On 2 April he replied to Liverpool:

Whatever people might tell you, I am not so desirous of fighting desperate battles; if I was, I might fight one any day I please...But I have looked to the great result of our maintaining our position in the Peninsula; and have not allowed myself to be diverted from it by the wishes of the allies, and probably by some of our own army, that I should interfere more actively in some partial affairs...I believe that the world in the Peninsula begins to believe that I am right... All I beg is, that if I am to be responsible, I may be left to the exercise of my own judgment: and I ask for the fair confidence of the Government upon the measures which I am to adopt.

There was one man in London who had complete confidence in Wellington, but he was slipping once more into the grip of porphyria. King George III wrote to his ministers telling them to allow Wellington 'to proceed according to his judgment...unfettered by any particular instructions which might embarrass him in the execution of his general plan of operations'.[34] The next year, however, the king went mad once more and an act of parliament created a regency, with the Prince of Wales becoming the Prince Regent.

Two events coming in swift succession the next month lessened the likelihood of Napoleon arriving personally in Spain, though neither made Wellington feel more at ease. Firstly, Napoleon's marriage to Princess Marie Louise on 2 April 1810 seemed to prevent Austria from

taking her place in any future anti-Napoleonic struggle; the corner-
stone of Pitt's original European coalition had been knocked away at a
blow. (When the Emperor of Austria, fearing the accusations of a
mésalliance with a Corsican upstart, asked permission to publish a con-
cocted genealogy to show that Napoleon's ancestors had reigned at
Treviso, Napoleon replied, apropos of Rudolf of Hapsburg who had
founded the dynasty in 1267: 'Permit me to be the Rudolf of my
dynasty.'[35] The Hapsburgs soon regretted the match, and have done
so ever since. A son of the last Empress of Austria told the writer that
his family do not 'regard it as our finest hour'. Tolstoy put the humiliating nuptials in characteristically carnal tones when he sneered that
'the Emperor of Austria is gratified that this man should take the
daughter of the Kaisers to his bed'.)

Wellington immediately recognised the dreadful implications for the
British war effort, already weighed down after seventeen years of conflict and now without Austria to help conduct a war of two fronts
against Napoleon. Writing to Brigadier-General Robert Craufurd two
days after Napoleon's nuptials, he said:

> The Austrian marriage is a terrible event, and must prevent any
> great movement on the continent for the present. Still, I do not
> despair of seeing at some time or other a check to the Buonaparte
> system. Recent transactions in Holland show that it is all hollow
> within, and that it is so inconsistent with the wishes, the interests,
> and even the existence of civilised society, that he cannot trust even
> his brothers to carry it into execution.[36]

This was a reference to Napoleon's problems with his younger brother
Louis, who had recently abdicated the throne of Holland in protest at
Napoleon's attempt to annex the country. Craufurd might have been
excused for thinking Wellington was clutching at straws.

The second great development of April 1810 was Napoleon's appointment of Marshal André Masséna to the command of the Army of
Portugal. 'Gentlemen,' Wellington told his officers, 'we are in the presence of one of the first soldiers of Europe.'[37] In a letter to Lord Mahon
years later, he described Masséna as the ablest French commander after
Napoleon, and he was also quoted as saying: 'When Masséna was
opposed to me, and in the field, I never slept comfortably.'[38] Napoleon
might not have been willing to present himself in the Iberian Peninsula
personally, but in sending Masséna – whom he nicknamed 'the spoilt
child of victory' – he was doing the next best thing.

André Masséna was born in Sardinian-owned Nice in 1758, possibly of Jewish origins. He was orphaned, became a cabin boy, then a sergeant-major, then a fruit-seller and smuggler, before being elected lieutenant-colonel of the 3rd Var Volunteers. He distinguished himself at the battle of Rivoli, commanded the Army of Switzerland and won the battle of Zurich in 1798, becoming a marshal of the first creation in 1804. He lost the sight of his left eye when Napoleon shot him in an accident in 1808, for which Berthier was prevailed upon to take the blame. In January 1810 he was made Prince d'Essling after his superb defensive engagement at the eponymous battle the previous year. He had also served with distinction at Wagram.[39]

At fifty-two, Masséna was therefore a very senior marshal as well as a remarkable character. His mistress Silvia Cepolini having brought him luck on the Italian campaign, he took another, Henriette Lebreton, out with him to the Peninsula. There is a debate among historians as to whether she wore the uniform of a dragoon or a hussar, but she was the wife of a captain on Masséna's staff and the sister of one of Masséna's former mistresses.[40]

Wellington was under no illusions about the importance of the outcome of the approaching onslaught. Writing to Dom Miguel Pereira Forjas in the spring of 1810, he repeated his earlier sentiments and foresaw with uncanny prescience the way the war would go:

> If we can maintain ourselves in Portugal, the war will not cease in the Peninsula, and if the war lasts in the Peninsula, Europe will be saved. I am also of the opinion that the position I have chosen for the struggle is good, that it is one calculated by its nature to defend the very heart of Portugal, and that if the enemy cannot drive us from it, he will be obliged to retreat, in which case he will run great risk of being lost, and at all events be forced to abandon Portugal.[41]

Napoleon was meanwhile keeping Masséna informed of what the British press was telling him about Wellington's army. Writing to Berthier on 29 May from Le Havre, he said that 'according to the news that we have from England, General Wellington is no stronger than 24,000 men, English and German, and the Portuguese are not quite 25,000'. Nonetheless he ordered Berthier not to attack Lisbon yet, but to spend the summer methodically capturing the fortresses of Ciudad Rodrigo and afterwards Almeida. As for 'le général anglais', as Napoleon still called Wellington, because he had fewer than three thousand cavalry it would be better for Masséna to attack in flat country rather than in country where cavalry operated at a discount.[42]

Masséna captured Ciudad Rodrigo on 9 July and Almeida – after the fortress's magazine exploded in a freak accident – on 27 August, from where he invaded Portugal. As he advanced, he sent back inflated reports of his successes, claiming, for example, that he had inflicted a thousand British casualties in fighting on the Coa river on 24 July, whereas the true figure deduced from the British muster rolls was only 360.

Up until Masséna began the siege of Almeida, Wellington still seems to have been under the impression that Napoleon would be commanding the invasion in person. 'We ought to take care to have a large fleet in the Tagus,' he wrote to Vice-Admiral Berkeley on 2 July, 'otherwise Buonaparte will strike a serious blow upon us, we may depend upon it. All the intercepted letters, and other intelligence, tend to show that he is making great naval exertions.'[43] To Craufurd on 13 July he suggested that a detachment of the Imperial Guard at Burgos 'appears to be stationed on the road, as if to protect the journey of Buonaparte to that place. If this be true, they are waiting for him.'[44] The next day he wrote to Liverpool: 'I should not be surprised if I was to hear that Buonaparte himself had come into Spain to direct these operations.'[45]

If Wellington was preparing himself psychologically for a clash with the emperor, Napoleon had meanwhile been behaving as if Wellington was already his prisoner. In 1810 there were 41,000 French prisoners of war held in Britain against 11,000 British and 17,300 Hanoverian prisoners held in France. From mid-April discussions started about a swap of these men, negotiated between a friend of the foreign secretary, Wellington's eldest brother Lord Wellesley, called Colin Alexander Mackenzie, and M. Moustier, the secretary of the Saxon legation in Paris, whom Napoleon had appointed to speak for France.

A letter from Napoleon to Moustier in the archives of the French foreign ministry at the Quai d'Orsay dated 30 June shows how staggeringly arrogant the emperor was about affairs in Portugal: 'It is possible that the English may not wish to set free all the French prisoners…You must affect to look upon their army as being actually in our power and you must not show any modesty in advancing this opinion.' Furthermore Moustier was instructed to emphasise to Mackenzie 'the utter folly of Wellington's presumption' in attempting to hold Portugal with forces 'which, whatever their numbers, are but a handful compared with the troops which France will lead against them'.[46]

With Napoleon effectively insisting that Wellington's undefeated army and his Portuguese allies should be included in the list of his prisoners, it was unsurprising that nothing came of the proposed exchange. Yet Napoleon dragged the negotiations out until August because 'he was impatiently waiting for news of the capture of Wellington's army by Masséna'.[47]

It was in August 1810 that the *Moniteur* published its jibe about Wellington, which nearly five years later he was to recall on the field of Waterloo, when it wrote: 'The sepoy general is waging war with all the ferocity he has learned in India, and shoots every poor Portuguese peasant who refuses to abandon his home.'[48] Whereas that might have been Wellington's policy in Malabar, it certainly was not on the retreat to Torres Vedras. Yet the phrase 'sepoy general' obviously rankled.

The following month Wellington learned from a very different source of Napoleon's low view of the British army, when he was sent a memorandum on the debriefing of General Moreau in America. Jean-Victor Moreau had succeeded Pichegru as commander of the Army of the North in 1795, and he later commanded the Army of Italy and the Army of the Rhine. A rival to Napoleon, Moreau had been banished from France for alleged complicity in a Royalist plot centred on General Pichegru, of which he was probably innocent, and lived in Morrisville, New Jersey, from 1804 until 1813, when he returned to Europe to fight for the tsar. According to the memorandum compiled by the British Foreign Office after interviews with Moreau in America: 'Neither Bonaparte nor Moreau have or had a high opinion of the British army, at least as to skill. The experience that army has acquired within a few years and the unquestionable proofs of courage and discipline they have given, may have ... altered their opinions.'[49]

Far from being caught out in the plains with virtually no cavalry, as Napoleon had hoped, Wellington conducted a scorched-earth retreat through Portugal towards the Lines of Torres Vedras. Napoleon famously remarked that an army marched on its stomach, but Wellington ensured that there would be nothing to fill French stomachs, burning everything of use that could not be carried away. It was a brutal form of warfare for the inhabitants of the ravaged regions, presaging the Total War of the next century. 'We are marching across a desert; women and children and old men have all fled,' Masséna reported to Berthier on 15 September, 'in fact, no guide is to be found anywhere.' Instead they found, in his phrase, 'an enemy behind every stone'. Masséna wished to shoot any Portuguese guerrillas – known as the *Ordenanza* – that he found, on the grounds that they were mere brigands and not in uniform, but on 24 September Wellington wrote to remind him that in the Revolutionary Wars 'you yourself added to the glory of the French army when commanding soldiers who had no uniform.'[50] It was relatively unusual for enemy commanders to correspond in this way, and Masséna backed down.

Napoleon attempted, at the distance of Fontainebleau, to interfere incessantly with the campaign. In one letter to Berthier of 29 September he ordered Soult to keep on the heels of the Spanish general, the Marquis de la Romana, and stop him crossing the Tagus. By the time the order arrived several weeks later, de la Romana's force had long crossed the river and had joined Wellington. Soult answered on New Year's Eve that, if he had followed the whole of Napoleon's orders about one regiment to the letter, 'that unit would never reach its destination and it would be surrounded immediately so that I could not go to aid it'.[51] It was one of the rare occasions on which a marshal answered the emperor back.

Napoleon's impatience was especially directed against Masséna, of whom he expected great things against Wellington. 'Tomorrow you must send an officer with a letter to Marshal Masséna, telling him to attack and to overthrow the English,' he told Berthier on 19 September, 'that Lord Wellesley has not more than 18,000 men, of which 15,000 are infantry and the rest cavalry and artillery; that General [Sir Rowland] Hill has not more than 6,000 men, and that it is ridiculous to think of 25,000 Englishmen holding the balance against 60,000 Frenchmen…Marshal Masséna has four times more artillery than he requires against the enemy.' At last Napoleon acknowledged that 'I am too far away, and the position of the enemy changes too often, for me to be able to give advice as to the manner of attack; but it is certain that the enemy is not in a position to resist. According to authentic news received from spies in London, if the 4,000 men at Cadiz are joined to the English army in Spain, it is only 28,000 strong.'[52]

Napoleon's letter, with its worryingly accurate estimates of Wellington's total force, led directly to Masséna's attack on Wellington at Busaco on 27 September. Masséna, like Napoleon, was over-confident. 'I cannot persuade myself,' he said on the 26th, 'that Lord Wellington will risk the loss of a reputation by giving battle, but if he does, I have him. Tomorrow we shall effect the capture of Portugal, and in a few days I shall drown the leopard.'[53] Masséna's lieutenants at the time, Ney, Reynier and Foy among them, threw themselves against Wellington's well-defended line and, in a classic use of lateral roads, reverse slopes and steady line fire against oncoming columns, Wellington won another victory. The Portuguese also distinguished themselves, and Wellington could afterwards continue his retreat to the Lines of Torres Vedras unhampered. Historians who persist in describing Busaco as a British defeat, because Wellington retreated afterwards, fail to recognise that, as his correspondence makes clear, he only ever intended it as a holding action designed to allow the army to enter the Lines of Torres Vedras in their own time and in good order.

Once safely there, Wellington was nearly impregnable. Six hundred cannon covered three lines of redoubts. Rivers were dammed, approaches destroyed, mountains scarped and signal-posts erected by several thousand Portuguese workmen. 'The greatest compliment to the strength of the Lines that can be paid', wrote the historian A. G. Macdonell, 'is simply to record that Ney gave them one glance and emphatically declined to attack them.'[54] If 'the bravest of the brave' wanted nothing to do with an assault, neither did Soult, who virtually refused to aid Masséna, but against Napoleon's orders spent nine days laying siege to Olivenza and nearly two months outside Badajoz.[55]

Masséna himself grumbled to his staff that he had not been told about the Lines, which Wellington had been secretly building for almost a year. 'To the devil with it,' he said in response to their explanations, 'he never built those mountains!' After an attempted assault failed on 14 October, Masséna convinced himself that Wellington's defences could not be attacked successfully, and wrote to Napoleon to say: 'The Marshal Prince of Essling has come to the conclusion that he would compromise the army of His Majesty if he were to attack in force Lines so formidable.' Soon afterwards, while the marshal was scouting near Redoubt 120, a British artilleryman nearly hit him with a well-aimed shell. Masséna raised his hat in salute and rode off. When Masséna finally lifted the siege, Wellington took the news with his customary sang-froid; he was shaving at the time and merely commented: 'Ay, I thought they meant to be off.'

Almost Napoleon's only source of information from Portugal since September came from British newspapers, which told him that, as of 17 October, 'Lord Wellington was with his army' and that Masséna had not yet given battle. He gave several orders expressing his discontent with the situation, still trying to fight an Iberian war of attrition from his palace outside Paris.[56] On 3 November he sent Berthier a series of orders for his armies in which appeared more than once the phrase 'as soon as the English have re-embarked', implying that he had no real idea of the realities of the situation outside Lisbon, where Masséna's army was running very short of food and was about to break up camp and retire to Almeida and Ciudad Rodrigo.[57] Wellington's destruction of the olive and orange trees and burning of villages and crops in Masséna's path had meant that the French could not live off the land outside the Lines through the winter. Some historians put the cost in terms of Portuguese lives lost to the starvation during the five-month siege at around fifty thousand – 2 per cent of the country's total population – but whatever the figure a very high civilian price was paid for Wellington's victory.[58]

It seems to have been Wellington's scorched-earth policy in the Peninsula which finally wrung out of Napoleon the first words of commendation that he ever employed towards Wellington. General Foy arrived in Paris on 22 November to report on the situation in Portugal. According to his letter to Masséna of 4 December, Napoleon 'recognised the difficulty of chasing the British' and showed great anxiety about the fate of the army.[59] In a subsequent interview with Foy, in which Napoleon ranted against the 'insubordination' of Ney and Junot and their defiance of Masséna, the emperor at last paid tribute to Wellington and his army. 'The English are full of courage and honour,' he conceded; 'they defend themselves well. Masséna and Ney do not know them but Reynier, whom they have beaten two or three times, knows them well. Wellington is admittedly a clever man. This total devastation of a country is cleverly conceived. I would not be able to do that with all my power.'[60] This has also been reported as: 'Only Wellington and I are capable of executing such measures.'[61]

The only time that the treasurer of the senate Jean-Antoine-Claude Chaptal, the Comte de Chanteloup, ever heard Napoleon praise Wellington's military talent was over the retreat to Lisbon. Noting his opponent's devastation of the route, destruction of windmills, burning of crops and rounding up of the whole population and livestock, Napoleon said:

> Here is a man who is obliged to retreat before an army which he does not dare fight, but he creates a desert of eighty leagues between the enemy and himself and slows down their march. He weakens the enemy by depriving them of everything. He knows how to destroy his enemy without fighting. In Europe there are only Wellington and

myself who are capable of such measures, but there is this difference between him and me, and that is that France ... would blame me, whereas in England they will approve.[62]

⌣

A new phase had opened in the relationship between Napoleon and Wellington. Hitherto Wellington had admired Napoleon militarily and despised everything else about him, while Napoleon had despised Wellington militarily as merely a 'sepoy general'. Since the 1810 retreat, and especially after Masséna was forced to break camp before the Lines of Torres Vedras, Napoleon did not demur at linking his own name with that of Wellington, albeit only in praise of their mutual ruthlessness.

Years later, speaking of his success at Torres Vedras, Wellington told Lady Salisbury: 'When a conqueror like Napoleon is once stopped, it is all over with him: he is like a snow-ball, he melts away.'[63] For all the pretentiousness of that remark – it was the snows of Russia in 1812 which destroyed Napoleon's power, not the Lines of Torres Vedras in 1810 – Wellington had successfully defied the emperor.

SIX

Will He? Won't He?
1810–1811

I can meet fate and destiny with courage; and, unless I change,
I shall very soon not move out of the way of a carriage.

NAPOLEON

fter the repulse of Masséna from the Lines of Torres Vedras a
new tone entered Napoleon's correspondence when referring to
Wellington. Gone were the assumptions of immediate British
re-embarkation or even capture; instead there was a hardheaded appreciation of the long-term threat Napoleon's empire faced as it haemor-
rhaged more and more troops, cash and resources in the Peninsula.
Napoleon even deigned to get Wellington's name and title right at last.
Although the propaganda references to Wellington and his army as a
'sepoy general' leading 'terrified leopards' continued in the *Moniteur*, in
private Napoleon discovered a new respect for Wellington's capabilities.
He was not, however, persuaded over the next eighteen months that
Spain was an important enough theatre for his personal presence.[1] His
devoted veterans, such as the cavalryman Baron Marbot, remained for
the rest of their lives 'convinced that Napoleon would in the end have
established his brother triumphantly on the throne of Spain if he had
been content to finish this war before going to Russia'.[2]

Wellington, an avid reader of the *Moniteur*, believed he could spot
from some paragraphs in the issue of 23 November 1810 what he
described to his brother Henry as 'a hint of the intentions of the
Emperor in respect to this country. Our position is evidently considered invulnerable; but they intend to endeavour to operate upon our
supplies.'[3] It was a shrewd assumption, because, although Napoleon
appreciated that he could hardly threaten the Royal Navy, which was
always able to resupply the British army, once Wellington had
marched as far from the sea as he had at Talavera, he lay open to

counter-attack. Far from hoping to seize Lisbon, Napoleon had to try, as he continued to fight the Peninsular War by correspondence course, to initiate engagements in west-central Spain, far from the coast.

Whenever Napoleon had intelligence from his spies or from the British press about where Wellington was or what he was doing he would immediately pass it on to Berthier, who in turn passed it on to the most interested quarter. On Christmas Day 1810, for instance, he told Berthier to warn General Foy that 'on 25 November Lord Wellington made a movement to menace the French army's right flank', and the following day he wrote from Paris to tell Foy that on 3 December 'Lord Wellington resumed his position at Torres Vedras... Send General Foy three copies of the *Moniteur* containing the news received from London yesterday.'[4] Since the news was at least three weeks old even before it was sent to the corps commanders in the field, the situation bordered on the ludicrous, not least because the despatches often had to be guarded by up to five hundred men. Napoleon was also personally editing Wellington's despatches from the Peninsula before inserting them in his own newspaper. 'As I have cut out several things from the despatch of Wellington which will be in tomorrow's *Moniteur*,' he wrote to Berthier on 4 January 1811, 'I am sending it to you complete.'[5]

It was fantastically frustrating for Napoleon's marshals to receive orders that were impossible to carry out, either because the military situation had altered since they were written or because the emperor failed to appreciate the nature of the terrain over which they had to fight, or because he held too low an opinion of the Spanish irregulars and the Portuguese regular forces, or because of the lack of good roads in such a large country, or because of shortage of cash, or because of a breakdown of intelligence about other French units. Central planning in Paris was an absurdity, but Spain had no centralised General Staff until 1812. The situation was not helped by Soult despising King Joseph. Insubordination was rife and at one point Napoleon attempted to command seven separate French forces in Spain from outside the country, with almost every commander seemingly incapable of getting on with his colleagues.[6] It was a textbook example of how not to fight a war, and would have hugely played into British hands even if Wellington had not himself been a military genius.

Yet Wellington rarely exhibited over-confidence. 'The French army is, without doubt, a wonderful machine,' he told his brother Richard in January 1811, and he elsewhere stated that 'France is not an enemy whom I despise, nor does it deserve that I should.' Yet when

Napoleon sent orders via General Foy for Masséna in February 1810 to build bridges across the Tagus, without hinting where the materials or opportunity to build them might come from, it is hard to doubt that the two successful months Napoleon had spent in Spain in 1808/9 had taught him all the wrong lessons about Iberian campaigning.[7]

⌐

Despite surviving at Torres Vedras, and despite the promise of future victories once Masséna had withdrawn, Wellington still found domestic opponents determined to belittle him. 'Who is there mad enough to expect that we shall be able to drive the French out of the Peninsula, either by arms, or by negotiation?' asked the leading Whig Sir William Fremantle in the Commons in February 1811. 'Where is the man, in his senses, who believes or will say that he believes, that we shall be able to accomplish this?'[8] Napoleonism was rife; the actress Elizabeth Inchbald, Sarah Siddons' great rival, was driven to furious distraction by the guns in Hyde Park whose salvoes announced Wellington's victories.[9]

Wellington left the Lines and by early April the French had been expelled from the whole of Portugal – except Almeida – and an invasion which had cost them twenty thousand dead was over. The Hyde Park guns were busy the following month, celebrating Wellington's defeat of Masséna at Fuentes d'Oñoro and Beresford's defeat of Soult at Albuera. Of the battle of Fuentes d'Oñoro, after which the French retreated but which they nonetheless claimed as a victory on the Arc de Triomphe, Wellington wrote: 'The most difficult one I was ever concerned in and against the greatest odds... If Boney had been there we should have been beat.'[10] In fact had Napoleon been there Wellington would probably not have given battle at such heavily unfavourable odds – 38,000 to 48,000 – but it is instructive that for Wellington the shadow of Napoleon even fell over battlefields on which he had been victorious. (Other French defeats engraved on the Arc de Triomphe include the battles of Corunna, Oporto and Toulouse.)

Masséna, who was forced to withdraw to Salamanca, complained in his bulletin that Wellington 'had employed all the resources of fortification against an attack made by main force', as though there was something ungentlemanly in such a thing. The *Moniteur* sneered at Wellington's 'prudence', but the fact remained that he was on the verge of gaining one of his greatest victories.[11] Napoleon decided to send out yet another marshal whom he hoped might take the measure of Wellington. On 10 May, five days after Fuentes d'Oñoro, Marshal Auguste Marmont took over the now inaptly named Army of Portugal. After the war Wellington met Masséna for dinner in Soult's house, and Masséna told him that the Englishman had given him all his grey hair, to which Wellington chivalrously replied: 'We were pretty level.' The Prince of Essling answered that Wellington had had the better of it – which was no more than the obvious truth.[12] Masséna managed to persuade himself that his failure was the result of Napoleon's jealousy of him, and blamed the requirement that the emperor's glory must 'always shine with the most brilliant lustre'.[13]

There was something almost pathetic about the way in which Napoleon, at St Cloud, wrote on 7 May to Berthier – very grandly entitled Prince de Neuchâtel et de Wagram, Major Général de l'Armée d'Espagne, despite also being based in Paris – to send him copies of English newspapers which stated that 'Wellington has crossed the Tagus.' He asked that they be sent on to Marmont and the Duc d'Istria (Marshal Bessières, commander of the Old Guard). Napoleon was concerned about the arrival of Wellington at the fortress of Badajoz, and asked to have the newspapers returned as soon as they had been copied by Berthier's office.[14] With over seven months to go before he began to make serious preparations for the Russian campaign, Napoleon was being criminally negligent in not sorting out the 'Spanish ulcer' himself. It was irresponsible, in both senses of the word.

Writing to Berthier again on 1 June about Wellington's marching with twelve thousand men to reinforce Marshal Beresford, Napoleon said his information came from British newspapers.[15] Yet by then Beresford had already defeated Soult at Albuera on 16 May, a defeat which Soult minimised to Napoleon later by claiming that only 2,900 French troops had died, when the true figure was over eight thousand.

Wellington could hardly believe that Napoleon would stay for ever at St Cloud rather than come out to fight him in the Peninsula. As he wrote to Beresford on 28 August: 'I have no doubt that unless the design has been altered since the end of June and beginning of July, we shall have the Emperor in Spain and <u>hell to pay</u> before much time elapses.' This might entail a return to Torres Vedras, especially if Napoleon were accompanied, as seemed inevitable, by large reinforcements. Wellington wrote that he had his force 'well in hand, and can have it on board again in a very few days'.[16]

Yet nothing happened, and Wellington started to impose his psychological dominance over the whole Spanish-Portuguese frontier theatre of the war. At Fuenteguinaldo on 25 September, when

Marmont had forty thousand men to Wellington's sixteen thousand, Marmont refused to attack, assuming that as at Busaco and elsewhere Wellington must have had large bodies of troops on the reverse slopes, when in fact he had not.[17] 'I am certain that if Buonaparte does not remove us from the Peninsula, he must lower his tone with the world: and I am equally certain that he will make every effort to avoid this necessity,' wrote Wellington four days later. 'He has a fleet, and does not want for armies; and he is just the man to sacrifice his fleet, and to make a great effort with his armies to effect this object.'

In the same letter he explained that he had armed Lisbon's sea forts 'as the only measure in my power at the time it was supposed that he was coming himself to take command of his armies'.[18] Although he could not be sure, it dawned on Wellington during September 1811 that Napoleon might not be coming after all. Nonetheless he used the threat of Napoleon's possible arrival to try to persuade the Government to keep him fully supplied, especially with ships to win a sea battle off Lisbon if necessary. By October, he could inform Lord Liverpool:

> I have no doubt but that Napoleon is much distressed for money. Notwithstanding the swindling mode in which his armies are paid, the troops are generally ten and eleven, and some of them twelve months in arrears of pay...It is impossible that this fraudulent tyranny can last. If Great Britain continues stout, we must see the destruction of it.[19]

From this period in late 1811, Wellington adopted a new, almost messianic tone in his descriptions of Napoleon and his system. His survival since April 1809 had led to his thriving militarily, and as the prospect of Napoleon arriving to give him 'hell to pay' receded, so his presentation of the war as a moral crusade increased. Previously it had been just another British military expedition, now Wellington began to portray it as a great righteous cause. This was partly because the Government was still under threat from the Whigs, and needed every good argument it could find; but also, now that he had beaten Delaborde, Junot, Victor, Soult and Masséna, and imposed his personality and will on the entire military scene, Wellington was confident not only of surviving but of being ultimately victorious. High-flown talk would have sounded ridiculous from one who was later forced speedily to re-embark; now Wellington felt confident enough to indulge in it freely.

Of course, he was vigorously talking up his own campaign. His letters deliberately emphasised that 'If I am right, the British army cannot be so advantageously employed as in the Peninsula.'[20] He quite consciously played up the personal role of 'Buonaparte' as Britain's opponent, only relatively rarely mentioning France, the French army or the French Government or Empire in his letters and official despatches.

In December 1811, for instance, he wrote three important letters about what he believed were Napoleon's intentions and capabilities in Spain. 'Buonaparte is still far from making the conquest even of that part of the Peninsula of which he has the military possession,' he told Lord Liverpool, 'and the people of the country are still disposed to resist whenever they see a prospect of advantage.'[21] From his headquarters in Freneda he told a political supporter that 'the sovereigns of Europe, and all who are willing to resist Buonaparte' must embark on a new type of warfare in which they 'will one and all persevere to the last, and either save all or lose all; with an entire conviction that the remainder, as it is called, will, in the course of events, be taken from them if they should cease to resist'. If, on the other hand, 'Buonaparte would be inclined or obliged to withdraw from the Peninsula', Wellington declared, he would then march over the Pyrenees into France itself.

One of the most impassioned letters that Wellington ever wrote about Napoleon was penned to Lord William Bentinck, the commander-in-chief of British forces in Sicily, on Christmas Eve 1811. It is remarkable for the unswerving confidence it showed in predicting a general reaction against Napoleon, even before the emperor had decided to invade Russia:

> I have, however, long considered it probable, that even we should witness a general resistance throughout Europe to the fraudulent and disgusting tyranny of Buonaparte, created by the example of what has occurred in Spain and Portugal; and that we should be actors and advisers in these scenes; and I have reflected frequently upon the measures which should be pursued to give a chance of success ... I am quite certain that the finances of Great Britain are more than a match for Buonaparte, and that we shall have the means of aiding any country that may be disposed to resist his tyranny.[22]

One country that showed herself more and more disposed to resist Napoleon's 'tyranny', at least insofar as she planned to withdraw from the Continental System, was Russia. Tsar Alexander I was, in the opinion of the great Napoleon scholar J. Holland Rose, encouraged by 'the continuance of the Peninsular War', thus making Wellington at least in small part responsible for the great events which were the primary cause of the eventual fall of Napoleon.[23]

In a long letter to Marmont on 13 December 1811, unsigned but carrying his handwritten corrections, Napoleon continued his policy of directing the Spanish campaign from Paris, even to the extent of ordering the marshal on the spot to establish his headquarters at Valladolid rather than Salamanca. Napoleon did not believe 'le général Wellington' would take the offensive after the rainy season, because 'the English have lost many and are finding it hard to recruit their army'. He instead believed that Wellington would simply content himself with the defence of Portugal.[24]

In this Napoleon again severely underestimated Wellington, and by ordering Marmont to disperse his forces and take over the responsibility for the western half of Old Castile, at precisely the time that he was removing troops for service in Russia and to reinforce Suchet in Valencia, the emperor weakened Marmont's Army of Portugal to the extent that Wellington could besiege Ciudad Rodrigo, which he captured on 19 January 1812 after only eleven days. 'Ciudad Rodrigo must be taken tonight,' was Wellington's laconic order, and so it was, with only five hundred casualties.[25]

In Paris Napoleon was watching carefully. In a single letter to Marmont of 18 February, going into minute detail about how to deal with the British offensive, he mentioned 'Lord Wellington' by name no fewer than seventeen times. He tried to anticipate all the various moves the British commander might make. 'If Lord Wellington directs himself towards Badajoz,' he wrote, 'let him go there.' He was confident that the great Spanish fortified city could withstand a very long siege, but in the event Wellington took it in under three weeks.

∽

The year 1812 was to be long, hard and ultimately disappointing for both Napoleon and Wellington, involving a dispiriting retreat for both men, begun within two days of one another in October. For Wellington, however, the retreat from Burgos was only a setback, whereas for Napoleon the retreat from Moscow represented a crushing reversal of fortune that signalled the beginning of the end for his Empire. Napoleon called Poland, from where he launched his invasion of Russia, 'the key to the vault'. And so it turned out, except that the vault was that of a graveyard rather than a treasury.

Wellington believed that France's war resources had started to dwindle as early as January 1812, long before he or anyone else had any inkling of Napoleon's ambitions in the east. Writing to

Lieutenant-General Baron Constant de Rebecque of the Dutch army, he argued that:

> One symptom of a sense of the failure of these resources is that Napoleon has recently seized upon the territories of Rome, Holland, and the Hanse Towns, and has annexed these states to France. By these means he has departed from a remarkable principle of his policy. In the early periods of his government he had not extended the dominions of France beyond what were called her natural limits of the Rhine, the Ocean, the Alps and the Pyrenees. It appeared that he was aware of the dangers to which all widely extended empires are liable; and he was satisfied with governing by his influence all these states, and those of the Confederation of the Rhine. He must at the same time have made up his mind to draw no resources from these States, excepting those of a military nature, stipulated by treaty; and indeed, the hopes of avoiding future plunder could have been the only inducement to these several States to enter into the Confederation.

In his attempts to delve into the mind of the man he now for the first time since the Convention of Cintra called 'Napoleon', Wellington argued that 'the futile disputes with his brother [Louis, King of Holland], the Pope, or the Senates of the Hanseatic towns' were not 'the cause of the departure from a remarkable principle of his early policy', and 'neither was it the dictates of a wild and extravagant ambition', otherwise he might have 'seized upon poor Switzerland'. Wellington believed that, not wanting 'to plunder Austria, Prussia, Russia or Denmark' any more than he already had, Napoleon had merely decided to plunder Holland, the Hanseatic towns and Rome, all of them rich but militarily powerless. As for Spain, 'it is completely plundered from one end to the other ... the cultivation in some parts ... is entirely annihilated'.[26] Setting aside the whiff of hypocrisy in feeling concern for Iberian agriculture when he had himself operated a scorched-earth policy during his retreat to Lisbon, Wellington was looking closely at and thinking deeply about Napoleon's war machine, and he suspected that it was already running out of important resources, including manpower.

Napoleon was meanwhile losing faith in Marmont, giving Berthier a long list of complaints from Paris on 20 February, not least that Marmont 'gives himself trouble because Lord Wellington sends one or two divisions towards Badajoz, although Badajoz is extremely strong, and the Duc de Dalmatie's [Soult's] army amounts to 80,000 men, and can be reinforced by Marshal Suchet; when, in short, if Lord Wellington were to march upon Badajoz, there would be a certain, prompt, and decisive method of recalling him...' Mr Lawrell, a member of the Whig club Brooks's in St James's Street, tended to agree with the emperor, betting Lord Kinnaird ten guineas on 1 April 'that there is a general engagement between Lord Wellington and the French before Badajoz is taken.' In fact Wellington took Badajoz on 6 April without Soult or Suchet being able to prevent him. (At Brooks's the members betted on anything, such as journeys to Abyssinia, Louis XVIII's restoration, the outcome of court cases, the state of George III's mental health, political appointments, who would survive whom, and the price of potatoes in Dublin.)

The ability of the French to bring off sophisticated combined operations was so circumscribed by 1812 that when the French army simply wanted to get a convoy of supplies from Bayonne to Madrid it found that the journey took thirty-seven days and required an escort of no fewer than four thousand troops.[27] It was impossible to co-ordinate operations effectively under such circumstances.

Wellington's storming of Badajoz after twenty days' siege, in three separate and costly attacks, was followed by an horrific orgy of looting and the wholesale rape of a convent within the walls. The people of Badajoz were believed not to have treated the British wounded well after the post-Talavera retreat, and their suspected francophilia was punished appallingly by the British troops, some of whom even fired on their own officers when they tried to end the pillaging. Wellington managed to get his men under control after nearly three days only because of fear of a French counter-attack; he even had a gallows erected in the town square to help sober up his men.

This was not a war crime on the cold-blooded scale of Jaffa, nor was it premeditated, like the killing of the Duc d'Enghien, but neither was it Wellington's finest hour. The disorder was not subdued, it subsided, and Wellington duly wrote to Liverpool about his men's undoubted gallantry – over 3,500 British casualties were sustained on the night of the storming – but made no mention of their later excesses. They were remembered by the townspeople, however, whose descendants in May 2000 refused to allow the Northumberland Fusiliers the right to put up a plaque on the wall of their city.[28]

The Napoleonic Wars might have been the Golden Age of Soldiering, with the most gorgeous uniforms and magnificent equipage, but they were no less concerned with the projection of terror than any other war in history. Gas, barbed wire, khaki and machine guns might have ruined the æsthetic of warfare, but, for all the glorious spectacle of the Grande Armée or Wellington's redcoats, it still came down to which organisation was the more efficient killing machine. The tortures practised by the Spanish guerrillas and the French reprisals for them were particularly horrific:

> A captive Frenchman might be buried with only his head above ground, to be used as a pin in a bowling match. As alternatives he might be hanged by his feet, sawn apart between two planks, skinned alive, boiled alive, impaled and then grilled over a camp fire, or cruci-fied upside down. Hospitals were favoured guerrilla targets; patients and medical personnel were massacred together. Women were usually mistreated; gang rape was only the introduction to torture. Even children might not be spared.

⤚

'His Majesty will go to Spain upon his return from Poland,' Berthier told Marmont on 16 April, but in the meantime Napoleon gave King Joseph supreme command in Spain, hoping that he might control the situation during the summer. At last the French army was under central, unified command in Spain, but under the wrong person. However much the marshals admired Napoleon for his military genius, they could not respect his elder brother. Worse still, Napoleon himself seemed to renege on his decision because, from the day he left Paris on 9 May to the day he returned there on 18 December 1812, the emperor did not contact Joseph at all, whereas he continued to send absurdly detailed orders to his other marshals in Spain, especial-ly Marmont. For all that he told Joseph 'to act with vigour, and to make yourself obeyed', he allowed other marshals to receive orders which enabled them to argue that they were carrying out the emperor's most recent instructions, of which Joseph knew nothing.[29]

In so wildly over-promoting his brother, a well-educated and well-intentioned but essentially weak man, Napoleon made a major error. The Spanish people never even did their king the honour of hating him, they merely despised him, nicknaming the ruby star on red sash of his Royal and Military Order of Spain the 'Order of the Aubergine'.

The battle of Salamanca, fought outside the city in north-west central Spain on 22 July 1812, in which Wellington defeated a momentarily over-extended French army under Marmont, was one of his greatest victories. Not trusting anyone else to explain his orders correctly, Wellington galloped the three miles from Teso de San Miguel to Aldea Tejada to give them to his brother-in-law Major-General Edward Pakenham and explain the situation personally. 'Ned, do you see those fellows over there? Throw your division into column, and drive them to the devil,' he ordered. The battlefield is dominated by two hills, the Greater and Lesser Arapiles, and the brilliance of Wellington's opportunist manoeuvre is immediately apparent to anyone standing on top of the Greater. The battle included some classic Wellingtonian tactics; he concealed his dispositions from the outset and Major-General Henry Clinton's 6th Division arranged in line also repulsed General Sarrut's division in column.[30]

One French general present, Maximilien Foy, probably the most experienced divisional commander in the French army in Spain, was deeply impressed with Wellington's victory. Six days afterwards he wrote in his diary:

> It raises Wellington's reputation almost to the level of Marlborough. Hitherto we had been aware of his prudence, his eye for choosing a position, and his skill in utilising it. At Salamanca he has shown himself a great and able master of manoeuvres. He kept his dispositions concealed for almost the whole day; he waited till we were committed to our movements before he developed his own; he played a safe game; he fought in the oblique order – it was a battle in the style of Frederick the Great.[31]

(Wellington had been greatly aided by the fact that Marmont had been wounded by a shell during the battle. Years later he organised a tour for Marmont around Woolwich Arsenal, where he met the magazine caretaker who had reputedly fired the shot. The man had later lost an arm at Waterloo and Marmont said to him: 'Ah, *mon cher*. We all have our turn.')

The road to Madrid now lay open to Wellington. He put out a General Order that could not have contrasted more with Napoleon's almost contemporaneous one just before the battle of Borodino. Small wonder that Wellington has been accused of emotional constipation when, after their great victory, in which two eagles, six colours and twenty guns were captured and fifteen thousand Frenchmen rendered *hors de combat* by death, wounds or capture, he addressed his army thus:

The commander of the forces returns his best thanks to the general officers, officers, and soldiers, for their conduct during the action of the 22nd instant. He will not fail to make the favourable report of them to HRH the Prince Regent, which they deserve. He trusts that the occurrences of yesterday will convince them that success in military operations depends upon the obedience of troops to their orders, and their steadiness in the ranks, which they should not, on any pretext whatsoever, be tempted to quit.

The victory at Salamanca started a general movement of French forces towards the Pyrenees and encouraged the Spanish to fresh efforts, while stilling criticism of the war back in Britain. The Prince Regent even later convinced himself that he had been personally present, and had led the charge of the 1st Dragoons of the King's German Legion disguised as Major-General von Bock.[32] 'Was that not so?' he once asked Wellington at dinner when he was king. 'I have often heard Your Majesty say so,' came the tactful reply.[33] (Fellow diners, though doubtless amused, must have been worried that George IV was about to suffer the same fate as his father. When, after his duel with the Earl of Winchelsea in 1829, Wellington was told that the king had wanted to take his place, the duke replied that in time he would claim to have done so.)

⤳

The story of the news of Wellington's victory at Salamanca as relayed to Napoleon is one of the great setpiece scenes of the Napoleonic epic, portrayed, among other places, in Book 3, Part 2, Chapter 26 of *War and Peace*. Just as Napoleon heard about the battle of Trafalgar shortly before Austerlitz, so he learned of Salamanca on the eve of Borodino. Colonel Charles Fabvier, Marmont's aide-de-camp, took thirty-two days to ride the 2,500 miles from Spain via Paris to Napoleon's headquarters outside the village of Borodino. There he told the emperor about the battle, and pointed out that the road through the Sierra Guadaramma mountain range close to Madrid was now open to the Allied army.[34] (In fact Wellington had entered Madrid in triumph before Fabvier arrived in Russia.)

Accounts sharply differ about Napoleon's reaction to the news. Baron de Marbot, aide-de-camp to five marshals in his time, states that it 'did much to cause [the emperor's] indisposition', particularly because 'when he had replaced Masséna in 1811 he gave out that he was going to beat Wellington', and this news now made Napoleon 'reflect that while he was invading Russia he was losing Spain'.[35] The historian General Philippe-Paul Ségur believes that Napoleon received Fabvier indulgently, but General Gaspard Gourgaud, on Napoleon's staff as *officier d'ordonnance*, said that the emperor 'gave vent to the sharpest dissatisfaction' at the news. Meanwhile General Montesquiou-Fézensac, who was aide-de-camp to Berthier at the time, recorded that 'despite his preoccupations' Napoleon kept Fabvier with him all evening. The ambassador to Moscow and Master of the Horse, the Marquis de Caulaincourt, merely thought that Russian affairs 'were just then too serious for the Emperor to pay much attention to the Duc de Ragusa's [Marmont's] reverses in the Peninsula'.[36] The next day Fabvier was wounded on the Great Redoubt at Borodino. 'A long way to go in search of a bullet' was Marbot's dry comment.

Arriving at Napoleon's camp along with the news of Salamanca came François Gérard's portrait of the King of Rome playing with a cup-and-ball and an imperial sceptre. Napoleon ordered that the painting be placed outside his tent for his soldiers to admire, and to contemplate for whom the campaign was ultimately being fought. 'Hide it away,' he rather poetically remarked just as the battle was about to begin. 'It is too early yet for him to look upon a field of battle.'[37]

A quarter of a century later, Wellington told an absurdly inflated version of the Colonel Fabvier story to Lord Ellesmere at Stratfield Saye. According to Wellington's account, Fabvier 'reached the French army about the time when Napoleon was taking up his quarters in the Kremlin', and, when the emperor discovered what his news consisted of, Fabvier 'was confined: <u>not</u> a normal arrest, but in strict confinement as a state criminal'. When finally Napoleon met Fabvier he asked how many troops Marmont had had, and on being told forty thousand, he is supposed to have retorted, 'Well, a man who has one million under his charge can hardly afford much attention to what happens to forty thousand at the other side of the world,' but then he sent Fabvier 'back to his seclusion'. Only when Napoleon received Wellington's own published report of the battle did he apparently send for Fabvier again, to tell him: 'I see by this account that the affair was a smart one and well contested. You may tell the marshal I am satisfied.'[38]

Virtually nothing in Wellington's version rings true, and is a good example of how the passing of time, in this case the tale was told in February 1836, can add barnacles to the bottom of a well-sailed story. Tolstoy's fictional scene, in which Napoleon 'made ironic remarks during Fabvier's account, making it understood that he had not expected matters could go otherwise in his absence', seems just as likely as Wellington's somewhat self-serving tale. Later in 1836 Wellington threw modesty entirely to the winds when he told Lord Mahon: 'It is quite certain that my opinion alone was the cause of the continuance of the war in the Peninsula. My letters show that I encouraged, nay forced, the Government to persevere in it. The successes of the operations of the army supported them in power.'[39] He added: 'I supported the Government much more than they supported me!' It was a vast exaggeration, unfairly blackening the names of Perceval, Castlereagh, Sidmouth, Liverpool, Bathurst, Canning and his own brother Richard, who had sustained him and ensured that he was regularly supplied with reinforcements, supplies, ammunition, weapons and not least large amounts of cash.

Huge British subsidies, nicknamed 'the cavalry of St George' by the French, were vital to victory in the Napoleonic Wars. Between 1808 and 1816 no less than £80 million was spent on Wellington's armies by the British Government.[40] As Liverpool's biographer has pointed out, 'to the end Liverpool and the rest of the Cabinet showed more understanding of Wellington's difficulties than he of theirs'.[41] The Government had, it is true, 'wobbled' in the spring of 1810 when Wellington's 32,000 men were faced by Masséna's 138,000, but after the battle of Salamanca domestic opposition to the Peninsular War significantly lessened.[42] Back in February Sir Thomas Turton had told the House of Commons that the conflict might last as long as the Peloponnesian Wars and the country could not bear the cost. In mid-May the MP for Sandwich Sir G. Warrender had wagered Lord Kinnaird five guineas at Brooks's Club that 'the present Administration are not in office this day fortnight', but after Salamanca the Government could breathe more easily.[43]

⌐

This is not the place to retell the story of the astonishing hubris that persuaded Napoleon that he could successfully invade Russia, even when he had not yet successfully vanquished Spain at the other end of Europe. Built on the grand scale himself, Napoleon's blunders were correspondingly enormous, and in Russia he squandered the most impressive fighting force since the days of Rome. Yet, in a pre-mechanised age, he did succeed in capturing the Kremlin, when 130 years later Hitler's Wehrmacht only managed to reach Moscow's outer suburbs. For all that he lost the campaign, Napoleon did after all add Warsaw and Moscow to the list of great cities through which he rode in triumph, which by then already included Madrid, Berlin, Vienna, Warsaw, Milan, Rome and Cairo.

(Napoleon's ride into Moscow provides a telling illustration of the limitations of oral history. At the time of the Romanovs' 300th anniversary in 1913, Tsar Nicholas II heard of a serf who had witnessed Napoleon's entry into the city. The serf, duly brought into the tsar's presence to relate his memory of that momentous and terrible day, was pensive for a moment before recalling that 'Napoleon was a very tall man with a long white beard.')

'Fortune is a woman,' Napoleon had told Marmont back in May 1796, 'and the more she does for me, the more I shall demand from her.' He had already been tremendously lucky in his career, as he had the decency freely to acknowledge, but by 1812 he had come to depend upon Fortune, and he asked too much of that notoriously inconstant goddess. 'I am not an ordinary man,' he once said, 'and the laws of morality and custom have therefore never been made for me.' Man-made laws might not apply, but the natural laws of geography and climate could not be altered for him, and it is thought that it was in Russia that the French were first obliged to acquire their taste for horsemeat. As with all the great tragic heroes, the emperor did not take his fatal step without being given a warning. The Marquis de Caulaincourt advised him in 1812 'that it was in Spain that he should first strike, if he persisted in his desire for this unfortunate war with Russia.' In reply, true to classic tragic dramatic form, Napoleon merely told his friend and adviser 'that I had turned [into] a Russian, and that I understood nothing of affairs.'[44]

Wellington watched the Russian campaign very closely, indeed almost obsessively at times, but he cannot be said to have affected it except very tangentially. Although a popular song published in Falkirk in 1813, set to the tune of 'Green Grow the Rushes O!', featured the stanza:

The Russian King to Britain look'd
For counsel, which he act'd 'pon;
And campaign plans were soon laid down
By gallant Gen'ral Wellington,

in fact Wellington had no direct involvement in the campaign beyond fighting the other war on the first front.[45]

Wellington was influential in another way, albeit indirectly. In May 1811 Tsar Alexander I was quoted as saying that in any future conflict with Napoleon: 'I intend to follow the system which has made Wellington victorious in Spain and exhausted the French armies – avoid pitched battles and organise long lines of communication for retreat, leading to entrenched camps.'[46] One historian of the Consulate and

Empire, Louis Madelin, recorded that 'Russian generals were already studying "Wellington's methods", which Russia was in a position to apply on a vast scale...From every point of view, nothing was more fraught with danger for Napoleon than the "lesson" of Torres Vedras.'[47]

It was certainly not true, as Sir Benjamin D'Urban persuaded himself in May 1812, that Napoleon had gone to Russia in order 'to throw the Peninsula and his defeats and disasters there into the shade'. In fact, although almost every other aspect of Franco-Russian relations was capable of being arranged peacefully, Napoleon insisted on the continuance of the Continental System, which attempted to blockade British trade, and the Russian adventure was launched to solidify it. Even in 1810, Britain received 80 per cent of her wheat imports from France or her allies and the System was in shreds. Yet, although Napoleon could probably have come to terms with the tsar over their other differences, his obsession with economic warfare and the restraint of Britain's trade impelled him towards by far his greatest blunder.[48] His obsession with closing Europe's ports to British commerce had dragged him thousands of miles into eastern Europe, far away from the sea but all too close to his nemesis.

Napoleon reached Moscow on 14 September 1812, after which large parts of it began to burn for no other reason than that, as Leo Tolstoy put it, 'a great city of wooden buildings abandoned by its inhabitants was certain to burn'. Napoleon stayed a little over a month, and the night before his departure he received one of his brother Joseph's aides-de-camp, Colonel Desprez, whom he had at first refused to see. 'You will realise that at this distance I can do nothing for the Armies of Spain,' he wrote to Marshal Clarke in Paris that day. 'You should make known to the King and to the Duc de Dalmatie [Soult] how little succour they can hope for, and how necessary it is, in their position, to act together, and diminish as much as possible the evils which a bad system has caused.'[49] No mention was made of who was responsible for creating such a 'system' in the first place.

Years later Wellington expressed the belief that, although Napoleon could never have maintained himself in Moscow all winter, 'he might at Smolensk, or rather Vitebsk. He might then have rallied the Poles into a kingdom and marched forward next spring, and then I think he would have succeeded.'[50] When in 1837 Lord Mahon asked why Napoleon could not simply have allowed himself to be cut off in Moscow throughout the winter, Wellington presented his answer in terms of politics rather than military strategy or supply, saying that a Parisian conspiracy centred on General Claude de Malet, which had

begun to manifest itself on 23 October, meant he had to return directly. 'In fact', said Wellington,

> if you look through his campaigns you will find that his plan was always
> to try to give a great battle, gain a great victory, patch up a peace, such
> a peace as might leave an opening for a future war, and then hurry
> back to Paris. This I should say was the great benefit of what we did in
> Spain – of what we did and enabled the Spaniards to do. We starved
> him out. We showed him that we wouldn't let him fight a battle at first,
> except under disadvantages: if you do fight, we shall destroy you; if you
> do not fight, we shall in time destroy you still.[51]

This penetrating analysis of Napoleonic strategy, since supported by
many scholars such as Correlli Barnett, shows how completely
Wellington understood his enemy.

Meanwhile Wellington was relating the latest rumours to his
youngest brother Sir Henry Wellesley, British ambassador to Spain,
which were often contradictory. 'The French in our front have two
reports,' he said on 1 November, 'one that the Russians are making
peace; the other that Buonaparte is marching to Petersburg,' neither
of which turned out to be true.[52] Napoleon actually began his retreat
from Moscow on 19 October.

In his papers for 22–28 November 1812 is Wellington's detailed
handwritten memorandum, entitled 'Notes on the French Army near
the Beresina', about which French corps commanders were where
during one week of the retreat. He could have discovered these
details only much later, and there is no indication of when it was
written, but its great attention to detail shows the fascination that
Napoleon's Russian campaign exerted over Wellington. Here is a
short excerpt:

> 22 Nov., 1812 – Napoleon at Toloczin: his army between that and
> Orsza ...
> 23 Nov. – Napoleon at Bobr ...
> 24 Nov. – Napoleon at Lochnitza ...
> 25 Nov. – Napoleon at Borisow ...
> 26 Nov. – Napoleon at Studianka
> 27 Nov. – ... The Guards and Napoleon recross the river, and
> [Marshal] Oudinot's division.

This handwritten, day-by-day analysis of Napoleon's whereabouts, identifying the slightly more southern route he chose for his retreat compared with the one used in his advance, hardly suggests, as some historians have claimed, that Wellington took little or no interest in Napoleon's campaigns.

Nor was Wellington out of Napoleon's thoughts during his retreat from Moscow. Caulaincourt records that in the Duchy of Warsaw in December 1812, after Napoleon had left the Grande Armée and was speeding back to Paris by sleigh after crossing the Niemen at Kowno, the emperor and his trusted adviser had a long conversation about general strategy.

'Doubtless it would have been better to have wound up the war in Spain before embarking on this Russian expedition,' admitted Napoleon, probably mindful of Caulaincourt's original warnings, 'though there is much room for discussion on this point. As for the war in Spain itself, it is not only a matter of guerrilla contests.'[53] He was still absurdly over-confident, even in the privacy of his own sleigh with one of his most loyal acolytes: 'On the day the English are driven out of the Peninsula, there will be nothing left of the war but isolated bodies of rebels, and one cannot hope to clear the country of those in a month or two.' It is true that Wellington was back on the retreat in late 1812, so Napoleon might have had some renewed cause for confidence, but the British were far from being 'driven out of the Peninsula', as he well knew. His comments reek of special pleading, not least because the quarter of a million Frenchmen Wellington and his allies had pinned down in Spain would have been invaluable to Napoleon during the retreat from Moscow.

'There is nothing to be done except hold the country and try to pacify it until I can myself put some vigour into the operations there,' Napoleon continued.

> Soult has ability; but no one will take orders. Every general wants to be independent, so as to play the viceroy in his own province. In Wellington my generals have encountered an opponent superior to some of them. Moreover they have made the mistakes of a school-boy...In fact, our momentary reverses in that war...have little effect on the general course of affairs, as I can change the course of affairs when I please. Events at present are giving Wellington a reputation. But in war men may lose in a day what they have spent years building up.[54]

That is just what the emperor was in the process of discovering.

Napoleon then rationalised the situation for himself, but not necessarily for Caulaincourt, by arguing that with the British – or 'English' as he always called them, regardless of the large Irish, Scottish, Welsh and King's German Legion contingents in the British army – busy in the Peninsula, they were not ravaging the coastlines of Brittany or Italy. At least in Spain, 'he knew where to look for the English; while if they were not occupied there he would be forced to prepare for them, and hold himself ready for defence against them, at every point'. He said he feared that thirty thousand English troops landing in the Pas-de-Calais or Belgium 'would do us much more harm than by forcing me to maintain an army in Spain'.[55] 'You would make a much worse outcry, my good Master of Horse,' Napoleon teased Caulaincourt, if the English arrived in Picardy and burned down his ancestral château of Caulaincourt. It was not a particularly strong argument, for until Wellington landed in Portugal the various British excursions on the continent had generally been unsuccessful.

Caulaincourt wrote that 'only the Emperor had been well-served throughout the retreat: that is to say that he always had white bread, linen, his Chambertin, good oil, beef or mutton, rice, and beans or lentils, his favourite vegetables'. The sleigh in which they rode had been bought for ten thousand francs from a Polish squire, and was driven by one of Napoleon's faithful Mameluke servants. Wellington employed even more servants in Spain than Napoleon had in Russia. He had three footmen (whereas Napoleon had to make do with two), five orderlies (Napoleon had two butlers), two valets (Napoleon had the same number), three cooks (Napoleon had the same), two hunts-men, a goat boy and three laundry women. By October 1813 the number of people attached to Wellington's headquarters, including military staff and servants, numbered no fewer than 417.[56]

The retreat from Moscow exemplifies the difference in strategy between Napoleon and Wellington. Of course it is unlikely that any parliamentary government would have embarked on a full-scale inva-sion of Russia at all, but, if ordered to do so, Wellington would never have treated Moscow in the talismanic fashion that Napoleon had. His constant concern for his lines of communication would have – as he suggested to Lord Mahon – stretched the campaign over several seasons rather than inclining him to attempt to win complete victory in just one. His constant willingness to retreat tactically and his early and ever present concerns about being cut off would probably have saved his army. We can know this better than most counterfactual conjectures, because in late 1812 Wellington was indeed involved in his own retreat, which forced him to finish the year back inside Portugal, precisely where he had started it.

SEVEN

Two Retreats, One Tragedy
1812–13

The battle of Wellington was the stroke of a battering-ram,
down went the wall in ruins. The battle of Napoleon was the swell
and dash of a mighty wave, before which the barrier yielded
and the roaring flood poured onwards covering all.

GENERAL SIR WILLIAM NAPIER

Although Wellington had enjoyed a tumultuous welcome into Madrid in August 1812, where he sat for his celebrated portrait by Goya, he was predictably unimpressed by his hosts. As he wrote to the secretary for war, the 3rd Earl Bathurst:

> I do not expect much from the exertions of the Spaniards, notwith-standing all that we have done for them...they are, in general, the most incapable of useful exertion of all the nations that I have known; the most vain, and at the same time the most ignorant, particularly of military affairs, and above all of military affairs in their own country.[1]

Wellington's contempt was to spawn a near-consensus among British Victorian historians that the Spanish had been almost incidental in the liberation of their own country, although the modern view is very different. The Spanish captured twice the number of French eagles as the British, they killed many more French troops and, despite several defeats of their regular army in the field of battle, they never surrendered. It was the first guerrilla war in modern history (as the etymology of the English word suggests), and its full implications for the conduct of future warfare were not appreciated sufficiently early by the French. By the twenty-first century guerrilla warfare has become so common that it is hard to recall quite how revolutionary it had been two centuries ago in the Peninsula.

It was a long, vicious but heroic movement of national resistance. Yet, speaking to Lady Salisbury at Hatfield in 1836, Wellington 'would not admit much merit in the battle of Baylen [in 1808], and said that Bonaparte had with reason been indignant with Dupont'. He then went on to castigate the various Spanish commanders, such as Silviera ('no general'), de la Romana ('totally deficient in military talent'), Palafox y Melzi ('a coxcomb') and: 'Of Albuquerque he spoke in disparaging terms and said he rejoiced when he was sent as ambassador to England.'

Insofar as Wellington was ever guilty of hubris it was in believing that after his successes in storming Ciudad Rodrigo and Badajoz he could take the fortified city of Burgos with only three siege guns. Five weeks of assaults all failed, and his sedentary position drew towards him all the French troops in the area, sixty thousand of them against his thirty thousand. When the time finally came to withdraw from what he called 'this damned place', errors were made, though not usually by him, and he had to extricate himself from what he later called 'the worst scrape I was ever in'. It was not until 20 November that he was safely ensconced back in Ciudad Rodrigo, from where he notoriously blamed his officers for the defeat, a fact that his authorised biographer, the Reverend G. R. Gleig, entirely omitted to mention.

It had been a blistering on-the-record attack, and was greatly resented by his officers. Wellington charged them with having allowed a situation to develop in which:

> discipline had deteriorated during the campaign in a greater degree than [he] had ever witnessed or ever read of in any army, and this without any disaster, any unusual privation or hardship save that of inclement weather ... and this unhappy state of affairs was to be traced to the habitual neglect of duty by the regimental officers.

Meanwhile Madrid had been abandoned, some six thousand men had been lost, and so, inevitably, the Whigs returned to the attack back home.

In a Commons debate on 3 December, the Radical MP Sir Francis Burdett described the withdrawal from Burgos as 'a most disastrous defeat', adding that 'the results of the campaign had been disaster and defeat'. He further decried the 'waste of life' in attacking Ciudad Rodrigo and Badajoz, and alleged – quite wrongly – that no breaches had been made in their walls. The leader of the Whig Opposition in the Commons George Ponsonby had already told the House: 'It is useless to carry on further an unprofitable contest: it is useless to waste the blood and treasure of England for an unattainable object; it has been proved that the power of England was not competent to drive the French out of the Peninsula.'[2] The Government stood loyally by Wellington, who in turn stood by them, saying in public: 'I see that a disposition already exists to blame the Government for the failure of the siege of Burgos... It was entirely my own act.'

(Napoleon, in a letter to Marshal Maret, who had replaced Champagny as foreign minister, wrote from Molodetchna on 4 December that although the resistance of Burgos had been 'une belle affaire militaire', all it actually proved was that such places could not be taken without siege artillery. He nonetheless believed that Wellington still posed 'une crise sérieuse'.)[3]

One must doubt whether Wellington believed in his own *mea culpa* at all, as in a single letter, to his former military secretary, now the Prince Regent's aide-de-camp, Colonel Sir Henry Torrens, he wrote of his senior subordinate officers:

> [Major-General Christopher Tilson-]Chowne should be removed...
> General Stewart... cannot obey an order... Either General Chowne
> or General Stewart must be recalled... There is a German General
> Löwe... who is by no means fit for service in this country. [Major-]
> General [J. H. C. von] Bernewitz ought not to be a General officer
> in this army. I don't want General officers in lieu of these. General
> Robinson might as well be ordered home... Indeed I don't believe
> he would be of any use.[4]

Although on 10 December Wellington wrote to Marshal Beresford, 'If Buonaparte has any money he will send out a fleet [to America] if he is wise. But he has no money,' very soon afterwards he discovered that Napoleon was very short of everything else as well.[5] The Empire had reached its greatest territorial extent in 1812, comprising forty-four million people in 130 departments not counting the four Catalan departments, six Illyrian intendancies and the twenty-four departments of the Kingdom of Italy.[6] Napoleon's imperium sprawled over the western half of continental Europe and included the allied Batavian Republic, the Confederation of the Rhine, the Helvetic Confederation, Piedmont, Parma, the Kingdom of Etruria, the Papal States, Venetian Istria, Hanover and Dalmatia. For the Russian campaign Napoleon crossed the Vistula river with 655,000 men from twenty nations, but by 1813 only 93,000 were left under his command. The Central Army Group, which took the worst beating, numbered 450,000 when crossing the Vistula, but was down to 25,000 crossing the Niemen on the way back. In all, around 370,000 of Napoleon's army had been killed and about 200,000 had been captured, of whom around half subsequently died. On top of that human catastrophe around two hundred thousand horses died and over a thousand cannon were lost.[7] The British army could have fought for another twenty years in the Peninsula before they managed to inflict such a level of damage.

Wellington heard the definitive truth about the Russian campaign, as opposed to the gossip of the gazettes and the speculations contained in intercepted mail, from Lord Liverpool, who wrote from his home Fife House on 22 December:

> There has been no example within the last twenty years, amidst all the extraordinary events of the French Revolution, of such a change of fortune as Buonaparte has experienced during the last five months. If there is any political speculation upon which reliance may safely be placed, we may now say that Russia is, for ages, alienated from France, and united to this country. The most formidable army ever collected by Buonaparte has been substantially destroyed; and it remains only to be ascertained whether he will be able to escape, and with what remnant of that army with which he entered Russia in June last.[8]

The prime minister added that the French cavalry was thought to 'have ceased to exist, except perhaps a small proportion of it, immediately attached to the person of Buonaparte'. Napoleon's whereabouts were inevitably the subject of a wager at Brooks's, between Mr Page who bet five guineas on 16 December that the emperor was in Russia that day, and General Sir Edward Howorth who thought him to be in France. Howorth won, and on 18 December Napoleon arrived in Paris, and immediately set about foiling the Malet conspiracy and then rebuilding his forces. His actions on that occasion belied a story that Wellington recounted about him years later, when in 1836 he told Lady Salisbury that, according to the finance minister Molé, Napoleon had said: 'If we had the energy and enthusiasm which existed at the beginning of the Revolution we might be able to recover it all, but that is over.'[9] In fact Napoleon acted with great vigour to resuscitate French greatness, even if it was probably too late by then.

With an emboldened Austria willing to wound her French ally but still afraid to strike, Wellington sent a message to Napoleon's father-in-law the Emperor Francis I saying: 'Lord Wellington expects at least to give employment to between 150,000 and 200,000 French troops in the next campaign.'[10] In his 1813 campaign, he watched Napoleon's activities carefully, in case the emperor suddenly left the German theatre to engage him directly in northern Spain or south-west France. He insisted on being kept closely informed on every political and military development, and made his views known on matters such as Napoleon's reconciliation with the pope in January 1813, prisoner exchanges – which he opposed as 'Buonaparte will find it very difficult to form another army' – and the Napoleonic campaigns in Germany.[11]

On the issue of possibly bribing Soult or some other French marshals to forsake Napoleon, Wellington showed what a low opinion he held of many of his opponents in the Peninsula:

> Depend upon it that very few French generals are to be bought, and Soult certainly is not in the market. He is now gone to France. I don't say this because I think French generals less venal than others, but because Bonaparte outbids everybody. That is the secret of his policy. I don't know what could be given to Soult equal to what he would lose by treachery to his present master. I admit that he and all of them hate Bonaparte and despise the whole race, but they cannot be so highly paid or get so much plunder from any other hand. They therefore serve him faithfully and most zealously.

That letter, of March 1813, was doubly significant because it was the first time that Wellington did Napoleon the honour of spelling his surname without the semi-insulting 'u'. It might have been a slip of the pen, because by 17 June 1813, writing of Napoleon's 'severe actions' at Bautzen in Germany between 20 and 22 May, he recorded: 'The victory is claimed by the French, royal salutes fired, etc., etc.; but I hear from the frontiers that Buonaparte lost 50,000 men in these actions...I suspect that there was hard fighting on the first two days, and none on the last, when Buonaparte turned them, and they retired.' (That is indeed precisely what had happened.)

↪

Wellington's greatest contribution to the Allied struggle against Napoleon in 1813 was made at his victory at Vitoria on 21 June, fought less than a hundred miles from the French border. It persuaded the Emperor of Austria and his foreign minister Count Clemens (later Prince) Metternich, that far from taking fresh reinforcements from Spain, Napoleon could only expect further dangers there, and at the very least Wellington had been correct in his prediction back in

January.[12] This, it is believed, helped tip the Austrians into outright opposition to Napoleon.

Before Vitoria the British army in the Peninsula had retreated as much as it had advanced; after it there would be no more hurried returns to Portugal. Nor could Napoleon have any further excuse for failing to recognise in Wellington a general worthy of his own mettle. To make the defeat more personally humiliating for Napoleon, it was his own brother Joseph who was in nominal overall command of the French forces. Joseph lost eight thousand men in the battle, as well as almost all his artillery and transport. Wellington had broken the French front line with a complicated but brilliant double-flanking movement. In all the French lost 151 guns, one hundred military wagons and two thousand prisoners.[13] There would have been many more prisoners had the army not indulged in wholesale looting of King Joseph's baggage train, from which around six million francs disappeared. It was there that the Spanish royal art collection was captured, so much of which is today to be seen on the walls of Apsley House.

The diplomatic victory was if anything still greater than the military one, with huge implications for the rest of Europe. Napoleon's victories at Bautzen and Lützen in 1813 were largely neutralised. 'It is easy to see that Lord Wellington's great achievements have produced as great a change in the atmosphere of Dresden and the North as it could have effected in Southern Europe,' wrote Sir Charles Stewart, Castlereagh's brother and the ambassador to Berlin.[14] British diplomats now spoke with far greater authority than before, when they had merely held the purse strings and contributed little else to the continental struggle. Once the fortresses of the Pyrenees had fallen, it was hoped that Wellington's army would erupt into southern France.

Napoleon, who heard the news of Vitoria earlier than the other sovereigns of Europe, ordered Caulaincourt 'to conclude a peace with Russia which could be glorious for the Power', and tried to keep the news secret as he also conferred with the Prussians over the promulgation of an armistice. In London, Castlereagh therefore had Wellington's report of the battle translated into German, Dutch and French and distributed as widely and quickly as possible on the continent.[15]

The Austrian envoy to Napoleon, Count Bubna, who got his copy in Dresden, sent it to Count Stadion in Vienna, who woke up Metternich in the middle of the night with the words: 'King Joseph is [expletive] in Spain!' Metternich later told Wellington that the Austrians' initial delight at the news 'subsided into a determination to denounce the armistice, and to enter the war against Napoleon, this time until Napoleon himself should be [same expletive]'.[16]

Wellington certainly never underestimated the effect of his own triumph, telling Croker in 1834 that it had 'freed the Peninsula altogether, broke off the armistice [being negotiated] at Dresden, and thus led to [the battle of] Leipzig and the deliverance of Europe'.[17] For all the immodesty of the remark, he was essentially correct. Napoleon's secretary Baron Fain described the news of Vitoria as 'l'influence fatale' on the Dresden negotiations, and Tsar Alexander I ordered a Te Deum to be sung in recognition of the victory, the first ever in an Orthodox church for a non-Russian victory. Beethoven meanwhile composed 'Wellington Sieg oder Die Schlacht bei Vitoria' (the Battle Symphony), which was dedicated to the Prince Regent. 'This absurd piece of propaganda music', says Beethoven's biographer in the *New Grove Dictionary of Music*, 'with its fanfares, cannonades and fugal treatment of "God Save the King", was thunderously acclaimed at two charity concerts on 8 and 12 December 1813.'

Napoleon was thoroughly rattled by Vitoria, but he did not at first seem to give Wellington any credit for the victory. 'All the blunders in Spain stem from my ill-advised kindness to the King, who, besides not knowing how to command an army, is in addition incapable of judging his own abilities accurately and of leaving the command to a soldier,' he wrote. Soult, who had been commanding the Guard in Germany, was ordered to leave Dresden that same evening and, travelling incognito under the name of an aide, get to Paris for further orders and thence go 'to take command of my armies in Spain'. Like Wellington, Napoleon, Castlereagh and Ney, Marshal Soult had been born in 1769. His wife the Duchesse de Dalmatie, who tried to prevent him going, was not to see him for a year. Meanwhile Wellington wrote to Liverpool commending the Portuguese, who had fought well at Vitoria, as 'the fighting cocks of the army', but could not forbear adding that this was owing more to 'the care we have taken of their pockets and bellies than to the instruction we have given them'.[18]

༄

It was after Vitoria that Wellington started being popularly compared to Napoleon. In the estimation of the biographer of Colonel Neil Campbell, the man who was to become Napoleon's gaoler on Elba the following year, 'the battle of Vitoria appears to have given rise, as might be expected, to much discussion; and many comparisons were in consequence drawn between the respective merits' of Napoleon and Wellington.[19] The two commanders began appearing in caricatures together: George Cruikshank drew them both in July 1813, and Thomas Rowlandson and Lewis Marks did so the following year. Napoleon had for years been ordering that caricatures be drawn of his opponents, usually showing Pitt the Younger, John Bull or, as he instructed Fouché in 1805, 'an Englishman, purse in hand', bribing the continental powers to fight France. He encouraged the use of cartoon propaganda in the French press, 'hence the constant attacks, often of the grossest conceivable nature, on George III and Queen Charlotte, the Prince Regent, the Dukes of York and Cambridge, Nelson and Wellington, and above all ... Pitt'.[20] Napoleon even used to suggest themes and individuals himself. It is inconceivable that Wellington would have deigned to interest himself in such an activity.

In the summer of 1813 Napoleon seems to have paid a compliment to Wellington far warmer than the grudging admission of 'a reputation' he had accorded him during the retreat from Moscow the previous December. On 4 June he had agreed the Armistice of Pleischwitz with the Allies, which ended on 17 August when hostilities resumed, this time with the Austrians on the Allies' side, they having signed the secret treaty of Reichenbach after the news of Vitoria.

In the course of the armistice, Napoleon held an epic nine-hour interview with Metternich on 26 June, ostensibly to arrange the details of what was going to be the Peace of Prague, but also in order to berate the Austrian foreign minister, whom he correctly suspected of wishing to backtrack. (The Reichenbach treaty was signed the very next day.) It was probably during this meeting at the Marcolini Palace, at which he notoriously told Metternich that he 'did not take much heed of the lives of a million men', that Napoleon seems to have made another admiring reference to Wellington's generalship.[21]

An undated letter from Lady Bessborough to her lover Granville Leveson Gower records that she had been dining the previous evening with Madame de Staël and Lord Kinnaird, having seen 'poor Madame Moreau' that morning. General Moreau, who had returned from America to serve the tsar, had been mortally wounded by a battery under Napoleon's personal direction while talking to Alexander I before the battle of Dresden on 26 August, and had died on 2 September after a double leg amputation, smoking a cigar throughout the operation. The letter can therefore safely be dated as having been written after his death. In it, Lady Bessborough said that Kinnaird had seen a 'Mr Vernon' at Vienna who had passed on the following information:

When B[onaparte] was representing to the Austrian foreign minister the folly of their going to war, among other reasons he urged their having no generals, and indeed that he scarce knew of any not of his own army. Then after a pause he added: 'Il y en a un – Mylord W[ellington], par example; voilà un général, mais aussi c'est le seul, qui a jamais su me comprendre, ou qui a jamais donné à deviser à mes maréchaux.'[22] ['There is one – Lord Wellington, for example; now there is a general, indeed the only one, though he has never understood me, and has never really tested my marshals.']

It was hardly a ringing encomium, but if Napoleon did indeed admire Wellington's generalship in June or July 1813, and it is only third-hand information that he did, he certainly blamed his brother for the defeat at Vitoria rather than giving Wellington any credit. In a letter to the police minister General Anne-Jean-Marie Savary in Paris, written from Dresden on 20 July, the emperor exploded with rage against the fleeing King Joseph, including the threat: 'If he were to come to Paris or to St Cloud, you would have to take steps to arrest him – he must be under no illusions on this point.' It was at this time that he withheld the Breguet watch from Joseph, in the action that struck Wellington as pathetically petty. As Napoleon continued to Savary:

Our misfortunes in Spain, as you will have seen from the English papers, are all the more serious because they are absurd: that is how the English themselves look at it. They are no dishonour to the army. The army has no general, and a supernumerary king. Ultimately (I admit) I am myself to blame. If I had sent the Duc de Dalmatie [Soult] to Valladolid to take over the command there – the idea did occur to me just as I was leaving Paris – this would never have happened.[23]

Napoleon's implication was that Soult was a superior general to Wellington, which seemed to be confirmed when the marshal launched his Pyrenees offensive after 25 July. With over seventy passes through the mountains, Wellington could not defend them all, but Soult was held back at the battles of Maya and Roncesvalles, which were fought by Wellington's subordinates while he oversaw the siege of San Sebastián. Napoleon ordered the *Moniteur* to announce that Soult had won a victory that had raised the siege with the capture of forty-two siege guns, when the truth was that General Sir William Stewart had lost four guns at the battle of Maya, but had nonetheless prevented Soult from breaking through into Spain.[24]

Wellington has been criticised for waiting for three months after Vitoria before crossing the Bidassoa river into France, the first invasion since the Prussians were halted at the battle of Valmy in 1792. One of his many good reasons for caution was that he was watching carefully what Napoleon was doing in Germany. 'I am very doubtful indeed about the advantage of moving any farther forward here at present,' he wrote to Bathurst shortly after crossing the border in October. 'I see that Buonaparte was still at Dresden on the 28th [August]; and unless I could fight a general action with Soult, and gain a complete victory, which the nature of the country would scarcely admit of, I should do but little good to the Allies; and, in retiring, should probably incur much loss and inconvenience.'[25]

Wellington did not want to be caught in southern France, deep inside enemy territory, with his still relatively small army, by a Grande Armée led by a Napoleon freshly returned from some great victory on the Elbe. Instead, on the same day that Wellington wrote to Bathurst, Napoleon suffered a crushing defeat at the battle of Leipzig – known as 'the battle of the Nations' – at the hands of the Austrians, Russians, Prussians and Swedes. Bavaria and Saxony subsequently joined the Allies. Ten days after Napoleon retreated from Leipzig to Mainz, Wellington crossed the River Nivelle. Part of Wellington's caution was explained by the need to take San Sebastián (on 31 August) and Pamplona (on 25 October), both to his rear. The lack of ready money for supplies in France, which Wellington insisted on paying for rather than plundering, as well as concerns that the Spanish might not allow him to retreat back over the Pyrenees, and a doughty rearguard action by Soult, all served to slow his advance.

There were also constant rumours that the Allies might possibly conclude yet another armistice with Napoleon, especially after he won the battle of Dresden on 26–27 August. Wellington told Bathurst that he feared such an outcome would mean that 'Buonaparte may be enabled to detach a large force against us. I hope they understand that if he should do so, and we should by accident be overpowered, which I do not think likely, he will not fulfil any expectations of favourable terms which he may have held out to them.' He further warned that if the continental powers again made peace with Napoleon he would once more have to withdraw deep into Spain.[26]

When Louis XVIII's nephew the Duc de Berri offered to join the Allies with twenty thousand Royalist soldiers in August, Wellington advocated acceptance as 'the interests of the House of Bourbon and of all Europe are the same, viz., in some manner or other, to get the better and rid of Bonaparte'. In his letter on the subject to Bathurst, he showed his extreme personal detestation of Bonapartism:

> He rests internally upon the most extensive and expensive system of corruption that was ever established in any country, and externally upon his military power, which is supported almost exclusively by foreign contributions. If he can be confined to the limits of France by any means, his system must fall.[27]

When Wellington crossed the Bidassoa river, almost exactly six years after General Junot had crossed it in the opposite direction in the original French invasion of Spain in 1807, the London painter Thomas Jones Barker advertised that he would be painting Wellington, along with his military secretary Lord Fitzroy Somerset (later Lord Raglan), 'uniform in size with the engraving of Napoleon and his aide-de-camp Rapp crossing the Alps in 1800, painted by Paul Delaroche'.[28] To London's print-buying public, at least, Wellington and Napoleon were now being seen as equals.

Wellington 'earnestly' opposed any prisoner exchanges, telling Bathurst on 9 November that although there were many old comrades he would like to see freed: 'Depend upon it, that Buonaparte is in the utmost distress for want of experienced officers and soldiers; and he would give two, or even three, of ours as for one of those we have, if he dared to do so.' As for getting the Spanish prisoners of war back, Wellington characteristically declared that he would 'prefer not to have them'.[29]

On 10 November 1813, the same day that Wellington defeated Soult at the battle of the Nivelle, Napoleon returned to St Cloud and asked the legislature in Paris to give him three hundred thousand more troops. A deputy objected to the phrase 'frontiers invaded' in the preamble to the request, which he thought might excite defeatism. 'Isn't it better in this case to tell the truth?' answered Napoleon. 'Hasn't Wellington entered the south, the Russians the north? Aren't the Austrians and Bavarians threatening us on the east?'[30] It is instructive that Napoleon mentioned Wellington by name, the other armies merely by nationality, further indication that, as he had admitted to Metternich that summer, he rated Wellington as the best of the Allied generals.

Napoleon was forced to conscript old men and teenagers – the latter nicknamed 'Marie Louises' – while Wellington kept over one hundred thousand French troops pinned down in south-western

France. Nonetheless the emperor managed to find 120,000 new recruits, as he fought some of the most brilliant campaigns of his career in the winter of 1813 and spring of 1814.[31] Wellington, speaking to Lord Mahon in 1831, said that he had read much about these campaigns and 'spoke in the highest terms of Napoleon's military genius'. On this occasion, noted Mahon, Wellington pronounced the word 'Bonaparte' without the 'u', 'à l'anglaise'.[32]

There can be no doubt that Wellington studied Napoleon's strategy in a way that Napoleon omitted to do with Wellington. This was done primarily on a 'know thine enemy' basis, as there is precious little indication that after the battle of Waterloo Wellington read anything at all about either Napoleon or the battle, besides Dr O'Meara's two-volume *Napoleon in Exile*. In a conversation with the diplomat George Chad in 1824, he reminisced about the period in late 1813 when he 'had been reading and studying a work upon France written by a man named Faber. It states that Bonaparte had no hold on the affections of the French people, nothing but force – military force – I read that book over several times and another work by Irving.'[33]

Gotthilf Theodor von Faber's 176-page book *Notices sur l'intérieur de la France* written in 1806 and published in St Petersburg in 1807 and in London in 1810, had been reviewed by Croker in 1811, who possibly drew it to Wellington's attention. It argued that France would overthrow Napoleon if given the opportunity. Partly as a result of his reading, when he invaded France two years later Wellington was determined to enter as a liberator of the French from Napoleonic tyranny, rather than as just another foreign conqueror. He soon persuaded himself that the country as a whole was ready for a restoration of Bourbon rule, and on 18 November he wrote to Lieutenant-General Sir Thomas Graham to say that 'The sentiments of the people in this part of the country respecting Buonaparte are exactly what one would suppose it to be under such a government as his. None, but the persons in office and the higher class of the officers of the army, are attached to him.'[34] (Graham, later Lord Lynedoch, was fanatically opposed to the French Revolution. His wife had been 'the beautiful Mrs Graham' painted by Gainsborough, and after her coffin was desecrated by drunken French National Guardsmen searching for contraband in 1792 he embarked on his brilliant military career partly out of a desire for revenge.)[35]

While Wellington was writing to Graham about Napoleon, the emperor was being teased about Wellington by Talleyrand. The former foreign minister was convinced that France needed to parley with the

Allies, and the minister of police General Savary urged Napoleon to sound Talleyrand out about conducting any such negotiations. In the course of their discussions, Talleyrand suggested that there was 'a certain English family' which, he believed, 'might aspire to anything in view of the glory it had achieved'. The European situation might be radically altered if France were to help that family 'become supreme' in Britain. Napoleon complained that Talleyrand 'was behaving as usual and that he couldn't guess what he meant', and asked him to be more explicit. According to Savary's account, Talleyrand then said: 'A man like Wellington may be acting with some ulterior motive. He must realise that if he lives on his reputation, he is bound to be forgotten very soon; he has many examples to go by, and a man as able as he won't stop as long as there is anything to be got.'[36]

The historian of Napoleon's tortuous relationship with Talleyrand describes this sally as 'the cruellest form of sarcasm'. By suggesting that Wellington was open to bribery in the way that many of Napoleon's own marshals were, or that he aimed for dictatorship in Britain as Napoleon had in France – 'he has many examples to go by' – Talleyrand was subtly holding Wellington up as a contrast to Napoleon in a way that amounted to an insulting rebuke. 'Before thinking of other people's ambitions,' replied Napoleon, affecting not to understand Talleyrand's meaning, or genuinely failing to, 'it was essential to be in a position to make oneself respected at home.' Very soon afterwards Napoleon broke with Talleyrand for ever.

Napoleon's secretary, Louis-Antoine Bourrienne, faithfully recorded the incident but also failed to appreciate Talleyrand's arch sarcasm, suggesting that Talleyrand genuinely believed in the value of 'working upon the ambition of the English family of Wellesley; and to excite in the mind of Wellington, the lustre of whose reputation was now dawning, ambitious projects which would have embarrassed the Coalition'. Of this 'extraordinary advice' – which is extraordinary only if taken at face value – Bourrienne said Napoleon 'did not adopt this proposition, the issue of which he thought too uncertain, and, above all, too remote, in the urgent crisis in which he stood'.[37] History was thus sadly denied the hilarious prospect of Napoleon attempting to bribe Wellington, perhaps with the promise of Murat's Neapolitan kingdom. (Wellington was in fact very vain about his lack of vanity, describing himself, in a conversation with Croker in 1852, as a 'conquérant sans ambition', adding 'I was almost king of Spain, but I handled my power with the greatest moderation and abstinence, and avoided every unnecessary exhibition of it.')

Unaware of Talleyrand's little *bêtise*, Wellington was meanwhile writing to Bathurst from St Jean de Luz in France on 21 November to reiterate his view that the French people were unanimous in 'an earnest desire to get rid of' Napoleon due to 'a conviction that as long as he governs, there will be no peace'. Yet he went on to make an extraordinary suggestion. After admitting that he had not so far heard 'any opinion in favour of the House of Bourbon', and stating that 'I am convinced that Napoleon's power stands upon corruption [and] that he has no adherents in France but the principal officers in his army and the *employés civils* of his Government,' he went on to say that nonetheless Napoleon should be allowed to retain the throne of France:

> Notwithstanding this state of things, I recommend to your Lordship to make peace with him if you can acquire all the objects which you have a right to expect...If Buonaparte becomes moderate, he is probably as good a sovereign as we can desire in France; if he does not we shall have another war in a few years; but if my speculations are well founded, we shall have all France against him; time will have been given for the supposed disaffection to his Government to produce its effect; his diminished resources will have decreased his means of corruption, and it may be hoped that he will be engaged single-handed against insurgent France and all Europe.[38]

Wellington gave as his reasons for this extraordinary advice the idea that the 'Powers of Europe require peace possibly more than France' and that 'it would not do to found a new system of war' upon his own views about what the French thought about Napoleon. Yet, even given his well-testified hatred of war, it is amazing that, after all he had said and written about Napoleon for so many years, Wellington should advise the British Government to make a negotiated settlement which would have left the emperor on the throne of France.

Only eleven days beforehand Wellington had lost 2,450 casualties (against 4,351 of Soult's) in the battle of the Nivelle, and he might have despaired of the chances of eventual peace. Yet on 13 November he had written to his brother Henry to say that, after the French had clashed with the Bavarians at Hanau, 'Napoleon's army is nearly destroyed.' The idea of Napoleon continuing to rule, especially as a 'moderate' or constitutional monarch, was a patent absurdity and Wellington's letter belies everything else he had written and said on the subject of the French emperor. If we did not know Wellington's high character better, we might almost be tempted to assume that Napoleon had indeed put Talleyrand's plan into operation.

If he did despair of the Allies' chances of ever finally crushing Napoleon, the defection on the night of 10 December, during the battle of the Nive in south-west France, of three entire divisions of German troops in Soult's army who had heard of Napoleon's defeat at Leipzig, must have reassured Wellington. As the historian of Napoleon's 1813 campaigns observes, events in Spain 'had great relevance to the Leipzig situation. The longer the French had to maintain an army there to oppose Wellington's advance into southern France, the fewer resources Napoleon could concentrate against the Allies in Germany.'[39]

Any doubts Wellington might have had about the war were certainly dispelled by New Year's Day 1814, when, having perused the latest Parisian papers, he wrote to Bathurst: 'As far as I can judge from Buonaparte's speech to the Legislative Body... you will have no peace now... Every day's experience here shows the desire of the people to shake off the yoke of Napoleon.'[40] If Wellington had momentarily 'wobbled' in his own determination to overthrow Napoleon, probably for humanitarian reasons, the opening of the 1814 campaign found him utterly resolute.

EIGHT

'Napoleon Has Abdicated'
1813–1814

What is a throne? A bit of wood covered with velvet.
NAPOLEON

In December 1813 Napoleon proposed that Ferdinand VII of Spain be released and restored to the Spanish throne, and if possible married off to his brother Joseph's eldest daughter Zénaïde. Although Ferdinand declined the marriage – he was twenty-eight, she was eleven – he did sign the treaty of Valençay which provided for all British and French troops to leave Spain. Ferdinand had no intention of respecting his obligations, and the Regency Government in Madrid swiftly repudiated it, but the treaty afforded Napoleon a face-saving formula by which he could try to withdraw the garrisons left behind Wellington in Catalonia and Valencia.

Wellington was unimpressed with Napoleon's plan, telling Bathurst: 'I have long suspected that Buonaparte would adopt this expedient; and if he had had less pride, and more common sense, and could have carried his measure into execution as he ought to have done, it would have succeeded.'[1] He cheekily concluded that the treaty had showed 'that Buonaparte is of the same opinion with me regarding the importance of our operations here'.

Wellington had been scathing about Napoleon's strategy at the time of the battle of Leipzig the previous October, saying that it had always seemed to him that:

if Buonaparte had not placed himself in a position that every other officer would have avoided, and had not remained in it longer than was consistent with any notions of prudence, he would have retired in such a state that the Allies could not have ventured to approach the Rhine.

They must not expect battles of Leipzig every day; and that which experience shows them is that they ought, above all things, to avoid any great military disaster.[2]

That had, after all, been the basis of his own successful policy in the Peninsula. 'If the Allies suffer no disaster,' he went on, 'the people of France will force him to make peace.' His overall view was that if 'you cannot make peace with Buonaparte in the winter, we must run at him in the spring'.

The longer Wellington spent in France, the more convinced he became of what he called 'the detestation of this man' by ordinary Frenchmen. By mid-January he was suggesting to Lord Burghersh, the Allied military commander at Frankfurt who had served on Wellington's staff in the Peninsula and had married his favourite niece Priscilla Wellesley-Pole, that the Allies should publicly declare for the Bourbons, and that if they did 'the whole of France will rise as one man in their favour', advice which was grossly over-optimistic. One advantage of reinstating the Bourbons on the throne – which Wellington said could be done 'with the utmost ease' – was that it would invalidate any further treaties such as Valençay. 'I think it probable that the Allies will at last be obliged to take this line,' he explained, 'as you will see the trick that Bony has endeavoured to play with his Treaty with King Ferdinand.' It was the first occasion on which Wellington had used Napoleon's nick-name in his official correspondence. Many of his letters home from this period advocate the restoration of the Bourbons, if not necessarily Louis XVIII himself. His apology for the length of his despatches – 'I had not the time to make them shorter' – invoked a paradox many writers will instantly recognise.[3]

It was also at this time that Wellington began forging Napoleon's currency. In what a century and a half later would be called a 'hearts and minds' policy, he was determined to win French support by paying for his supplies. When the local French victuallers started to refuse to accept Spanish or Portuguese cash for the goods they were – luckily for them – allowed to sell to the British army, Wellington asked his commanders whether they had any former counterfeiters in their units. It is a comment on the recruitment policies of the British army of the day that no fewer than forty of them came forward, and very soon Spanish dollars were being converted into Napoleonic five-franc pieces. The people whom Wellington had the previous July only semi-affectionately described as 'the scum of the earth' clearly had their uses.[4]

The series of victories Napoleon won over the Russians, Prussians,

Austrians and Westphalians at Champaubert, Montmirail, Château-Thierry, Vauchamps and Montereau between 10 and 18 February were, in Wellington's opinion, 'very brilliant, probably the ablest of all his performances'. Even that encomium had a sting in its tail, however. In 1823 the diarist Charles Greville reported Wellington's view that had Napoleon:

> possessed greater patience he would have succeeded in compelling the Allies to retreat; but they had adopted so judicious a system of defence that he was foiled in the impetuous attacks he made upon them, and after a partial failure ... he got tired of pursuing a course which afforded no great results, and ... threw himself into the rear of the Grand Army. The march upon Paris entirely disconcerted him and finished the war. The Allies could not have maintained themselves much longer, and had he continued to keep his force concentrated, and to carry it as occasion required against one or other of the two armies, the Duke thinks he must eventually have forced them to retreat, and that their retreat would have been a difficult operation. The British army could not have reached the scene of operations for two months. The Allies did not dare attack Napoleon; if he had himself come up he would have attacked him, for his army was the best that had ever existed.[5]

Wellington's view remained unchanged by 1831, when he told Mahon how the study of Napoleon's 1814 campaign 'has given me a greater idea of his genius than any other. Had he continued that system a little longer, it is my opinion that he would have saved Paris. But he wanted patience – he did not see the necessity of adhering to defensive warfare. I have been obliged to do it for many months together – and he threw himself imprudently on the rear of the Allies. Then, of course, they marched on Paris.'[6]

In both estimations of Napoleon's great string of victories, Wellington inserted himself into the argument. Yet, as the respected Napoleonic scholar Felix Markham has pointed out, Wellington's judgment failed to get to the heart of the matter. Napoleon supposed that Paris would stand firm as a fortified base against the Allies, leaving him free to operate against their flanks and rear. It was only because Paris had not the heart for a prolonged resistance, after twenty-two years of war, that his strategy failed.[7] With Talleyrand still at large in the capital, and declaring himself president of a provisional government as soon as Napoleon had left the city, there was little the emperor could realistically have done.

Wellington was one of those who advocated a straight drive on Paris by the Allies, opposing any 'broad front' policy as likely to be turned by Napoleon to his advantage.[8] He was too far south for Napoleon to worry about him overmuch during the 1814 campaign, beyond ordering Marshal Clarke on 23 February to write to Soult that 'qu'avec de belles troupes il doit battre Lord Wellington, mais que dans les circonstances actuelles il faut avoir un peu plus de décision et de vigeur' (with such fine troops he should beat Wellington but in the current circumstances determination and vigour are also necessary).[9]

From 5 to 19 February the Allies attempted to persuade Napoleon to return France to her 1792 borders at a congress at Châtillon, but when it proved fruitless on 9 March Austria, Russia, Prussia and Britain signed the treaty of Chaumont, undertaking not to negotiate any separate peace with France before Napoleon's abdication. Wellington, who did not then know the treaty had been signed, wrote to Lord Liverpool on 4 March saying that any such 'declaration from us would, I am convinced, raise such a flame in this country as would soon spread from one end of it to the other, and would probably over-throw him ... I cannot discover the policy of not hitting one's enemy as hard as one can, and in the most vulnerable place ... He would cer-tainly overthrow the British authority in Ireland if it was in his power.'[10]

Napoleon was warned by his arch-chancellor Cambacérès in early March that Wellington was about to enter Bordeaux, although it was presented to him as entirely the result of the treachery of the authori-ties there.[11] In fact Wellington took the city on the 12th, but, fighting for his throne before Paris, there was nothing that Napoleon could have done. Wellington, meanwhile, was inundated with false rumours about Napoleon, complaining to Colonel Bunbury of the War Office on 1 April – the appropriate day for it – that 'I have been told twenty times that Buonaparte was dead, that he had died of a wound, was poisoned, was dead of the gravel, &, &, that the Congress [of Châtillon] was dissolved, that there was an insurrection in La Vendée, in Brittany, &, &, the whole being false.'[12] (The 'gravel' was a painful urinary disease of the day.)

Outside Toulouse on Easter Sunday, 10 April 1814, Wellington fought one of his fiercest battles of the war, defeating Soult once again but losing 4,568 men to Soult's 3,236. Recalling to George Chad years later how General Picton had lost five hundred men by attacking in disregard of his orders, Wellington ruminated: 'Buonaparte would have approved of it, because he did not care for the lives of his men;

we were obliged to husband them.'[13] Soult withdrew the next day to Carcassonne, leaving most of his guns and 1,600 wounded, and at noon on 12 April Wellington entered the city of Toulouse. He found that the stone eagles had been pulled off the administrative buildings there and Napoleon's statue had been thrown out of the window of the Capitol. He saw the Bourbon white flag flying everywhere, 'and everybody wearing the white cockade' of the Legitimist monarchy of Louis XVIII.[14]

At 5 p.m. that day Colonel Frederick Ponsonby of the 12th Light Dragoons, the emissary from Allied headquarters, found Wellington in his shirtsleeves, pulling on his boots. 'I have extraordinary news for you,' Ponsonby said. 'Ay, I thought so. I knew we should have peace; I've long expected it,' answered Wellington. 'No; Napoleon has abdicated.' 'How abdicated!' Wellington cried. 'Ay, 'tis time indeed. You don't say so, upon my honour! Hurrah!' Wellington then turned on his heel and snapped his fingers in a triumphal pastiche of a flamenco dance. The Peninsular War was over.

In 1838 Wellington told Lady Salisbury that, if Napoleon had not abdicated, he would have taken Bayonne and marched up the coast towards the Loire, attended by naval transports along the way.[15] As it was, on the day Wellington heard of the emperor's abdication, Napoleon himself attempted to commit suicide, drinking from a phial of poison he had hung on a string around his neck ever since he had nearly been captured by Cossacks on the retreat from Moscow. The mixture of opium, belladonna and white hellebore had gone off in the intervening two years; it merely left him retching and ill.[16]

Although Napoleon hoped to take his own life he certainly did not want others to take it for him, and one of the stipulations of his abdication was that a British officer should protect him on the way to the Mediterranean island of Elba off the west coast of Italy, and reside there as a commissioner once he had landed. Colonel Sir Neil Campbell, a Peninsular veteran, was therefore attached to him as an Allied commissioner to guarantee his safety from Royalist mobs and Maltese pirates. When Campbell arrived at Fontainebleau he found:

a short active-looking man, who was rapidly pacing the length of his apartment, like some wild animal in his cell. He was dressed in an old green uniform with gold epaulettes, blue pantaloons, and red topboots, unshaven, uncombed and the fallen particles of snuff scattered profusely upon his upper lip and breast.[17]

Napoleon and Campbell fell to talking about the Peninsular War, and the ex-emperor said of the British army, 'You have acted your part well there,' before discussing the sieges of Ciudad Rodrigo, Badajoz and San Sebastián.

Once Napoleon had bid his tearful farewell to his Imperial Guard in the grand court at Fontainebleau on 20 April 1814, complete with embracing of eagles, kissing of flags and the proclamation of his intention 'to write the history of the great achievements we have performed together,' he and Campbell set off for Elba. At a breakfast in the course of the journey, at Briare, Napoleon 'enquired anxiously as to the reports of an affair which had occurred since the occupation of Paris between the armies of Wellington and Marshal Soult. He passed high encomiums upon the former, inquired as to his age, habits, etc.' When Campbell, who had served under Wellington, described his former commander's 'great activity', Napoleon observed: 'C'est un homme de vigeur dans la guerre. Pour bien faire la guerre, il faut en avoir comme cela' (He's a man of vigour in warfare. To fight well, you have to have some of that). His conversation then turned to military subjects 'and events connected to the British army, on which he seemed to reflect with the deepest interest; but he did not once touch upon the operations of the other Allied armies'.[18]

Napoleon went on to state: 'I have been your greatest enemy – frankly such; but I am no longer.' His praise of Wellington might only have been part of a new campaign for Britain's friendship, but if so there was little to be gained from speaking to a relatively minor official at breakfast. It is far more likely that, as with his reported remarks to Metternich the previous year, Napoleon had been forced to admire what Wellington had achieved in the Peninsula.

By April 1814 the facts were unanswerable, and it would have taken the blindest prejudice on Napoleon's part to deny Wellington's contribution to the Allied victory. What had started as a minor irritation for Napoleon had become a festering sore in the Iberian Peninsula – an 'ulcer' in his own words – and was by 1814 a major military threat to his southern flank.[19] 'A man, to be really great, no matter in what order of greatness,' Napoleon once said, 'must have improvised a portion of his own glory, and shown himself superior to the events which he has brought about.' Wellington had done exactly that in the Peninsula, and it seems from subsequent conversations with Campbell that Napoleon appreciated as much.

In 1808 Napoleon had estimated that his Spanish adventures would cost him the lives of around twelve thousand men in all. In fact the overall cost to France has been estimated at 240,000, an average of nearly one hundred men per day over seven years. Wellington in contrast computed that he lost 36,000 men over six years – 'killed, prisoners, deserters, everything' – and told Lord Mahon in 1836 that 'It would have been infinitely greater but for attention to regular subsistence. The French armies were made to take their chance and to live as they could, and their loss of men was immense. It is very singular that in relating Napoleon's campaigns this has never been clearly shown in anything like its full extent.' In 1810 no fewer than 320,000 French and French-allied troops were tied down in the Peninsula, with two hundred thousand still there when Napoleon desperately needed them in Germany in 1813.

Of course this was by no means all, or even principally, the work of Wellington or the British army. Spain had experienced a fully national resistance to Napoleonic rule. Indeed, in the early stages Wellington expressly stated that 'Our business is not to fight the French army … but to give occupation to so large a portion of it as we can manage and leave the war in Spain to the guerrillas.' 'In war,' said Napoleon, 'the moral is to the physical as three to one.' In the Peninsular War Europe caught its first true glimpse of Napoleonic vulnerability; the first cracks in the continental edifice appeared there as the whole theatre became a source of danger, weakness, frustration and demoralisation for the French Empire. This cannot all be put down to Wellington – Sir John Stuart's victory at the battle of Maida in 1806 and Lord Henry Paget's at Sahagun in 1808 had been significant – but he achieved victory time after time.

It cannot be overemphasised that the Napoleonic Wars were not won by the British army: 'It was not the Spanish ulcer, but the Russian coronary which destroyed Napoleon.'[20] The Peninsula represented a terrible drain on Napoleon's resources, but it was containable for as long as he did not get drawn into a war on two fronts. At his greatest point Wellington commanded no more than 75,000 men in total, and tactical excellence was easier to deliver when he personally knew all his regimental commanders, in a way that would have been impossible if he had commanded an army nine times the size, as Napoleon had in Russia.[21]

Wellington attributed his success in part to 'the want of information by the enemy's General officers', telling Samuel Rogers: 'Everywhere I received intelligence from the peasants and the priests. The French learnt nothing.'[22] In fact the French had learnt much from the British press, but Napoleon found it very hard to discover the truth from his own marshals, complaining of one report that it had as much complicated stuffing as the insides of a clock.[23] There were many factors to which Napoleon could, and at first did, ascribe France's Peninsular defeats at the hands of the 'sepoy general'. The Royal Navy's seapower afforded great logistical advantages; his marshals were almost uniformly jealous of one another; the population were, in his own phrase, 'bandits led by monks' who did not sue for peace once Madrid had fallen; the terrain was, beyond Spain's central plains, unsuitable for setpiece warfare; Joseph Bonaparte did not have the necessary kingly qualities; above all, perhaps, Napoleon never went there himself after January 1809, and so Wellington 'never had to face the might and combined-arms coordinated attacks of the veteran Grande Armée in its heyday'.[24]

By 1814 Wellington had defeated no fewer than six of Napoleon's twenty-six marshals – Jourdan, Marmont, Masséna, Ney, Soult and Victor – as well as a whole raft of his generals, including d'Erlon, Foy, Gazan, Junot, Kellermann, Laborde, Marchand, Reille and Reynier.[25] Many of these men were to hold high military posts during the Waterloo campaign, and needed their resolve stiffening on the morning of the battle itself.

'In war one sees one's own troubles,' Napoleon once said; 'those of one's enemy one cannot see.' Yet Wellington made it his priority to be concerned with what he could not see, that which was 'on the other side of the hill'. It is no coincidence that he was so often portrayed with a telescope in his hand rather than a sword or baton, for with his mastery of topography it was his most effective weapon. His great attention to logistical detail also explains much. The famous dictum ascribed to Napoleon about large armies in Spain starving and small ones being defeated did not apply to the British army. Wellington's large army of seventy thousand in 1813 was well provisioned, while the small ones he commanded in 1808, 1809 and 1810 were unbeaten.

Yet Napoleon's hagiographers regularly refuse to give Wellington due credit for his Peninsular achievements. In his book on the French marshalate, the Napoleon-worshipper A. G. Macdonnell stated:

> Probably no general in history has ever had such an easy task as Wellington had. Working on interior lines, with a mercenary army, in a country where every peasant and priest was at once an ally, a source of information, and an active assassin, with a constant flow of supplies from England, and with the complete command of the sea, the Duke of Wellington had the game in his hands, and yet it took him nearly six years to advance from Lisbon to the Pyrenees.[26]

Wellington was almost always outnumbered and was particularly deficient in cavalry. He had a total of 240 cavalry at Vimeiro and still only 5,900 by the time of Vitoria. Until the battle of Salamanca, partly out of prejudice and partly out of necessity, he generally employed his cavalry for intelligence-gathering, piquet duty, foraging and escorts, not considering that they had distinguished themselves at either Vimeiro or Talavera.[27] Criticisms that Wellington was not a good offensive general are also very wide of the mark, however regularly made by hostile historians. Of his fourteen major Peninsular battles, only five were essentially defensive, the rest were offensive and there were also four major sieges. Wellington's crossing of the Bidassoa river and his chasing of Masséna in March and April 1811 should also be seen as offensive manoeuvres.[28]

One person who was in no doubt about the effects of the Peninsular War was Napoleon himself, who on St Helena told his confidant and 'ghost-writer' Emmanuel, Comte de Las Cases:

> That unlucky war ruined me; it divided my forces, obliged me to multiply my efforts, and caused my principles to be assailed…All the circumstances of my disasters are connected with that fatal knot: it destroyed my moral power in Europe, rendered my embarrassments more complicated, and opened a school for the English soldiers.[29]

Wellington himself had not taken a single day's leave from April 1809 to April 1814. When he finally arrived in Paris on 4 May, having bid a typically curt farewell to his men at Bordeaux, he felt he deserved some pleasure and was determined to enjoy it. In the meantime, as a postscript to a letter to his brother Henry, he was able to write: 'I believe I forgot to tell you that I was made a duke.'

At Lord Aberdeen's party a week after Wellington had arrived in Paris, someone mentioned that he had never been opposed to Napoleon across a field of battle. 'No, and I am very glad I never was,' replied Wellington instantly. 'I would at any time rather have heard that a reinforcement of forty thousand men had joined the French army, than that he had arrived to take command.'[30] It was considered at the time a generous sentiment to those Allied generals who had been defeated by Napoleon, but the figure of forty thousand men was one he was to repeat several times over the years, and there can be no reason to disbelieve what he said. It is important not to pay too much attention to the actual figure of forty thousand, however, as it might have been simply a contemporary metaphor meaning 'many', not unlike the biblical 'forty days and forty nights', rather than an accurate and considered measure of actual battlefield force. Napoleon is on record as having said that the Italian people were not worth the lives of forty thousand Frenchmen, and that a Bourbon government in France was not worth forty thousand British lives, so the figure needs to be considered in its colloquial as well as military context. Nonetheless, for all his criticisms of some aspects of Napoleonic strategy, in 1814 Wellington undoubtedly admired Napoleon the soldier as much as he despised and detested Napoleon the political phenomenon.

Someone who agreed with Wellington's analysis – only quibbling over the numbers involved – was Napoleon himself. In her memoirs, Napoleon's stepdaughter and sister-in-law, Queen Hortense, recalled that at dinner alone with the emperor and Marie Louise on 24 January 1814, as four hundred thousand Austrians, Russians and Prussians converged on France, she unsubtly observed that the emperor had only fifty thousand troops with which to oppose them. Thumping the table, Napoleon shouted that, because he was there to lead them, 'That makes one hundred and fifty thousand!'

NINE

Evenings on St Helena, Nights in Paris

1814–1815

I have always admired Mithridates contemplating the
conquest of Rome when he was vanquished and a fugitive.

NAPOLEON

Wellington arrived in Paris just in time to see the Russian and
Prussian Guards march past King Louis XVIII. The French
king deluged him with glorious presents, including two large
Sèvres vases, a Sèvres *déjeuner* and a tray originally destined for
Napoleon's mother, Madame Mère, entitled *A Hunt in the Forest of
Compiègne*, which featured Napoleon and his Mameluke servant Roustam
Ali wearing the costume of the imperial hunt and following the hounds.[1]

To his surprise, as he considered it 'a situation for which I should
never have thought myself qualified', Wellington was appointed British
ambassador to France in July. Not only was he unqualified, but it also
seemed a staggeringly tactless action by the British Government to
appoint as ambassador the man responsible for so many French
defeats and deaths, a bovine choice for what was usually a diplomatically deft ministry. As ambassador, Wellington tried to persuade the
French to abolish the slave trade, something that Louis XVIII's ministers found impossible to do. When Napoleon returned he simply
abolished it overnight.[2]

Wellington now needed a grand British embassy. His eye fell upon
the huge home of Napoleon's sister Pauline Borghese, the Hôtel
Charost at 39 rue du Faubourg St Honoré, close to the Elysée and the
Quai d'Orsay. Austrian officers who had been billeted there had left
the cellars dry, and Wellington was almost put off by the sheer size of
the place, writing to Castlereagh's half-brother Sir Charles Stewart in
July: 'The Prince Borghese's house is so very large that, however
much I may wish to have it, as thinking it the only home that I have

ever seen that would perfectly answer, I feel a great disinclination to apply to the Government to purchase it. I must therefore give up all thought of it.'[3] Fortunately for British ambassadors in Paris ever since, Stewart raised the necessary eight hundred thousand francs, which was fifty thousand less than Pauline had originally asked, but twice what she gave for it in 1803. Wellington signed the inventory on 26 August and moved in at once. The first payment was made in October and the last in 1816.

Wellington seems to have known Pauline well enough to address her by her Christian name in their correspondence, visiting her several times in Paris and teasing her mildly over their mutual friend Mary Bagot, the sister of Lady Fitzroy Somerset and Lady Burghersh. He called her a 'heartless little devil' but he hung a rather revealing portrait of her in his bedroom.[4] She was the first of several of Napoleon's relations whom he cultivated, also calling upon Napoleon's sister-in-law Queen Hortense, to whom he was 'most deferential'.[5]

For his embassy cook Wellington hired a Frenchman who had been in Napoleon's employ. According to Gleig this man 'knew perfectly how to select materials for a banquet and how to deal with them when chosen'. It was probably a piece of gastronomic triumphalism to take on this particular cook, for Wellington cared little for the culinary arts and according to Lord Ellesmere could scarcely tell rancid butter from fresh.[6] He had been greatly amused in Flanders in 1794 when a Guards officer warned him that he might occasionally have no dinner at all on campaign, emphasising: 'I mean literally no dinner, and not merely roughing it on a beefsteak and a bottle of port wine.'

When not carrying out his diplomatic duties, Wellington would enjoy hunting excursions with the French royal family. On one occasion he donned gold lace and jackboots and took them on a special expedition to Napoleon's hunting lodge at Rambouillet.[7] At a dinner in May 1814 he made tangential contact with Napoleon's wife Marie Louise, after her lady of the wardrobe, the Comtesse de Luçay, asked General Junot's wife the Duchesse d'Abrantès to introduce them at a dinner party.[8] He got to know the empress directly at the Congresses of Vienna and Verona. Wellington's closest contact with Napoleon in Paris, however, came when he slept with not one but two of the emperor's mistresses.

↜

Josephina 'Giuseppina' Grassini was born in Varese in Lombardy in

April 1773, making her four years younger than Napoleon and five years younger than Wellington. After studying opera in Milan she made her début in Parma in 1789 in Guglielmi's *La pastorelle nobile*. A contralto, in 1800 she appeared at La Scala in Milan in three comic operas, but realised that her natural talent was for powerful dramatic and tragic roles, and over the next decade she performed the work of Zingarelli, Cimarosa, Portogallo, Bertoni, Mayr and Nasolini, in the opera houses of Vicenza, Venice, Milan, Naples and Ferrara. Her voice was 'narrow in range but of great power and volume, unusually flexible for its weight and always used with taste and musicality'. By the time Napoleon first heard her in 1797 she was one of the most admired Italian divas of the day.[9]

It was her looks as much as her considerable dramatic ability that made her the most fêted person in Milan after Napoleon himself. 'Her thick and finely pencilled eyebrows stood out in sharp contrast to the ivory whiteness of her face … her movements showed both charm and majesty.'[10] She had 'fine expressive eyes, large regular features, fine teeth, and tragic dignity'.[11] The word most often used to describe her figure was 'voluptuous'. Yet Napoleon at that time had eyes solely for Josephine, and showed no interest in Grassini when she sang for him on the Isola Bella on Lake Maggiore in 1797.

Napoleon entered Milan on campaign three years later, by which time he knew of Josephine's infidelity with Hippolyte Charles, and had himself already been unfaithful to her in Egypt. When he responded to her attentions after a concert at La Scala in July 1800, Grassini mock-scolded him for showing no interest in her before, saying that in 1797:

> I was in the full glory of my beauty and talents. I was the only topic of conversation; I blinded all eyes, and inflamed every heart. Only the young general remained cold, and all my thoughts were occupied by him alone. How strange it seems! When I was still worth something, when the whole of Italy was at my feet, when I heroically spurned all homage for a single glance from your eyes, I could not obtain it. And now, now you let your gaze rest upon me, today, when it is not worthwhile, when I am no more worthy of you![12]

Napoleon clearly thought differently, because when his chief of staff General Berthier arrived for a working breakfast the following morning the woman who was soon to become famous as 'La Chanteuse de l'Empereur' was already present. (Later that same day

Napoleon lectured two hundred Roman Catholic priests on the text: 'No society can exist without morality, therefore it is only religion which can provide a strong and enduring support for the state.')

Napoleon arranged for Grassini to follow him to Paris, but so as not to alert Josephine an official bulletin was published saying that 'the famous Billington, Grassini, and Marchesi...will proceed to Paris where they intend giving a series of concerts'.[13] Josephine, it was said, 'allowed herself to be deceived by it'.[14] At Les Invalides on Bastille Day 1800, Grassini sang an ode to the liberation of Italy written on Napoleon's orders by the great French composer Étienne-Nicolas Méhul. The 'Chant National du Quartorze Juillet 1800' was composed for two full-sized choirs and orchestras and a third group of high voices accompanied by two harps and solo horn, and is credited as 'a notable ancestor of Berlioz's *Requiem*, written for performance in the same building'.

Admirers said that to hear Grassini was to listen 'not to a singer but to a Muse'.[15] She sang at Malmaison and at the War Ministry's fête to celebrate the anniversary of the battle of Marengo, prompting a widespread revival of Italian music in Paris. 'Who should more fittingly celebrate the victory of Marengo', asked the *Moniteur* rhetorically in 1801, 'than those whose peace and happiness are thereby assured?'

Napoleon greatly appreciated music and the human voice, although he himself sang out of tune. He bestowed the Order of the Iron Crown on the great Italian singer Crescentini, and also gave Grassini fifteen thousand francs per month as he (rather wittily) installed her as his mistress in a guest-house on the rue Chantereine. Grassini wanted to become Napoleon's openly avowed mistress, but for both political and personal reasons the first consul wanted to keep the affair secret, so fairly soon she took on a lover, a twenty-two-year-old violinist from Bordeaux called Rode.

Rode was understandably nervous of the Corsican emperor finding out, yet when he did he acted very generously, and in March and October 1801 Grassini and Rode performed with his permission in the Théâtre de la République, where the receipts amounted to 13,868 francs on the latter occasion alone. The lovers then left for an extended and triumphant tour of Germany, Italy and the Netherlands. Napoleon had clearly not entirely forsworn her, however, as in 1803 Josephine was writing to her friend Madame de Krény to ask whether she might send her maid Julie to spy on Grassini on her return to Paris, and complaining:

I am so unhappy, dearest…every day there are scenes with Bonaparte, and for no reason…I tried to guess the explanation and learned that la Grassini has been in Paris for the last week. Apparently she is the cause of all my troubles…Please try and find out where that woman is living, and whether he goes to her or she comes to him.[16]

It seems that she came to him at the Tuileries, which must have been doubly galling for the soon-to-be-empress. Because of her bad teeth, Josephine 'affected a mysterious, tight-lipped, Mona Lisa smile', which Napoleon's affair with Grassini could only have made yet tighter.

Grassini then spent three seasons in London. The Comtesse de Boigne, in exile in England, who often sang at private houses with her, recorded that:

She was the first professional singer who had been admitted to London society. To great talent she added extreme beauty, and a sound common sense which enabled her to adapt her behaviour to any company in which she found herself. The Duke of Hamilton allowed her to become intimate with his sisters. The Count of Fonchal, the Portuguese ambassador, gave delightful parties, which were eagerly awaited. Not only was she invited to concerts, but to all society meetings, even to those of special cliques. She was an excellent actress, and her principles of singing were admirable.[17]

Lady Bessborough agreed with the Comtesse de Boigne's estimation of Grassini, telling Granville Leveson Gower in May 1805 how superior her acting was to that of Mrs Siddons, and that 'The whole House rings again with applause' after a performance of *Thabala the Destroyer*.[18] Thomas De Quincey called Grassini's voice 'delightful to me beyond all that I have ever heard. Yes; or have since heard; or shall ever hear.' High praise from an opium-eater.

When Grassini returned to Paris, Napoleon welcomed her back with a thirty-six thousand franc salary and a fifteen thousand franc 'bonus' as *prima donna* at – ironically enough – the Théâtre de l'Impératrice. He even paid 1,200 francs for a box at her and Rode's concerts. Along with other miscellaneous gifts she is estimated to have cost the French taxpayer seventy thousand francs per annum between 1807 and 1814, and it is hard to believe that these enormous sums solely covered her services to song. When she was robbed of a diamond-encrusted portrait of the emperor on the Côte d'Or in 1807, two of the four Swiss deserters responsible were executed by the local

National Guard commander, to whom Napoleon awarded the *légion d'honneur*.[19] Napoleon was also present in November 1813 when she appeared as Horatia in *Gli Orazi* at the Théâtre-Italien.

The following year Grassini became one of Wellington's Parisian mistresses, as far as it is possible to be certain about things in an era before telephoto lenses and DNA-testing. The Comtesse de Boigne, Charles Greville, Madame de Staël, Lady Bessborough and Lady Shelley all took it entirely for granted that Grassini was Wellington's mistress in Paris, as have most post-Victorian historians, and given his incomprehensible and unhappy marriage to Kitty Pakenham it does seem very likely. At forty-one, Grassini was not the luscious twenty-seven-year-old Napoleon had first enjoyed at Milan, but she was by all contemporary accounts still tremendously attractive, personally and sexually.

Grassini stated that *ce cher Villainton*, as she called him, did not need to be asked twice, as Napoleon had, but also that he was meaner with his money than Napoleon had been with France's. Her bills at Leroy, the court *modiste*, dressmaker and milliner where Wellington paid off her accounts, show how drastically she had to cut back under the new regime. In December 1815 they came to only 529 francs and 64 centimes. (Equally, she might have been gratified to learn that the same month the Duchess of Wellington's account there came to a mere 380 francs.)

Stories that Grassini offered to go to Elba with Napoleon are heavily discounted, and by November 1814 Lady Bessborough was writing to her lover Leveson Gower about the Duchess of Wellington, to say that the duke 'is behaving very ill to that poor little woman, not on account of making her miserable or the immorality of the fact, but the want of *procédé* and publicity of his attentions to Grassini'.[20] This is confirmed in the *Memoirs* of Grassini's friend and favoured composer Blangini, who was also the *cavaliere servente* of Pauline Borghese. He recalled:

> When Madame Grassini attended informal gatherings at Lord Wellington's she declaimed and sang scenes from *Cleopatra* and *Romeo and Juliet*. Alone in the centre of the salon she gestured as if she was on stage and using a big shawl she dressed up in different ways. I cannot remember if, during these sessions, she sang the arias which end with a *sguardo d'amor*; but what I am certain of is that Lord Wellington was enchanted, in ecstasy.[21]

By the spring of 1816 the Comtesse de Boigne was no longer entranced by her former singing companion, and complained that on one occasion Wellington:

> conceived the idea of making Grassini, who was then at the height of her beauty, the queen of the evening. He seated her upon a sofa mounted on a platform in the ballroom, and never left her side; caused her to be served before anyone else, made people stand away in order that she might see the dancing, and took her into supper himself in front of the whole company; there he sat by her side, and showed her attentions usually granted only to princesses. Fortunately, there were some high-born English ladies to share the burden of this insult, but they did not feel the weight of it as we did, and their resentment could not be compared with ours.[22]

To the end of her life, Grassini, who retired in 1823 and lived in Paris and Milan until her death in June 1850, would talk of her affairs with Napoleon and Wellington. She 'preserved to the last some relics of the beauty which had fascinated the hero of Marengo', as well as some more tangible relics of her career, leaving more than half a million lire in her will. 'See this snuffbox,' she would tell visitors, 'Napoleon gave it to me one morning at the Tuileries where I had paid him a visit. "This is for you, you are a fine creature," he would say. Ah, why would he not listen to me and patch things up with *ce cher Villainton?*'[23]

To sleep with one of Napoleon's mistresses might be considered an accident, but to sleep with two might suggest a pattern of triumphalism in Paris, especially after Wellington had also bought Napoleon's sister's home, engaged Napoleon's cook, called upon his sister-in-law, received presents of his image, and placed a picture of Napoleon's sister in his bedroom. (Louis XVIII's brother the Comte d'Artois – later King Charles X – commented that the picture of Pope Pius VII hanging between those of Grassini and Pauline Borghese reminded him of 'Our Lord between the two thieves'.)

Marguerite Josephine Weimer was born in 1787, making her eighteen years younger than Napoleon and Wellington. She was only fifteen, or possibly just sixteen, when in Nivôse Year XI of the Revolution – between 21 December 1802 and 19 January 1803 – Napoleon seduced her at St Cloud after she played Clytemnestra in *Iphigenia in Aulis* at the Comédie Française. His affair with Grassini now over, Napoleon seems to have been amused by Weimer – whose stage name was 'Mademoiselle George' – as much as he was impressed by her beauty and figure and youth.

Napoleon treated Mademoiselle George – whom he called 'Georgina' – generously if boisterously, once pushing forty thousand francs down her cleavage, presumably in notes. They had a two-year affair during his consulship, which infuriated Josephine, but as Napoleon once put it: 'Exclusivity is not in my nature.' Josephine was particularly unamused when Mademoiselle George, acting in *Cinna* at the Théâtre Français, declaimed the line, 'If I have seduced Cinna, I shall seduce many more,' and the audience at once rose to applaud the first consul, who was sitting in his box with Josephine. The affair ended in 1804. When years later Alexandre Dumas the Elder asked Mademoiselle George why, she answered, with slightly more poetry than accuracy: 'He left me to become an emperor.'[24]

After spending some time in Russia between 1808 and 1812 – an anecdote about her appears in the opening scene of *War and Peace* – George returned to Paris. It was there that she met Wellington after Napoleon's abdication and, still aged only twenty-seven, is thought to have had an affair with him. The Radical politician and friend of Byron John Cam Hobhouse records her in April 1814 as being 'very large but with a fine face and strong lines with expressive action, so as now and then to remind me of Mrs Siddons'. Wellington's affair with her is not so well documented as that with Grassini, but it is generally accepted to have taken place.[25]

Weimer died in 1867 at the age of eighty, but unlike Grassini she had not invested her wages of sin wisely. At the time of the 1855 Paris Exhibition she was reduced to applying for the post of manageress of the Lost Umbrella Office, which was (rather cruelly in the circumstances) refused.[26] Perhaps her greatest service to history was to have compared Napoleon's and Wellington's performances as lovers, judging that 'Monsieur le Duc était de beaucoup le plus fort' (The duke was much the stronger).[27] In his master's defence, Caulaincourt recorded that, although it was true that Napoleon had 'had Mademoiselle George and a few other women' during his marriage to Josephine, such affairs were only 'a distraction which afforded him but little amusement'.[28]

Nor were Grassini and George the only people connected to Napoleon whom Wellington is thought to have tried to seduce. Madame Juliette Récamier, the former mistress of Napoleon's brother Lucien, was reckoned one of the greatest beauties of Paris. She rejected Napoleon's attentions, but not those of Prince Augustus of Prussia or of the writer Benjamin Constant. Wellington paid court to her in June 1814, and she kept his letters. 'Each time I see you, I leave you more impressed with your charms and less inclined to give my attention to politics!!!' read one. 'I shall call on you tomorrow…in spite of the dangerous effects such visits have upon me.' She later claimed to have rejected Wellington when he promised that he would take revenge on Napoleon, who was reputed to have ill-treated her. 'Je l'ai bien battu,' he apparently told her before the beautiful French patriot closed the door on him.[29] This seems unlikely, as by June 1814 Wellington had never faced Napoleon, let alone beaten him, but however much of her story one believes it seems that Wellington was unable to succeed where Napoleon had failed.

⤶

While Wellington was enjoying himself in Paris making his own highly idiosyncratic collection of Napoleona, the emperor was on Elba. In May 1814 Castlereagh reported Napoleon's landing there to Wellington, with the warning that 'during the voyage on one occasion his mind seemed still to cherish hopes as to France'. In August Lord Liverpool wrote to say that Louis XVIII would like to send Napoleon further afield than a few miles off the coast of Italy. Talleyrand agreed, and over the following months St Lucia, Trinidad and the Azores were privately and unofficially canvassed as possible ultimate destinations.

Sir Neil Campbell, one of the Allied commissioners who accompanied Napoleon to Elba, had several conversations with the sovereign of the tiny isle, who had been allowed to retain the title of emperor, however ludicrous it might have sounded at the time. A few of their talks were highly instructive about the admiring attitude Napoleon had by then adopted towards Wellington. Campbell had twice been mentioned in despatches in the Peninsula, from where he had been invalided out when he was wounded after the siege of Burgos. (A better soldier than he was a minder, Campbell was to be mentioned in despatches again after Waterloo and went on to become governor of Sierra Leone.)

On 16 September 1814, after asking Campbell whether a British regiment was stationed in Nice, Napoleon told him about a recent dinner party in Paris at which his former imperial chaplain, the Archbishop of Malines, had denounced him as a fool and a bad general. According to Napoleon's source, a Frenchman present had pointed out that Napoleon had enjoyed great success during his Italian campaigns. 'Lord Wellington had remained silent during the whole time of this conversation, but when the same gentleman referred to him for his opinion, he replied that the success which the Emperor had obtained in the last campaign, between the Seine and the Marne, was equally great.' According to Campbell, Napoleon 'appeared to be highly flattered by the praise thus accorded to him by the Duke of Wellington, and asked me whether he was not generally reserved in conversation. I replied that he was certainly not talkative!'[30] In the same conversation, Napoleon denounced Mariotti, the French consul at Leghorn in Tuscany, as 'a Corsican adventurer', which implies a lack of irony on his part and great powers of self-restraint on Campbell's.

For all his satisfaction at Wellington's praise of his 1814 strategy, Napoleon believed, as he told Campbell on 31 October, that 'The appointment of the Duke of Wellington as ambassador at Paris was an open insult and injury to the feelings of the French people. He, who had been one of the most successful instruments against them, could not be considered in any other light.'[31] It is hard to gainsay Napoleon, and Louis XVIII's very pronounced fondness for Wellington, who was correctly suspected of occasionally interfering in French politics, merely made matters worse. Public opinion was alienated, especially when Wellington failed to pay for the crop damage caused by his hunting expeditions. 'La gloire de Wellington' was also known to irritate Marshal Ney, although Soult, Masséna and Foy consented to receive their former antagonist. Foy spent an hour with Wellington on 26 October, where they discussed 'la guerre'.[32]

Wellington was under no illusions about the discontent prevalent in the French army after the first Bourbon Restoration. 'Buonaparte left an army of a million men in France,' he wrote to the veteran French soldier General Dumouriez who was in exile in Britain in November 1814, 'other than officers in prison in England and Russia. The King cannot maintain a quarter of them...All those not employed are discontented.'[33] When sentries insisted on presenting arms to Napoleon's veterans who wore the medal of the *légion d'honneur*, despite its being against orders and subject to disciplinary charges, the practice finally had to be officially condoned. Napoleon told Campbell that 'the Bourbons have very few partisans in the army', while he enquired whether there were any British troops in Genoa. He was 'at pains to point out that he had no personal motives or expectations'; as he told his brave and honourable but somewhat naïve commissioner: 'I am a dead man.'

During the winter of 1814/15 the Casa Mulini, Napoleon's official residence on Elba, proved the ultimate tourist destination for British Whigs, who visited in order to be able to say they had met Napoleon, and to report back his words of wisdom. In his turn, the Emperor of Elba received his British visitors and pumped them for information about British domestic politics and troop dispositions along the Mediterranean coastline, where he planned to land as soon as the political situation in France seemed ripe for his return. As a result of these meetings we know much of what Napoleon was thinking at the time, or at least what he wanted his erstwhile and prospective British sympathisers to think he was thinking.

Talking to the pro-Reform Whig the Hon. George Venables Vernon and the Whig MP for Lincoln John Fazakerley in a four-hour interview on 18 November, Napoleon said: 'They are brave fellows, those English troops of yours; they are worth more than the others. Next to them, I consider the Prussians the best, but I have always found myself able to defeat the Continental troops with very inferior troops.'[34] Venables Vernon, the eldest son of Lord Vernon, who later sat as a Whig MP for Derbyshire South, reported to the Whig grandee the 3rd Marquess of Lansdowne that Napoleon had also praised Britain's form of aristocratic government, saying 'I tried to form one, but that was a thing which required time. Chemists have a species of powder out of which they can make marble, but it must have time to become solid.'

In a three-and-a-half-hour interview with Campbell on 4 December, Napoleon cited 'Wellington pressing forward from Toulouse' as one of several reasons why he had abdicated the previous April, but he added that 'he would not have done so had not Marmont deserted him'.[35] Marshal Marmont, the Duc de Ragusa, had surrendered his entire corps six days after negotiating a truce which had allowed the Allies into Paris. His action inspired the colloquial French verb raguser, meaning 'to betray'. Wellington took a more generous line with the man he had defeated at Salamanca, explaining to Lady Salisbury in 1836 that 'Napoleon had released all his generals from their allegiance, and [Marmont] was the first who acted upon it, that was all.'[36]

Napoleon enjoyed descanting upon the story of his immediate past, blaming the Duc d'Enghien's death on Talleyrand (while 'showing very little emotion or regret at the circumstances itself'), telling a visitor Captain Adye, who had served under Nelson at the battle of the Nile, of his plans to invade Britain and separate Ireland from her, and generally showing, in Campbell's opinion, that 'his thoughts seemed to dwell perpetually on the operations of war'.[37]

On the morning of Monday, 6 December, Napoleon spent three and a half hours talking to Hugh Fortescue, Viscount Ebrington. The nephew of the former prime minister Lord Grenville, Ebrington was also related to William Pitt. After Eton and Brasenose College, Oxford, Ebrington had become MP for Barnstaple aged twenty-one in 1804, and by 1814 he was MP for Buckingham. In 1809 he had been appointed aide-de-camp to Wellington but was unable to take up his appointment. General Druout, the governor of Elba, passed on Ebrington's request for an interview with the emperor, and, when it was granted, Napoleon's first question was about whether the French were content. To Ebrington's non-committal reply 'comme ça', Napoleon said:

> They cannot be; they have been too humbled by the peace; they have had a king imposed on them, and imposed by England. Lord Wellington's appointment must be very galling to the army, as must the great attentions shown him by the king, as if to set his own private feelings up in opposition to those of the country. If Lord Wellington had come to Paris as a visitor, I should have pleasure in showing him the attentions due to his great ability [*grande mérite*], but I should not have liked him being sent to me as ambassador.[38]

Napoleon then discussed the Bourbons, the House of Lords as a bulwark of the British constitution, old British families (the Fortescues can trace themselves back to the Norman Conquest), Alexander I's duplicity, the King of Prussia ('un caporal'), the mediocrity of the Archduke Charles, the retreat from Moscow, Marmont's treachery, the relative merits of Soult, Davout and Masséna, Talleyrand's supposed advice to him 'to have the Bourbons assassinated', the Italians ('lazy and effeminate'), the deaths of d'Enghien and Pichegru (neither of which was apparently his fault), his fortuitous escape from circumcision while adopting Mahomedanism in Egypt, and the Jaffa massacre, which he effectively admitted.

Napoleon evidently enjoyed his *tour d'horizon* and found it useful, because Ebrington was soon invited back. At dinner two days later, Napoleon 'entered a good deal into the state of parties' in Britain, asking if any was sufficiently Jacobin to celebrate the execution of King Charles I. Ebrington thought not, adding that indeed there were probably more Jacobites who revered him than Jacobins who reviled him. Napoleon then talked of the various prominent Whigs he had met in Paris during the Peace of Amiens in 1802–3, including Charles James Fox, the Duke and Duchess of Bedford, Lord Holland and Lord Erskine. He blamed the British for breaking the Peace, and then spoke of the advantages of polygamy in the colonies. This – circuitously enough – brought him round to Anglo-American relations. He thought the renewed warfare with the United States had weakened Britain's voice at the Congress of Vienna, where the Powers were trying to draw up a lasting post-Napoleonic continental settlement.

In four hours alone with Napoleon, making seven and a half in all, Ebrington had about as comprehensive a discussion as it was possible for a non-acolyte to hold. Yet only a matter of days afterwards, Napoleon met Lord John Russell, Whig MP for Tavistock and scion of one of the greatest Whig families in England, as well as a future British prime minister. Over half a century later Russell recalled that Napoleon:

was dressed in uniform – a greatcoat, single-breasted, white breeches, and silk stockings. I was much struck by his countenance – eyes of a muddy colour and cunning expression; the fine features which we all know in his bust and on his coins; and, lastly, a most agreeable and winning smile. He was very courteous in his manner.[39]

During their ninety-minute discussion, Napoleon and Russell talked of the latter's family, the allowance he received from his father the 6th Duke of Bedford, the state of Spain and Italy and the arrangements for the pacification of Europe then under discussion at Vienna. Then Russell described how:

Napoleon seemed very curious on the subject of the Duke of Wellington. He said it was a great mistake of the English Government to send him [as] ambassador to Paris. 'One does not like to see a man who has beaten one.' He had never sent as ambassador to Vienna a man who had entered Vienna as an officer of the French invading army. As I had seen a good deal of the Duke of Wellington in Spain, Napoleon asked me what were likely to be his occupations. I answered that during his campaigns the Duke had been so much absorbed by his attention to the war that I did not well understand how he could give his mind to other subjects. He remarked, as if he thought I was inclined to think lightly of military talents, 'Eh bien, c'est un grand jeu, belle occupation!'[40]

(Count Lebzeltern, the Austrian ambassador to Rome, hotly denied the truth of Napoleon's second assertion. General Antoine-François Andreossy, for example, had been inspector-general of artillery at Napoleon's headquarters in the 1805 campaign, but later became ambassador to Vienna in 1808–9 and governor of the city during the French military occupation.)

John Cam Hobhouse's diary for 30 December 1814 recorded: 'A gentleman, who has lately seen Napoleon, [reported] that Napoleon said to him, "There are but three generals in the world: myself, Lord Wellington and that drunkard Blücher."'[41] The gentleman in question might possibly have been Russell, but could not have been John Macnamara, who only went to Elba a fortnight later. Macnamara also had a conversation with Napoleon about Wellington. It is hard to avoid the assumption that the Emperor of Elba was planning his escape from his Lilliputian island, and was sizing up his most formidable opponent.

At their meeting on either 13th or 14 January 1815, Napoleon told Macnamara that Wellington was 'a brave man' and said he 'would sooner trust him with one hundred thousand men than any of his own generals, even Soult; but it was very foolish sending him to the Court of France to face those whom he had humbled'. Macnamara then asked why the French generals talked so slightingly of Wellington. Napoleon replied, 'Because he has humbled them one after another,' before changing the subject to how the English felt about the Bourbons.[42] Napoleon's answer to Macnamara was apposite, because it was to apply to Napoleon himself. When Wellington was merely beating his subordinates, Napoleon could afford to be objective about his talents and bravery. Only after Wellington had beaten Napoleon himself did the emperor become viciously contemptuous.

Although Napoleon still saw Wellington in a subordinate capacity to himself, as equal to the best of his best marshals, it is quite clear from both the Macnamara conversation and from the others he held with British subjects while on Elba that his thoughts then about Wellington and the British army were very different from those he expressed in derisory terms at the Le Caillou farmhouse only five months later. Wellington also had the satisfaction of knowing that Napoleon held him in high regard, for on 9 February 1815 Lord Liverpool sent him the notes he had made of 'a private letter detailing an interview with Buonaparte at Elba, the latter end of January'. (As Macnamara only saw Napoleon in mid-January, he was probably not Liverpool's correspondent.)

According to the letter, Napoleon had predicted that Britain could not afford to keep a large standing army on the continent, and she 'should probably lose on the first *coup de canon*, and a battle lost before Brussels would open the road to Holland'. (This was an illuminating insight into Napoleon's later strategic concept for the Waterloo campaign.) After blaming the treacherous marshals Augereau and Marmont for forcing his abdication, Napoleon said Blücher 'was a brave man, but no general...of [the Austrian field marshal Prince zu] Schwarzenberg he appeared to have no better opinion...the Duke of Wellington he praised', before going on to criticise the Spaniards.[43]

Whether or not Napoleon knew that such conversations were being reported back to His Majesty's Government, he was clearly willing, in conversations with Sir Neil Campbell, George Venables Vernon and John Fazakerley MP, Lord Ebrington MP, Lord John Russell MP, John Cam Hobhouse's unnamed 'gentleman', John Macnamara and Lord Liverpool's 'private' correspondent, to make a series of positive, and on occasion frankly admiring, references to Wellington.

Napoleon also regularly expressed great interest in the dispositions of British troops in southern Europe, the state of French public opinion vis-à-vis the Bourbons, and the progress of the negotiations in Vienna, all of which implied that he was planning to return. He could only have been encouraged by the fact that, by the close of 1814, the Congress was on the verge of collapse because Russia was demanding a large portion of Poland, Prussia wanted all of Saxony, while Britain, France and Austria had refused to concede either. On 1 January 1815 Castlereagh warned Liverpool that the Prussians were fortifying Dresden and 'organising their army for the field', and very shortly afterwards he, Metternich and Talleyrand agreed to a secret three-Power pact against Russia and Prussia.[44]

It seemed as if only one event could unite the various factions in Vienna, and, when Campbell left for a twelve-day visit to Florence to consult his ear-doctor, it happened. Napoleon took advantage of a gentle southerly breeze to escape from Elba and sail for France, landing at Golfe Juan near Cannes at 3 p.m. on 1 March 1815. Madame Mère recounted how, the night before his escape, Napoleon asked for her advice. 'Go, my son,' she recalled telling him, 'fulfil your destiny, you were not made to die on this island.'[45] As in the utterances of the Delphic oracle, there was an ironic ambiguity to her prophecy.

TEN

A Hundred-Day Dash
for *La Gloire*
March–June 1815

I am always the same; men of my stamp never change.

NAPOLEON

Wellington was fortunate not to have been in Paris in early March 1815 when the news arrived that Napoleon had landed on the coast of Provence near Cannes. He had been sent to the Congress of Vienna as a plenipotentiary, and so was not forced ignominiously to pack his bags and quit the French capital, a bad psychological start to any campaign. Instead he was in the Austrian capital on 7 March when he received the despatch from Lord Burghersh, the British minister in Florence, informing him 'that Buonaparte had quitted the island of Elba, with all his civil and military officers, and about 1,200 troops'. Wellington later recounted how he had 'immediately communicated this account to the Emperors of Austria and Russia, and to the King of Prussia, and I found among all a prevailing sentiment, of a determination to unite their efforts to support the system established by the Peace of Paris'.

They also agreed, because they did not know exactly where Napoleon had gone, 'to postpone the adoption of any measure till his further progress should be ascertained'.[1] Wellington reported to Lord Castlereagh that he was confident that 'if unfortunately it should be possible for Buonaparte to hold at all against the King of France, he must fall under the cordially united efforts of the sovereigns of Europe'. He later recalled to Samuel Rogers the spirit of sang-froid which the various royalties adopted on receipt of the news, saying that he had communicated it 'to every member of the Congress, and all laughed; the Emperor of Russia most of all'.[2] Lord Clancarty, who was assisting Wellington in Vienna at the time, told Castlereagh a very different story on 11 March, however: 'We were at Court the night of the arrival of Burghersh's despatch... and though there was every attempt to conceal apprehension under a masque of unconcern, it was not difficult to perceive that fear was predominant in all.'

Rumours and conjecture abounded as to where Napoleon was headed, although anyone who had studied his career, and appreciated the discontent prevalent in the French army, ought to have guessed Paris. Yet some said America, others that he would join King Joachim of Naples (that is, Joachim Murat) in Italy; it was even thought he might return to Elba, as though the whole exercise had been a prank or unauthorised sailing trip. Wellington remembered that 'none would hear of France. All were sure that in France he would be massacred by the people when he appeared there. I remember Talleyrand's words so well: "Pour la France – non!"'

As so often when everyone agrees on something, everyone was wrong. Gradually the news arrived at Vienna that not only had Napoleon not been massacred by the people, but he had been welcomed by a significant and growing proportion of them, enough to force Louis XVIII to quit Paris on the night of 19/20 March. In later years Wellington enjoyed telling the story of how Père Elisie, the man whose job it was to dress the king's bloated gouty legs, came to be left behind as the royal party departed for Ghent. He also worked for the Duc de Duras, and although everyone else connected with the *ancien régime* was desperately scrambling to escape the city, Duras was 'too imbecilic to appreciate the danger'.[3]

Although Wellington later claimed to Lord Mahon that he had known all along that Napoleon would head for Paris and that the Bourbons would leave, it seems from the contemporary evidence that he waited for hard news just like everyone else.[4] On 13 March, for example, he wrote to Burghersh to say: 'Bony's conduct is very extraordinary, and in my opinion certainly the *effet d'illusion*...I...am working at a great exertion in case things should become serious in France. But I think the King will settle the business himself, which is the result much to be wished.'[5] That same day Wellington, along with the plenipotentiaries of Russia, Spain, Portugal, Sweden, Prussia and Austria, signed a declaration outlawing Napoleon. It stated:

> In reappearing in France with projects of troubles and upheavals, he has deprived himself of the protection of the laws and manifested in the face of the universe that it cannot have peace with him. The Powers declare that Napoleon Bonaparte is placed outside civil and social

relations, and that as an enemy and disturber of the peace of the world, he has delivered himself over to *la vindicte publique.*

These last two words meant 'public justice', but were interpreted by Wellington's enemies in the House of Commons to mean 'public vengeance'. On 3 and 15 April a series of Opposition speakers in parliament condemned Wellington for signing the declaration, arguing that further war with France was unnecessary since Napoleon had been summoned to power by the people of France, disgusted by Bourbon misgovernment. Samuel Whitbread MP claimed that the Allies' declaration had undermined the authority of parliament, contravening English common law and amounting to a 'sanction for the doctrine of assassination'.[6] Napoleon naturally published all such favourable speeches in the *Moniteur.* In fact what seems to have been intended by the declaration was that Napoleon was stripped of his sovereign immunity, thus rendering him liable to prosecution in the municipal courts of the European powers. It is doubtful, however, that much grave thought went in to the declaration during this emergency, and that it was more a propaganda tool to emphasise Napoleon's lack of legitimacy.

On the legal aspect at least, Whitbread might well have had a case against the declaration, because under English law due process had to be undergone before anyone could be 'outlawed, imprisoned or executed'. The whole question was to re-emerge later that year, when Napoleon was prevented from landing in England to ensure that he did not fall within the jurisdiction of the English courts. Whitbread also proposed a motion on 28 April which sought to stop the resumption of a war which he predicted would last another twenty years, during which the chances of a British victory would become 'weaker by the day, while the chance of Napoleon every day grows stronger'. Only three weeks before the battle of Waterloo, Whitbread voted against the payment of subsidies to the Allies for such 'an insane project' as war against France.[7] At Brooks's Club Colonel Ponsonby gave Mr Howorth 'ten guineas to receive one hundred guineas should Louis XVIII or any Bourbon be reinstated on the throne of France in the course of twelve months'.

Someone who claimed that Wellington was in Paris in March 1815 was the courtesan and author Harriette Wilson, who reported being visited by him at her residence at 35 rue de la Paix, one evening 'in a gay equipage. He was all over orders and ribbons of different colours, bows and stars and he looked pretty well,' but Wilson went on to state that Wellington 'was no inducement for me to prolong my stay in Paris

...as Bonaparte was now on his way from Elba'. Her account of her affair with Wellington is shot through with inaccuracies, although the argument put by Wellington's apologists that he would have been more likely to visit her in plain clothes than in his finery is a weak one. The debate about whether to wear one's decorations to assignations was not resolved even by 1852, when the journal of Edmond de Goncourt records that the politician Henri, Comte Siméon et de Lurde argued that it was right to wear decorations to a brothel, on the grounds that 'if you do, they give you the women who haven't got the pox'.[8]

Having entered Paris on 20 March, Napoleon held a meeting at the Tuileries with Hugues-Bernard Maret, his private secretary and prospective new secretary of state, and Cambacérès, his arch-chancellor. He had not by then heard of the Vienna Declaration, but said: 'Let us not forget that the sovereigns at the Congress are not my only enemies. The European oligarchies fear me, and they have enough representation at Vienna. Castlereagh and Wellington will stir them up against me and they will come to a decision to make war, so we must prepare for this.'[9] One of his first acts was to check the amounts of money available in the French Treasury, and to spend it on a heavy rearmament programme. He then set about appointing a government and announcing a series of liberal constitutional measures.

Two days later Wellington wrote to Burghersh from Vienna: 'I am going into the Low Countries to take the command of the army, as soon as I shall have settled here a treaty something like the Treaty of Chaumont...Other matters here are going on but slowly.'[10] To his brother William on 24 March he showed yet more sang-froid: 'You will have seen what a breeze Buonaparte has stirred up in France. We are all unanimous here, and in the course of about six weeks there will be not fewer than 700,000 men on the French frontier.' Sure enough, the following day a treaty was signed in Vienna by which the four Powers – Russia, Prussia, Austria and Britain – all agreed not to make any more separate peace agreements with Napoleon. They also each pledged to contribute 150,000 troops to the coming campaign, with Britain making up in cash what she could not provide in manpower.

While they might have been unanimous in Vienna, back in Britain the Radicals and some Whigs had yet again fallen for the Napoleonic programme. By abolishing the slave trade (at least in name), promising civil liberties and promulgating a constitution drawn up by the liberal politician Benjamin Constant, Napoleon once again easily took in a large number of Britons on the political left. William Cobbett's *Weekly Political Register* hailed the emperor's new government as 'essentially

Republican', and Radicals drew parallels between Napoleon returning from Elba and William of Orange landing in England in 1688.

By supporting renewed war against Napoleon, Lord Grenville split the Whig party between his faction and the Foxite Whigs under Earl Grey. Pro-Napoleonic publications such as the *Statesman* – whose editor was relieved from debt in May 1815 by a roll call of anti-war grandees such as Samuel Whitbread MP, the Duke of Bedford, Sir Francis Burdett MP, Lord Holland, the Marquess of Tavistock and Earl Grey – argued that Napoleon was 'legitimate' and had been called to the throne of France by 'the universal voice, or consent, at least, of the people'. So incorrigible were they in support of Britain's enemy that, if anything, Napoleon's fall sent him yet higher in the Radicals' esteem, and a (post-Waterloo) letter of August 1815 published in Cobbett's *Register* claimed that his regime had been 'one of the grandest instances of legitimate government that ever was proposed and adopted for the welfare of a country'.

Meanwhile, Wellington was still in Vienna on 26 March, writing to Lord Bathurst about the optimum number of members of the Order of the Bath (reckoning 180 as the maximum).[11] He finally set off on the 29th, skirting around France on Castlereagh's orders, and assumed command of the Anglo-Allied army – the combined British, Dutch, Hanoverian and Brunswicker forces – at Brussels on 5 April. Just before Wellington left Vienna, Tsar Alexander placed his hand on his shoulder and said: 'C'est pour vous encore de sauver le monde' (It's again up to you to save the world).[12]

When Wellington was appointed to the Anglo-Allied command he took with him as the Russian liaison officer on his staff General Carlo Pozzo di Borgo, an acknowledged expert on Napoleon.[13] If anyone could help Wellington understand Napoleon's intentions and actions, it was he. Pozzo di Borgo was five years older than Napoleon and Wellington, and had been the Bonaparte family's lawyer on Corsica, on intimate terms with them for many years. Unlike Carlo Bonaparte he had stayed loyal to Paoli, however, and became head of Corsica's civil government during Paoli's rule and then president of Corsica's council of state when the British ruled the island. Forced to live abroad after France recaptured the island in 1796, he headed the list of people drawn up by Napoleon as liable to immediate arrest. He became a lifelong opponent of Napoleon, first from Vienna until 1804 and then as an agent for the tsar.

After the treaty of alliance between France and Russia signed at Tilsit in 1807, Pozzo di Borgo was forced to retire, but he was recalled by the tsar in 1812, and by 1814 he was Russian minister in France, being present at the Congress of Vienna.[14] He fell out with the tsar over Russia's obdurate demands concerning control over Poland, which he thought unreasonable, and so Alexander I was more than willing to allow him to join Wellington's staff as the resident Napoleon-expert. Napoleon claimed to have offered Pozzo di Borgo an olive branch during the Hundred Days, but on St Helena he admitted to having received no reply.

Pozzo di Borgo stayed close to Wellington during the battle of Waterloo, during which he was unhorsed, and the duke mentioned him in his post-Waterloo despatch as having 'rendered me every assistance in [his] power'. To what extent this included reading Napoleon's mind for Wellington is sadly unrecorded, but he did write to Louis XVIII for Wellington, advising him to return to Paris as soon as possible.[15]

From an entry in the journal of the MP Thomas Creevey for 22 April it is clear that Wellington was still unsure about what was going on in Paris. Creevey, a fiercely partisan Radical, had taken his wife to Brussels for a rest-cure, which was not, considering what was about to happen, a very clever choice of city. Meeting at Lady Charlotte Greville's party there, for the first time since they had sparred in the House of Commons over Indian politics ten years previously, Wellington told Creevey that he believed 'that a republic was about to be got up in Paris by [Interior Minister General Lazare] Carnot, Lucien Bonaparte &, &, &'. Creevey naturally asked whether Napoleon had consented to this, but Wellington merely replied that 'he had no doubt it would be tragedy by Buonaparte, and that they would be at him by stiletto or otherwise in a very few weeks'. Creevey thought that the odds must be in Napoleon's favour over any such clique, 'but my Lord would have it B[onaparte] was to be done up out of hand at Paris: so *nous verrons*'. Creevey assumed Wellington 'must be drunk; but drunk or sober, he had not the least appearance of being a clever man'.[16]

Whatever Wellington thought might be happening in Paris, he was insistent that, as he told his brother Henry on 28 April, 'if we only leave Buonaparte alone, we shall have him more powerful than ever in a short time…If we are stout we will save the King, whose government affords the only chance of peace.' Ever the Legitimist, he feared that Vienna and London were moving towards a position in which the Bourbons' cousin the Duc d'Orléans took the French throne as 'a middle term between Buonaparte and the Bourbons'.[17]

At the important Tirlemont conference on 3 May, Wellington and the Prussian field marshal Prince Gebhard von Blücher had discussed the overall strategic coordination of the Anglo-Allied and Prussian armies in the event of a French attack. Together they commanded around 210,000 men, which old Marshal 'Vorwärts' considered quite enough to justify an offensive operation. Wellington, however, having studied Napoleon's 1814 operations around Paris and been deeply impressed by them, wanted to wait for a few more months when their troops could be joined in a general invasion of France by Schwarzenberg's 210,000 Austrians, Frimont's 75,000 Austrians and Barclay de Tolly's 150,000 Russians.[18]

As well as concern about Napoleon's defensive abilities and the dangers of attacking him piecemeal, Wellington wanted more time for reinforcements to be brought over from Britain and across the Atlantic. Much of his old Peninsular army was stationed in Canada, Ireland and America, or was on the high seas, and he feared that the troops he had available in the Low Countries were of relatively inferior quality. As he wrote to Bathurst on 4 May:

> It will be admitted that the army is not a very good one: and, being composed as it is, I might have suspected that the generals and Staff formed by me in the last war would have been allowed to come to me again; but instead of that I am overloaded with people I have never seen before; and it appears to be purposely intended to keep those out of my way whom I wished to have. However, I'll do the best I can with the instruments which have been sent out to assist me.

It was only one of many such grievances Wellington expressed about his army, both before and even after the battle of Waterloo. As at least twenty British battalions had seen Peninsular service, and only three regiments were brand new, Wellington was perhaps exaggerating the defects of his army. Few generals tell their political masters that they have quite enough troops for the tasks allotted to them. Furthermore, to have it on record that he had 'not a very good' army might enhance his reputation in victory and perhaps partly protect it in the event of defeat. Eighteenth-century generals were also quasi-politicians, and none more so than Wellington.

A week later, writing to the Peninsular veteran Sir Henry Hardinge, whose job it had been to watch Napoleon's movements since the escape from Elba and who was now the British liaison commissioner with the Prussians, Wellington predicted relatively accurately

Napoleon's strength in the coming campaign (which was 122,000) when he said: 'I reckon the force with which Buonaparte can attack this country at 110,000 men.'[19] Yet the next day he told his brother that 'Buonaparte cannot venture to quit Paris. Indeed, all accounts give reason to hope that, even without the aid of the Allies, his power will not be of long duration.'[20] Reams have been written about how much Napoleon underestimated Wellington during the coming campaign, but it is also true that from the moment that Napoleon landed at Golfe Juan, and embarked on the adventure that saw him reach Paris in under three weeks without a shot being fired, install himself as emperor, reconstitute his army and government, and then unleash his lightning attack on Belgium, Wellington consistently underrated Napoleon. For as Balzac said of the Napoleon of March 1815: 'Before him did ever a man gain an Empire simply by showing his hat?'

Napoleon showed more than just his hat at the ceremonials of the Champ de Mai, which – like Cambridge's May Week – actually took place in June. A massive military display, with powerful religious overtones and civil and administrative undertones, accompanied Napoleon's proclamation that 'I have been summoned to the throne by my anger at seeing sacred rights, won by twenty years of victory, scorned and cast aside, by the cry of injured honour, by the will of the people.' Two hundred eagles and eighty-seven banners of the National Guard were massed before an altar, and Napoleon arrived to 101-gun salutes fired from the Tuileries, Les Invalides and the Pont d'Iéna. In brilliant sunshine he mounted a throne, dressed in his velvet coronation robes and an extravagantly plumed hat, and asked his troops to swear an oath 'to surpass yourselves in the coming campaign, and die to a man rather than permit foreigners to dictate to the Fatherland'. They swore by acclamation, amid cries of 'Vive l'Empereur!' (Today the National Guard banners can now be seen at Apsley House and Stratfield Saye, having been presented to Wellington by Louis XVIII in 1816.)

⁓

The Waterloo campaign began in reality on 13 May, when Napoleon took the decision to strike north to capture Brussels. A crushing victory, he hoped, would achieve a number of political objectives, including heartening the people of France, bringing down the Liverpool ministry in London, dismembering the Seventh Coalition against France, opening the way to Holland and encouraging the Belgians to rise in his support. 'A great victory,' as the National

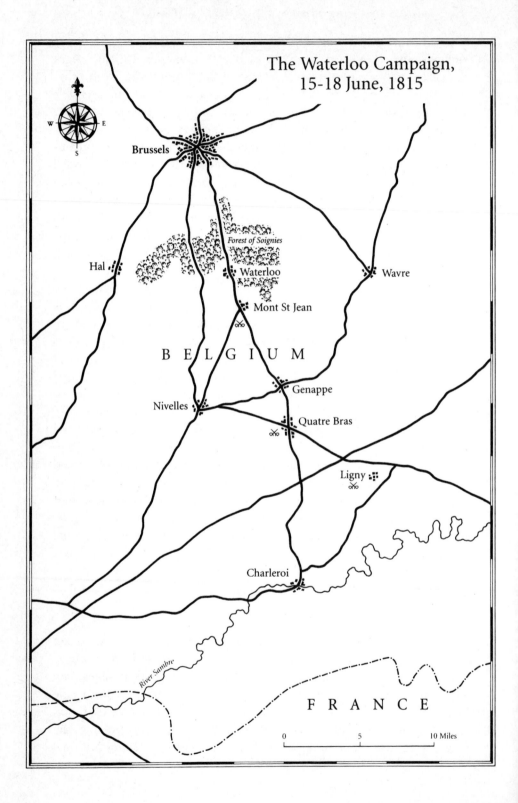

Guard's commander General Mathieu Dumas put it, 'nothing less than the destruction of the English army, could alone re-establish the ascendancy of his genius, the fascination of his glory, and justify the rashness of his enterprise.'[21] A defeat for Wellington would moreover avenge France's Peninsular humiliations while proving Napoleon's primacy over his own marshals.

It has been suggested by no less a Napoleonic scholar than Dr David Chandler that the emperor deliberately fielded his 'second team' of marshals in the Waterloo campaign because he desired an emphatically personal victory, one that could not be ascribed to Davout, say, or Suchet.[22] It sounds unlikely, but, whatever the reason, Napoleon was unlucky with his subordinate commanders in the campaign and moreover made errors in placing them in the posts he did. He had severely limited options since only seven marshals had rallied to him. His veteran chief of staff Berthier had decided not to rejoin his former master's standard, and on 1 June he died after falling from a window in Bamberg in Bavaria. He had been standing on a chair in his children's nursery window, watching Russian troops manoeuvring outside. There are credible theories that he was defenestrated, and others that he jumped out of remorse for having abandoned the emperor, but however it occurred he was not about to fill the key place as chief of staff of the Army of the North, which on 9 May went to Soult.[23]

Although Napoleon once said 'Exiled kings never pardon on their return to the throne,' he did forgive Soult, who had been minister for war and governor of Paris under Louis XVIII, as well as Ney, who had famously boasted in March that he would bring Napoleon back to Paris in an iron cage. It did not help that Soult and Ney, effectively Napoleon's second and third in command during the Waterloo campaign, loathed one another. Ney was only recalled at absolutely the last possible moment, Sunday, 11 June, to command the left flank in the Waterloo campaign, and he is widely considered to have been suffering from battle fatigue (although this is denied by his biographers and many adherents). His appointment was also partly political, to encourage further supporters of the Bourbons to defect to Napoleon, as well as to put heart into the army because of his formidable military reputation.[24]

Junot had gone mad through syphilis and had committed suicide, jumping from a window in July 1813. Two months earlier Bessières had died on the eve of the battle of Lützen from ricocheting roundshot that hit him in the chest. Murat's offer to fight for Napoleon was refused because of his treachery the previous year, despite his probably still being the world's finest commander of cavalry.

Suchet, the one marshal to leave the Peninsula with a Spanish title and his reputation intact – perhaps because he had never had to face Wellington – was sent off to command the Army of the Alps guarding France's eastern frontier. It has been seen as a waste of one of Napoleon's most talented marshals. Similarly, the trustworthy Davout was left behind in Soult's old post of war minister and Paris governor, rather than employed in the vital Waterloo campaign. Two of his best field commanders were therefore deliberately absented from the Army of the North by Napoleon.[25] Marshal Brune, whose career had been on the wane since being dismissed as governor of the Hanseatic Towns for republicanism, was appointed to command the Army of the Var. It is thought that Napoleon made these dispositions because he 'believed the shock of his sudden invasion would send Wellington and Blücher reeling back and that Brussels would fall without a difficult campaign. The important fighting would come later, against the Austrian and Russian invaders.'[26] However it is just as likely that he felt that this might be a long campaign, in which case it would be important to have good men in charge in Paris, the Alps, the Var and so on. Ney, whom he understandably did not trust, he kept close by him on campaign rather than in a position of political authority in Paris or elsewhere. That, and his choice of Davout for Paris was an interesting comment on his political vis-à-vis his military priorities, the former taking precedence.

Of the other marshals, Macdonald and Gouvion Saint-Cyr refused Napoleon's call, and Victor, Oudinot, Augereau and (hardly surprisingly) Marmont declared for Louis XVIII. Mortier joined Napoleon but due to sciatica he had to give up his command of the Imperial Guard to General Antoine Drouot. This had the effect of denying to Napoleon Drouot's expertise in gunnery – a loss felt all the more dearly at Waterloo when the commander of the Guard artillery was killed early on in the battle.[27]

Perhaps Napoleon's most fateful decision relating to the marshalate, however, was taken on 26 April when he awarded a baton to General the Marquis de Grouchy, originally in charge of the cavalry reserve. Davout opposed Grouchy's promotion to such an important post, which carried with it the likelihood of an independent command, but Napoleon went ahead nonetheless.[28] As it turned out, Grouchy had neither the despatch nor the luck that Napoleon demanded from his marshals.

In his great northern offensive, therefore, Napoleon had good marshals missing, other marshals in the wrong posts, spent marshals present, an over-promoted marshal in a key position and one ill marshal depriving a good non-marshal of his proper post. As

Wellington told Creevey in early June, he did not expect to receive any deserters from Napoleon's army, except 'we may pick up a marshal or two, perhaps, but not worth a damn'.

Despite these drawbacks, Napoleon's success in moving his 89,000 infantry, 22,000 cavalry, 11,000 artillerymen and 366 guns from their many various cantonments around France on 6 June to be ready to cross the Sambre river into Belgium at dawn on 15 June – across bridges the Allies ought already to have destroyed – was, in the opinion of most military historians, nothing short of brilliant.[29] Moreover, despite Wellington's later protestations to the contrary, it took the Allies largely by surprise.

Although it is notoriously difficult to establish Napoleon's exact state of mind when it comes to overall strategy in May and June 1815 – and his own later writings on the subject are not much help – it seems clear that he hoped to smash the hinge between the Anglo-Allied and Prussian armies, leaving himself free to manoeuvre against whichever seemed the weaker and to make space in order to finish off the other one later. He would thereby be able to use his numerical superiority over each force, so long as he did not have to fight both simultaneously, in which case he would be drastically outnumbered. His success in using the strategy of the central position to get his army into a ten-mile-square box between the Anglo-Allied and Prussian armies before they fully appreciated the situation therefore cannot be gainsaid, and rates along with the finest of his 1814 manoeuvres. Yet, although Wellington and Blücher were surprised by Napoleon, it was also their choice to fight at Quatre Bras and Ligny respectively.

Napoleon's moves early in the campaign suggest that he preferred, other things being equal, to take on the Prussians first. He later said that he thought Blücher's 'hussar complex' would inspire him to close up with Wellington if defeated, whereas Wellington's cautious nature and Peninsular experience would mean that, if defeated, the Anglo-Allied army would automatically fall back along their lines of communication towards the Channel ports, so 'although Blücher would risk all to help Britain, the British army would not be risked for Prussia'.[30] To an extent all warfare is psychological, as Napoleon knew better than anyone, and in his reading of his two opponents' characters he was not far off the mark. Yet the theory breaks down in its application, because if it really was Napoleon's view of the situation he ought to have engaged Wellington first, not the Prussians. Had he defeated Wellington and sent the Anglo-Allied forces back towards Antwerp and the Channel ports, he would then have been free to deal with the Prussians at leisure. The truth was that Napoleon was acting opportunistically, taking his chances as and when they occurred.

Wellington's reputation for defending his lines of communication was well established by 1815. Even the most cursory examination of his Peninsular strategy – for example at Salamanca where he attacked Marmont partly to prevent himself from being cut off from Portugal – would have told Napoleon how he would have reacted. So concerned was Wellington that Napoleon might try a western flanking movement around Mons that he fortified the town and left a substantial body of men – numbering no fewer than seventeen thousand – at Hal, where they could not possibly have taken part in the battle of Waterloo. Blücher, on the other hand, was far less predictable; anglophobic Prussian officers such as Generals von Gneisenau and Ziethen might have advised a retreat towards the Rhine in the event of a defeat.

Napoleon's explanation for his thinking also fails to take into account the fact that, when he did defeat Blücher at the battle of Ligny on 16 June, he assumed that the Prussians were retreating eastwards, 'Hussar complex' or not. As with so many of his statements on St Helena, Napoleon was creating an *ex post facto* rationalisation for his defeat that would not damage the Napoleonic myth he sought to nurture. Also, after the Prussians were defeated at Ligny, the British did indeed retreat along their lines of communication, back towards Brussels. If Napoleon's strategy was actually based upon his reading of his opponents' characters he did not get either man wrong; he merely underestimated 'that drunkard' Blücher's resolve to continue supporting Wellington after Ligny. When Wellington arrived at Quatre Bras on Blücher's extreme right flank on 16 June, and then withdrew north-westwards towards the slopes of Mont St Jean, it must have seemed to Napoleon that his original plan – if such it was – was being borne out in detail.

Wellington has been accused of not paying sufficiently methodical attention to Napoleon's strategy. An historian of the Hundred Days has castigated him, saying that he 'could not be bothered to study carefully Napoleon's battles and the reasons for his extraordinary success year after year', and as a result was too cautious in the opening stages of the campaign.[31] Yet it is clear from his many oral references that Wellington had studied Napoleon's campaigns, especially those of 1814, but had come to the conclusion that the lesson to be learned was that no generalisations could be derived about what Napoleon might do in any given situation. He knew that caution was no bad stance to adopt in the face of such an enemy. Napoleon had fought over sixty battles by the time of Waterloo, and can only really be said to have lost ten –

Bassano II, Caldero, Acre, Aspern-Essling, Krasnoi, Teplitz, Leipzig, Craonne, Laon and Arcis-sur-Aube – if one takes Eylau and Borodino as either draws or Pyrrhic victories. Extreme caution in the presence of such a phenomenon was no more than common sense.

For all his reading of Napoleonic strategy in the past, Wellington rightly thought it could only be of very limited use when dealing with the emperor in the present, as different circumstances had produced very different tactics from Napoleon, and probably would again. In some of his battles, Napoleon had relied on flanking movements, in others on the central thrust, in others on a combination of the two. As some comments made after Waterloo suggest, Wellington was expecting some far more imaginative tactics from Napoleon than those he had hitherto encountered from his opponents in the Peninsula.

Wellington appreciated the opportunist and improvisatory nature of much of Napoleonic strategy, for which no amount of study could have properly prepared him. In April 1838 he told Lady Salisbury 'a curious anecdote' about Field Marshal Prince Karl Philipp Wrede, the best Bavarian soldier of the era, whom he had met in 1814 at the Congress of Vienna. Wrede had fought under Napoleon from 1805 until his defection to the Allies in 1813, serving at the battles of Eylau, Friedland and Marengo, and during the Russian campaign. Wrede once asked Napoleon about his theory of strategy and tactics, only to receive the reply: 'Je n'en ai pas. Je n'ai point de plan de campagne' (I don't have them. I don't have a campaign plan). Wellington agreed with Wrede's analysis, saying: 'And it was true, he had no plan; all he required was that his troops should be assembled and posted as he directed, and then he marched and struck a great blow, defeated the enemy, and acted afterwards as circumstances would allow.'[32] (Wrede was years later the victim of one of those regular honours mix-ups which are so enjoyable for those not concerned, when his Order of the Bath somehow went instead to the Prince de Condé due to the bad handwriting of a certain Colonel Percy, leaving Wrede mortified.)

The evidence therefore suggests that, as he entered what came to be called the Waterloo campaign, Wellington believed Napoleon had no set strategy beyond the obvious one of trying to capture Brussels and expel the Allies from Belgium (then called the United Netherlands). Impromptu genius would dictate his great opponent's actions, and natural caution would be of more use than dogmatic adherence to any theory about what Napoleon had done in the past. Wellington had not been reluctant to fight great engagements in India or occasionally in the Peninsula when the prospects of advantage dictated, but he would try to avoid fighting one if heavily outnumbered by the French in the Low Countries, not least because he had grave doubts about the quality of his own army and none at all about that of Napoleon's.[33]

Wellington therefore withdrew after the battle of Quatre Bras on 16 June 1815, when he could not expect any help from the Prussians to the east, but not from the slopes of Mont St Jean, where Waterloo was fought two days later, when he knew he could. He certainly never underestimated Napoleon once the campaign was under way in earnest, writing: 'I can now put 70,000 men into the field, and Blücher 80,000; so that I hope we should give a good account even of Buonaparte.'[34] The word 'even' is instructive; Wellington was in no doubt that he was up against the best that the French Empire had to offer.

Yet as late as 13 June Wellington did not believe that Napoleon was really on his way. 'There is nothing new here,' he told Lord Lynedoch. 'We have accounts of Buonaparte joining the army and attacking us; but I have accounts from Paris on the 10th, on which day he was still there, and I judge from his speech to the Legislature that his departure was not likely to be immediate. I think we are now too strong for him here.'[35] This was not mere complacency on Wellington's part, so much as doubt that Napoleon would risk all in going north and an assumption that he would hear about it as soon as he had.

Yet it was not until 3 p.m. on 15 June that Wellington heard for sure that Prussian outposts south of Charleroi had been attacked, by which time Napoleon had been on the offensive for the nine hours since dawn.[36] Bad staff work seems to have been responsible, and Wellington and others privately blamed various individual Prussians for the delay, possibly unfairly.[37] Wellington was very concerned about what turned out to be French feints to the north-west, which he feared until quite late on might cut off his lines of communication with the all-important Channel ports. That evening Wellington certainly admitted, as he told the Duke of Richmond during the celebrated ball on the night of the 15th, that 'Napoleon has humbugged me, by God! He has gained twenty-four hours' march on me.'[38] Yet in later years he took great offence at any insinuation that Napoleon could have done this. On one (possibly apocryphal) occasion, when asked by the painter Pickersgill during a sitting, 'Were you surprised at Waterloo?', he answered: 'No but I am now!'[39] It might, of course, have been because he took the question entirely literally, and differentiated his being surprised on the afternoon and evening of the 15th at the start of the campaign with the accusation that he had been surprised at the battle of Waterloo itself three days later, which of course was not the case.

(Pickersgill had apparently asked the question in order to bring 'a degree of animation into his sitter's countenance'. It clearly worked.)

There might also have been a degree of inventive hindsight in Richmond's reminiscences, because after the 'humbugged' remark Wellington is also supposed to have said, 'I have ordered the army to concentrate on Quatre Bras, but we shall not stop him there, and, if so, I must fight him here,' as he placed his thumbnail on the map over Waterloo. This reeks of anecdotal embroidery, not least because late on the 15th Wellington had ordered his troops to concentrate to the south and west of Brussels and at Nivelles, but not all at Quatre Bras where they would be most needed the next day. 'Wellington cannot concentrate his scattered forces before the 17th,' said Napoleon on the 15th, and he was largely correct.[40]

Wellington has been criticised for his immediate dispositions after receiving hard news of Napoleon's attack, because they were not in accordance with what had been agreed with Blücher at Tirlemont on 3 May. What does seem clear is that he was excessively concerned about an attack in the west, cutting off his lines of communication between Brussels and the Channel ports. A relatively small British expeditionary force marooned on a hostile continent faced disaster. Dr Chandler finds it difficult to discover any convincing explanation for Wellington's initial miscalculation, saying an appreciation of French interests ought to have convinced the duke that Napoleon was hardly likely to attack the open British flank, for the net result of any such move would have been to drive the British in upon the Prussians, thus causing 'a decidedly unfavourable preponderance of allied strength against l'Armée du Nord'.[41]

Wellington's supporters argue that he was not caught off guard at all: because it was 'sheer guess work' which of the three roads to Brussels Napoleon would choose – via Tournai, Mons or Charleroi – Wellington, by keeping his army well back from the French frontier, gave himself time to concentrate before counter-attacking. Fortunately for him, on Friday, 16 June all that had hitherto gone right for Napoleon began to go wrong. After the brilliant staff work necessary to get the army into position in Belgium, problems arose when two corps ran into one another on the 15th, causing unnecessary congestion. Then, during the battles of Ligny against the Prussians and Quatre Bras against the Anglo-Allied army, Comte Drouet d'Erlon's I Corps was permitted through bad staff work to march uselessly between the two battlefields arriving at neither, just when it might have been decisive on either. Ney's (entirely reciprocated) hatred of Soult might have been at fault, but whoever was to blame the phantom of Berthier – who would never have allowed such an blunder – was hovering over the campaign.

In one sense General d'Erlon ought to be regarded as almost as crucial a figure in denying Napoleon victory in the Waterloo campaign as Marshal Grouchy has since become. Had d'Erlon's twenty thousand men arrived at Ligny the Prussians would have been utterly routed, rather than simply defeated, and thus rendered incapable of giving Wellington any significant assistance two days later. Equally, had d'Erlon arrived at Quatre Bras Wellington might well have been defeated. Two days later, had d'Erlon taken and held the ridge on Wellington's centre-left at the battle of Waterloo he would have split the Anglo-Allied line before the Prussians had arrived in force. D'Erlon's failure to arrive at either battle on 16 June – the responsibility for which is disputed but which has been split between Ney and Napoleon – was almost as important as Grouchy's own epic non-appearance at Waterloo. Indeed, had d'Erlon been effectively committed on the 16th (particularly at Ligny) then the issue about Grouchy would have been superfluous, or even non-existent.

Although Napoleon and Wellington never met or corresponded, and only ever fought one engagement against one another, it seems that Wellington did catch sight of Napoleon just before the battle of Ligny. He had left Brussels at 7.30 a.m. on 16 June, and brought his army to the crucial crossroads of Quatre Bras by 10 a.m. He then rode off to the Prussian positions, reaching them at around 1 p.m. According to the 1857 memoirs of General von Reiche, Ziethen's chief of staff, Wellington overlooked the Prussian dispositions from the mill at Bussy, enquiring 'what measures had been taken or were in hand. At this moment we noticed in the distance a party of the enemy, and Napoleon was clearly distinguishable in the group. Perhaps the eyes of the three greatest military commanders of the age were directed on one another.' Wellington told Hardinge, who was attached to Blücher, that the Prussians should withdraw 'under shelter of the rising ground', predicting that otherwise they would get 'damnably mauled' by the French artillery.[42] He ended his visit by promising to bring his army to Ligny, 'provided I am not attacked myself'.

It turned out that Wellington was indeed attacked in force, and lost 4,700 men to Ney's 4,300 at Quatre Bras, and therefore could not assist Blücher, who lost 16,000 men to Napoleon's 11,500 at Ligny that day. The Prussian troops, who had been left in front of the French batteries, were indeed 'damnably mauled', and although Blücher started the day with 84,000 men and 224 guns over a seven-mile battle front, by the end of the day twenty-one guns had been lost and nine thousand troops had decamped eastwards to Liège, effectively quitting the campaign altogether.

Yet under the cover of darkness much of the retreating Prussian army had managed to stay intact, and instead of making off towards the Rhineland, as Napoleon had hoped and assumed, the bulk of it retreated northwards towards Wavre. This crucial decision had been taken by the chief of staff Gneisenau, despite his scepticism about Wellington's intentions and the danger of being cut off from ammunition and food supplies, and it was later fully endorsed by Blücher who had been concussed in a fall when his horse was shot and he had been ridden over by French cavalry. In a rare resort to hyperbole, Wellington later described Gneisenau's order to go northwards rather than eastwards as 'the decisive moment of the century'.[43]

Napoleon, who had been unwell that morning, had gained his last victory, but it was not the rout he needed, and that he believed it to be. 'The Emperor has just won a sweeping victory over the English and Prussian armies under the command of Lord Wellington and Marshal Blücher,' announced the *Moniteur*. 'The army is now entering the village of Ligny beyond Fleurus in pursuit of the enemy.'

At Quatre Bras, Wellington's drawn engagement with Ney had prevented Napoleon being reinforced at Ligny. Ney had been defeated by Wellington at Busaco and he and General Reille delayed their attack at Quatre Bras because they believed that the duke had adopted the same reverse-slope tactics, hiding his main force. It turned out that Wellington was bluffing, and after very stiff fighting on 16 June the Anglo-Allied army was able to withdraw in good order the next morning. In a textbook example of 'breaking contact with the enemy' he brought his army back towards the slopes of Mont St Jean, over which he had ridden on his journey from Brussels the day before and which he is credited with having reconnoitred as a suitable battleground only the previous year.

Quatre Bras had seen Wellington in some serious personal danger of capture, as he had also been at Talavera, Sorauren and just before Salamanca. Unlike Napoleon by this time, Wellington did not stay at the rear during his battles. Yet it is untrue to suggest, as some anti-Bonapartist politicians and historians have over the years, that the emperor was kept entirely out of danger. A horse near to Napoleon was hit by a stray shot during the battle of Waterloo, and Wellington always personally discounted accusations of Napoleon's supposed cowardice there.[44] Apart from any other considerations, Napoleon occupied a very different role from Wellington. Whereas Wellington was an agent of the British Government, and therefore ultimately expendable, Napoleon personified the French Government and it would have been politically irresponsible to expose him to the risk of capture or death.

〜

'I may lose ground,' Napoleon used to say about his campaigns, 'but I shall never lose a minute.' Yet on the morning of Saturday, 17 June 1815 his unaccountable lethargy lost him perhaps his best chance of victory. Had he joined Ney at dawn on 17 June and attacked Wellington – who only had around fifty thousand troops at Quatre Bras at the time – he could hardly have failed to overwhelm him. Instead he wasted many valuable hours inspecting his troops and the battlefield of Ligny, waiting for news about Wellington and Blücher and even discussing political reports from Paris. This loss of the initiative was disastrous, and still worse was his decision at around 11 a.m. to split his forces by sending Marshal Grouchy off with 33,000 men and no fewer than ninety-six cannon to follow the Prussians in what at least initially turned out to be the wrong direction. 'Had Napoleon attacked the Anglo-Allied army with his whole force and succeeded in defeating it,' suggested the military historian General Sir James Shaw Kennedy, a Peninsular veteran and then a captain attached to the 3rd Division, 'there could be little question of his being able to defeat afterwards the Prussian army.'

Yet Napoleon showed unnatural torpor that morning, and even though both Soult and Grouchy tried to dissuade him, he instructed the latter to, in the words of one listener, 'follow up those Prussians, give them a touch of cold steel in their hinder parts, but be sure to keep in communication with me by your left flank'.[45] The written order was less colloquially phrased:

> You will pursue the enemy. Reconnoitre his march, and tell me of his movements, that I may penetrate his designs. I shall move my head-quarters to Quatre Bras, where the English still were this morning...It is important to discover what Wellington and Blücher mean to do, and whether they meditate uniting their armies to cover Brussels and Liège by risking the fate of a battle.[46]

Since their defeat the previous day, the Prussians had gained a four-teen-hour head start over Grouchy. Misunderstandings occurred as to which French units should set off first, so that by the end of the day Grouchy had covered only seven miles and had not yet discovered the true line of the Prussians' retreat. The job ought to have been done by a far smaller force, with Napoleon keeping the bulk with him for use against Wellington, especially, as his written order seems to suggest, as he had not ruled out the possibility that his two enemies might still unite. It was one of the few errors that he was willing to acknowledge on St Helena, saying: 'I should have left only [Lieutenant-Colonel Comte Claud] Pajol, with [a]...division of the VI Corps, in pursuit of Blücher, and taken all with me.'[47] Splitting his forces in the vicinity of an expected great battle was something the emperor had long decried in other commanders, yet he himself did just that the very day before Waterloo.

Napoleon desperately needed to know whether the Prussians had retreated northwards or eastwards after their defeat at Ligny, yet he had entirely failed to develop the one invention that might almost immediately have furnished him with such vital information. Hot-air balloons had been used by the French army since 1793 to carry despatches over the heads of the enemy and were employed for observation purposes at the battle of Fleurus, fought only a few miles from Ligny in 1794, but five years later Napoleon had disbanded the French balloon corps. Although the technology was in its infancy, by 1815 balloons might have allowed Ney to spot Wellington's reverse-slope bluff at Quatre Bras, and permitted Napoleon to discover that the Prussians were moving towards Wavre after Ligny. They might even perhaps have helped Napoleon to spot the appearance of Bülow's corps in time to withdraw in good order after the opening stage of the battle of Waterloo, although it did suddenly emerge from a wood.[48]

When Napoleon set foot in Paris for the first time, aged fifteen in October 1784, the *Journal de Paris* was celebrating in verse the Montgolfier brothers' successes in ballooning of the year before:

Man soars to the ranks of the gods,
To make the world tributary
To the daring of his genius.[49]

Had Napoleon's undoubted genius dared to continue the Revolution's experiments with ballooning, the Waterloo campaign might well have turned out differently. It was only behind a screen of cavalry that Wellington managed to slip away from Quatre Bras on the morning of 17 June, after all, a covering manoeuvre that would have been instantly perceptible from the air.

Although Lieutenant-Colonel John Money set up a British balloon observation corps in 1785 it did not gain much support either. There were, admittedly, several major problems associated with the military application of early ballooning – not least the flammability of hydrogen – but had enough thought, effort and resources been devoted to its development these could well have been overcome.[50] For example, the use of granulated zinc as an alternative to iron filings would have caused far fewer problems. From the 125-foot-high Lion Mound constructed (to Wellington's chagrin) in the 1820s as a memorial to the Prince of Orange, one can easily observe the battlefield of Waterloo almost in its entirety. A balloon need not have gone any higher than that to provide Napoleon with the invaluable news that Grouchy had failed to head off the Prussians. As it was, commanders relied for their information on the luck and sense of direction of an officer on horseback, and to a very great degree during the Waterloo campaign they were let down. The intelligence work was abysmal on both sides, due to the paucity of reconnaissance by light cavalry and lack of accurate reporting. On one occasion, Wellington complained that a messenger from the Prussians was so fat that he could not cover thirty miles in thirty hours.[51]

Grouchy, the grandest of all the French marshals by birth – Prince Poniatowski being Polish – was not, for all his fine qualities as a cavalry commander when under others' instructions, a good independent commander. He was further hamstrung by vague and contradictory orders of the type that Berthier would never have sent. Whosever fault it was – and the debate still rages, nowadays with added vigour in cyberspace – Grouchy left with almost one-third of Napoleon's total force on the morning of 17 June effectively exiting the campaign, failing to prevent the Prussians from appearing on the field of Waterloo the following day. (He did, in fact, fight a tough action against Blücher's rearguard at Wavre, but by then it was too late for him to influence the only battle that mattered.)

Did Napoleon fatally underestimate Wellington by giving Grouchy so large a force? It is a common criticism, but if Grouchy had managed to prevent any Prussians from turning up on 18 June the size of the force might have been justifiable. It cannot be assumed that Wellington would have given battle on the slopes of Mont St Jean had he not been in receipt of Blücher's promise to support him with almost the whole Prussian army later that day. On balance, Napoleon can be considered to have taken a grave but calculated risk by despatching Grouchy with the huge force he did, but was wrong in sending him in the direction he did as late as he did.[52]

Napoleon's ill-health has been regularly cited as the explanation for his disastrous torpor on the morning of 17 June, with some French historians presenting it as a major reason why he seemed to perform less impressively than in his earlier campaigns. In particular it has been alleged that the emperor suffered from a disease called acromegaly, which is said to induce both torpor and over-optimism.[53] This disease, caused by a tumour of the pituitary gland which then secretes enormous amounts of growth hormones, leading to gigantism, does not produce over-confidence at all, only diabetes. By 1815 'Bony' was a very inappropriate nickname for Napoleon indeed, but although on Elba he joked that no one of his size could be thought ambitious, he was certainly not suffering from gigantism, however stout and puffy-cheeked he had become.[54]

In the past Napoleon had suffered from an inflammation of the bladder and urinary tract which had made riding difficult at the time of Borodino, but he had ended the Russian campaign in excellent health. He was not ill on Elba, and as his aide-de-camp during the Waterloo campaign, General Comte Auguste Flahaut de la Billarderie, wrote to Thiers in 1862 after the appearance of the author's volume relating to 1815: 'You were right in asserting that at no period of his life did the Emperor display more energy, more authority or greater capacity as a leader of men.'[55]

On the night of 16/17 June Napoleon did suffer from haemorrhoids, which 'had prolapsed and were strangulated outside the anus. In a short time if unreduced they would have become thrombosed and oedematous, causing great pain,' especially when the emperor was in the saddle. Only his brother Jérôme, surgeon Baron Larrey and valet Louis Marchand were permitted to know of this condition, and the truth did not emerge until Jérôme mentioned it just before his death in 1860. Today we cannot tell whether on that occasion Larrey used leeches, a lotion of 15 per cent lead subacetate in boiled distilled water, or simply warm water bathings with clean flannels (not sponges), which were the favoured remedies of the day.[56] Whichever method was employed, by 8 a.m. on the 17th Napoleon was up, dressed and in the saddle, and therefore inflamed piles cannot be blamed for his failure to attack Wellington that morning.

Other afflictions known to have affected Napoleon during his career were constipation (for which he used to 'apply three or four leeches'), cystitis and exhaustion, but most such medical explanations seem to hint at apologists' *ex post facto* rationalisations for his defeat, employed largely to try to keep their hero's military reputation intact.[57] Napoleon might well not have been feeling his very best during the campaign – he had swallowed a phial of poison only the previous year – but his health cannot really be held up as a primary factor in his defeat. He did not, after all, decide to detach 33,000 men under Grouchy because he was suffering from piles. The great Napoleonic scholar J. Holland Rose concluded his detailed examination of Napoleon's health in 1815 by saying that he 'was in his usual health amidst the stern joys of war... During the campaign we find very few trustworthy proofs of his decline and much that points to energy, resolve and great rallying power after exertion.'[58]

Having finally joined Ney on 17 June and moved his army northwards towards Brussels and behind Wellington's, Napoleon slept at Le Caillou farmhouse that night, hoping that Wellington's army would still be at Mont St Jean the next morning. Even at this distance of time it seems astonishing that, when the dawn of the 18th revealed the Anglo-Allied army still in position, neither Napoleon nor anyone else on his staff seems to have guessed that this might be because Wellington knew that the Prussians were on their way in force. If Napoleon had the slightest inkling that that was the case he could have recalled Grouchy immediately, but, although Soult suggested it, he refused. Grouchy was not ordered to return to Napoleon's main force until the Prussians were actually spotted on the field, by which time it was much too late. The decision to let Grouchy operate far out to the east broke another of Napoleon's cardinal military maxims of warfare: 'The army must be kept assembled and the greatest possible force concentrated on the field of battle.'

If it is true that Napoleon despised Wellington as an over-cautious commander, why did he not wonder why the duke's army had remained in position on the night of 17/18 June, and then guess that Blücher's proximity was the reason? Perhaps he believed Wellington thought his position, with its slopes and reverse slopes, an easy one to defend. Or perhaps he believed his opponent could not face the humiliation of ceding Brussels, affording the emperor a triumphant entry into the city and an easy propaganda victory. Also, just as the gambler subconsciously feels that wagering ever larger sums will enable him eventually to cover his mounting losses, so Napoleon – with far more justification – might have felt that detaching Grouchy with so large a force might have proportionately increased his chances of settling his score with Wellington free from outside interference on his eastern flank. Napoleon had, after all, asked much of Fortune many times before in his extraordinary career, and she had usually favoured him. Why should this time be any different?

PART II

Waterloo and its Aftermath

ELEVEN

'Thank God, I Have Met Him!'
18 June 1815

The art of war is a simple art; everything is in
the performance. There is nothing vague in it;
everything in it is common sense;
ideology does not enter into it.

NAPOLEON

If one had been present at the breakfast at Le Caillou farmhouse at eight o'clock on the morning of Sunday, 18 June 1815, it would have been easy to understand why Napoleon made the infamous remark to Soult that 'Because you have been beaten by Wellington, you consider him a great general. And now I tell you that Wellington is a bad general, that the English are bad troops, and *ce sera l'affaire d'un déjeuner.*' Far from expressing over-confidence, as is constantly assumed, the emperor was displaying his irritation at what sounded like the defeatism of a series of his Peninsular generals. As he had told his brother Joseph back in 1809, it was always wrong to praise the enemy, 'for to do so is to take away from oneself; in war morale is everything'.[1]

Thus when his generals began extolling the British army just before the battle, and urging a strategy of manoeuvre rather than the a massive frontal assault he had already decided upon, the emperor had little alternative but to snap at his chief of staff in that contemptuous way. He had not personally fought the British since Toulon twenty-two years earlier, and it was natural for him to ask General Reille for his views about their capabilities, but the answer he received – 'I consider the English infantry to be *inexpugnable* [impregnable]' – was unacceptably defeatist talk on the very morning of what was clearly going to be a major engagement.

Soult's remark, 'Sire, l'infanterie anglaise en duel c'est le diable' (Sire, in a straight fight the English infantry are the very devil), was no better. At this distance of time we cannot know the mood in the room, or the gestures or murmurs of support perhaps given by the other

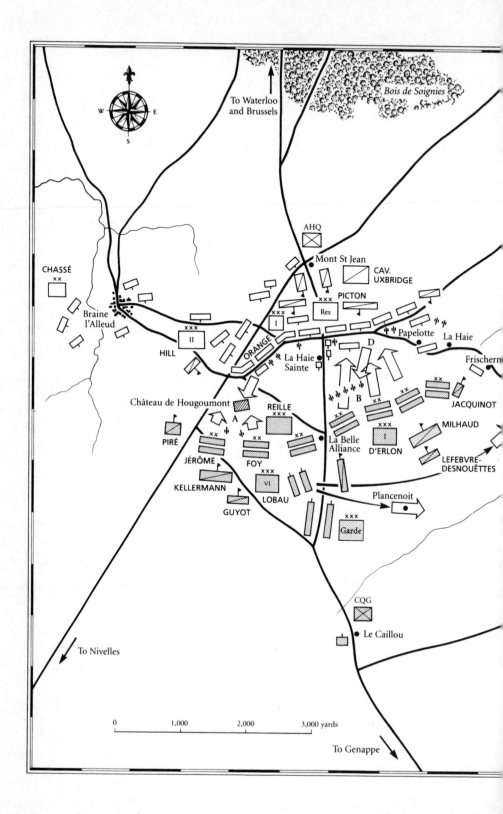

Bois de Soignies

To Waterloo
and Brussels

AHQ

Mont St Jean

CAV.
UXBRIDGE

CHASSÉ

PICTON

Res

I

Papelotte

La Haie

Braine
l'Alleud

ORANGE

Frischern

II

HILL

La Haie
Sainte

D

JACQUINOT

Château de Hougoumont

REILLE

B

MILHAUD

PIRÉ

A

La Belle
Alliance

D'ERLON

LEFEBVRE-
DESNOUËTTES

JÉRÔME

FOY

KELLERMANN

VI

LOBAU

Plancenoit

GUYOT

Garde

CQG

Le Caillou

To Nivelles

0   1,000   2,000   3,000 yards

To Genappe

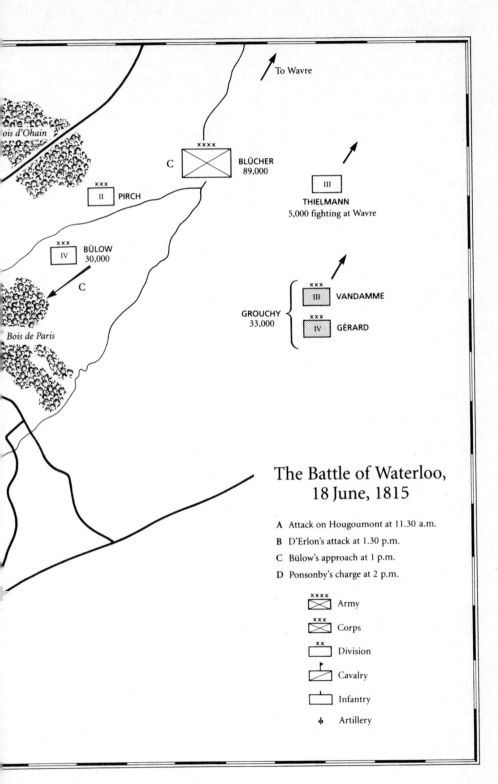

To Wavre

C · BLÜCHER
89,000

III
THIELMANN
5,000 fighting at Wavre

II · PIRCH

IV · BÜLOW
30,000

C

Bois de Paris

ois d'Ohain

GROUCHY
33,000
{
  III · VANDAMME
  IV · GÉRARD
}

The Battle of Waterloo,
18 June, 1815

A Attack on Hougoumont at 11.30 a.m.

B D'Erlon's attack at 1.30 p.m.

C Bülow's approach at 1 p.m.

D Ponsonby's charge at 2 p.m.

⊠ Army

⊠ Corps

▭ Division

▱ Cavalry

▭ Infantry

⊣⊢ Artillery

Peninsular veterans present such as Ney, Foy and d'Erlon.[2] Thus Napoleon's retort, which has consigned him to the judgment of history as absurdly over-confident on the morning of Waterloo, and genuinely contemptuous of Wellington, is in fact perfectly understandable given the exigencies of the moment. Like everything else to do with this extraordinary man, his pre-battle statements need to be seen in the context of the prevailing circumstances.

The evidence that Napoleon did not really consider Wellington a 'bad general' is elsewhere overwhelming, given his earlier remarks to Chanteloup, Caulaincourt, Metternich, Campbell and several British visitors to Elba. Are we to assume that in mid-1815 Napoleon's views of Wellington suddenly and completely changed, simply because he had surprised him at the start of the campaign and forced him to retreat from Quatre Bras? Seen in the context of a morale-boosting pre-battle harangue to cautious and nervous generals, Napoleon's remarks are entirely explicable, and should not have been taken so literally by so many historians.

The generals had every reason to be nervous. Napoleon had turned down Soult's request for an immediate recall of Grouchy's force, and those who had served in the Peninsula well knew Wellington's reputation for selecting topographically advantageous defensive positions. In his private journal for 23 September 1811, Foy had written: 'I think the English infantry superior to our own in equal numbers and on a limited battle front. This opinion I keep carefully to myself: it is better the rank and file should despise the enemy as well as hate him.' Although the British infantry were not in anything like equal numbers to the French at Waterloo, it was a very limited front indeed. Foy had even met Wellington while Napoleon was on Elba and 'nous avons parlé guerre'.[3] The Peninsular veterans knew exactly what they were up against.

For his own part, Wellington also showed great confidence in the outcome. His friend the Spanish attaché General Alava, joining him early that morning, recalled thinking to himself, 'I wonder how he feels and looks with Napoleon opposite,' and was soon rewarded with an answer when Wellington put up his telescope and, sweeping over the enemy's ground, declared: 'That fellow little thinks what a confounded licking he'll get before the day is over.'[4] His similar comment to Müffling, about showing Napoleon what a 'sepoy general' was capable of, displayed great optimism.

Looking spruce – the shaving mirror he used that morning can be seen in the National Army Museum in Chelsea – the 'Beau' was ready. He later even claimed that 'If I had had my old Spanish [that

is, Peninsular] infantry, I should have attacked Buonaparte at once,'
which although probably not literally true – the Prussians were still a
long way off and his position was of use only in defence – also implies
a very positive state of mind.[5] Since shortly before dawn, when he
heard from Blücher that almost the whole of the Prussian army would
be falling on Napoleon's right flank later that day, Wellington was
happy to defend the strong position he had adopted.[6] In later years he
often used to laud the slopes of Mont St Jean, with their two well-
placed and fortifiable farmhouses, as ideal ground on which to fight.

The thunderstorm of the previous evening and night did something
to dampen the ardour of the Anglo-Allied infantry, yet the twelve
thousand or so Peninsular veterans among them could recall that there
had been similarly atrocious weather before Wellington's victories at
Salamanca, Sorauren and Vitoria. On the advice of his artillery expert
General Drovot, who stated that the mud made the positioning of the
guns difficult and slow, Napoleon decided to postpone the attack for
over three hours.

In 1995 the 180th anniversary re-enactment of the battle was similarly preceded by a torrential downpour the previous night, and the
seas of mud forced the organisers to re-route marches down metalled
roads that had not existed in 1815. Wheeled heavy artillery would have
fared far worse than men on foot and horseback, so it is unfair to
blame Napoleon for the decision to put off the attack until nearly
noon, especially as his refusal to recall Grouchy proves that he had no
idea of the proximity of the Prussians.[7] Yet, as Napoleon himself had
once said: 'The loss of time is irretrievable in war.' From breakfast-
time onwards he was running out of time, although he himself had no
inkling of it. Had he attacked at daybreak, as Wellington expected, he
would have had five extra hours in which to try to break the Anglo-
Allied lines before the arrival of the Prussians, but with his guns being
manhandled through the rain-sodden fields, sometimes up to their
axles in mud, that option was effectively closed to him. On St Helena
he was to blame the previous night's rainfall for his defeat, among a
score of other factors and personalities.

Instead of attacking, Napoleon reviewed his troops in a massive
demonstration of high morale, while the ground slowly hardened for
his cannon. Inspecting his troops on horseback, he received 'the most
exceptional manifestation of mass enthusiasm he had encountered
since the days of Austerlitz' ten years earlier.[8] The cheering of 'Vive
l'Empereur!' might have been intended to weaken the morale of
Wellington's army as much as to hearten his own troops, and

contemporary accounts suggested that it depressed and intimidated many Anglo-Allied soldiers who witnessed it, although not the Peninsular veterans. At Fuentes d'Oñoro a lull in the fighting had been used simultaneously by the French to hold a parade and by the British to play a game of football.

Napoleon had not far short of 72,000 men, and according to Wellington it was:

> the finest army he ever commanded; and everything up to the onset must have turned out as he wished. Indeed he could not have expected to beat the Prussians, as he did at Ligny, in four hours. But two such armies as those at Waterloo have seldom met, if I may judge from what they did on that day. It was a battle of giants! A battle of giants![9]

Of course it was in Wellington's interests to emphasise the quality of the French army he beat, and the Grande Armée Napoleon took into Russia in 1812 was probably superior, but on most objective analyses Napoleon's 1815 army was also a superb fighting force. There are those who argue that the latter army was in fact better, on the grounds that the 1812 army had had many foreign units, whereas several French regiments had been committed to Spain that year. Furthermore, few French troops in 1815 had not received a baptism of fire the previous year. They were largely volunteers loyal to Napoleon, and keen to exact revenge for the humiliations they felt had been visited on France over the previous twelve months.

Wellington had a far less elevated view of his own polyglot army, complaining how few British troops there were – 23,990 out of 67,660 – only about half of whom had seen Peninsular service. 'Many of my troops were new,' he said afterwards, 'but the new fight well, though they manoeuvre ill.' He knew he could also implicitly rely on the 5,800 men of the King's German Legion. Some of his other troops – his composite force spoke five languages – were not considered first-class soldiers. The 17,000 Dutch–Belgian troops were not wholly trusted politically; the 2,800 Nassauers had been fighting for Soult as recently as 1813; and many of the 11,000 Hanoverians and 5,900 Brunswickers were raw recruits. Although the numbers on paper – Napoleon's 71,947 to Wellington's 67,660 – were not widely different, Napoleon's army was generally considered to be much superior on paper, in terms of quality, experience, homogeneity and even motivation. Furthermore, Napoleon's preponderance in cannon – 246 to Wellington's 156 – was another important factor in his favour.[10] Yet

Wellington had been regularly outnumbered in the past, and, compared to some of his Peninsular battles, these were some of the best numerical odds he had ever enjoyed.

Although Napoleon reconnoitred the terrain and the enemy lines, and sent his engineer General Haxo to study their fortifications and earthworks (Haxo found virtually none), he did not fully appreciate the strength of the position Wellington had adopted on the slopes of Mont St Jean. He later complained on St Helena that he had not had a particularly clear view of the battle. One French historian has stated that, if he had only sent observers up to climb trees, he might have 'perceived that the north side of the plateau descended to a pocket where reserves might be hidden – a favourite tactic of Wellington'.[11] It was, at least once the rain began to clear at about 8 a.m., perhaps the ideal time to have raised an observation balloon. There was talk of Napoleon using an observation tower, and one is actually depicted on some contemporary maps of the battlefield and mentioned in visitors' accounts, but no written source mentions Napoleon ever climbing up one, and it is not even certain exactly where it was located.

Napoleon could, however, see how small the battlefield was and how difficult it would have been for him to manoeuvre even had he wished to take the advice General Reille gave at the Le Caillou conference. Of all his many battlefields, Waterloo was one of the smallest. With the hamlets of Papelotte, Smohain and La Haie and the château of Frischermont to the east, and the Bois de Paris beyond, and the village of Braine l'Alleud in the west, and with the two fortified farmhouses, La Haie Sainte and Hougoumont in between, Waterloo was, at six square miles, a very cramped area for nearly two hundred thousand people to fight in.

Including the cavalry on its extreme wings, the whole battle front was little over three miles across, whereas at Austerlitz it had been seven miles long, Bautzen twelve, Dresden eight, Friedland nine, Jena-Auerstädt seven, Leipzig twenty-one, Ligny seven and Wagram twelve miles long. Only the battle of the Pyramids had seen a tighter front.[12] Equally, Wellington was used to larger battlefields; Vitoria was twelve miles long and Fuentes d'Oñoro fifteen, but at Waterloo he needed to box Napoleon in as far as possible, so as not to have his flanks turned by the more numerous and manoeuvrable French. His selection of battlefields was always skilful, in particular those of Vimeiro, Talavera, Salamanca and Orthez, and the slopes two and a quarter miles south of his headquarters at Waterloo were no exception.[13] As Müffling delightedly recalled only six days after the battle:

Before we arrived there I said to the Duke, 'If only there were an appropriately weak point in the right flank of your position, so that Bonaparte might assail it right furiously, and neglect his own right wing to such an extent that he should fail to discover the march of the Prussians!' And see! When we arrived there, there lay the advanced post of Hougoumont, upon which he did indeed fall.[14]

Hougoumont was only 'an appropriately weak point' insofar as it was dangerously forward from the rest of the Anglo-Allied lines; otherwise it was highly defensible. But it did distract attention from the advance of the Prussians at the other end of the battlefield. The ground Wellington had chosen was flat only insofar as it was not actually hilly; this was the Low Countries after all. Deployed squarely across the main Charleroi-Brussels road, his army occupied numerous spurs, folds and inclines in the land, which are very pronounced when one walks the ground but were not significant enough to be mentioned on the two maps available to Napoleon in 1815. With low escarpments and indentations not imme-diately obvious to the attacker, this was perfect Wellingtonian country. Although 'ridge' is a somewhat grand term for the mildly steep incline upon which Wellington placed the bulk of his army at Mont St Jean – and from the French positions it does not look too steep – it certainly permitted him to practise his reverse-slope manoeuvre of concealing his troops from too much direct artillery fire.[15]

Because Wellington was often on the offensive in the Peninsula, especially at the end of the campaign, the reverse-slope technique was not constantly used by him, but it was employed to good effect at Vimeiro and Busaco and partially also at Talavera, Fuentes d'Oñoro and Sorauren, so Napoleon had little excuse not to be *au fait* with its implications.[16] Yet as one historian has put it: 'Although well suited to Wellington's system of defence, there was little in the ground itself likely to impress Napoleon with an idea of its strength, or the difficulty in forcing it.'[17]

Behind Wellington was the forest of Soignies; he afterwards stated that he had deliberately chosen to fight with a forest in his rear so that his army could retreat into it if necessary, hampering any pursuit by French cavalry. By contrast, Napoleon argued that it would have spelt ruin to have withdrawn through the forest, turning any retreat into a certain rout. At the battle of Leipzig two years earlier, he had fought in front of an impassable stretch of swamp with only one bridge across it, yet Wellington was probably more accurate in his assessment of the risks attendant on fighting with a forest behind him than Napoleon.

For then, as today, the forest had little brushwood underfoot, and was intersected by several roads.[18]

Wellington expected Napoleon to manoeuvre more than he actually did at Waterloo. 'I should have turned the flank,' he said a few weeks after the battle when discussing Napoleon's options. 'I should have kept the English army occupied by a demonstration to attack, or perhaps by slight attacks, while I was in fact moving the main body by Hal on Brussels.'[19] It was a view he was to repeat regularly for the rest of his life. The town of Hal lay eight miles due west of Waterloo and, in order to prevent any such wide outflanking movement, Wellington left over seventeen thousand men there under the command of Prince Frederick of the Netherlands and Sir Charles Colville of the 4th Division. Although only about 15 per cent of this large detachment was made up of British troops, the majority being Dutch-Belgian militiamen, Wellington could undoubtedly have done with these men at Waterloo, almost as much as Napoleon needed Grouchy's corps.

Yet although Wellington has been criticised by several military historians for leaving so significant a force on his extreme right flank, unable to affect the battle once it was joined on the 18th, and has even been accused of being 'obsessed' with guarding against a non-existent threat to the eastern approach to Brussels, there were very sound reasons for the positioning of the Hal detachment. He needed a defensive fallback position in the event of defeat, or in case the Prussians failed to arrive. Moreover he had no foreknowledge that Napoleon would attack head on, while examination of the emperor's earlier strategic form would suggest that he might try to turn the Anglo-Allied lines. To be cut off from the Channel ports just as Napoleon entered Brussels might have spelt disaster.

It was largely due to Napoleon's reputation as a supreme strategist that Wellington posted quite so many men at Hal; Lord Ellesmere noted in 1847 that Wellington 'thought then, as he thinks now, that Napoleon ought, after Quatre Bras, to have manoeuvred in that direction in order to draw the British army away from the Prussians, with the ulterior chance of acting between them'.[20] Because Wellington could not be certain that Napoleon did not know where the Prussians were, he had to make allowances for every possibility. 'It would be rash to assume that the Emperor would fall into the error made by Junot at Vimeiro, by Victor at Talavera, by Masséna at Busaco, by Soult at Sorauren, and make a frontal attack.'[21] Yet that is basically what happened. Afterwards, on St Helena, Napoleon claimed that it had been his own strategy of sending troops towards Hal that had forced Wellington to weaken his own army by reinforcing the town, but the French historian Henri Houssaye has proved this to be 'a complete fabrication'.[22] Wellington acted in anticipation of Napoleon on this occasion, not in reaction to him.

Otherwise, Wellington's plans very much depended on Napoleon's, as he freely admitted to the commander of his cavalry Lord Uxbridge when he was asked about them the day before the battle. Uxbridge, having discussed the matter with Alava, broached the subject with some delicacy with Wellington, as it presupposed that the duke would have been killed or incapacitated. Considering the large number of Wellington's staff and subordinates who were killed or wounded the next day – Uxbridge himself was maimed – it was a perfectly reasonable question to have asked. Nonetheless Wellington, who disliked Uxbridge for having eloped with his sister-in-law, answered him sarcastically, saying: 'Who will attack the first tomorrow – I or Bonaparte?' Uxbridge naturally replied 'Bonaparte.' 'Well,' came the response, 'Bonaparte has not given me any idea of his projects, and as my plans depend on his, how can you expect me to tell you what mine are?'

Although in one account of this conversation Wellington apparently then softened and said that he knew Uxbridge would do his duty, by August 1837 he was telling Lady Salisbury that he had considered Uxbridge's question 'impudent'.[23] In the meantime, however, he had sacked Uxbridge (by then the Marquess of Anglesey) from the lord-lieutenancy of Ireland in 1829 for being too pro-nationalist. Uxbridge in his turn complained to the historian Captain William Siborne in 1842 that at Waterloo 'I received no order from the Duke of Wellington to make the first charge or any other during the day,' and that the order to take overall command of the cavalry was only made on the morning of the battle, and 'These are *all* the orders I ever received from the Duke during this short campaign.'

'In war,' ran one of Napoleon's many martial maxims, 'the simplest operations are the best and the secret of success lies in simple manoeuvres and in taking measures to ensure against surprise.' Yet at Waterloo his operations were just too simple, relying on his huge central battery to break Wellington's centre just as it had 'knocked loose Blücher's centre at Ligny'.[24] If anything, Wellington was actually disappointed when he came to test his mettle against the best, only to find that the best France had to offer was no better than the rest of his marshals had been in the Peninsula.[25] As Sir Andrew Barnard, who was wounded at Waterloo, recalled at Apsley House in 1845: 'The Duke said of Napoleon during the action: "Damn the fellow, he is a mere pounder after all."'[26]

Napoleon was willing to make a diversionary attack against Hougoumont, hoping to draw Wellington's reserves into the fight for the farmhouse. His main assault would then take place after a tremendous preliminary barrage on Wellington's centre-left, where he hoped to break the Anglo-Allied line, supporting his onslaught when gaps appeared with his own reserve, heavy cavalry and Imperial Guard. At Wagram Napoleon's battery of one hundred guns had successfully mauled the Austrian lines, so at Waterloo, with two and a half times that number of cannon, he not unreasonably hoped to smash through Wellington's. He was expecting, despite what he had told George Venables Vernon on Elba, to fight Wellington in much the same way as he had fought the continental armies in the past.

It was far too conservative an approach. Wellington's reverse-slope technique, which meant that many of his men were simply not visible to the French artillery, was a perplexing new problem for Napoleon that required radical thinking. The central assault had worked at Rivoli in 1797 and Leipzig in 1813, but it was hardly an imaginative tactic, especially against a commander who was later to say: 'I never took so much trouble about any battle.' Wellington had only had nine hours' sleep in ninety over 15–18 June, but he had very carefully adjusted his line with great attention to detail, interspersing British units among the Dutch-Belgian ones in order to give them heart.[27]

The attack on Hougoumont at around 11.30 a.m. – hardly do two accounts agree when the battle actually began – was commanded by Reille and under him Jérôme, who commanded a division. Such was the resistance of the British Foot Guards within the walls and orchard of Hougoumont that it began later in the day to draw in French reserves instead of British. 'If you start to take Vienna – take Vienna' was another of Napoleon's maxims that he was to violate that day. A battle within a battle, Hougoumont was defended throughout the day and Wellington was never forced significantly to weaken his position in reinforcing it. In all around 3,500 Anglo-Allied troops tied down 8,000 Frenchmen there in eight hours of fierce fighting. 'The success of the battle turned upon closing the gates of Hougoumont,' Wellington wrote years later when awarding £500 to one of the men responsible. (The rector of Framlingham in Suffolk left money in his will to 'the bravest man in the British army at Waterloo', and Wellington had been called upon to adjudicate.)[28]

Napoleon's 'Grand Battery' opened up at around noon, and was heard by Grouchy at the village of Walhain. He was eating strawberries with a group of senior officers and, despite a sharp disagreement with General Gérard, he decided not to march towards the sound of the guns but to carry on northwards towards the Prussians at Wavre, obeying to the letter Napoleon's original orders of the previous day.

Even before 1 p.m., Napoleon's staff noticed movement on the extreme right flank of the battlefield, where dark-clad troops seemed to be issuing from the woods near Chapelle St Lambert. Initial hopes that this might be Grouchy's corps, and that Wellington was therefore doomed, were dashed when reports arrived that, according to a captured corporal of the Silesian Hussars, the troops debouching on to the battlefield were in fact thirty thousand Prussians under General Count von Bülow. Moreover, the French right flank and rear were largely unprotected from any such incursion. The news effectively meant that Napoleon had overstayed his welcome on the stage of History, but he apparently took it with commendable sang-froid, sending reserves to bolster his position in the east. 'Ask me whatever you like, except time,' he had once said, 'it is the only thing beyond my power.' There is some dispute about exactly when the hussar divulged his information; it might even have been before the Grand Battery's initial bombardment.

Yet Napoleon does not seem to have considered simply calling off the attack on Hougoumont and withdrawing in good order before the combined Anglo-Allied-Prussian armies, to fight another day. With Grouchy now at last recalled to the field he might have been able to reverse the situation later on, for as the military historian Karl von Clausewitz was to write of warfare: 'No human activity is so continuously or universally bound up with chance.' Napoleon was not so committed to a general assault by 1 p.m. that it could not be broken off, yet he decided to allow Ney to carry on with the attack, presumably in the hope that it would succeed before the bulk of the Prussian army arrived. If so, it was an act of hubris almost equivalent to his decision to invade Russia.

It is otiose to argue whether Wellington could have won Waterloo without the aid of the Prussians, for it was only ever fought on the assumption that they would arrive. Before the First World War, Kaiser Wilhelm II, with characteristic gracelessness, stated that Blücher had 'rescued the English army from destruction at Waterloo', but, as J. Holland Rose pointed out, that made no more sense than 'to say that in a pugilistic encounter the right hand saves the left from a thrashing'.[29] The Prussian contribution was a central feature of the decision to fight on the slopes of Mont St Jean, and therefore to minimise Blücher's contribution, as the military historian Colonel Chesney wrote in 1869, 'robs Wellington of his due' because he had prepared with Blücher 'this fatal stroke of war; and not to understand or to ignore this, is to miss the real design with which the fight was joined'. Nonetheless British, French and German historians have continually interpreted the events from their own (usually chauvinistic) viewpoints.

Despite having failed to weaken Wellington's centre in his attack on Hougoumont, Napoleon decided to unleash Comte d'Erlon's vast infantry force at around 1.30 p.m., hoping to break the Anglo-Allied line. A slight variation of the classic column seems to have been adopted for the attack by the divisional commanders, but not so significant an alteration as greatly to increase the firepower it could bring to bear. The 'column of deploying battalions' was the compromise they most probably reached. Napoleon had once warned Foy about the disadvantages of the column as a formation, saying it could break through only if there had been a 'very superior' artillery bombardment beforehand, yet at Waterloo d'Erlon was sent ahead towards troops who had not been demoralised by a preliminary bombardment that had largely passed over their heads, not least because Wellington had ordered them to lie down behind the reverse slopes.[30]

Perhaps in earlier days Ney, whom Napoleon had appointed battlefield commander, might have insisted on a different formation, but the bulk of France's best troops had been lost in Russia three years earlier and 'as the quality of the French infantry deteriorated, their generals had occasional recourse to huge, divisional squares and columns'.[31] These were intended to get as close to the enemy as possible and then deploy into line by fanning out. Yet at Waterloo d'Erlon's column never had the chance. The enormous blocks of soldiers, each approximately 175 men wide and 25 men deep, provided an ideal target for the British lines ranked two men deep, who came up to the crest of the slope just as d'Erlon's force approached.[32]

The largest single infantry assault in the Peninsula had been the French attack at Albuera that consisted of eight thousand men. Now Wellington's men had to face d'Erlon's vast, dense, multi-divisional attack of around twice that number, mounting the slope towards them to the beat of the drum. With high crops in the field and mud underfoot it was slow work, but the sight and sound must still have been unnerving, even for veterans. D'Erlon had fought at Fuentes d'Oñoro, Vitoria, the Pyrenees, Nivelle and Nive, and, although some mystery exists about the exact formation that he adopted at Waterloo, it seems he tried a hybrid about six hundred yards wide designed to combine the advantages of the column's manoeuvrability and the line's firepower.[33]

Wellington was unimpressed with the French tactics, remarking after the battle, 'They came on in the same old way, and we sent them back in the same old way,' which considering that d'Erlon had at least attempted to employ a better formation than the traditional solid column seems somewhat unfair. D'Erlon got close to the top of the ridge, but although supported by cuirassiers of Milhaud's IV cavalry division he had not time to react before Uxbridge's heavy cavalry brigades charged through hedges as they neared the summit. Uxbridge ordered Lord Edward Somerset, who commanded the Household Brigade (comprising the 1st and 2nd Life Guards, Royal Horse Guards and 1st King's Royal Dragoon Guards), and General Sir William Ponsonby, who commanded the Union Brigade (comprising the 1st Royal Dragoons, 2nd Scots Greys Dragoons and 6th Inniskilling Dragoons), to attack, placing himself too far forward in the Household Brigade's charge. Two minutes later, or so Captain Alexander Clark-Kennedy of the 1st Royal Dragoons told Captain Siborne, and d'Erlon might indeed have broken through. Yet Wellington's line held, and the British heavy cavalry then put the French to flight in that vital sector of the battlefield, with only the French rearguard having time to form square. The two British cavalry brigades attacked an infantry force over five times their number, scattered them, took two eagles and captured three thousand prisoners. But then they rode on too far.

To his great and lasting regret, Uxbridge could not hold back his cavalry, who subsequently charged the Grand Battery and silenced over fifteen cannon. They were heavily counter-attacked by French lancers and cuirassiers, losing Ponsonby and the commanding officer of the Scots Greys, and sustaining most of the 44.5 per cent casualties they suffered that day. 'Well, Paget, I hope you are satisfied with your cavalry now,' commented a sour Wellington, even though Uxbridge's brigades had broken d'Erlon's assault at the very point when it might have cut through the centre-left of his line. In fact Uxbridge had good reason to ignore Wellington's sarcasm and feel well satisfied, for as a modern historian has pointed out: 'Such was the effect of the charge that the French would not attack in any great strength to the east of the main Brussels road for the rest of the day. This left Wellington free to concentrate on the assaults on his right and centre. The struggle here was so intense that one cannot believe that Wellington would have been able to hang on had the French been able to launch further attacks against his left.'[34]

As Ney tried to reform the survivors of d'Erlon's mauled and demoralised corps, Wellington reinforced his front line from his reserves. After failing in his initial attack on La Haie Sainte at 3.30 p.m. – it was defended by the King's German Legion, which held out for another three hours before running out of ammunition – Ney launched a series of heavy and light cavalry charges against the British infantry, which formed around twenty squares. Just as Ney had not supported d'Erlon with cavalry, this time he failed to support his cavalry charges with infantry, and the cavalry exhausted themselves by galloping around the squares, failing to penetrate any. There were very few examples of cavalry breaking squares – horses simply would not charge at a bristling wall of bayonets – but squares were in turn vulnerable to artillery and enemy infantry. Ney failed to deploy the case-shot from the horse artillery which could have severely damaged the Anglo-Allied squares, or the infantry which could have poured withering fire into a formation that by its geometrical nature was ill able to respond. Instead the French cavalry made about fourteen in-effective but tiring charges, circling the squares, the heavy horses moving more and more slowly as the muddy ground was churned up underhoof. They finally ceased at around 5.30 p.m., too fatigued to support Foy's abortive infantry assault on Wellington's right.

By this time the leading brigades of Bülow's corps, debouching in ever greater numbers from the Bois de Paris, were starting to drive back Comte Lobau on Napoleon's right flank, and were later to take Plancenoit (although later on it was retaken by the Imperial Guard). Wellington, wearing his plain blue civilian frock-coat, white buckskin trousers, hessian boots and unplumed cocked hat with its cockade insignias of Britain, Spain, Portugal and the Netherlands, was every-where during the battle, in contrast to Napoleon who delegated far too much immediate operational control to Ney.

At one stage in the battle an artillery officer 'came up to the Duke, and stated that he had a distinct view of Napoleon...that he had the guns of his battery well pointed in that direction, and was prepared to fire. His Grace instantly and emphatically exclaimed "No! No! I'll not allow it. It is not the business of commanders to be firing upon one another."' Another account of the incident is more specific. 'There's Bonaparte, Sir, I think I can reach him, may I fire?' 'No, no, generals commanding armies have something better to do than to shoot at each other.'[35] Whatever the military advantages that might have accrued from the death of Napoleon at that point, including a massive blow to French morale, it was the correct political decision. Napoleon needed to be defeated on the field of battle for his myth to be tar-nished and French revanchism stymied. To have been killed in an 'ungentlemanly' way, let alone on Wellington's personal orders, would have forever left the suspicion that Napoleon would have won the battle. After the First World War a *Dolchstosslegende* (stab-in-the-back myth) emerged in Germany, which explained the events of 1918 in terms of treachery at home rather than defeat in the trenches. How much more potent would the French myth of Napoleonic omnipotence have been had he died at Wellington's hands in the early stages of the battle of Waterloo.

⤳

Both Napoleon and Wellington rode Irish-bred horses during the battle. Wellington's charger Copenhagen carried him throughout the day. Napoleon – who covered only a fraction of the ground – seems to have ridden at least three or four horses, including Marie, Desirée and his favourite, Marengo, which was foaled at Wexford in 1796. The 14.1-hand grey purebred Arab is thought to have been lightly wounded in the hip while carrying Napoleon at the end of the day, so the emperor switched to another horse before leaving the field. (After its death in 1832 two of Marengo's hooves were made into snuffboxes, one of which is still used in the Household Brigade's dining quarters at St James's Palace. The rest of its skeleton is on display in the National Army Museum.)[36]

Wellington's and Napoleon's personal activity during the battle could not have contrasted more. Wellington was forty-six, Napoleon forty-five, yet Wellington acted as energetically as a man in his twenties, Napoleon as lethargically as someone in his sixties. Wellington's exertion was terrific, he was personally present at many of the scenes of the greatest crisis, as proven by the terrible toll among those closest to him during the battle. An aide-de-camp Charles Fox Canning was killed. Another, Colonel Sir Alexander Gordon, was mortally wounded at his side. Colonel Sir William De Lancey of his staff was in close proximity to Wellington when he was struck down. Lord Fitzroy Somerset lost an arm to a sniper's bullet fired from the roof of La Haie Sainte while standing beside Wellington. The Austrian attaché Baron Vincent was wounded and the Spanish attaché Alava suffered a 'contusion'. Uxbridge's aide-de-camp was close by Wellington 'when I was knocked off my perch by a cannon-shot which carried off a portion of my neck, paralysed my right ear and right nostril'.[37] Uxbridge himself lost a leg while actually talking to Wellington, who nonetheless escaped the day entirely unscathed. Small wonder, therefore, that in his despatches and then to at least four different women over the ensuing years, the duke put down his survival that day to the self-evident fact that 'the finger of Providence was upon me'.

Although Wellington did not personally attend the fighting at Hougoumont or at the eastern end of the battlefield, he continually rode back and forth between Hougoumont and La Haie Sainte, entering squares on occasion and constantly rallying his troops, giving orders to their commanders and directing batteries where to fire.[38] Napoleon, by contrast, ceded operational control to Ney, partly so as to deal with the oncoming Prussian threat himself, and kept in one place too much, acting on others' information rather than riding out to see the situation for himself. He later complained that Ney's cavalry charges had not been authorised, yet he did nothing to prevent them taking place from virtually right in front of him. Indeed it is inconceivable that Ney could have launched Kellermann's cavalry or Milhaud's corps without Napoleon's approval. This deputising of front-line leadership meant, in the view of one historian who speaks for many, 'that Bonaparte himself had only a loose, sluggish and half-blind control over his army'.[39]

The fall of La Haie Sainte to Ney at around 6.30 p.m. created a new crisis for Wellington, upon which Napoleon signally failed to capitalise when he refused Ney's request for troops to help break the Anglo-Allied line directly behind the farmhouse. With Wellington's centre now taking a terrible beating from a battery Ney had placed a mere three hundred yards away, it seemed possible that a gap might at last appear. Yet Napoleon refused to send the Imperial Guard forward, telling Ney's messenger sarcastically: 'Some troops?! Where do you expect me to get them from? Do you want me to make them?' Lobau's VI Corps had been committed to the right flank. Reille's II Corps was mired down outside Hougoumont. D'Erlon's I Corps was broken and the horses of the IV Cavalry Corps were blown. If a general has only one great decision to take after a battle starts – when and where to commit his reserve – Napoleon had lost his capacity to take it. His first priority was to deal with the Prussian threat in the east, so a great – some argue potentially a battle-winning – opportunity was allowed to lapse.[40] It never returned. Napoleon had once said: 'In war there is only one favourable moment; the great talent of the commander consists in seizing it.' He had missed his, which he probably would not have done had the Prussians not been enfilading the right of his line so vigorously.

Asked if he ever saw Napoleon on the battlefield, Wellington answered: 'No, I could not – the day was dark – there was a great deal of rain in the air.'[41] The closest they seem to have come to one another was at about 7.30 p.m. when Napoleon at last decided to commit the Middle Guard to the assault. He rode to the gentle inner slope on the left of the Charleroi road that overlooked La Haie Sainte – now in his hands – which provided the best view for his whole line. The Guard marched past him up the road and 'as they approached, he pointed significantly to the Allied position; a gesture which drew forth renewed shouts of "Vive l'Empereur!"'[42] Almost simultaneously, Wellington rode up to Captain Napier's Foot Battery posted on the immediate right of General Sir Peregrine Maitland's Brigade of Guards and ordered its officer to make ready. 'The message had scarcely been communicated when the bearskin caps of the leading divisions of the column of Imperial Guard appeared just above the summit of the hill.'

Wellington later told Samuel Rogers that during Waterloo, 'Buonaparte I never saw: though during the battle we were once, I understood, within a quarter of a mile of each other.' From their opposing viewpoints, they both witnessed what happened next. Siborne estimated that three hundred French Guardsmen must have died in a single minute as a result of the furious, sustained and accurate firing from the 1st Foot Guards and the cannonading from Captain Napier's battery, firing at a range of only forty to fifty yards. The Imperial Guard were not supported by cavalry, were actually outnumbered by Wellington's infantry which met them, came uphill by battalion rather than *en masse*, enjoyed no artillery bombardment in support of their assault, and advanced in hollow square formations which allowed for only a fraction of the firepower of the British. Wellington's line even curved inwards on to the Middle Guard for maximum concentration of firepower. No amount of French bravery and *esprit de corps* could alter these damning fundamentals.

Wellington later described as ridiculous a story that at around 8 p.m. in the last square near La Belle Alliance farmhouse General Cambronne had cried, 'The Guard dies but doesn't surrender!' 'Never, certainly, was anything so absurd as ascribing that saying to Cambronne,' he said, not least because the general had in fact surrendered, and then invited himself for dinner at Wellington's headquarters after the battle. (Wellington refused to eat with someone who had conspicuously betrayed the Bourbons.) In fact of course most of the Guard neither died nor surrendered; the great majority of the 'Invincibles' retreated tenaciously before the onslaught, before breaking ranks and escaping the field.

Wellington then raised his hat to signify a general advance on all fronts. The incredulous French cry 'La Garde recule!' was replaced by

'Sauve qui peut!' as the whole Anglo-Allied force swept forward. 'No cheering, my lads,' ordered Wellington, 'but forward and complete your victory.'[43] He insisted on the French being given no opportunity to rally anywhere on the field. When British regiments came up against unbroken French infantry, Wellington demanded that the momentum be kept up, correctly sensing they would not stand. Two brigades of light cavalry under Major-General Sir Hussey Vivian and Major-General Sir John Vandaleur helped chase the French army from the field.

At around 8.15 p.m., Napoleon having quitted the scene, Wellington met Blücher at La Belle Alliance farmhouse. It would have made a politically perfect name for the battle, and was not surprisingly Blücher's own choice. Major-General Vivian wanted it called 'the battle of Mont St Jean' after the place where it was in fact fought, but Wellington decided to name it after his own headquarters some two and a quarter miles away, which, if not particularly logical, was surely his prerogative.

After the battle was over and safely won, Wellington 'two or three times relaxed for an instant, and allowed the mask of stern self-discipline to fall from his face. "Thank God, I have met him!" he cried. "Thank God, I have met him!" The convulsive working of his hands betrayed the intense emotion by which he was stirred.' The very *ad hominem* nature of that repeated statement – mentioning Napoleon rather than France or the French army – is of a piece with his comments before the battle and his remark about Napoleon being 'a mere pounder' during it. Wellington was acutely conscious of the personal nature of the clash between himself and France's greatest commander. The two men's trajectories – which had been rising in Wellington's case since 1810, and falling in Napoleon's since 1812 – had at last intersected. Their lives had finally collided, and Wellington's response was 'Thank God I have met him!', as though he would always have doubted his own superiority as a general if he had not.[44] Wellington had, along with Blücher, administered the *coup de grâce* that had been awaiting Napoleon ever since Russia had swallowed up his Grande Armée. The duke was under no illusions about the importance of his own role in the affair, and displayed no false modesty when he told Creevey the very day after the battle: 'By God! I don't think it would have been done if I had not been there.'[45] For all the vanity the remark seems to display, it was probably no more than the truth.

TWELVE

Wellington Protects Napoleon
(and His Own Reputation)
June–July 1815

Wellington had always been baneful to Bonaparte,
or rather the rival genius to France,
the English genius, barred the road to victory.

CHATEAUBRIAND

'My Lord,' wrote Wellington to the secretary for war Lord Bathurst in his great Waterloo despatch on the morning of 19 June 1815, 'Bonaparte having collected the 1st, 2nd, 3rd, 4th and 6th Corps of the French army, and the Imperial Guard and nearly all the cavalry, on the Sambre...advanced on the 15th, and attacked the Prussian posts...at daylight in the morning.'[1] Wellington then skated over the fact that he had been, in the word he used to the Duke of Richmond, 'humbugged', by saying that when he heard of Napoleon's having crossed the Sambre 'in the evening of the 15th' he had 'immediately ordered the troops to prepare to march, and afterwards to march to their left'. This somewhat obscured the central point, that he had heard in the afternoon, and that they had originally been ordered to concentrate to the south-west of Brussels, and not, as had been agreed with Blücher, to the south-east.

Wellington's reference to the battle of Ligny was similarly misleading. Highly complimentary to Blücher, he stated that the Prussian army had 'maintained their position with their usual gallantry and perseverance' and then the Prussian commander had 'determined to fall back to concentrate his army upon Wavre; and he marched in the night, after the action was over'. Wellington had not been present during the fighting, and therefore had an excuse for dressing up his ally's defeat in this generous way. (The Prussians had been forced from the field and Blücher, recovering from concussion in a barn after having been ridden over by French cavalry in the retreat, in fact only confirmed Gneisenau's order to head northwards to Wavre long after it had been taken, though Wellington might well not have known this on the 19th or not have thought it relevant.)

Ignorance of the truth might also have led Wellington to state that 'The enemy made no effort to pursue Marshal Blücher,' when in fact of course Grouchy had been detached with 33,000 men and ninety-six guns to do just that. The (surely unintentional) effect of this misstatement was to have led the readers back in Britain – and the despatch was reproduced in almost every newspaper in the land – to assume that Napoleon must have attacked Wellington with his entire army, rather than just two-thirds of it. Later on Wellington does refer to Napoleon having sent his III Corps 'to observe' Blücher, which contradicted his earlier statement but anyhow hardly altered the overall impression.

When Wellington wrote that Blücher had 'promised me that, in case we should be attacked, he would support me with one or more corps, as might be necessary', he did the Prussian commander-in-chief something of a disservice. In fact Blücher had told Wellington that 'Bülow's Corps will set off marching at daybreak in your direction. It will be immediately followed by the Corps of [Lieutenant-General Georg] Pirch. The Ist and IIIrd Corps will also hold themselves in readiness to proceed towards you.' No mention of 'as might be necessary' or 'in case we should be attacked' – they were on their way. In the event the I and III Corps came also, with around fifty thousand Prussians staving in Napoleon's right flank and following up the victory in place of the exhausted Anglo-Allied army.

Wellington reported the battle of Waterloo as having started at 10 a.m., when according to almost all other sources it did not actually start until about one and a half hours later. Once again, he had every possible excuse – people did not check their timepieces during cannonades, and he was writing the very day after the battle – yet the overall result was that his readers gained the impression that he had had to hold out for over six and a half hours before the Prussians arrived in force, when in fact it had been around five.

Wellington stated that 'the march of General Bülow's corps, by Frischermont, upon Plancenoit and La Belle-Alliance' had not 'begun to take effect' until 'about seven in the evening', which also did a grave disservice to the advance Prussian units which had been fighting heavily since about 4 p.m. and had taken Plancenoit, been driven from it by the Imperial Guard, and had then retaken it by 7 p.m. Wellington had not visited that sector of the battlefield, and his account once again led the domestic British gazette or newspaper reader to underestimate the Prussians' role. It is true that there were fuller, yet almost *pro forma*, tributes to the Prussian contribution at the end of the despatch, but no more than might be expected for an ally with whom he was still actively on campaign and jointly preparing to march upon Paris.

Wellington further stated that at 'about seven in the evening' he could perceive the fire of Bülow's cannon, and 'as Marshal Prince Blücher had joined in person with a corps of his army to the left of our line by [the Bois d']Ohain, I determined to attack the enemy, and immediately advanced the whole line of infantry, supported by the cavalry and artillery', before which the French 'fled in the utmost confusion'. Once again, an impartial reader might have supposed from this that it was Blücher's appearance at 7 p.m. rather than the Prussian troops' active engagement on the battlefield for several hours which encouraged Wellington to finish off the French.

Blücher 'sent me word this morning that he had taken sixty pieces of cannon belonging to the Imperial Guard, and several carriages, baggage, etc. belonging to Bonaparte'. Apart from the mention of Napoleon in the first sentence of the despatch, this was the only reference Wellington made to his great adversary in the whole report. A long list of officers' names was then given as having been killed or wounded. (Blücher's official despatch, by contrast, was highly personalised, with several references to 'Napoleon'.) Off the record, Wellington was much more forthcoming, writing to his brother William the same day: 'You'll see the account of our desperate battle and victory over Boney. It was the most desperate business I was ever in … and never was so near being beat.' To Marshal Beresford he wrote that Napoleon had 'just moved forward in the old style, in columns, and was driven off in the old style', a line he was to repeat. The victor of 'Bloody Albuera' would have known exactly what that meant.

'It gives me the greatest satisfaction to assure your Lordship that the army never, upon any occasion, conducted itself better,' wrote Wellington to Bathurst, 'and there is no officer nor description of troops that did not behave well.' Unless he was writing solely about the British contingent, this was simply untrue, and he knew it at the time. Yet he must have been referring to his entire Anglo-Allied army, because in the previous sentence he had commended the Prince of Orange for his 'gallantry and conduct'. It was, once again, perfectly understandable that Wellington should not have wanted to draw attention to those officers and troops who had behaved badly, but the fact remains that he well knew that several had.

As Wellington was himself to remark years later to Samuel Rogers, the Nassau Brigade actually fired 'a few shots after me as I rode off', once he had failed to persuade them to stay in an orchard when the French were 'close by'. He had even lamented to his staff at the time: 'And with these men I am to win the battle.' He believed that since the Brigade had defected to him *en masse* on 10 December 1813, 'and knowing as they now did, that Buonaparte was in the field, their dread of him must have borne some proportion to the courage with which he had formerly inspired them'.[2]

Uxbridge also had 'the strongest reason to be excessively dissatisfied with the general commanding a brigade of Dutch heavy cavalry and with a colonel commanding a young regiment of Hanoverian hussars' because, while he was actually advancing to the charge at one point in the battle, his aide-de-camp Captain Horace Seymour had to inform him that the Dutch cavalry were not following them. As the Household Brigade retained its position, the Dutch cavalry were moved away immediately, to prevent demoralisation. Furthermore, the commander-in-chief of the Belgian cavalry calmly told Uxbridge that his men were 'too dispirited' to attack the French.[3] Colonel Hacke of a Hanoverian regiment, the Duke of Cumberland's Hussars, was actually court-martialled and cashiered after his unit failed to charge in support of the 2nd Life Guards, but instead turned and rode off the field of battle, with Hacke at their head. The colonel even told Uxbridge's astonished aide-de-camp that his men's horses were 'their own property' and since they were volunteers they would 'move to the rear' in defiance of Uxbridge's express orders.[4]

It was a sorry story, but not one that for political reasons could be alluded to in the despatch. Hanover shared a sovereign with Britain in King George III, and with a campaign still possibly ahead of him Wellington could not consider offending his allies. These were, more-over, relatively minor incidents in the battle, in which the various Allied contingents in general fought bravely, especially the King's German Legion. Nonetheless, Wellington probably knew that it was simply not accurate to state that 'there is no officer nor description of troops that did not behave well'.

Wellington's peroration in praise of Blücher and the Prussians has usually been described as very warm and generous:

> I should not do justice to my own feelings, or to Marshal Blücher and the Prussian army, if I did not attribute the successful result of this arduous day to the cordial and timely assistance I received from them.

The operation of General Bülow upon the enemy's flank was a most decisive one; and, even if I had not found myself in a situation to make the attack which produced the final result, it would have forced the enemy to retire if his attacks should have failed, and would have prevented him taking advantage of them if they should unfortunately have succeeded.[5]

Yet, seen in the context of his earlier remarks, this was still – except for the first sentence – somewhat mealy-mouthed. Examination of the sub-clause 'even if I had not found myself in a situation to make the attack which produced the final result' shows that Wellington, for all his praise of Blücher's 'cordial and timely' help, did not wish his readers to gain the impression that he could not have won Waterloo without the Prussians, or that it became winnable only once they had arrived. He acknowledged the 'decisive' nature of Bülow's assistance, but claimed that the Anglo-Allied army was anyhow 'in a situation to make the attack which produced the final result'.

Readers of the despatch could hardly divine from it that Napoleon had been steadily withdrawing reserves and the Guard away from Wellington's front ever since first spotting the Prussians at 1 p.m., only ninety minutes or so after the attack on Hougoumont had begun, and was so denuded of troops by 6.30 p.m. that he could not follow up opportunities on his northern front, such as the fall of La Haie Sainte. (However, we cannot be sure that Wellington knew this for certain himself.) Nor could readers have gleaned the true extent of the harsh fighting on the eastern part of the battlefield, or the full contribution of the Prussians in following up the victory. Indeed Wellington's readers might have been forgiven if they read the generous and unqualified sentence of testimony to Blücher as a fine-sounding but almost formulaic praise of an ally, of a type which abounded in such post-battle reports of the day. When the American envoy to London read the despatch he found it so free of uplifting rhetoric that he assumed that Wellington had actually lost the battle.

It is perhaps unfair on Wellington to place this despatch under too microscopic or structuralist a textual analysis. We do not have his notes or earlier drafts – if indeed there were any – to let us know what was going through his mind as he wrote it. Nor can he be expected to be entirely objective at such a moment. Many close comrades had died or were dying, he was physically shattered and even tearful, the mud of the battlefield was still on his boots, he had slept the previous night on a pallet because his favourite aide-de-camp Colonel Sir

Alexander Gordon lay dying on his bed, he was still on campaign having nothing but a shrewd guess as to where Napoleon had gone, Grouchy was still in the field, and he had important security and political considerations to take into account in deciding what to report. To expect a finished, entirely factual, finely tuned account of the tumult of the previous four days was too much to ask of anyone. It was certainly a far more accurate account than that which appeared in the *Moniteur*, which referred to the battle of Mont St Jean as having been 'funeste' (dire), but 'glorieuse pour les armées françaises'.

Yet Wellington wanted his despatch to stand for ever as the standard historical record of Waterloo, the only account to which anyone could give any credence. For the whole of the rest of his life he poured unending scorn on anyone and everyone who tried to write about the campaign, and the examples of his contempt for all other historical accounts are legion. Writing to Sir John Sinclair in April 1816 asking him not to publish an account of the defence of Hougoumont, Wellington said: 'The battle of Waterloo is undoubtedly one of the most interesting events of modern times, but the Duke entertains no hope of ever seeing an account of all its details which shall be true.'[6] A fortnight later he told Sinclair: 'I am disgusted and ashamed of all that I have seen of the battle of Waterloo. The number of writings upon it would lead the world to suppose that the British army had never fought a battle before; and there is not one which contains a true representation, or even an idea, of the transaction...'

Another would-be writer was sharply recommended by Wellington 'to leave the battle of Waterloo as it is. You may depend upon it you will never make it a satisfactory work.' Comparing the writing of the history of a battle to that of a ball, he said that some individuals might recollect 'all the little events by which the great result is the battle lost or won; but no individual can recollect the order in which, or the exact moment at which, they occurred, which makes all the difference as to their value or importance'. He wound up snorting that there were so many versions of the battle that he sometimes even 'doubted whether he had been there himself'.

The person who was most keen to rewrite the story of what he called the 'battle of Mont St Jean' was Napoleon. As after every setback to his career, he had left his army and dashed back to Paris. Arriving at the Elysée Palace at 5.30 p.m. on Wednesday 21 June, he was met on the steps by Caulaincourt, a man to whom 'he could pour out the sorrow in his heart and the intensity of his spirit'. As he got into his bath, he ordered Caulaincourt to assemble the Council of

Ministers and to reprimand Ney and Grouchy for their failure to obey orders. 'But for a traitor's desertion, I would have annihilated the enemy at the outset of the campaign,' he said, referring to the Royalist General Louis Bourmont's defection on the first day. He also blamed his right flank for having 'failed in its duty. Well, all is not lost. After feats of great valour, panic seized the army.'[7] Ney, Grouchy, Bourmont, the 'right flank' and 'panic' – these were the first of a large number of scapegoats Napoleon was to blame for his defeat. Yet, whatever the excuses, France was tired of war, and there was not the political will left to support Napoleon in yet another campaign, as the Council of Ministers and the French parliament, the Chambers, soon made abundantly clear to him.

That evening, Napoleon received his Polish mistress Countess Marie Walewska and their son Alexandre, as state papers were being burned and Marchand was packing up the emperor's personal effects. Alexandre Walewski played with Louis-Napoleon, the son of Napoleon's brother ex-King Louis of Holland and Josephine's daughter Queen Hortense, as the crowds outside cried 'Vive l'Empereur! Ne nous abandonnez pas!'[8] (The previous day Wellington had predicted to Dumouriez, 'I think that this is the end of Bonaparte. We are hard on his heels ...')

At noon on Thursday, 22 June 1815, Napoleon abdicated in favour of his son the King of Rome, whom Bonapartists thereafter called Napoleon II. Davout stood in silence as he watched the document being signed. He had been ready to disband the Chambers by force the previous day, but Napoleon did not call on him to do so, as he said he did not want to try to 'rule by the axe' and provoke civil war.[9] Instead, somewhat unrealistically, Napoleon hoped to be asked to command the army as an apolitical general.

Friday, 23 June saw Wellington writing to Uxbridge to say: 'We have dealt Napoleon his death-blow. From all I learn, his army is totally destroyed; he can no longer stand up to us ... He can only hang himself.'[10] It is paradoxical that almost the first time that Wellington used Napoleon's imperial name was on the day after it had been forsworn. The Chambers, urged on by the ubiquitous Fouché, who had become president of the five-man Commission of the Government, insisted that Napoleon leave Paris. The next day Davout, as minister of war, visited the Elysée to inform the furious ex-emperor of their decision. Napoleon refused to shake Davout's hand, but went to Malmaison, the country house outside Paris that had once belonged to Josephine. He was never to see Paris again.

On Sunday, 25 June, Louis Bignon, France's temporary foreign minister, was sent to Wellington, possibly on Fouché's orders, to ask for safe-conduct for Napoleon who 'desired to retire without delay to the United States of America', along with some family members and a small retinue. Wellington told Bignon, and subsequently also Fouché, that he had no authority from the British Government to provide any such safe-conducts and could only receive Napoleon as a prisoner of war. He simultaneously warned Castlereagh to have the ports blockaded even more closely than usual.[11] To Paris' requests for peace, Wellington answered that he 'could not consider the abdication of an usurped power in favour of his son, and his handing over the government provisionally to five persons named by himself, to be that description of security which the Allies had in view, and therefore I continue my operations'.[12]

Although, as Wellington told Bathurst, 'All accounts concur in stating that it is impossible for the enemy to collect an army to make head against us,' that did not prevent him from continuing to complain about the state of his own army, describing it, only one week after the battle of Waterloo, as 'the worst equipped, with the worst staff, ever brought together', although as ever he excepted his Peninsular veterans from criticism. When the news arrived that the Prince Regent had been pleased to appoint himself captain-general of the Life Guards and Blues in recognition of their conduct in the battle, Wellington merely commented: 'His Royal Highness is our sovereign and can do what he pleases; but this I will say, the cavalry of other European armies have won victories for their generals, but mine have invariably got me into scrapes.'[13]

Far more magnanimous was Wellington's absolute refusal to allow Napoleon to be handed over to the Prussians, who were keen to execute him. On 27 June, General Count von Gneisenau wrote from Compiègne to Major-General von Müffling, Wellington's Prussian liaison officer:

The French general De Tromelin is at Noyons, with the intention of proceeding to the headquarters of the Duke of Wellington to treat for the delivering up of Bonaparte. Bonaparte has been declared an outlaw by the Allied Powers. The Duke of Wellington may possibly (from parliamentary considerations) hesitate to fulfil the declaration of the Powers. Your Excellency will therefore direct the negotiations to the effect that Bonaparte may be delivered over to us, with a view to his execution. This is what eternal justice demands, and what the declaration of 13 March decides; and thus the blood of our soldiers killed and mutilated on the 16th and 18th [at Ligny and Waterloo] will be avenged.[14]

Later that day Gneisenau also instructed Müffling to inform Wellington that the Prussian High Command had told the Provisional Government in Paris that they would only agree to a truce under six swingeing conditions, the first of which was 'the delivering up of Bonaparte alive or dead'. He added that he had said that Prussia was waging war against Napoleon and that 'After having destroyed him, we no longer care' who the French put in his place, be it the Bourbons or a republic.[15]

When Müffling dutifully but regretfully passed on these messages to Wellington:

> The Duke started at me in astonishment, and in the first place disputed the correctness of this interpretation of the Viennese declaration of outlawry, which was never meant to incite to the assassination of Napoleon … As far as his own position and that of the Field Marshal [Blücher] with respect to Napoleon were concerned, it appeared to him that, since the battle they had won, they were become much too conspicuous personages to justify such a transaction in the eyes of Europe … 'Such an act would hand down our names to history stained by a crime, and posterity would say of us, that we did not deserve to be the conquerors of Napoleon; the more so as such a deed is quite useless, and can have no object.'[16]

Wellington flatly refused to allow Napoleon to be 'destroyed' like some rabid animal, and wrote to Sir Charles Stuart, the British minister at the Hague, on 28 June to say that he would not negotiate Napoleon's departure for America. He added: 'Blücher wishes to kill him; but I have told him that I shall remonstrate and insist on his being disposed of by common accord. I have likewise said that … if the Sovereigns wished to put him to death they should appoint an executioner, which should not be me.'[17]

Blücher and Gneisenau were unpersuaded. A convinced anglophobe, the latter complained of Wellington's 'theatrical magnanimity' in sparing Napoleon's life, and even stated that the duke's humanitarianism was a pretence cloaking his desire to keep alive the man whose career had so extended British 'greatness, prosperity and wealth'.[18] On 29 June Gneisenau further wrote to Müffling, who entirely sympathised with Wellington, to say that it had been Blücher's intention 'to execute Bonaparte on the spot where the Duc d'Enghien was shot' – the courtyard of the Château de Vincennes – but out of deference to Wellington's wishes 'he will abstain from this measure'. He nonetheless still wished Müffling to ensure that Napoleon 'may be delivered up to us', in order, he wrote, to save the British from feeling 'embarrassed'.

Writing to Davout the previous day, Napoleon made clear his intention to await arrest at Malmaison, 'until decision on his fate had been made by the Duke of Wellington', hoping 'that no action unworthy of the nation and its Government will be taken against him'.[19] Talleyrand, who had also insinuated himself back into office, told Stuart, who told Wellington, that the British decision not to execute Napoleon 'will guide [that] of the King, if his fate should come under consideration in the Council'.[20] It was therefore very much Wellington's personal intervention that saved Napoleon's life during those crucial two weeks in late June and early July 1815. Wellington later told Samuel Rogers how much he would have liked to have met Napoleon at this time: 'I regret it much; for he was an extraordinary man.'

The war was not yet officially over, however, and Wellington made it clear to the French commissioners for the armistice that, 'after consulting Marshal Prince Blücher, His Highness agrees with me that, in the present circumstances, as long as Bonaparte is at liberty and while operations are still carrying on, hostilities cannot be stopped'.[21] Wellington was unconvinced by the French protestations of pacifism, and feared that a reorganisation of the army might be taking place under the cover of the negotiations. The Allied armies therefore continued warily to approach Paris.

On 1 July Napoleon left Malmaison for Rochefort near the River Charente's estuary on France's west coast, still hoping that he might be able to quit Europe for America. He had, after all, been fortunate in evading the Royal Navy during his Egyptian adventure in 1798 and in skipping Elba the previous year; so who could tell whether he might not escape on a frigate to the much-mooted destinations of Mexico, Buenos Aires or even California?[22] (Joseph Bonaparte escaped on board the American brig *Commerce*, which he had chartered under the name of Bouchard for eighteen thousand francs on 25 July. Although the brig was twice inspected by British boarding parties during the voyage, his false papers escaped detection and he landed in New York on 28 August, although that was hardly an option open to the instantly recognisable ex-emperor.)

By the Convention of St Cloud on 3 July, France finally capitulated to the Allies. It left Wellington virtually the dictator of France. During the negotiations, Davout insisted on a special clause being inserted in the treaty, after Louis XVIII had proclaimed that he would 'reward the good and apply the law against those who are guilty'. Under Article XII it was therefore agreed that:

> The persons and property of individuals shall ... be respected, and the inhabitants, and all other persons resident in the capital, shall continue to enjoy their rights and liberties without being molested, or any inquiry made, respecting their employments which they follow, or may have followed, or their political conduct or opinions.[23]

This, it was hoped by both sides, would prevent a policy of Royalist retribution against those who had gone over to Napoleon in the Hundred Days. It did not prevent the Prussians wrecking Marshal Ney's country estate, however, and much worse was to follow.

When the veteran politician the Marquis de Lafayette visited Wellington at this time, in order to ask what he intended to do with the Chambers, the duke curtly replied that he:

> would readily answer his question if he could point out to me any instance in which Napoleon or any other French commander, having entered Vienna, Berlin, or any other foreign capital, had ever answered – or indeed even allowed to be put to him – any one question as to what he intended to do in any respect whatever.[24]

The point was made. (Wellington later considered Lafayette's support for the revolutions of both 1789 and 1830 as 'a striking instance [of] how seldom men profit by experience'.)

Back in Britain, Lord Liverpool was meanwhile writing to Castlereagh from Fife House to say that 'there are three questions which occur to every person one meets', the first of which was: 'What is to become of Bonaparte?' Liverpool personally had no moral qualms about taking 'the most easy course', which was to 'deliver him up to the King of France, who might try him as a rebel', and then execute him. If Napoleon tried to set sail, Liverpool assumed that 'we have a good chance of laying hold of him', and seemed to have little difficulty about Louis XVIII's 'clear right to consider him a rebel, and to deal with him accordingly'.[25]

On the very day he entered Paris for his Second Restoration on 8

The ultimate trophy: Canova's statue of Napoleon that stands
in the stairwell of Wellington's London home, Apsley House,
the gift of a grateful nation in 1815

The Duke of Wellington, painted by Sir Thomas Lawrence

The Emperor Napoleon, painted by Delaroche

The six French marshals who Wellington defeated in the Peninsular War:

André Masséna

Jean-Baptiste Jourdan

Auguste Marmont

Michel Ney

Nicolas Soult

Claude Victor

Wellington's political allies:
Left Robert Jenkinson, 2nd Earl
of Liverpool, *Below* Robert
Stewart, Viscount Castlereagh

Two mistresses shared by Napoleon and Wellington: *Right* Giuseppina Grassini, *Below* Josephine Weimer ('Mademoiselle George')

Le Caillou farmhouse, where Napoleon held the pre-battle
conference on the morning of Waterloo

Longwood House, where Napoleon eked
out his exile on St Helena

Field Marshal Prince Gebhard
Leberecht von Blücher, whose
steadfastness on 18 June 1815
ensured Wellington won the battle

Jean-Baptiste Drouet, Comte d'Erlon,
whose actions on 16 and 18 June
1815 ensured Napoleon lost the
campaign

Europe's political weathervanes:
Left Prince Clemens von
Metternich, *Below* Charles-
Maurice de Talleyrand,
Prince de Benavente

Left King Louis XVIII of France, *Below* Tsar Alexander I of Russia

Queen Hortense of Holland, the
daughter of Josephine and wife of
Louis Napoleon

Napoleon's sister, Pauline
Bonaparte, Princess Borghese

The brothers: *Left* Richard
Colley, Marquess Wellesley,
Below Joseph Bonaparte,
King of Spain

The clause in Napoleon's will which left ten thousand francs to M. Cantillon, Wellington's would-be assassin

The Vendôme column in Paris,
shortly after being pulled down
by the Communards in 1871

July, Louis XVIII ordered Fouché – the former regicide whom Wellington had persuaded the king against his better instincts to re-appoint – to arrest Napoleon. That evening the king waved to the crowds from the window of the Tuileries, standing alongside Wellington and Castlereagh, finding it impossible to converse with them, so loud were the acclamations of the turncoats in the crowd.[26] Earlier that same evening Napoleon had gone to Fouras, a small fishing village at the mouth of the Charente river, where he embarked upon the French frigate *Saale*.

Although Wellington was unwilling to see Napoleon executed by the Allies, there is evidence to suggest that, after Waterloo, he did not mind his great opponent dying a hero's death in battle. He was present at a meeting in Paris on 12 July that agreed a form of words to authorise the Royal Navy to sink Napoleon's ship should he attempt to evade the blockade. Wellington agreed this policy with Castlereagh, Talleyrand, Fouché, the French minister of marine the Comte de Jaucourt, and the naval secretary to the first lord of the Admiralty, John Wilson Croker, who 'held the pen' (or acted as secretary). According to the letter Croker wrote the next morning to Rear-Admiral Sir Henry Hotham, the senior naval commander in the Basque Roads whose intimate knowledge of the Biscay coast proved invaluable at this time, Napoleon had embarked on 'one vessel; of a small squadron … anchored under the forts of the Isle d'Aix, ready to escape at the first opportunity'.

The Comte de Jaucourt had informed the meeting that 'the escape of Buonaparte's squadron' from the Charente was 'impossible', so Hotham was instructed to plan for 'the capture of Buonaparte'. This was to be done peacefully if possible; however, it was made abundant-ly clear that Wellington and Castereagh had authorised the use of force, and had countenanced with some equanimity the prospect of Napoleon dying in a sea battle. For as Croker told Hotham:

Lord Castlereagh feels that it is of the most urgent importance to seize Buonaparte, but he also feels that the safety of His Majesty's ships ought not to be compromised beyond the ordinary risk of a naval engagement, and he is sincerely desirous of avoiding the effusion of blood, which, however, he is inclined to think may be best effected by bold and decisive measures; and if the ship in which Buonaparte may be, should, by an obstinate resistance, drive you to extremities, he feels that you ought not, for the sake of saving her or any one on board her, to take any line of conduct which should increase in any degree your own risk. The consequences of the resistance will be chargeable on those who may make it.[27]

Wellington and Castlereagh were thus quite prepared to accord Napoleon a death at sea, and were unwilling to jeopardise British sailors' lives in too risky an attempt to capture him alive.

The same day that Croker was writing to Hotham, Napoleon wrote the Prince Regent a short letter which bears repetition in full:

> Your Royal Highness, exposed to the factions which distract my country and to the enmity of the greatest powers of Europe, I have ended my political career, and I come, like Themistocles, to throw myself on the hospitality of the English people; I put myself under the protection of their laws, which I claim from Your Royal Highness as the most powerful, the most constant, and the most generous of my enemies. Napoleon.

After signing the letter he remarked to Marchand: 'There is always a danger of entrusting oneself to one's enemies but it is better to risk relying on their sense of honour than to be in their hands as a prisoner of war.' This was especially true in the case of the Prussians. His enemy Chateaubriand's scornful comment on Napoleon's attempt to liken himself to the great Athenian statesman was: 'Go then, Themistocles, and sit quietly by the British hearth, whilst the soil has not yet finished drinking the French blood shed for you at Waterloo!'

The idea of Napoleon reaching England, and thus coming under the automatic protection of her common law, including the right of trial by jury, appalled the Liverpool ministry. The pro-Napoleon Whigs and Radicals in parliament could be relied on to support their hero's legal rights, even after Waterloo. On 23 June, after Castlereagh had moved a motion thanking Wellington and proposing a vote of £200,000 for a palace to be built for him, Samuel Whitbread denounced the war as one 'into which this country had neither occasion nor right to enter' and Sir Francis Burdett spoke of 'the injustice and inexpediency of the present war'.[28]

On the night the news of Waterloo arrived in London, Major-General Sir Robert Wilson and Lord Grey were at Brooks's demonstrating 'satisfactorily to a crowded audience that Boney had 200,000 men across Sambre, and that he must be then at Brussels'. Just as Wilson was reading aloud a letter announcing that the British population of Brussels was fleeing to Antwerp, 'the shouts in the street drew us to the window' to hear the crowds celebrating Wellington's victory. 'Nothing could be more droll than the discomfiture of our politicians at Brooks's,' the Hon. H. Bennett MP wrote to Thomas Creevey. (Wilson went to Paris soon afterwards to become a Bonapartist version of the Scarlet Pimpernel, and spent six months in a French gaol for helping Napoleon's friend and postmaster-general the Comte de Lavalette to escape Bourbon 'justice'. An apostle of Bonapartism, Wilson became a Whig MP in 1818.)

Wellington enjoyed telling stories of the Whigs' discomfiture at his victory. In 1838 at Walmer Castle he recalled that 'when the truth came out of our having won, Lord Sefton went to Lady Jersey and said to her "Horrible news! They have gained a great victory!"'[29] Byron also tried to minimise Wellington's success by pointing out on 7 July 1815 that the duke had to 'thank the Russian frosts, which destroyed the <u>real élite</u> of the French army, for the success at Waterloo'. The day before, Samuel Whitbread, with everything he stood for in dust and all that he had predicted proved wrong, had the rare decency in a politician of committing suicide.

⌒

On 15 July 1815, a month short of his forty-sixth birthday, Napoleon boarded the Royal Navy frigate HMS *Bellerophon*, to be received by Captain Frederick Maitland and officially taken into British custody as a prisoner of war. The Napoleonic Wars were over. Between five and six million combatants and civilians had perished across the European continent since France had declared war on Austria on 20 April 1792, more than twenty-three years before.

Captain Maitland wrote a *Narrative* of Napoleon's sojourn on the *Bellerophon*, in which he described his prisoner-guest as he stepped aboard:

> He was then a remarkably strong, well-built man, about 5' 7" high, his limbs particularly well formed, with a fine ankle and very small foot, of which he seemed rather vain, as he always wore, while he was on board the ship, silk stockings and shoes. His hands were also very small, and had the plumpness of a woman's rather than the robustness of a man's. His eyes light grey, teeth good; and when he smiled, the expression of his countenance was highly pleasing; when under the influence of disappointment, however, it assumed a dark gloomy cast. His hair was of a very dark brown, newly approaching to black, and though a

little thin in top and front, had not a grey hair amongst it. His complexion was a very uncommon one, being of a light sallow colour, differing from almost any other I have ever met with. From his having become corpulent, he had lost much of his personal activity, and, if we are to give credit to those who attended him, a very considerable portion of his mental energy was also gone. It is certain his habits were very lethargic while he was on board the *Bellerophon*.[30]

Wellington was delighted by the news of Napoleon's surrender. 'Exactly one month after his invasion of the Low Countries', he wrote to Lady Frances Wedderburn-Webster, 'and only one battle, he has been obliged to give himself up to the nation with which he had been at war during his whole career.' Despite his passing over of the battles of Quatre Bras, Ligny and Wavre, Wellington was justifiably proud of the Allies' achievement. 'I congratulate with all my heart the first general in the world,' Louis XVIII had told him, although during Napoleon's lifetime Wellington always accorded his enemy primacy, at least in public. When the king asked after Wellington's age, the duke replied that he had been born in 1769. Louis XVIII replied: 'And so was Bonaparte. Providence owed us this compensation.'

The fighting war over, the war of mythologies had already begun. Only seven weeks after Waterloo, Napoleon-tourism was well under way. Lord Uxbridge's niece Georgina Capel wrote to her mother that on her visit to the battlefield, 'at a distance we saw the telegraph erected by Buonaparte and where they say he mounted to view the fight'. By July souvenir hunters had already gouged the musket balls and grapeshot out of the elm under which Wellington had watched part of the battle, and later the tree itself was cut down to make commemorative snuffboxes, a chair and even a toothpick-case.[31]

The question of what to do with Napoleon occupied many minds both official and unofficial. British newspapers speculated that he might be taken to the Tower of London or Dumbarton Castle; Metternich told Marie Louise that he would probably be imprisoned in Fort St George in Scotland, while Talleyrand suggested the Azores as a final destination. Lady Shelley's journal for July 1815 states that at a party in Paris Wellington said he believed 'that Bonaparte ought to be shut up at Fort St George, as, by the laws, his life cannot be forfeited. The Duke brought us home in his carriage, and stayed for some time conversing about the situation relative to the surrender of Bonaparte.'[32]

Wellington was not ultimately involved in the choice of St Helena, which was made by the Government in London. On 21 July, Lord Liverpool wrote to tell Castlereagh that he had spoken to Lord Melville, the first lord of the Admiralty, and John Barrow, the permanent secretary, and the latter 'recommends St Helena as the place in the world best calculated for the confinement of such a person'.[33] It was thus a British civil servant's recommendation, rather than that of Wellington or a politician, which consigned Napoleon to St Helena. Barrow had sailed on Greenland whalers and travelled widely in China and Africa, and his mastery of cartography had earned him a place at the Admiralty, from where he had risen to the senior post. He was a founder of the Royal Geographical Society and his opinion on St Helena's suitability, principally due to its great distance from anywhere else, was respected.

Liverpool's view was that 'the situation is particularly healthy' and with luck Napoleon 'would very soon be forgotten'. The second prediction was soon proved very wide of the mark. The prime minister still hoped that Louis XVIII might 'hang or shoot Bonaparte as the best termination of the business', but if that was 'impracticable' St Helena would be the next best option. By the time General Beatson, who had been governor there, wrote to Liverpool a week later also to recommend St Helena's suitability, the decision had already been taken.[34]

Wellington recalled in 1851, in a letter to Croker, that Napoleon's fate 'was never mentioned as a subject for consideration' at the Congress of Vienna, and that the former emperor could have had no inkling of it, because if he had 'he would have avoided to expose himself to capture on his passage to the coast of France'. Wellington certainly did not oppose the choice. When he had visited St Helena in 1805 he had told a friend that 'the interior of the island is beautiful and the climate apparently the most healthy that I have ever lived in'.[35]

Napoleon and his adherents there, however, always assumed that Wellington was the man behind the British Government's decision, perhaps because they knew that he had visited the island ten years before. As Napoleon told O'Meara in September 1817: 'Have you heard that Lord Wellington was the person who first proposed to send me to St Helena?... If it be true, it will reflect but little honour upon him in the eyes of posterity.'[36] Another reason Napoleon's circle assumed Wellington was involved seems to have been that General Charles-Tristan, Comte de Montholon heard it from another of Napoleon's suite, Emmanuel, Comte de Las Cases, who got it from his wife the Comtesse, who had heard it from her friend Lady Clavering who lived at 19 Portland Place in London, and who had herself heard it as a rumour.[37]

Lady Clavering, since 1791 the wife of the 8th baronet Sir Thomas Clavering of Axwell, County Durham, was the daughter of Jean de Gallais, Comte de la Sable of Anjou, and she kept in clandestine touch with her countrywoman the Comtesse de Las Cases via James Scott, the Las Cases family's mulatto servant. He had letters written on taffeta silk sewn into his waistcoat to attempt (on one occasion in vain) to escape British detection. Lady Clavering's guesswork about Wellington was not much to go on, but for the resentful and suspicious French mini-court on St Helena it was enough.

On board the *Bellerophon* Napoleon did not like to speak about Wellington, but Captain Maitland asked another of the twenty-six-strong suite, General Comte Bertrand, what the emperor thought of the duke. 'Why,' replied Bertrand, 'I will give you his opinion nearly in the words he gave it to me: "The Duke of Wellington, in the management of a great army, is fully the equal of myself, with the advantage of possessing more prudence."'[38] Years later this appreciation was passed on to Wellington by his friends Charles and Harriet Arbuthnot, but without the qualification that it had come third hand.[39] It was almost the last time Napoleon was ever reported to have had a good word to say about his opponent.

In one of the notebooks used at his military academy in 1788, in a jotting on British possessions worldwide, Napoleon had written: 'Sainte Hélène – petite île', and then left the rest of the page blank. For the former master of a continental land mass, Napoleon's life was strangely bound up with islands. He was born on Corsica, fought against Britain, married a woman from Martinique, returned to war over Malta, was exiled to Elba, was defeated by a man born in Ireland, and, as St Helena hove into view on 14 October 1815, he could have guessed that that was where he would die. 'It is not a pretty place to live,' he told another member of his suite, General Gaspar Gourgaud.[40] 'I would have done better to have stayed in Egypt.'

THIRTEEN

Shepherding the Scapegoats
1815–1816

Death is nothing, but to live defeated is to die every day.

NAPOLEON

On 7 August 1815 Napoleon, who had been transferred from
the *Bellerophon* to HMS *Northumberland* for the journey, set sail
for St Helena. While on board, and also after landing, he was
often engaged in conversation with a Dr William Warden, who took
detailed notes of what he said. In his *Letters from St Helena*, published
two years later, Warden recorded:

Ever since I had enjoyed an occasional communication with
Napoleon I had never ceased to be animated by a strong and curious
desire to learn his opinion of our renowned commander. I had repeatedly heard that he did not withhold it, but I could never ascertain the
fact on any certain authority. The present moment [shortly after
landing] appeared to afford me the opportunity I had so anxiously
sought; as he seemed to be in a temper of more than usual communication and courtesy, though I have never had reason to complain of
either. At all hazards I resolved to make the trial; as it might be the
only opportunity I should ever possess. 'The people of England', I
said, 'appear to feel an interest in knowing your sentiments respecting
the military character of the Duke of Wellington. They have no
doubts that you would be just; and, perhaps, they may indulge the
expectation that your justice would produce an eulogium of which the
Duke of Wellington might be proud.' Silence ensued: I began to think
I might have gone too far; for it is most true, that I had never before
addressed him without looking him full in the face for a reply, but my
eyes dropped at the pause, and no reply was made...At the same

time, he did not appear to be in the least displeased, as in a few minutes he renewed the conversation with this enquiry: 'You mentioned a Review – what does it contain?'[1]

They then discussed a recent edition of the *Quarterly Review*.

Brigadier-General Sir George Bingham, commander of the 2nd Battalion of the 53rd Regiment which had been selected to guard Napoleon, recalled that in a conversation on 16 August with Rear-Admiral Sir George Cockburn Napoleon had deigned to discuss Waterloo, saying 'that he should not have attacked Wellington on the 18th, had he supposed he would have fought him; he acknowledged that he had not exactly reconnoitred the position; he praised the British troops...he denied that the movement of the Prussians on his flank had any effect'. Napoleon went on to claim that the cry of 'Sauve qui peut!' had been raised by the 'malevolent' (rather than the genuinely terrified), and had it not been dark by then he would have 'thrown aside my cloak, and every Frenchman would have rallied round me; but darkness and treachery were too much for me'.[2]

The bare outlines of an explanation of Waterloo that largely exculpated Napoleon were beginning to emerge, with 'darkness and treachery' joining Ney, Grouchy, Bourmont, the 'right flank' and 'panic' as at least the initial scapegoats. Already contradictions were appearing, with Napoleon blaming the 'right flank' in his conversation with Caulaincourt on 21 June, but denying it 'had any effect' on the battle's outcome in his conversation with Cockburn two months later. Only one explanation for the defeat was never once proffered by Napoleon; that Wellington had simply out-generalled him on the day. Nor is the explanation of 'darkness' valid; at 7.30 p.m. on a mid-June day in western Europe dusk is still far off. Napoleon also, with perhaps more reason, blamed the pre-battle rainstorm. 'Oh God!' he exclaimed while on St Helena. 'Perhaps the rains of 17 June had more to do with the defeat of Waterloo than we think! If I had not been so exhausted I would have spent the whole night on horseback. The apparently most trivial circumstances have often the greatest effect.'

Napoleon was not ungenerous to all his enemies; on St Helena he made favourable references to Blücher, the Archduke Charles and Admirals Nelson, Cochrane and Sir Sidney Smith, among others. With Wellington, however, he developed a complete blind spot. Going over the defeat in his mind again and again, as his Mediterranean soul passed five and a half years on his mid-Atlantic rock, to which he wrongly believed Wellington had assigned him, bitterness entered his soul until he could not bring himself to think objectively about his opponent. Las Cases noticed that 'In general the Emperor disliked speaking of Lord Wellington. He seemed carefully to avoid pronouncing his opinion on him; feeling, no doubt, the impropriety of publicly depreciating the general who had triumphed over him.'

In his remarks to Las Cases about 'that unhappy war in Spain', for example, Napoleon blamed himself for taking the wrong political decisions about dethroning the Bourbons there, but rarely mentioned his marshals' string of military defeats at the hands of Wellington. The list of people to blame for Napoleon's downfall grew longer and longer in his exile. In May 1816 d'Erlon, Ney and 'junior staff officers' were held to be at fault. By February 1817 they were joined by Murat, Vandamme, Mortier and Grouchy again. Fouché and Soult were later added to this veritable herd of scapegoats. Napoleon's reinterpretation of himself and his battles renders St Helena, in the eyes of his biographer Albert Guérard, 'the most successful of his campaigns', because 'He had his wish: his empire is dust, but his fame has lost none of its splendour.'[3]

In his desire to set the record awry, Napoleon regularly bent the truth. It is true that he had few reference works on the island, and relied too much on his often faulty memory, but there was a good deal of sheer propaganda too. 'My only wish is that my time may mark the beginning of the era of representative government,' the ex-despot had told his secretary Louis-Antoine Bourrienne, and on St Helena he told anyone who would listen – which meant everyone – that had he won Waterloo he would have instigated a generation of world peace.[4]

On St Helena he also produced an entirely fictitious Order of the Day for when he took up command of the Army of Italy.[5] He blamed the Spanish and 'weak-minded admirals' for all of France's naval defeats, never acknowledging the superiority of the Royal Navy. Dictating to Montholon, Napoleon had Admiral Brueys as master of the Mediterranean from August 1799, when in fact he had been killed at the battle of the Nile the previous year. He gave all Marlborough's victories to Prince Eugene, got Admiral Sir Roger Curtis' name wrong, claimed that the whole of Moscow had burned down in 1812, and misplaced Ney's headquarters in the Waterloo campaign.[6] He indulged endlessly in counterfactual history – 'If I had had Bessières at Waterloo my Guard would have brought me victory' – and so on. He was also intensely sarcastic about Grouchy, who he said had 'solved the apparently undiscoverable secret of being on the morning of the 18th neither on the battlefield of Mont St Jean nor on that of Wavre'. (In fact Grouchy had engaged the Prussian rearguard at Wavre shortly after 4 p.m.)[7]

Of course it is impossible to say how bitter Wellington might have become had *he* lost the battle of Waterloo, surrendered and been exiled by Napoleon. Judging from his comments on the supposed tardiness of his promotion in India and his references to his officers' failings during the retreat from Burgos, and from his criticisms of his cavalry as 'galloping at everything', we can fairly safely predict that he could have been similarly caustic about Blücher and the Prussians had they not arrived in time.

When Napoleon did finally comment to Las Cases about Wellington on St Helena his opinion was predictably damning:

Ah, he owes Blücher a great deal. Without him I've no idea where His Grace, as he's called, might be, but of course I would not be here. His troops were admirable, his strategy deplorable. Well, it would be better to say that he had none. He placed himself in a completely impossible position; and, the strangest thing, it is that which ended up saving him. Had he been able to start his retreat he would have been lost. He remained master of the battlefield, that is without doubt; but was it due to his troop dispositions? He received the fruits of a great victory, but had his genius created this?... His glory is all negative, his faults are enormous. He, the European general given such huge responsibilities – having in front of him an enemy as quick, as daring as I am, to leave his troops thinly spread, sleeping in a capital and to be taken by surprise!... No, Wellington has but one special talent; he has no creativity; Fortune has done more for him than for herself... His victories, their results, their influence will remain imprinted on history; but his reputation will be brought down even whilst he lives.[8]

From these and many other remarks made on St Helena, it can be deduced that Napoleon was a deplorably bad loser. In their staccato intemperance they ring true, but they also lack logic and precision. This was a rant, occasioned in this particular instance by Napoleon's suspicion that Wellington had been responsible for the choice of St Helena.

In fact Wellington rather sympathised with Napoleon and privately deplored his treatment at the hands of Major-General Sir Hudson Lowe, St Helena's governor (who was also born in the same year as Napoleon and Wellington). It was almost a studied insult to Napoleon to appoint a former commander of the Corsican Rangers to the post, considering that it was a unit composed of anti-Bonapartists from his home isle. Lowe had also served under Blücher at Leipzig and had carried the news of Napoleon's abdication to London in 1814, for which the Prince Regent had knighted him. His fussy, suspicious, indecisive, pedantic and generally quotidian personality had got on Wellington's nerves in the 1815 campaign (the duke had once been heard to mutter 'Damn fool' under his breath when the quarter-master-general took an age to study a map in the Low Countries). After a ridiculous row about the Prussians, Wellington sent Lowe off to Genoa, where he arrived on the day of the battle of Waterloo.[9]

On St Helena Lowe went out of his way to clash with Napoleon and the admittedly highly obstreperous French contingent around him. Although there is in the National Army Museum a gold watch given to Lowe by Napoleon, the two men met only four times and relations steadily worsened between 'General Bonaparte', as Lowe insisted his illustrious prisoner be called, and his pernickety gaoler.

Although the rows between Napoleon and Lowe constitute only a footnote to a footnote to History, Wellington emerges relatively well from them; he told Creevey in 1818 that, although 'Buonaparte is so damned intractable a fellow there is no knowing how to deal with him,' Lowe had employed 'absurd' means to ensure he did not escape. Wellington believed a 'mere handful of men' could easily have covered the three or four places on the island from which Napoleon could have embarked and set sail, a point he emphasised to Lady Shelley, who recorded that 'Having taken these precautions, the Duke proposed to give Bonaparte the whole range of the island as his prison-house.' All Lowe had to do, according to Wellington's scheme, which he also regularly proposed to others, was to ascertain 'every night in what part of the island Bonaparte would sleep. In the Duke's opinion his plan would have insured Bonaparte's safety, without the odium caused by the petty annoyances to which he was subjected.'[10]

Wellington thus had little regard for Lowe, and when prime minister he refused to give him either the governorship of Ceylon or the £1,500 per annum pension which Lowe craved. Only in February 1833, when Lord Teynham criticised Lowe in a House of Lords debate, did Wellington stand up for his former subordinate, describing him as 'a highly respectable officer', which Lowe clearly did not consider to be damnation with faint praise because he thanked the duke profusely.[11] By then Lowe was in such bad odour in France that, when Alexandre Dumas the Elder's play *Napoléon Bonaparte* was performed in Paris, the actor playing Lowe had to be given police protection.

Writing soon after Napoleon's death, Lord Holland complained that, although Wellington might privately have expressed some regret about the way Lowe had treated Napoleon, this:

was never conveyed to the quarters where it might have rectified the mistake and alleviated the sufferings of the prisoner. Wellington preferred the odium of abetting the oppression of a great man to the hazard of losing Royal favour or incurring the resentment of official pride, by an act of humanity and generosity. He must abide by the consequences. History, if she does not brand him as an accessory in the guilt, will describe him in this instance as deficient in that magnanimity which is incapable of it.[12]

In fact History has done nothing of the sort, as Napoleon's treatment after his surrender was no part of Wellington's responsibilities at the time.

⌒

While Napoleon languished on St Helena, guarded by, among others, a soldier who went by the name of Edward (later General Sir Edward) Pine Coffin, Wellington was enjoying the delights of Paris quite as much as he had the previous year. Giuseppina Grassini was in town that summer, as were Lady Charlotte Greville and Lady Frances Wedderburn-Webster. Wellington continued his Napoleon-tourism, taking the twenty-eight-year-old Lady Shelley to Malmaison one August evening. As she recalled, 'when we reached the conservatory it was quite dark. We had great fun in going through it, with two or three wretched candles. A storm came on, with vivid flashes of lightning. The Duke brought me home.'[13]

As well as Napoleon's hunting lodge, Wellington visited Napoleon's clock-maker Breguet (incidentally the craftsman who made the gold watch given to Lowe). Napoleon had frequented Breguet's workshop, and Wellington had a watch made there which, according to Captain Gronow, 'on touching a spring at any time, struck the hour and minute'. It cost Wellington three hundred guineas and he carried it for many years. (Gronow, an Etonian Welshman with sybaritic tendencies, had fought in the Peninsula and had been aide-de-camp to General Picton. He was tremendously vain, but was a fine raconteur with a good memory.)

In pursuing what he called his 'paternal attitude' towards France, Wellington opposed the imposition of a Carthaginian peace settlement upon the defeated country, and generally supported the more liberal French politicians against the reactionaries grouped around the king's younger brother, the Comte d'Artois.[14] He also gave the British antiquary Colonel Woodford a strong hint that he should stop disinterring the French knights who had fallen at the battle of Agincourt four centuries earlier.

When he first entered Paris, Wellington also managed to preserve the Pont d'Iéna from the francophobe wrath of Blücher. Napoleon's bridge over the Seine had been built between 1806 and 1813 to commemorate his greatest victory over Prussia. Blücher 'was most determined' to destroy the bridge, in direct contravention of Article IX of the St Cloud Convention, arguing that 'the French had destroyed the pillar at Rossbach and other things, and that they merited this retaliation. He also said that the English had burned Washington, and he did not see why he was not to destroy this bridge.' Wellington recognised that it would be a grave insult to the French and visited his former liaison officer General von Müffling, who was now governor of Paris, to ask him to persuade Blücher 'to abandon this design'.

The Prussians were out for revenge for the devastation caused by Davout's corps after the battle of Jena, and, as Captain Gronow observed, on the way to Paris after Waterloo the Prussian army had:

> committed fearful atrocities on the defenceless inhabitants of the villages and farms which lay in their line of march...We found that every article of furniture in the houses had been destroyed in the most wanton manner: looking-glasses, mahogany bedsteads, pictures, beds and mattresses, had been hacked, cut, half-burned and scattered about in every direction; and, on the slightest remonstrance of the wretched inhabitants, they were beaten in a most shameful manner and sometimes shot.

Wellington and Müffling designed a plan to prevent Blücher carrying out his intentions, and posted British sentries on the bridge, with orders not to leave their posts even if the Prussian sappers should arrive to mine it. This is often credited with having saved the bridge, but it seems that at least three explosions did take place, which nonetheless failed to destroy the Pont d'Iéna.

On 13 July John Croker wrote to his wife to say that he had personally seen 'the marks of the explosion' on the bridge, for as Wellington told the diarist Charles Greville: 'The Prussians arrived, mined the arches, and attempted to blow the bridge, sentries and all. Their design, however, was frustrated and the bridge received no injury.' The Napoleonic eagles within laurel wreaths visible on the sides of the bridge had survived to taunt Blücher. Talleyrand and Louis XVIII tried to gain credit with the people of Paris for protecting the bridge, and to save Teutonic face it was renamed the Pont des Invalides, but it was Wellington who persuaded Blücher to wait until the King of Prussia arrived in Paris to pronounce on the bridge's future. It survived.

Blücher then turned his vandalistic attentions towards the column that Napoleon had erected in the Place Vendôme. 'I saw that I had gone out of the frying pan into the fire,' Wellington recalled to Grenville on a rainy day during a shooting trip five years later.[15] On 1 October 1803 Napoleon had ordered that 'In the centre of the Place Vendôme in Paris a column shall be erected similar to that in honour of Trajan in Rome.' It was to be 17 feet in diameter, 143 feet high and encrusted with a spiral band on which were to be 108 allegorical bronze figures each 3 feet tall representing the departments of the republic. A statue of Charlemagne was originally going to be placed on top. By March 1806 Napoleon decided that it should be renamed the 'Austerlitz' column and he requisitioned a number of Austrian and Russian cannon captured in the battle to be recast as bas-reliefs. A bronze statue of Napoleon himself, dressed as a Roman emperor crowned with laurels, was now to grace the semi-circular platform on the summit. On Napoleon's birthday celebrations on 15 August 1810 it was unveiled to the delight of huge crowds.

Thereafter the column became a Bonapartist shrine and symbol. On 14 January 1814, Royalists placed a placard on the plinth which read, 'Pass by quickly, he is going to fall,' and a month later a crowd cried 'Vive la colonne!' in response to rumours that the Allies intended to demolish it. On 4 April 1814, two days after the Senate had declared that Napoleon had forfeited the throne and two days before he abdicated it, a crowd attempted to pull the statue off the top. Napoleon's former mistress 'Madamoiselle George' happened to be driving past in her carriage at the time, and was only with difficulty prevented by a friend from getting out to remonstrate. With the Parisian press calling her the 'Corsican widow' and audiences hissing her stage performances, it was doubtless for the best.

The crowd found that ropes alone could not dislodge the statue, so once the Allies occupied the capital the tsar's aide-de-camp gave Launay, the original caster of the statue, orders to return it to his studio. When Napoleon returned from Elba the following year the column was the scene of wild celebrations by Parisians. After Waterloo, Wellington managed to protect it by appealing to the tsar's and King of Prussia's senses of mercy and political expediency, so another Parisian landmark was saved from desecration. Wellington personally admired the column, and asked in 1817 that instead of the City of London 'presenting me with a silver column [they] ought to erect a column of the dimensions of that in the Place Vendôme in some square in London. If they present me with a silver column they should take the scale of that in the Place Vendôme and whatever may be the size adhere to it.'

The column continued to be a focus for Bonapartist sentiment, and was pulled down by the Paris Commune on 16 May 1871 after the fall of Napoleon III. (According to the diarist Edmond de Goncourt, the method used, a bevel-cut at the base, was designed by an engineer who needed the six thousand francs reward to give to his mistress, a woman of particularly easy virtue called Ménier who had been abandoned by her rich protector because of her infidelity.)[16] The column was rebuilt in 1873, and stands – slightly cracked – in the Place Vendôme today, bearing the inscription: *Monumentum Belli Germanici Anno MDCCCV.*

⤶

A major blot on Wellington's reputation has long been his refusal to interfere in the judicial murder of Marshal Ney and Napoleon's aide-de-camp General le Comte de La Bédoyère by the Bourbons. Louis XVIII had not been party to the St Cloud Convention, and therefore did not consider himself bound by its stipulations regarding a general amnesty for those who had fought for Napoleon. Ney had not just changed sides, but had prior to his defection notoriously promised the king that he would bring Napoleon back to Paris 'in an iron cage'. It was an entirely unnecessary remark to have made, and of course, as Marshal Jacques Macdonald pointed out, 'he would never have sullied his reputation by putting it into execution'.[17] Ney was high on the Bourbons' list of people upon whom they wished to wreak vengeance. The 'White Terror' was an ugly thing: when Royalists captured Marshal Brune in August 1815 he was lynched and his corpse was then used for target practice. In the same month de La Bédoyère was also shot for treason.

When Ney was arrested on his country estate, Wellington felt he could not interfere in what was essentially a matter of French domestic politics. Article IX of the St Cloud Convention was held, slightly legalistically, to give immunity only to those resident in Paris. Despite having signed the Convention, and being the most influential man in France at the time, and possessing Louis XVIII's gratitude in abundance, Wellington decided not to intervene, for which he has since been castigated by many. His bitter political enemy Lord Holland, who always gave the worst possible interpretation to his actions, said of Wellington's signature on the Convention that 'when a construction of a doubtful passage might have saved one of the first officers of the age, he gave it the meaning least favourable to the conquered party and left a man with whom he once coped in the field of honourable war to be taken off by the hands of the executioner'.[18] He went on to imply that Wellington was jealous of Ney's superior reputation for generalship, and Byron later added insult with his unsubtle verse in the ninth canto of *Don Juan*:

> Glory like yours should any dare gainsay,
> Humanity would rise and thunder 'Nay!'

When Ney's wife Aglaé begged Wellington to help save her husband, the duke 'regretfully declined' to involve himself in a matter between the French king and his subjects, and the marshal was duly shot on 8 December 1815. Louis XVIII had pointedly snubbed Wellington shortly beforehand, and Wellington was reputed to have said: 'I could only have asked it as a special favour to myself; and when I had been insulted in this manner, and was not on terms with the King, I could not think of asking favours of him.'[19] (The froideur between duke and king was short lived; in that same month Louis XVIII's ministers only just prevented him from presenting Wellington with the magnificent estate of Grosbois between Paris and Fontainebleau, arguing that it was tactless so to honour France's conqueror.) A more chilling explanation of Wellington's refusal to save Ney came out at Stratfield Saye in April 1838, when Lady Salisbury recorded that 'Speaking of Ney, he said it was absolutely necessary to make an example.'[20] *Raison d'état* thus seems to be the true explanation why Wellington failed to act in the gallant way expected of the former foe of 'the bravest of the brave'.

Napoleon reportedly received the news with indifference, although he later recognised the propaganda advantages of mourning his 'murdered' lieutenant. Entirely bound up with his own troubles, he initially said Ney had been a fool who deserved his fate, not least because he had refused to lend him money during his Elban exile.[21] Only when the opportunities for blaming the Bourbons and the 'English oligarchy' for the death of his once favourite marshal became apparent did Napoleon begin to accord Ney a foremost place in the Napoleonic pantheon, while still blaming him for his tactical failures at Waterloo.

On 6 December 1815 Napoleon was 'in good spirits' because he had received the British newspapers up to mid-September. 'The greater confusion there is in France, the greater chance he fancies there is on his being allowed to return,' Bingham told his journal, 'as he thinks the English Government will be obliged to recall him to compose the confusion that exists in that unhappy country.'[22] It was a delusion that must have comforted Napoleon, but it amounted to no more than that.

⤳

'Poetry, painting, and sculpture must lie,' Napoleon once said; 'but they should lie with grandeur, charm, and splendour.' He certainly greatly resented the efforts made by Wellington to rectify the question of the art works looted by the French over the previous quarter-century and placed in the Musée Napoléon at the Louvre. The art collection that Napoleon had amassed during his campaigns was immense. Between 1796 and 1814 he removed 506 major works from Italy alone, and almost all his conquests involved the plundering of art.[23] The greatest spectacle in the history of the Louvre was Napoleon's marriage to Marie Louise in the Salon Carré in 1810, which featured a bridal procession down the Grande Galerie. According to the drawing made by Benjamin Zix, the paintings they walked past that day included works by Rubens taken from Alost in Belgium and Antwerp Cathedral, a Francia from Parma, Raphaels from Bologna and the Vatican, as well as Peruginos from the Vatican and Cremona.

On 18 September 1815 Wellington sent British officers into the Louvre to prise from its director-general, Vivant Denon, the art that had been looted over the previous quarter-century and to restore it to its rightful owners.[24] The Allies had specifically refused a proposed clause in the St Cloud Convention guaranteeing art against restitution, yet the Parisians were furious at what they saw as the desecration of what was admittedly the finest art collection ever brought together in one place. They willingly believed the rumour that Wellington had personally been at the Louvre 'unhooking and taking down the pictures which Napoleon had accumulated from every corner of Europe'.[25] Louis XVIII was incensed by the policy, and his nephew the Duc de Berri denounced Wellington as an 'upstart', a status which apparently 'accounts for his vulgarity in sending back so many valuable articles to their rightful owners'.[26]

The king particularly could not see why the four bronze horses of St Mark, removed by Napoleon from the Piazza di San Marco in Venice, should be taken down from the Arc de Triomphe du

Carrousel at the Louvre by a company of British sappers and returned to Venice. Wellington told Castlereagh he was 'giving the people of France a great moral lesson', that their 'national vanity' over these 'trophies' would not be indulged.[27] Lord Holland argued that the removal of the art was a 'stain on the character of the Great Captain of the Confederacy', but his view was not generally accepted by non-Frenchmen.

Wellington's own trophies of the Napoleonic Wars fill his two large homes Apsley House on Hyde Park Corner and Stratfield Saye in Hampshire. He had a keen artistic eye and took a close personal interest in the hanging of his pictures. The vast majority of the best works came from the Spanish royal collection captured from King Joseph at the battle of Vitoria, which a grateful King Ferdinand VII allowed him to keep with the gracious words, 'His Majesty, touched by your delicacy, does not wish to deprive you of that which has come into your possession by means as just as they are honourable.' The 165 works included pictures by Titian, Correggio, Watteau, Murillo, Velasquez, Caravaggio, Poussin, Raphael, Breughel, Rubens, Dürer, Van Dyke and Leonardo. As well as being given works of art by admirers, Wellington bought them in post-war Parisian sales and occasionally also commissioned them himself.

By far the greatest single item of Napoleana in Wellington's extensive collection was Antonio Canova's eleven-foot statue of the emperor as the Roman god of war Mars in the pose of an Hellenic athlete, standing naked but for a figleaf and cloak, which today stands at the foot of the main staircase at Apsley House. The contract for the statue was signed on 1 January 1803, when the first consul was at the height of his powers and looks, but was not delivered until 1811, by which time both Napoleon's fortunes and his physique had suffered a decline. (During the statue's conception, an Englishman had written to Canova to complain that the great neo-classical sculptor was 'profaning his chisel for a little monster whose figure was as ignoble as his stature was low and his character odious'.)

Fashioned from a single perfect block of Carrara marble, Napoleon holds a lance in one hand and a small globe surmounted by winged Victory in the other. The composition 'much displeased' Napoleon, according to his secretary the Baron de Méneval, because of 'the want of resemblance in the head, and its nudity', and on the emperor's orders it was hidden away in the Louvre and not exhibited. The figure of winged victory had its back turned upon Napoleon, which was also deemed ominous. Pope Pius VII was under the impression that, as he told Wellington's friend Lady Shelley, 'the ladies of Paris were so angry at its nudity that it had to be concealed'. It was an explanation from the 'old gentleman' – who she thought 'spoke oddly for a pope' – that struck Lady Shelley as displaying a 'marvellous naïveté' about the true nature of Parisian womanhood.

In 1816 the British Government bought the statue from the Louvre for 66,000 francs, and the Prince Regent presented it to Wellington. Once the floor above the Apsley House cellars had been strengthened, the huge structure was transported there with Canova sending instructions for its installation. Once again, many French were outraged. Méneval complained that the bottom of the stairs was 'a spot very unworthy of it', and argued that the siting 'does little honour to the delicacy of feeling of the victor'. He was infuriated when he heard that the statue had been used by the duke's visitors 'to hang cloaks and hats on'. Chateaubriand was similarly angry: 'This deification seems more appropriate to a vain caretaker than to an honourable warrior,' he wrote. 'General, you did not conquer Napoleon at Waterloo. All you did was wrench asunder the last link in an already broken chain of destiny.'[28] The Reverend G. R. Gleig, who knew Wellington well, averred in the final sentence of his authorised biography of the duke that Wellington's siting of the statue had not been intended to belittle his rival, and although it was 'an unfortunate one no doubt [it] has no signification whatsoever'. It was well cared for, and when the figleaf fell off during the Blitz the shocked housekeeper contacted the Wellesley family immediately.[29]

Although the Canova statue was Wellington's most important piece of Napoleana, there were plenty more items, and, unlike the statue given to him by a grateful nation, these others were mostly acquired by the duke himself. It is thought that Napoleon's sword had been given to him by Blücher. Made by Napoleon's goldsmith Biennais, it is today on display at Apsley House along with its three scabbards. In one upstairs room, the Portico Drawing Room, there are no fewer than three paintings of Napoleon. That of the first consul by Laurent Dabos was a gift from a Mr Fleming, who in 1824 had been invited to dinner by mistake in place of another man of the same name. Although Wellington's messenger requested the return of the invitation card, Fleming refused, went to the dinner and was received by the duke. The portrait was sent as an *amende honorable*. Another, entitled *Napoleon in the Prison of Nice in 1794*, was bought by Wellington in 1841 for £21 from the painter Edward Matthew Ward RA.[30] The third is a life-sized bust portrait after Gérard of Napoleon wearing the uniform of a colonel of foot grenadiers and the grand cross of the *légion d'honneur*, which was bought or presented to the duke before 1830.

Napoleon also features in the right foreground of Sir William Allan's ten-foot-long painting of the battle of Waterloo that Wellington specially commissioned in 1843, with the duke himself appearing on the left horizon. (This was as seen from the French side of the battlefield; the companion painting seen from the Anglo-Allied side hangs at Sandhurst.) There is also a painting of Pauline Borghese by Robert Lefèvre that shows the emperor's sister's nipples very clearly through her white chemise, and a large bronze equestrian statue of Napoleon given by the Comte Alfred d'Orsay. There were plenty of paintings of Napoleon and his family in Wellington's collection. Paintings by both Gérard and Lefèvre of King Joseph were captured at Vitoria, a painting of Josephine by Lefèvre was bought by Wellington from Comte d'Orsay for £100 in 1851, and there was Swebach's *Passage of the Danube by Napoleon before the Battle of Wagram*. A bust of Napoleon by Alessandro Triscornia, probably bought at the sale of the belongings of Napoleon's uncle Cardinal Fesch in 1817, stands in the hall at Apsley House.

In beautiful rosewood cases mostly specially commissioned by Wellington is kept the finest early-nineteenth-century continental porcelain collection in Britain. The Sèvres factory produced a splendid 'Egyptian' dinner service for Napoleon in 1802, providing a (well-sanitised) visual record of the 1798 campaign, and the emperor presented it to Tsar Nicholas I. In her divorce settlement, Josephine was awarded thirty thousand francs to buy herself some Sèvres porcelain and she commissioned an identical service, but she rejected the design when it was completed as 'too severe'. Louis XVIII presented this second service of 102 pieces to Wellington in 1818 with the sublime understatement: 'Do little gifts keep friendship alive.'[31]

The private library at Apsley House has remarkably few books on Napoleon or Waterloo; Wellington was not generally interested in reading about the battle and was almost universally scornful of those accounts he saw. There are, however, his personally annotated volumes of Dr Barry O'Meara's *Napoleon in Exile*. Number 1, London, as Apsley House used to be designated before a more prosaic postcodal system intruded, also boasts sixty-six flags blessed by Napoleon at the Champ de Mai ceremony a fortnight before the Waterloo campaign. The flags, with their Napoleonic bees, eagles and 'N' motifs in laurel leaves, were also the gift of Louis XVIII to Wellington.

Wellington commissioned Lefèvre to make copies of his famous portrait of Napoleon; there are no fewer than three in his collection. A life-sized one, acquired by Wellington before 1820, shows the emperor aged forty-four in the blue uniform of a French general, wearing red facings, gold epaulettes and the sash and star of the grand cross of the *légion d'honneur*. At Stratfield Saye there is a bust of Napoleon as first consul by the sculptor Houdon. Towards the end of his life, Wellington allowed himself to be painted contemplating it. In the hall hangs a large print of the battle of Waterloo by J. W. Pieneman, in which Napoleon is visible, as well an 1808 miniature by C. Châtillon of Napoleon and another miniature of King Joseph in the Small Drawing Room. In the Print Room Wellington personally chose Benjamin Robert Haydon's 1830 representation of Napoleon on Elba looking out over the Mediterranean, which was then pasted above his desk by his daughter-in-law. In the gallery at Stratfield Saye is a four-foot-high gold and black marble bust of Napoleon as a Roman emperor, also bought in the sale of Cardinal Fesch's works of art.

Like that at Apsley House, the library of Wellington's country house has few books on Napoleon that were bought by him, although there are plenty that were collected by Lady Charles Pierrepoint (*née* Wellesley) long after the duke's death. One book that was in Wellington's library, however – according to the 1838 catalogue in which the emperor is characteristically listed under 'Buonaparte' – was the three-volume *Histoire de Jean Churchill Duc de Marlborough* (1808) by Archdeacon William Coxe. This book originally came from Napoleon's library at St Cloud, and was presented to Wellington in July 1815 by Colonel John Gurwood, the soldier who later edited his correspondence. One forbears to ask whom Gurwood paid for it, or whether it was simply victors' loot in much the same way – although of course on an altogether different scale – as the Louvre paintings. Napoleon clearly had more than one copy of Coxe's work, because in the month before he died he donated an English-language version to Captain Engelbert Lutyens of the 20th Regiment of Foot, to be placed in the regimental library. (So small minded was the governor of St Helena that this led to the removal of Lutyens from duty at Napoleon's residence, Longwood.) Napoleon must have missed the St Cloud copy, however, as he had General Bertrand translate the book into French.[32]

Bound in green leather with Napoleon's coat of arms embossed in gold on the cover, along with the customary imperial eagle, sceptres, *légion d'honneur* and a huge crown, the book offers no indications that it was read either by Napoleon or by Wellington. One book that does carry pencilled annotations, and was donated to Wellington by its author Lewis Goldsmith in 1811, was *The Secret History of the Cabinet of Bonaparte including his Private Life, Character, Domestic Administration, and his Conduct to Foreign Powers: Together with the Secret Anecdotes of the Different Courts of Europe, and of the French Revolutions*, a rabidly anti-Bonapartist work. (One of the anecdotes marked – we cannot tell whether by Wellington or someone else – was the tale of a rabbit shoot arranged for Napoleon that went hilariously wrong. A thousand tame rather than wild rabbits were bought for the emperor's sport, which when he arrived mistook him for the man who brought them their daily lettuce. Instead of fleeing to be shot they mobbed him, and he was forced to dash back to the safety of his carriage.)

Another book taken from Napoleon's library at St Cloud soon after his 1814 abdication was a *Précis historique de l'exécution du traité de Lunéville*, which had been published in 1801. Whether these possessions of Wellington's were conversation pieces, memorabilia, trophies or all three, they together constitute a remarkable amount of Napoleana amassed by a man who was continually held up as a model of Victorian modesty and self-effacement. Napoleon's busts, statuettes, flags, books, portraits, his sword, his watch, his cook, his sister's house, his statue, two of his mistresses – short of having the emperor himself in an iron cage in the hall at Stratfield Saye, Wellington could hardly have had more trophies of the man he had defeated. A truly modest man does not turn his home into a shrine to his own achievements, but it was certainly an unmistakable way of emphasising and commemorating his victory over someone who had sneeringly referred to him as a 'sepoy general'.

⮔

Some time in 1816 Wellington was asked by a friend of Sir Walter Scott's whether during the battle of Waterloo he had often looked over to the woods from where the Prussians were expected to issue. 'No,' came the answer. 'I looked oftener at my watch than at anything else. I knew if my troops could keep their position till night, that I must be joined by Blücher before morning, and we would not have left Buonaparte an army next day.' What, asked his interlocutor, if his position on the slopes had been forced by the French? 'We had the wood behind to retreat into.' But if that had been forced also? 'No, no...we could have made good the wood against them.' It is clear that what Napoleon regarded as Wellington's greatest tactical weakness at the battle, the forest of Soignies to his rear, Wellington viewed as a source of strength.

As Wellington enjoyed his time in Paris in 1816, Napoleon went over in his mind again and again what had gone wrong the previous year. 'I committed an error in assembling the Chambers,' he said to General Gourgaud in February. 'Everything depended on Waterloo.' Nine days later he told his companion while out riding: 'If I hadn't been foolish enough to let myself be beaten at Waterloo, all would be well. I can't even now conceive how that defeat happened. But don't let's talk any more about that.'[33]

Napoleon nonetheless simply could not leave the subject alone. Only a week later, on 24 February, he was telling Gourgaud that he ought to have assembled the five thousand Imperial Guardsmen in Paris along with the trustworthy section of the National Guard, harangued them, and then used them to dissolve the Chambers when he returned to Paris after Waterloo. 'Blücher and Wellington could not have arrived in time,' he insisted to a privately doubtful Gourgaud, and he said he would have amassed one hundred thousand men to fortify the right bank of the Seine over the following fortnight. The egomania was total; speaking of Josephine to O'Meara two days later, Napoleon even said: 'She, poor woman, fortunately for herself, died in time to prevent her from witnessing the last of my misfortunes.'

Rear-Admiral Sir Pulteney Malcolm succeeded Admiral Cockburn as naval commander of the Cape Station, which included St Helena, in June 1816. Napoleon enjoyed Malcolm's company and the two men saw much of one another before the admiral left the island in July 1817. Lady Malcolm was the daughter of Hon. William Elphinstone and the niece of Admiral Lord Keith, and as Whig social figures the couple knew the Lansdownes, Hollands and Hobhouses. Napoleon liked Clementina Malcolm and her family, and enjoyed teasing her about her Scottishness, but he probably did not know that after every meeting she diligently wrote up their conversations, giving us a fine account of what Napoleon was thinking and saying in this early period of his exile. In one conversation alone, held on 25 June 1816, Napoleon and Malcolm discussed Admiral St Vincent's age and gout, gout in sea officers in general, income tax (which the Corsican Ogre thought 'good and productive'), the poems of Ossian and the tactics of Nelson.

While a house called Longwood was being made ready for him to move into on 10 December, Napoleon resided at The Briars with the Balcombe family, with whom Wellington had stayed on his return from India in 1805. Malcolm received a letter from Wellington in Paris, written on 3 April 1816, saying: 'You may tell "Bony" that I find his apartments at the Elysée-Bourbon very convenient and that I hope he likes mine at the Balcombes'. It is a droll sequel to the affairs of Europe that we should change places of residence.'[34] Wellington was of course joking; Malcolm was not really intended to pass on so cruel and insulting a message.

Soon after Wellington wrote that, a rumour went around Europe that Napoleon had escaped to America. 'We must expect all sorts of him as long as our Earth is burthen'd with him,' wrote Georgina Capel to her mother on her way to see Wellington; 'the only regret I feel is that he had not fallen into Old Blücher's hands and then we should have done with him *pour toujours*.'[35]

Napoleon had not escaped, but was sitting in his bath on 8 May fighting the June 1815 campaign yet again. 'I ought to have stopped on the 16th at Fleurus; beaten the Prussians the same day, the 16th, and then the English on the 17th,' he told Gourgaud from his tub. 'D'Erlon's movement did me great harm.' This realisation that his inaction on the morning of 17 June, and the error which had d'Erlon marching fruitlessly between battlefields the day before, had been disastrous accords closely with modern estimations of the campaign. For, had d'Erlon's presence helped Napoleon utterly to rout Blücher at Ligny, the Prussians could not possibly have arrived at Waterloo, and Wellington would probably not have fought before Brussels, but would have withdrawn his expeditionary force to the Channel ports for yet another British re-embarkation from the continent.

Three days later, on 11 May 1816, Napoleon dictated some notes on Waterloo for a book Gourgaud published in 1818 entitled *La Campagne de 1815*. 'The Emperor is very calm when dictating,' Gourgaud told his journal that day, even though it 'rends my heart by reminding him of our defeat'.[36] Anniversaries meant much to Napoleon. His orders of the day rarely failed to mention them if they augured well; for example, the anniversary of the battle of Austerlitz was never allowed to pass without its memory being used to enthuse his troops. So on 18 June 1816 he was in predictably contemplative mood. A daughter had been born to the Comtesse de Montholon at 6 p.m., and Napoleon consented to stand godfather to the baby, to be called Hélène-Napoléone. After dinner, which surprisingly enough never lasted more than about forty minutes on St Helena, Napoleon reminisced to Las Cases about the events of the previous 18 June:

'Incomprehensible day!' said he in a tone of sorrow; 'Concurrence of unheard-of fatalities! Grouchy! Ney! D'Erlon! Was there treachery or only misfortune? Alas! Poor France!' Here he covered his eyes with his hands. 'And yet', said he, 'all that humans could do was accomplished!' A short time afterwards, alluding to the same subject he exclaimed, 'In that extraordinary campaign, thrice, in less than a week, I saw the certain triumph of France and the determination of her fate slip through my fingers. Had it not been for the desertion of a traitor I should have annihilated the enemy at the opening of the campaign. I should have destroyed him at Ligny if my left had only done its duty. I should have destroyed him at Waterloo if my right had not failed me. Singular defeat, by which, notwithstanding the most fatal catastrophe, the glory of the conquered has not suffered, nor the fame of the conqueror been increased: the memory of one will survive his destruction, the memory of the other will perhaps be buried in his triumph!'[37]

This utter refusal to accord Wellington any credit for the victory, indeed the sentiment that Wellington's reputation might indeed actually suffer from it, was recorded in every telling detail by the acolyte Las Cases.

Only a fortnight later, Napoleon returned to the subject of Waterloo in a long conversation with Sir Pulteney Malcolm on 4 July. Malcolm introduced some of his naval officers to Napoleon, who talked to them for two and a half hours about incidents in his life, as well as about the present 'unsettled' state of Europe. The subjects included the battle of Trafalgar, the Basque Roads, the Toulon fleet and his 1805 invasion plans. During the conversation Napoleon leaned on a window 'in great good humour and frequently laughed out loud'. When the subject turned to Waterloo, he said:

Wellington ought to have retreated, and not fought that battle. For had he lost it, I should have established myself in France, but had I been obliged to follow the English and Prussians, in the end I must have been beaten by the junction of the Allied armies. Wellington risked too much, for by the rules of war I should have gained the battle. I calculated that General Grouchy would have kept the Prussians in check until I beat the English; and he ought to have done so.

Malcolm, who had commanded a naval squadron off the French coast during the 1815 campaign, said that Wellington must have feared that the Belgians would join Napoleon, and asked why he had not attacked on the right of the English and cut them off from the sea. Napoleon replied that he had:

taken into consideration the character of the two generals; one was an hussar, the other an officer of method, who would not move his army without reflection, nor without his supplies. If he had first attacked the English, the Prussians would have been on him at full gallop; and as everything depended on the first onset, he thought it best to begin with the Prussians, believing the English would be somewhat slower, particularly as their cavalry was at some distance from the point of attack. He said that his troops fought well; some few officers were traitors but not a single soldier.

He also said that 'two courses lost him the battle – Grouchy's failing in dealing with the Prussians, and his great charge of cavalry being made half an hour too soon, but they performed nobly'.[38] (After this criticism of Ney, Napoleon went on to praise the English aristocracy as superior to the old French nobility.)

Other accounts of this conversation exist, and, although they differ in some minor respects, they agree on the central feature – that Napoleon claimed he determined his Waterloo strategy according to his reading of Wellington's and Blücher's different military psychologies. Captain Henry Meynell of HMS *Newcastle*, who accompanied Malcolm, records Napoleon as saying 'a General always calculates on the characters of the officers opposed to him'. The Russian commissioner on the island, Count Balmain, reported to the tsar that Napoleon had said of Blücher: 'That drunken hussar, impatient to distinguish himself, would have left everything to succour England ... But although the Prussians did much, the day belongs to Wellington.'[39] Yet this is at best second-hand information, and Balmain never met Napoleon himself, and most probably only had this from Malcolm.

Napoleon's admission that Waterloo was Wellington's victory appears nowhere else. In Las Cases' account of the same conversation, Malcolm is supposed to have told Napoleon: 'The English thought the battle lost, during the whole day, and they acknowledge that it would have been so, but for Grouchy's error.'[40] (Napoleon's regular references to Blücher's drinking might have come from the knowledge of the Prussian hussar's imprisonment for drinking and gambling decades earlier.)

From the Malcolm account it is clear that Napoleon had already worked out in his own mind the explanations for his defeat, blaming a large number of disparate factors and individuals, including, albeit occasionally and parenthetically, himself for not following up Ligny vigorously enough. Wellington was accorded credit only in one (second-hand) account, but any generosity of spirit towards the victor that might have existed quickly receded, and was not seen again in Napoleon's lifetime. He generally wished to portray Wellington as having made an error in ever having fought the battle of Waterloo at all, but also as a plodding, cautious, over-promoted staff officer, in contrast to the dashing, loyal – if supposedly drunken and ambitious – Blücher.

Napoleon made nine 'observations' about the campaign, which he dictated to Gourgaud and which were finally read to his entourage on 26 August. 'What pages!' recorded Las Cases, who clandestinely got them off the island and into print in France. 'They are sickening… The destinies of France suspended by so thin a thread!'[41]

Napoleon's first observation was that France had needed a dictator to reunite the Chambers, quell the Royalist revolt in the Vendée region and restore the country's honour and independence, and that he himself had clearly been that man, judging by the way he stole a march on Wellington and Blücher and surprised them in a manner that 'cannot be underestimated'. The second observation also concerned Napoleon's 'great rapidity and ability' in the opening stage of the campaign, as he moved the Grand Armée between Blücher and Wellington. He congratulated himself on the fact that 'Ce plan fut conçu et exécuté avec audace et sagesse' (This plan was conceived and executed with audacity and wisdom). In his third observation scapegoats began to be introduced. 'The character of several generals had been weakened by the events of 1814;' he wrote, 'they had lost the audacity and resolve and confidence that had brought them so much glory and success in the past.' Next, III Corps was specifically singled out for arriving at Charleroi three hours late on 15 June and Ney was taken to task for 'hesitating' before seizing the Quatre Bras crossroads the following day. 'Always first into the fire, Ney neglected those troops not in his line of sight,' chided Napoleon, before going on to state that the bravery of a commander-in-chief had to be different from that expected of a *général de division*, which in turn should be different from that of a captain of grenadiers, his implication being that Ney had not learned this. Yet he also claimed, quite without justification, that Ney had destroyed Wellington's 5th Division on its arrival from Brussels.

Never has the French soldier shown more courage, more esprit and enthusiasm [declared Napoleon of the battle of Waterloo]; he was full of the feeling of this superiority compared to all the other soldiers of

Europe. His confidence in his emperor was total and had perhaps grown, but he was suspicious and mistrustful towards the other generals. The treasons of 1814 were ever present in his conscience. Every movement he did not understand worried him and he thought himself betrayed.

The fourth observation concerned the treachery of General Bourmont on 14 June and the fear among his troops that there might be more treason afoot. At the start of the battle an old corporal had warned Napoleon that Soult was a traitor, in the middle of it an officer had told Soult that General Vandamme had gone over to the enemy and at its end a dragoon had told Napoleon – again entirely falsely – that General Phénin had also defected. Napoleon put the cry of 'Sauve qui peut!' during the final rout down to treachery and stated, equally fancifully, that although some officers had 'disparu' from the field, many private soldiers who had been wounded committed suicide when they realised the extent of their emperor's defeat.

Napoleon's fifth observation concerned Grouchy's failure to 'culbuter' (overthrow) the Prussian rearguard after Ligny. He claimed that after Grouchy had moved north he had been left with 69,000 men to engage Wellington's supposed 90,000. 'If the Anglo-Dutch army had beaten the 69,000 which marched against it,' he suggested, writing in the third person, 'we could have reproached Napoleon for having miscalculated, but it is true, as even his enemies admit, that without the arrival of Blücher the Anglo-Dutch army would have lost the battle between 8 p.m. and 9 p.m.' Of course Napoleon's British enemies admit nothing of the sort, but his self-justification in several of the nine observations is intimately bound up with his desire to portray Wellington as a bad general. The rest of the fifth observation was taken up with blaming General Guyot for launching a cavalry attack without orders, Grouchy for not arriving on the battlefield and Mortier for having sciatica, which Napoleon complained was 'extremely inconvenient'.

Blücher came in for severe criticism in the sixth observation, for having contravened several fundamental rules of warfare during the Waterloo campaign. Having lost at Ligny, the Prussians should have withdrawn along their supply lines or have joined up with Wellington, but they ought not to have struck northwards towards Wavre. Napoleon was outraged by Blücher's conduct, which was unpredictable and thus disastrous for the French, who had effectively lost him on 17 June, and there is something comic about the emperor complaining that his victorious opponents failed to observe the conventions of warfare. Wellington, he argued in his seventh observation, should have concentrated his cantonments around Brussels, and not have given battle at Quatre Bras at all, where he 'exposed his troops to defeat as they arrived'. The duke, who was referred to as 'le général anglais', ought to have stayed at Waterloo and united his army, as the French could not have arrived until 17 June. In fact, had Wellington not advanced to Quatre Bras he would only have given Ney the opportunity to join with Napoleon on the 16th and annihilate the Prussians, forcing him to retreat to Antwerp. This was the emperor's plan all along, but he could hardly complain if Wellington did not fall in with it.

In his eighth observation, Napoleon argued that 'the English general's decision' to give battle on 18 June was 'against his nation's interests' on the grounds that with her military commitments in India and America, Britain should not have exposed the flower of her youth 'with such lightness of heart in such a deadly struggle'. He then took the Allies to task for daring 'to risk the success of their cause in a risky battle with a force which was more or less equal, and where all the odds were against them'. He further insisted that 'If the Anglo-Dutch army had been destroyed at Waterloo, what good would it have been to the Allies to have had this large number of armies ready to cross the Rhine, the Alps or the Pyrenees?' – he was no doubt assuming that he would have been able to defeat each of them piecemeal. The whole argument smacks of the counterfactual style of history, to which he was so prone on St Helena.

Napoleon was on safer ground when he argued that 'The English general took the decision to give battle at Waterloo based only on the co-operation of the Prussians, but this co-operation could not take place until the afternoon. He was therefore exposed alone from 4 a.m. until 5 p.m. That is to say for thirteen hours. A battle does not normally last longer than six hours; therefore this co-operation was illusory.' Furthermore, Wellington had no idea that Grouchy had been detached and therefore had no reason not to assume that he was faced by the whole French army of over one hundred thousand men. In Napoleon's opinion this, too, ought to have dissuaded him from fighting on the slopes of Mont St Jean. Had the French attacked at 8 a.m., Napoleon believed, the Prussians would have arrived in time only to be repulsed themselves. 'In one day the two armies would have been destroyed,' wrote the ex-emperor, indulging in much wishful thinking. D'Erlon and Grouchy were then jointly blamed for allowing the

Prussians to escape Ligny in good order, whereas if Blücher had been properly routed on 16 June 'the Anglo-Dutch would have had to carry the effort alone of 69,000 French during the day of the 18th; and there can be no Englishmen who would not agree that the result of this struggle was uncertain, and that their army was not arrayed in a manner to take the full brunt of the imperial army for four hours'. In fact, of course, there were (and are) plenty of Englishmen who would vigorously contest that assertion, pointing out that Wellington's dispositions that morning were masterly.

Napoleon went on to blame the rain: 'During the night of the 17th/18th the weather was horrible, which made the ground unusable by 9 a.m. This loss of six hours from daybreak was all to the enemy's advantage. But could their general trust his fate to the weather?' In his denunciation of Wellington's willingness to take unacceptable risks on the 18th, Napoleon went on to ask:

> Could the English general be sure that the Marshal [Grouchy] would lose his way in such a strange manner? The conduct of Marshal Grouchy was as unforeseeable as if his army had been swallowed up by the ground. If Marshal Grouchy had been on the battlefield of Mont St Jean, which the English and Prussian generals believed during the night of the 17th/18th and the whole morning of the 18th, and the weather had allowed the French army to attack by 4 a.m., by 7 a.m. the Anglo-Dutch army would have been cut up, dispersed and defeated.

When he arrived on the field, Blücher 'would have suffered a similar fate'. Equally, if Grouchy had been in position to attack the Prussians at Wavre at dawn on the 18th, they could never have reinforced Wellington's army at Waterloo, which 'would have been utterly beaten by the 69,000 Frenchmen who opposed them'.

Napoleon was even unwilling to accord Wellington any credit for his selection of ground, and for almost anything else. 'The position at Mont St Jean was badly chosen,' he insisted, and 'during the battle the English general did not draw from his numerous cavalry', an absurd observation, unless he meant Sir Hussey Vivian's corps, which was held in reserve and did invaluable work during the rout at the end of the battle. (Of course Napoleon, who had left the field by then, could not have known this.) The former emperor argued that Wellington 'did not believe he would be attacked on his left, he believed he would be attacked on his right', whereas the duke's dispositions on the morning of the battle showed that he was equally prepared for either eventuality. It is impossible to escape the conclusion that Napoleon was rather clutching at straws in this part of his denunciation of his opponent's tactics, and there is an element of hypocrisy in his blaming Wellington for holding his cavalry in reserve only a few paragraphs after he had complained of Guyot's behaviour in denying him the opportunity to do the same thing himself.

The ninth and last observation concerned the overall strategy of the Waterloo campaign, with Napoleon arguing that Wellington and Blücher ought to have moved further north, reunited before Brussels itself and given battle there, leaving a force in the forest of Soignies to slow down and break up the French advance. This would have allowed Wellington to collect further regiments on their way from America to Brussels via Ostend, and would probably have deterred Napoleon from attacking altogether, being outnumbered, he calculated, by two hundred thousand Allied troops to one hundred thousand French. 'This certainly would have been the most advantageous situation for the Allies,' he asserted. Whatever the merits of this particular argument, Napoleon cast them aside in his peroration, a vicious and in many ways ridiculous – coming as it did from the vanquished – attack on the victor's capacities as a soldier, who was at least finally mentioned by name. 'From 15 to 18 June the Duke of Wellington was constantly manoeuvring in a manner that pleased his enemy, he did nothing that his enemy feared he would do,' wrote Napoleon. 'The Anglo-Dutch army had been saved twice during the day by the Prussians…On this day 69,000 French had beaten 120,000 men; their victory was torn away from them between 8 p.m. and 9 p.m. by 50,000 [Prussians].' On top of his other undoubted achievements, Napoleon was clearly a fine revisionist historian.

Yet even writing these observations failed to exorcise Wellington and Waterloo from Napoleon's thoughts. On 4 September, talking to O'Meara about 'the English mode of besieging towns', he said that Wellington's 'immense sacrifice of men at Ciudad Rodrigo and Badajoz by no means compensated for the capture of these places'. A month later he fantasised to O'Meara about Wellington losing Waterloo. 'What a state would England have been in!' he said. 'The flower of your army destroyed, for not a man would have escaped.' If neither Grouchy nor the Prussians had arrived, Napoleon believed that:

> the English army would have been destroyed; they were defeated before midday. I would have gained everything; I had gained

everything. I beat the Prussians; but accident, or more likely destiny, decided that Lord Wellington should gain it, and he did so. It was fortunate; accident and destiny favoured him. I could scarcely believe he would have given me battle, because, if he had retreated, as he ought to have done to Antwerp, I must have been overwhelmed by three or four hundred thousand men coming against me, and against whom I could not possibly resist.[42]

Napoleon then once again mentioned Wellington's decision to fight with a forest to his rear, saying it was *'coglioneria* [foolhardy] ... to hazard a battle in a place where, if defeated, all would have been lost, for he could not retreat'. As Napoleon yet again insisted:

He would have been altogether destroyed; besides, he suffered himself to be surprised by me. He ought to have had all his army encamped from the beginning of June, as he must have known that I intended to attack him: he might have lost everything by it: it was a great fault on his part; but he has been fortunate, and everything he did will meet with applause.

Napoleon then agreed that his intention had been to try to bring down the Tory ministry in London, which he believed would have been the 'immediate' result of destroying Wellington's army. The British public, he believed, would have said that 'it mattered nothing to them whether Napoleon or Louis reigned in France', and was certainly not worth forty thousand British lives.

With Britain knocked out of the coalition, 'the Saxons, Bavarians, Belgians, Wirtemburghers, and others would have joined me; the Russians would have made peace'. After that, 'I would have been quietly seated on the throne, I would have made peace with all.' It must have been a comforting delusion, but in fact the Seventh Coalition would probably have held together after an Allied defeat in June, and even victory at Waterloo would not have saved Napoleon from the vast Allied armies that were converging on France in the summer and autumn of 1815. The European Powers had seen through Napoleon; they were not again about to make the old mistake of concluding separate peace treaties with him.

When the (incorrect) news arrived on St Helena that Wellington had joined the Liverpool ministry, Napoleon fumed further. On 16 November, speaking of his arch-enemy Lord Castlereagh, he told Las Cases that 'Wellington has become his creature! Can it be possible that the modern Marlborough has linked himself in the train of a Castlereagh, and yoked his victories to the turpitude of a political mountebank? It is inconceivable! Can Wellington endure such a thought? Has not his mind risen to a level with his success?'

Contrary to his usual practice with regard to Wellington, on this occasion Napoleon 'yielded, without reserve, to the full expression of his feelings'. We cannot at this remove tell whether the phrase 'the modern Marlborough' was said sarcastically, but his subsequent remarks suggest that it probably was. Furthermore the short, aggressive sentences imply that he was once again indulging in little less than a rant to Las Cases. For now, on 16 November 1816, Napoleon poured out his feelings of resentment to his faithful Las Cases, with 'a degree of warmth which I had never before witnessed in him. His gestures, his features, his tone of voice, were all expressions of the utmost indignation'. Listening to the ex-emperor 'in astonishment' Las Cases heard that Wellington had been responsible for the choice of St Helena, and in Napoleon's opinion:

It is conduct well worthy of him who, in defiance of a solemn capitulation, suffered Ney to perish – Ney, against whom he had so often been engaged on a field of battle! For my own part, it is very certain that I gave him a very terrible quarter of an hour. This usually constitutes a claim on noble minds; his was incapable of feeling it. My fall, and the lot that might have been reserved for me, afforded him the opportunity of reaping higher glory than he has gained by all his victories... Wellington possesses only a special type of talent: Berthier also had his! In this he perhaps excels. But he has no ingenuity... How different from Marlborough, of whom he seems to consider himself as the rival and equal. Marlborough, while he gained battles, ruled Cabinets and guided statesmen; as for Wellington, he has only shown himself capable of following the views and plans of Castlereagh. Madame de Staël said of him, that when off the field of battle, he had not two ideas. The salons of Paris, so distinguished for delicacy and correctness of taste, at once decided that Madame de Staël was right; and the French plenipotentiary confirmed that opinion.[43]

It was an explosion of bile unworthy of one so great as Napoleon Bonaparte, however much the bracing mid-Atlantic winds had chilled his warm Mediterranean blood.

FOURTEEN

A Shrinking Colossus
1817–1821

If such a man as Frederick the Great, or any other man of his cast, were
to take to writing against me, then it would be a different thing; it would
then, perhaps, be time for me to be moved; but as for all the other writers,
whatever be their talents, their efforts will be in vain. My fame will survive:
and when they wish to be admired, they will sound my praise.

NAPOLEON

'I will tell you what will happen when I'm dead and gone, say in
thirty years,' Napoleon told Admiral Malcolm on 11 January 1817.
'They, the Bourbons, will be obliged to raise a monument to my
memory in France; has not your Regent made one for the Stuarts?'
Malcolm answered that indeed he had. Yet, if anything, Napoleon
had underestimated; by 1840 there was a splendid monument to his
memory at his burial-place in Les Invalides, although it was built by
the Orleanist King Louis-Philippe, whose cousins the Bourbons did
not last on the French throne a decade after Napoleon's death.

Soon after this prediction, Napoleon made another. To Captain
Meynell he said that Wellington's abilities 'would one day be of bad
consequence to the English nation, who would expect more from their
army than they had the capacity for, when not guided by superior
knowledge'.[1] After his long tenure as commander-in-chief from 1842
(when he was seventy-three) until his death in 1852, Wellington did
indeed leave the British army ill prepared to fight in the Crimea two
years after he had gone, especially once his chosen successor and
former military secretary, Lord Raglan, had taken over. In a sense it
was fortunate that the Crimean War did not break out during
Wellington's watch at Horse Guards, as otherwise his reputation could
not have failed to be damaged by it.

'At present the King only governs under Wellington,' Napoleon told
Admiral Sir Pulteney Malcolm of Louis XVIII in January, adding that
'there was no real nobility in France, no aristocracy, no leaders of
party'.[2] He did not expand upon his own responsibility for this state of

affairs. The next month he found yet another excuse for his defeat at Waterloo. 'If I had delayed my attack I should have had twelve thousand extra men drawn from the Vendée,' he told Gourgaud on 24 February; 'but who would have guessed that the Vendée could have been so easily pacified?... It is Fate that beat me at Waterloo. The campaign ought to have succeeded. The English and Prussians were taken by surprise in their cantonments.'[3]

Napoleon did indeed have a point; the Vendée region in southern France had in the past risen in support of the Bourbons and had been bloodily suppressed only after many months of desperate resistance. Yet it is doubtful that he would have been stronger had he waited until the Vendée had been pacified, because British reinforcements were also arriving in force in the Low Countries in June 1815. (Over the next six months on St Helena the number of men that Napoleon claimed he had been deprived of at Waterloo because of the Vendée swelled from twelve to thirty thousand.)

At Napoleon's request, Brigadier-General Sir George Bingham, the friendly commander-in-chief of the troops stationed on the island, gave Gourgaud an English book about Waterloo, which Napoleon devoured the moment it was translated. As soon as he had finished it, Napoleon summoned Gourgaud into Longwood's billiard room to hear another series of explanations for the defeat at Waterloo. 'It was a great mistake to employ Ney,' said the Emperor.

> He was unhinged. His past had robbed him of all his energy...I ought to have placed Soult on the left...The eyes of everyone were fixed on Blücher. He knew full well that rewards would be lavished on him, were he to sacrifice himself for the English...I ought not to have employed Vandamme. I ought to have given to Suchet the command I entrusted to Grouchy...Mortier, by leaving the command of the Guard to Beaumont, did me great harm. I ought to have placed Lobau there. Drouot had too much to do... [General Comte de] Friant was incapable of turning the Guard to good account, he is a good soldier but that's all.

Napoleon further criticised Soult for not being as good a chief of staff as Berthier.[4] Several of these criticisms were valid, and have subsequently been supported by military historians, but of course Napoleon was ultimately responsible for the distribution of all the commands he had itemised.

While dictating his memoirs to Gourgaud the following month, Napoleon said that 'he couldn't see the battle very well. He wanted, as at [the battle of] Montmirail, to make a perpendicular attack, and to lead it himself: but Bülow's arrival forced him to remain in a central position. Ney didn't understand this attack.' The theory that Napoleon did not fully appreciate the topography of Waterloo is an intriguing one that re-emerges from time to time. The expert Philip Haythornthwaite believes that one explanation of Napoleon's remark might be that it was a reference to Wellington's 'favourite tactic of deploying as much as possible of his army on the reverse slope of a ridge...Napoleon would only have been able to see clearly those forward elements of Wellington's army deployed on the top of the ridge, or on its forward slope...It was probably the first time in his career that Napoleon had come across such a deliberate use of concealment and it could well have frustrated him as much as it did his marshals who had to contend with it in the Peninsula.' By contrast, when Sir Watkyn Williams Wynn moronically asked Wellington whether he had had a good view of the battle, the duke testily replied: 'I generally like to see what I am about.'

Napoleon returned to the subject of Wellington on 25 March when he was discussing the intricacies of the British peerage with Admiral Sir Pulteney and Lady Malcolm at Longwood. 'He could not understand about Scotch peers being made English peers,' recorded Captain Meynell, and Malcolm explained that since the 1801 Act of Union some Scottish peers had become peers of the United Kingdom. 'He seemed anxious to understand the different degrees of English nobility,' and 'spoke of the titles of Wellington and Nelson and asked who Nelson's title had gone to'.[5] To choose those two, one who had taken his title from a Somerset village, and the other who had taken his surname for his title, could only have further confused the emperor, especially once Malcolm also instanced Earl St Vincent, whose title derived from the cape off which he won his great victory. This might, however, explain why Napoleon had taken so long to get Wellington's nomenclature correct in his Peninsular despatches.

The following day Napoleon came up with the same old reasons for his defeat at Waterloo, but found someone entirely new to blame. 'The plan of the battle will not in the eyes of the historian reflect any credit on Lord Wellington as a general,' he told Dr O'Meara. Wellington should not have fought while the Allies were divided, ought to have encamped before 15 June, should not have fought with the forest of Soignies behind him, and had allowed himself to be surprised. Yet, because of Grouchy's 'great tardiness and neglect in executing his orders' and because General Comte Guyot, who commanded the heavy cavalry, had 'engaged without orders and without my knowledge', he was defeated.

Guyot's action, said Napoleon, robbed him of his reserve and thus any means of rallying his army once Wellington began his general advance at around 7 p.m. 'The youngest general would not have committed the fault of leaving an army entirely without reserve,' he said, but whether it had been 'in consequence of treason or not, I cannot say'. This was a grave slander against Claude-Etienne Guyot, who had retained his command of the Guard's *grenadiers à cheval* under the First Restoration, but who had loyally rejoined Napoleon during the Hundred Days. The idea that the heavy cavalry suddenly charged without preparation or any direct orders is also preposterous – in fact they manoeuvred almost directly in front of Napoleon, who could have prevented the attack from taking place at almost any time. With Ney acting as Napoleon's designated battlefield commander, no direct orders from the emperor himself were required or expected, as he presumably well knew when he was dictating his criticisms. In the rewriting of the events of 18 June 1815, few were to be spared in the attempt to protect the myth of Napoleonic omniscience.

'If Wellington had entrenched himself,' Napoleon told O'Meara, 'I would not have attacked him. As a general his plan did not show talent. He certainly displayed great courage and obstinacy; but a little must be taken away even from that, when you consider that he had no means of retreat, and that, had he made the attempt, not a man of his army would have escaped.' Napoleon believed that Wellington was 'principally indebted for his victory' to 'the firmness and bravery of his troops', a judgment from which the duke himself would probably not have differed, but also to Blücher's arrival. Napoleon believed Blücher deserved 'more credit as a general; because he, though beaten the day before [in fact on the 16th], assembled his troops and brought them into action in the evening. I believe, however, that Wellington is a man of great firmness. The glory of such a victory is a great thing; but in the eye of the historian his military reputation will gain nothing by it.'[6] Of all the predictions Napoleon was so fond of making on St Helena, this must rate as his worst.

Napoleon grossly overestimated the size of Wellington's army. On the morning of the battle he had told his generals that the Anglo-Allied army – or 'the English' as he always called them – outnumbered the French by 'one-fourth' (that is, they numbered around 90,000, when in fact it was closer to 68,000). On St Helena he told O'Meara that he himself had had seventy thousand men of whom fifteen thousand were cavalry, which was fairly accurate, as one might expect, but that 'Lord Wellington had under his command about ninety thousand and 250 pieces of cannon,' which was a wild exaggeration. He admired 'the English as being able to take care of my own' but 'thought little' of the rest of the Anglo-Allied troops. (In this, except for the excellent King's German Legion, Wellington might also not have demurred too much.) Napoleon also believed that Wellington had had between thirty-five and forty thousand specifically 'English' (that is, British) troops, when the true figure was closer to twenty-four thousand. When he saw Bülow's corps arrive, he said he had still thought the odds were 'eighty chances out of a hundred in my favour'. (In fact at the time he had told Soult that he estimated them at sixty-forty.)

The closest Napoleon ever got to praising Wellington on St Helena came when he grudgingly admitted to O'Meara that 'all generals were liable to err, and that whoever committed the least number of faults, should be esteemed the greatest, and that he [Wellington] had committed them as seldom as others'. It was hardly a ringing encomium, but it was the best Wellington was to get.

On 30 March Napoleon and Gourgaud spent four and a half hours in the morning until 10.30 a.m. working on the manuscript of *La Campagne de 1815*. There had been a froideur between the two men, which General Bertrand told Gourgaud had been due to the fact that Gourgaud had quarrelled with Las Cases, and was probably now quarrelling with Montholon. Napoleon's companions in exile were a disputatious and difficult lot, each vying for the regard of their master. With little else useful to do, except to refight Waterloo with him, they regularly fell out among themselves over trifles.

⤴

While Napoleon was fretting about Waterloo, Wellington was putting pressure on Austria to prevent Napoleon's son from inheriting the Duchy of Parma on the death of Napoleon's wife Marie Louise. In late 1816 Tsar Alexander had revealed to the British – without Metternich's knowledge – the existence of a secret but unratified treaty of 31 May 1815 by which Austria, Russia and Prussia had agreed to allow the King of Rome to become the Duke of Parma on Marie Louise's death. The Spanish meanwhile wanted Parma to revert to the infanta, Marie Louisa, the ex-Queen of Etruria, and afterwards to her son. If Madrid got its way the King of Rome – who was also called the Prince of Parma and (by Bonapartists) Napoleon II – would get nothing. The tsar revealed the treaty because Russia had changed sides, wanting a naval station on the Mediterranean from which she could threaten Turkey, something Spain might afford her but Austria would not.

It was Wellington who attempted to offset the danger of an Austro-Spanish clash, by putting pressure on Baron von Vincent, the Austrian ambassador in Paris who had been his liaison officer at Waterloo. Wellington emphasised the injury to Austria's commercial interests in the Mediterranean that might result through hostilities with Spain, and said that he was soon leaving Paris for London and that unless it was dealt with beforehand, Austria might be forced to succumb to *force majeure*. 'You may be convinced that once I have taken my departure, you will never get this matter settled,' he warned. Vincent feared that, with Wellington gone, the Spanish, Russians and French might impose harsh conditions on Austria.

By the treaty of Paris of 10 June 1817, the King of Rome was disinherited, though not specifically by name, and it was agreed that Parma would revert to Maria Louisa on the death of Marie Louise. 'We specially excluded the name of the young Napoleon from the treaty in order to avoid making him a public person,' Wellington reported.[7] As it was, the King of Rome – who on his mother's insistence was now created Duc de Reichstadt – died in July 1832, predeceasing Marie Louise by fifteen years. She, in the meantime, had anyhow lost Parma in a revolution in 1831. In December 1940, Hitler brought Reichstadt's body from Vienna to be deposited next to his father in Paris, in a romantic but fairly naïve attempt to curry favour with Occupied France.

⤳

While his boy was being disinherited by Wellington, Napoleon was still pondering the might-have-beens of the battle of Waterloo. He told O'Meara that it was 'very probable' that had Murat been in charge of the cavalry that day, instead of Ney, France would have won. 'I could not be everywhere,' he told the scribbling surgeon; 'and Murat was the best cavalry officer in the world. He would have given more impetuosity to the charge. There wanted but very little, I assure you, to gain the day for me.'[8] Once the British had formed squares to receive the French cuirassiers, Murat could not have broken them any more than did Ney, unless he had brought up infantry or artillery.

On 20 September, in a discussion with O'Meara about the greatest generals of history, Napoleon ranked Turenne the greatest, Marlborough 'great', Frederick the Great 'beaucoup' and Saxe 'a mere general'. Of course such an opportunity to criticise Wellington could not be lost, and Napoleon said:

> Judging from Wellington's actions, from his despatches, and above all from his conduct towards Ney, I should pronounce him to be *un homme de peu d'esprit, sans générosité, et sans grandeur d'âme* [a man of little spirit, no generosity, and without grandeur of the soul]. Such I know to be the opinion of Benjamin Constant and Madame de Staël...I think history will judge him to be *un homme borné* [a narrow-minded man].'9

That Napoleon judged the views of de Staël and Constant to be worth while, despite having exiled one and been overthrown by the other, shows how deep his loathing of Wellington was by then, as well as his residual respect for the views of Parisian intellectual salon society. He anyhow seems to have been misinformed about the views of Madame de Staël, who had written to Wellington as recently as 7 May to say that 'the conviction has spread that you sincerely intend to do good to poor France, and, in fact, to conquer is not enough, one must build in order to be the first man of modern times'.

On 20 October, having spent the morning dictating to Montholon his thoughts on Marlborough's Italian campaigns, Napoleon sent for Gourgaud to discuss the topic to which his mind constantly returned. 'Waterloo was lost because Grouchy failed to rejoin us,' he lamented. 'Poor France! – to be beaten by those rascals. But it's true – they had already beaten us at Crécy and Agincourt. I felt too confident of beating them. I had guessed their numbers, but probably I ought to have waited another two weeks. Perhaps I was wrong in attacking. Russia and Austria would certainly not have acted against me.'10 In fact the Austrians and Russians were on their way with vast armies to do exactly that.

Not only was Wellington not allowed any credit for winning Waterloo, but by 9 November Napoleon even discounted one of his important Peninsular victories, the battle of Busaco. Napoleon told O'Meara that Marshal Masséna had been so ill in Portugal that he could not sit on horseback or inspect his troops, neither of which was true. He put down Masséna's defeat to his 'not being able to reconnoitre properly', adding that 'had Masséna been what he was formerly, he would have been able to follow Wellington so closely as to be able to attack him, while entering the Lines [of Torres Vedras] before Lisbon, before he could have taken up his position properly'. It was true that Masséna failed to carry out a proper reconnaissance of Wellington's position before the battle of Busaco on 27 September 1810, but this was not due to ill-health.

'I cannot persuade myself', the over-confident Masséna had grandiosely declared to his staff the day before, 'that Lord Wellington will risk the loss of a reputation by giving battle. But if he does, I have him. Tomorrow we shall effect the capture of Portugal, and in a few days I shall drown the leopard.' That night, as Wellington slept in his cloak among his troops on Busaco Ridge, Massséna was with Madame Lebreton in their tent, through the flaps of which aides-de-camp had to shout urgent information.

Such was the anger Napoleon directed against Wellington by the end of 1817 that he even described his former antagonist as a 'coward'. He told Gorgaud that the Bonapartist letter-writer Madame Fortunée Hamelin had reported from Paris 'that Wellington has no courage. He acted out of fear. He had one stroke of fortune, and knows that such fortune never comes twice. He knows well enough what would happen in a year or two if I were at the head of a hundred thousand Frenchmen.'[11] (Born in 1776 in Santo Domingo, Madame Hamelin married an army contractor at sixteen but thereafter, in the words of the editor of her correspondence, 'the marital state did not constitute too heavy a burden upon her', and she became intimate with a number of prominent men of the First Empire.[12] She is thought possibly to have had an affair with Napoleon himself, and certainly idolised him and stayed in contact with his court when he was on St Helena.)

Napoleon's self-delusion went a stage further the next month when in January 1818 he told O'Meara that 'Those English who are lovers of liberty will one day lament with tears having gained the battle of Waterloo.' His rationale was that while he had proposed making education available to all, even the peasantry, Europe was now in the hands of 'triumvirs, associated together for the oppression of mankind, the suppression of knowledge and the restoration of superstition'. Lady Holland would have agreed; that year she bought a bronze Canova bust of Napoleon and erected it on a nine-foot column in the grounds of Holland House, with an inscription proclaiming that on a 'distant, sea-girt island, harsh men the hero keep'.

Wellington himself never denied that some of Napoleon's reforms had been beneficial for France. On a journey through the country in August 1818 he had an hour and a half's 'very agreeable' conversation with

Thomas Creevey, 'principally about the improvements going on in France, which had been begun by Bonaparte – land, etc., etc....' (During their 130-mile trip, Creevey – a true Radical – hated the 'scanty' fare, 'commonest' champagne and 'dirty maids' at their uncomfortable, 'miserable concern' of an inn, whereas the Tory duke 'seemed quite as pleased and well satisfied as if he had been in a palace'.)

Nor was Wellington generally disrespectful of the French army's conduct at Waterloo, usually taking pains to praise it in what one listener called 'the highest terms'. Only on one occasion is he recorded as being anything but complimentary, when at Stratfield Saye in March 1820 he told the diplomat George Chad that militarily he had never seen the French 'behave ill, except at the end of the battle of Waterloo; whole battalions ran away and left their arms piled, and as for Cambronne he surrendered without a word'.[13] It was a harsh judgment; for when asked by a woman whether British soldiers had ever run away he had once answered: 'Madam, <u>all</u> soldiers run away.'

∽

In the early hours of Friday, 11 February 1818, on the rue des Champs Elysées, a gun went off in the direction of Wellington's carriage as it turned into the narrow entrance to his residence. Wellington did not lower his carriage window as he assumed it had been a sentry's musket discharging by mistake, but closer inspection revealed that he had been the subject of an assassination attempt. The Parisian police arrested Marie-André-Nicolas Cantillon, a Bonapartist sub-lieutenant of hussars whose alibi quickly broke down. As he could nonetheless not be proved to have been at the scene, at least to the satisfaction of the (Parisian) jury, he was acquitted and merely demoted to sergeant, prompting Wellington to comment wryly to Lord Clancarty: 'In these virtuous days the greatest crime a man can be guilty of is to denounce the crime of another, even though the crime should be a plot to assassinate a third person!'[14]

To add to the threat of corporeal assassination, Wellington had to deal with the character assassination that Lord Byron meted out to him after 1819, when his poem *Don Juan* was published. In the ninth canto, Byron, who could forgive Wellington neither for defeating his hero nor for sleeping with more than one woman he himself coveted, penned several slighting references to the duke, such as:

And I shall be delighted to learn who,
Save you and yours, have gained by Waterloo?

Never had mortal man such opportunity,
Except Napoleon, or abused it more:
You might have saved fallen Europe from the vanity
Of tyrants, and been blest from shore to shore.

Oh Wellington,
Waterloo has made the world your debtor –
(I wish your bards would sing it rather better).

And now – what is your fame? Shall the Muse tune it ye?
Now – that the rabble's first vain shouts are o'er?
Go! Hear it in your famished country's cries!
Behold the world! And curse your victories!

You did great things: but not being great in mind,
You left undone the greatest – and mankind.

Though as an Irishman you love potatoes,
You need not take them under your direction;
And half a million for your Sabine farm
Is rather dear! – I'm sure I mean no harm.

Byron did indeed mean harm, but he inflicted none as Wellington heartily despised all the Romantic poets. 'I hate the whole race,' he said. 'There is no believing a word they say…There never existed a more worthless set than Byron and his friends – poets praise fine sentiments and never practise them.'[15]

(Byron, travelling in a replica of Napoleon's coach that he had commissioned, etched his name on the wall of Hougoumont, a fact that the 1838 edition of *Murray's Handbook for Travellers on the Continent* was keen to point out to tourists. In a conversation with his cousin Captain George Byron and his half-sister Augusta in 1816, Byron said that after due consideration he regarded himself as 'the greatest man existing'. When his cousin interjected, 'Except Bonaparte,' the poet exclaimed: 'God, I don't know that I do except even him!')

Wellington was hardly more impressed with Fleury de Chaboulon's *Memoirs of the Private Life, Return and Reign of Napoleon in 1815*, which was published in 1820 and attempted to prove, among other things, that the Prussians had won Waterloo. The author had been the sub-prefect of Rheims who had travelled to Elba in February 1815 to brief Napoleon on the level of discontent in France. Commenting on the book to Lady Shelley, Wellington rather ungratefully said that 'Blücher's chief merit in that affair consisted in avoiding an engagement with Grouchy's inferior force. He kept in mind the all-important object of joining the English, in order that the Prussians may profit by their victory.' The rest of the conversation was spent in mocking Blücher's 'strange hallucination' that he had been made pregnant by a Frenchman. 'The Duke of Wellington assures that he knows this to be a fact,' wrote Lady Shelley, who had the decency to admit that 'While we laugh, our hearts reproach us.'[16] In fact, Blücher – who was prone to fits of melancholia and who died that year – had declared himself to be have been made 'pregnant by an elephant', a Berlin colloquialism of the day meaning to go a little mad, and was not intended as a serious claim of pachydermal penetration. It is true that Blücher had at one point claimed that the French had heated the floor of his room to force him to walk on tiptoe.[17]

Earlier that month, having heard from Lord Ellesmere that Sir Hudson Lowe was mistreating Napoleon on St Helena – information that Ellesmere had received from his cook – Wellington had written: 'I always thought Lowe was the most unfit person to be charged with the care of Buonaparte's person. But I don't believe your cook's stories. On the contrary, I believe Buonaparte is in very good health, as well provided for as a man can be on St Helena.'[18] Wellington had the previous month read Napoleon's *Observations* on Waterloo as published by Las Cases, which were sent to him from Paris by Baron von Vincent. He described the book as 'very interesting. I haven't the slightest doubt it comes from Bonaparte. I do not say he wrote it, because it is better written than he could write, but he furnished the facts and gave the ideas; and I think he wrote a part, above all the chapter [Number 8] on observation.'

Although Wellington did not deign to comment point by point on Napoleon's observations on that occasion, he did discuss the Waterloo campaign in detail with the diarist Charles Greville on a carriage journey to shoot at Lord Granville's country home Wherstead that December. He said that 'Bonaparte was certainly ignorant' of the contingent he had left at Hal and that 'The French army was the best army that was ever seen and that in the previous operations Bonaparte's march upon Belgium was the finest thing that was ever done – so rapid and so well combined.'

In Wellington's estimation, Napoleon's 'object was to beat the armies in detail, and this object succeeded insofar as he attacked them separately'. The duke then admitted that 'they certainly were not prepared for this attack, as the French had previously broken up the roads by which their army advanced; but as it was the summer this did not render them impassable'.[19] This was hardly any sort of *mea culpa*, yet he was giving a very honest account, almost admitting, for the first time since the Duchess of Richmond's ball, that he had indeed been surprised by Napoleon on 15 June.

As a fascinated Greville went on to record: 'He says that Bonaparte beat the Prussians in a most extraordinary way, as the battle [of Ligny] was gained in less than four hours; but that it would probably have been more complete if he had brought a greater number of troops into action, and not detached so large a body against the British corps.' Wellington estimated Ney as having had forty thousand men at Quatre Bras – in fact there were 24,000 in action but 44,500 in the near vicinity – and he said 'that the attack was not so powerful as it ought to have been with such a force'.

Greville then asked about Napoleon's errors in the campaign. Wellington replied that 'he thought he had committed a fault in attacking him in the position of Waterloo; that his object ought to have been to remove him as far as possible from the Prussian army, and that he ought consequently to have moved upon Hal, and to have attempted to penetrate by the same road by which the Duke himself had advanced. He had always calculated upon Bonaparte doing this, and for that purpose he had posted twenty thousand men ... at Hal.' (In fact it had been closer to seventeen thousand.) Wellington went on to say that his position at Waterloo had been 'uncommonly strong' because of the 'admirably situated' farmhouses of Hougoumont and La Haie Sainte.

By January 1821 the European situation had so . worsened that Wellington seems to have considered Napoleon's overthrow a mistake, for the first time since his extraordinary letter to Bathurst of November 1813 suggesting that Napoleon be allowed to keep his throne. Speaking to Metternich's mistress Princess Lieven, the wife of the Russian ambassador to London, while playing piquet (a card game for two), Wellington commented on the Bourbons' ousting of the King of Naples: 'None of that family is any good. As long as the Bourbons hold four thrones there will be no peace in Europe. We have made a tremendous mistake in getting rid of Bonaparte. He is the man we ought to have had. We should not be so badly off with him as we are without him.' Princess Lieven wrote to Metternich the next day: 'The last remark is not new to me; for the past year he had returned to this idea at every available opportunity.'[20]

It might well be that Wellington's repeated comments to the princess should be taken at face value, but a far more likely explanation is that the duke was trying to impress on Metternich via Princess Lieven – whom he intensely mistrusted – the gravity of the Neapolitan situation and of other European issues, using the spectre of Napoleon's possible reintroduction on to the world scene by the British to underline his seriousness. Equally they might have been said largely for their shock value, and given too literal an interpretation by the princess.

Far less serious was the 'very odd story' he told Harriet Arbuthnot that March about how in 1812 Napoleon had tried to distract the French from the Russian humiliation by making the Paris *corps de ballet* dance 'without their undergarments!' (Wellington later apologised for this absurd tale.)[21] He made a more seemly crack at a dinner in the Admiralty on 6 May in the company of the Duke of York, the Marquess of Huntly and John Croker. In a discussion about the cuirass, the cavalry breastplate of which Wellington did not approve, he was asked whether the French cuirassiers had not 'come up very well at Waterloo'. 'Yes,' he replied, 'and they went down very well too.'

No one around the Admiralty dining table knew it that evening, or indeed were to know it until early July, but at 5.49 p.m. the previous day – Saturday, 5 May 1821 – Wellington's great opponent had breathed his last. As Las Cases was told, 'at the very instant when the cannon was announcing the setting of the sun, his great soul quitted the earth'.[22] Lowe was petty to the end and beyond; he objected to the presence of the word 'Napoleon' on the tombstone, along with the former emperor's dates and places of birth and death, and insisted on the addition of the word 'Bonaparte'. Montholon and Bertrand decided that they would prefer no inscription at all to one that denied their master's imperial status.

Wellington's spirit was even present at the interment. It was said that at Napoleon's military funeral at noon on 9 May the British regimental flags that were dipped to his coffin bore the battle honours of Talavera and the Pyrenees.[23] (Certainly when Chateaubriand years later visited the Plantation House from where the government of St Helena was conducted, he saw a portrait of Wellington and pictures of his battles, along with a glass-fronted cabinet containing a piece of the Waterloo elm tree. It had somewhat incongruously been placed between an olive branch gathered from the Mount of Olives and some ornaments worn by South Sea islanders.)

The news of Napoleon's death arrived in London on 4 July, but caused little stir. Mrs Arbuthnot recorded how it made 'much less sensation than the death of Lady Worcester', Wellington's beautiful twenty-eight-year-old niece who had succumbed to an inflammation from having a cold bath after dancing at a ball at the Prince Regent's London residence Carlton House. When Wellington called on Mrs Arbuthnot, he made the hardly modest remark: 'Now I may say I am the most successful general alive.'[24]

It is not certain exactly where Wellington was when he heard the news of Napoleon's death, but for many years he enjoyed telling the tale that he had been at Madame Craufurd's salon in Paris. According to the version he told Lord Mahon in 1831, Lady Salisbury in 1833 and Thomas Raikes in 1843, he was present with Talleyrand when Madame Craufurd exclaimed, 'Mon Dieu, quel événement!' (My God, what an event!), to which the famous wit replied: 'Ce n'est pas un événement, c'est une nouvelle' (It's not an event, it's an item of news).[25] Mahon noted that, in telling the anecdote, Wellington pronounced the emperor's name as 'Napoléon, à la française'.

In fact it is doubtful that Wellington was actually present at all, or even in France when the news arrived. Talleyrand was at the Russian ambassador Pozzo di Borgo's house at the time, and received it via Sir John Strafford and the French foreign minister Etienne Denis Pasquier. 'Both affected indifference and then spoke of Bonaparte in a detached way,' reported Strafford, who made no mention of Wellington being present, as he surely would have had he been.[26] For three of Napoleon's greatest enemies to have attended the same gathering and to have heard of his death there would have made irresistible copy for Strafford, who had been twice wounded serving under Wellington in the Peninsula and had commanded the 2nd British Brigade at Waterloo. Wellington's has all the hallmarks of an invented anecdote, of which Talleyrand inspired many.

On 6 July, two days after the news was received in London, John Cam Hobhouse recorded in his diary that he was 'glad to hear that the Duke of Wellington the other night at Almack's [Club] talked with great admiration of Napoleon', which seems to place him in London at the time the news was received. Three days later, on the 9th, the Duchess of Wellington wrote that she was contemplating suicide over her husband's ill-treatment of her and his threats of separation, but her letter gives no hint of where Wellington was at the time.[27]

Wellington was in London on 27 July when King George IV, who had succeeded his father the previous year, dined with him. Afterwards he went on to 'a magnificent ball at Almack's', given by the French ambassador extraordinary, the Duc de Grammont, and he wore the Order of St Esprit, the highest Bourbon chivalric decoration, which had been bestowed upon him by Louis XVIII and was reputed to be worth £25,000. Its two largest diamonds had once been in Louis XIV's St Esprit and had later been mounted in Napoleon's sword. (When the order was suppressed after the 1830 revolution, Wellington had the two gems made into earrings for his daughter-in-law.)[28]

The following year, in October, Wellington attended the Congress of Verona, which had been assembled to discuss the worsening situation in Spain. He had already had an opportunity of conversing with Napoleon's eleven-year-old son, the Duc de Reichstadt, in Vienna in September. 'I passed part of the day in his company,' he reminisced to Lord Mahon eighteen years later. 'He seemed a fine lad – educated just like the archdukes.' Mahon asked whether the ex-King of Rome seemed to be aware of the influence Wellington had had on his fate. 'I cannot tell,' replied the duke, 'he was civil to me.'

So too was Reichstadt's mother, Marie Louise, with whom Wellington played écarté for gold napoléon coins that November, 'the word "Napoleon" frequently passing between them in payments for the game'. When Wellington went to dine with Napoleon's former wife he found that they had once had the same chef. Having worked for Napoleon, he had entered Wellington's service after Waterloo and left it when the Allies withdrew from France in 1818, only to seek employment with Marie Louise again. Having heard from him Wellington's favourite dish, Marie Louise said to the duke that she was 'very sorry indeed that I could not get any roast mutton for you'. Although they had met briefly at Schönbrunn during the Congress of Vienna, they had not encountered one another there much, not least because Marie Louise still sympathised with her husband while he was on Elba. She clearly was not entirely committed to him, however. Wellington heard years later that she had said that the duke 'little knows the service he has done me by winning the battle of Waterloo', because she had become pregnant by her one-eyed aide-de-camp General Count Adam von Neipperg, whom she later married, and if Napoleon had won 'she feared she would have had to have returned to him in that state'.[29]

It was the publication of the terms of Napoleon's will that seems to have permanently soured Wellington's view of the ex-emperor, which until then he had little qualms about burnishing.[30] Hitherto, the greater a commander Napoleon was deemed to be, the greater was the reputation of his eventual vanquisher. Yet the fifth clause of the fourth codicil of Napoleon's will, written in his own hand and signed and sealed at Longwood on 24 April 1821 – when he knew he was dying – completely changed Wellington's attitude towards the reputation and memory of his former antagonist.

The clause read:

Item: Ten thousand francs to the sub-officer Cantillon, who has undergone a trial upon the charge of having attempted to assassinate Lord Wellington, of which he was pronounced innocent. Cantillon had as much right to assassinate that oligarch as the latter had to send me to perish upon the rock of St Helena. Wellington, who proposed this outrage, attempted to justify himself by pleading the interests of Great Britain. Cantillon, if he really had assassinated that peer, would have excused himself, and have been justified by the same motives, the interests of France, to get rid of a general who, moreover, had violated the Capitulation of Paris [that is, the St Cloud Convention] and by that had rendered himself responsible for the martyrs Ney, La Bédoyère, etc; and for the crime of having pillaged the museums, contrary to the text of the treaties.[31]

Ten thousand francs was worth about £500 in 1821, a useful sum for an unemployed veteran. Elsewhere in the same codicil, Napoleon had given one hundred thousand francs 'to the widow, son or grandson of our aide Muiron, killed at our side at Arcola, covering us with his body'; one hundred thousand francs to the son or grandson of Baron du Thiel, who commanded the Auxonne academy which Napoleon had attended; one hundred thousand francs to the descendant of General Dugommier, his commander-in-chief at Toulon who had helped him up the important first rungs of the military ladder; and one hundred thousand francs to the descendant of Gasparin, the Convention deputy who had 'protected and authorised' Napoleon's plan to capture the city.

Yet because the generous terms of the 1814 abdication no longer applied after his Hundred Days' adventure – as Napoleon well knew – there was no money to pay off these and many other bequests, which totalled 6.81 million francs, although Lady Holland did receive a gold snuffbox which the pope had given Napoleon in 1797. Napoleon also left other angry denunciations behind; an earlier codicil dated 21 April stated that 'the unfortunate result of the two invasions of France, when she still had so many resources left, is to be attributed to the treason of Marmont, Augereau, Talleyrand and Lafayette'. Napoleon's brother

Louis, who finally settled in Italy after Holland was annexed in 1810, wrote books under the pseudonym Comte de St Leu, one of which angered Napoleon so much that he wrote in his will: 'I pardon Louis for the libel he published in 1820; it is full of false assertions and falsified documents.' Their brother Lucien interpreted this as actually meaning: 'I do not pardon my brother, and I invite all my friends to share my resentment.'[32]

Napoleon's cry of rage against Wellington from beyond the grave was unworthy of him. It was also unfair, as in fact Wellington had saved Napoleon's life from the Prussians and Royalists after Waterloo, and had played no part in the choice of St Helena as his final destination. Yet Napoleon could not have known this, and as Ferdinand Gregorius wrote in his work *Corsica* in 1855: 'Not to avenge oneself is held to disgrace a Corsican. The obligation of vengeance is with them a natural sentiment, a consecrated passion.' Napoleon had spoken of the assassination of Wellington before. After O'Meara had told him that his incarceration on St Helena was deemed 'useful' to the British Government, Napoleon had exploded:

> Would it not have been <u>useful</u> to me to have procured the assassination of Nelson or Wellington? Would it not have been <u>useful</u> to the French nation to get rid of all the Allied troops by poisoning the bread and water? Would it not be <u>useful</u> to them to assassinate Wellington? It is not the utility of an act which is to be considered, it is its justness.[33]

The Cantillon bequest lowered Napoleon in the eyes of many of his admirers. Like the execution of the Duc d'Enghien, it was held to show all too clearly his Corsican antecedence; it looked like the action of a *bandito* or a *mafioso* rather than a statesman and emperor. Even John Cam Hobhouse had to admit that it was 'a criminal error' which 'gives proof of a selfish malignity unworthy of a great man and a great soldier'.[34]

The bequest had a predictable effect on Wellington himself. In 1826, having driven past the parish pump at Aldgate in his carriage, he told John Croker:

> All those codicils to his will in which he bequeathed millions to the right and left, and amongst others left a legacy to the fellow who tried to assassinate me, is further proof of his littleness of mind; the property he really had he had already made his disposition of. For the payment

of all those other high-sounding legacies, there was not the shadow of a
fund. He might as well have drawn bills for ten millions on that pump
at Aldgate. While he was writing all these magnificent donations, he
knew that they were all in the air, all a falsehood. For my part I can see
no magnanimity in a lie; and I confess that I think one who could play
such tricks but a shabby fellow.[35]

Five years later, when Lord Mahon observed that the Cantillon
bequest had been the 'greatest blot' on Napoleon's character,
Wellington agreed, shaking his head with a 'sad and serious expression', sorry that his old adversary had so fallen below the level of
events.

Cantillon received some money from Napoleon's executors, in small
instalments between 1823 and 1826, through legal representation in
the French courts. He does not seem to have pursued his claim for the
total figure. His wife did, however, and in August 1854 demanded the
balance from the commission set up to honour the terms of Napoleon
I's will. The commission declared Napoleon I to have been of
unsound mind when dictating this particular codicil. Madame
Cantillon's claim for 1,200 francs was rejected by the commission in
April 1855; perhaps it was felt that paying it would hardly have gilded
the lily of Anglo-French amity at a time when the two allies were
fighting in the Crimea together. Cantillon died in July 1869 without
pressing for further funds.[36]

FIFTEEN

Remembering with Advantages
1822–1835

Soldiers generally win battles;
generals generally get the credit for them.

NAPOLEON

In February 1822, the under-secretary for war, Sir Robert Horton, fetched from the War Office some papers to amuse Wellington and Harriet Arbuthnot about what Napoleon had told Las Cases he would have done had the then Prince Regent responded positively to his 'Themistocles' letter and allowed him to retire to England. Mrs Arbuthnot recalled how they showed that Napoleon had

> depended greatly upon his *succès de société*, thought that he should soon have gained *l'opinion publique* and would soon have been restored to his former power. These were his feelings when he was writing to the Regent, 'J'ai terminé ma carrière politique'! He must have thought John Bull a greater fool than he really is.

Wellington was therefore under no illusions about Napoleon's mendacity when later that year Dr Barry O'Meara published his two-volume work entitled *Napoleon in Exile, or A Voice from St Helena, The Opinions and Reflections of Napoleon on the Most Important Events of his Life and Government in his Own Words, by his Late Surgeon*. Wellington bought it as soon as it was published and even had it bound, which he did not always do. Dedicated 'with Her Ladyship's permission' to Lady Holland, it was a pæan to O'Meara's former patient and full of criticisms of his enemies. From Wellington's extensive pencilling in the margin of the volumes in the Apsley House library it is easy to ascertain which parts most interested him.

O'Meara reproduced a flattering Romanesque cameo portrait of

Napoleon in profile for his frontispiece, in which a handsome emperor wore a laurel crown, and the text added that it was 'an excellent like-ness' and had been presented to O'Meara by Madame Mère, showing her son before the battle of Marengo, 'previous to the time when Napoleon became corpulent'. Across the text Wellington scribbled: 'A Lye. See the … of the day.' Unfortunately most of the sentence is illeg-ible, but it seems that Wellington denied that Napoleon had been as good-looking as his propaganda portraits suggested.[1]

After that, Wellington marked every distortion made by Napoleon as recorded by O'Meara. He put a cross beside the claim that the first consul had ordered Admiral Brueys to enter Alexandria Harbour in 1798, implying that it would have prevented the disaster of Nelson's victory at the Nile. In fact only a week before the battle Brueys had urged Napoleon that his fleet's security depended upon an immediate refit at Toulon, which expert advice Napoleon had ignored.

Similarly, Wellington marked Napoleon's claim that the Congress of Vienna had secretly decided to move him from Elba to St Helena in 1814, which it was claimed 'contributed to determine Napoleon to attempt the recovery of his throne'. Napoleon's denigration of Soult as 'an excellent minister at war, or major-general of an army' who did not have the stuff of an independent commander in him, also rated a pencil mark. Wellington also noted Napoleon's declaration that after Waterloo he had wanted to live in England or America 'in the most profound retreat … a stranger to every political occurrence', as well as Napoleon's opinion that Longwood was 'the worst abode in the world' on 'the worst part of the island'.

Whenever Napoleon mentioned the Waterloo campaign, Wellington marked the passage. 'Before twelve o'clock I had succeed-ed,' stated Napoleon, 'everything was mine, I may say, but accident and destiny decided it otherwise.'[2] In fact the battle had not even begun much before noon. Wellington also marked Napoleon's allega-tion that in 1802 the British ambassador to Paris, Lord Whitworth, had offered him a bribe of thirty million francs to give up French claims over Malta, although in fact this probably did occur, as Whitworth had written to the British Cabinet about the necessity for a 'douceur' for Napoleon and a 'consideration' for his immediate entourage. Wellington also marked the much more unlikely suggestion that on his return from Elba he had an agreement with the Emperor of Austria that 'if I gave him up Italy, he would not join the coalition against me', a deal only ruined by 'that *imbécile*' Murat. As Austria was an integral part of the coalition then based in Vienna it is very unlikely that this was anything more than Napoleonic wishful thinking, or mischief-making.

Wellington also marked Napoleon's claim to have been so badly wounded above the knee during the Italian campaign that the surgeons thought it might be necessary to amputate his leg, and that he had often been wounded but it had always been kept secret.[3] In fact Napoleon was hardly ever scathed in battle, only ever receiving two mild wounds at Toulon in 1793 and Ratisbon in 1809.

Napoleon's further contention that Marshal Oudinot had offered his services in 1815, and even took an oath of allegiance, was particularly malicious; in fact Oudinot had remained conspicuously loyal to the Bourbons and did very well as a result, commanding the Royal Guard and becoming minister of state. Similarly, Wellington noted Napoleon's statement that the battle of Copenhagen in which Nelson captured sixteen Danish ships-of-the-line had not inconvenienced him, and was of 'but little consequence. I had plenty of ships and only wanted seamen.' (In fact eighteen ships-of-the-line had been burned, sunk or captured by Nelson, wrecking Napoleon's naval plans for years into the future.) Wellington was also sceptical about Napoleon's boast that he had once 'continued at his labours for three days and nights, without lying down to sleep'.[4]

Napoleon's assertion that Louis XVIII had asked for the return of his throne after the battle of Marengo, and that he had replied that it 'could not be effected without his having passed over the bodies of five hundred thousand Frenchmen' was noted by a clearly doubtful Wellington, although this had in fact happened. In 1800 Napoleon had written back to Louis XVIII that it would have resulted in one hundred thousand corpses – not five hundred thousand – but in the event of course the death toll was considerably higher than either figure.

Wellington also noted Napoleon's contention that the Anglo-Allied army at Waterloo had numbered 90,000 men and 250 cannon, a huge inflation of the correct figure of 68,000 and 146 cannon. There is also a cross in the margin beside the sentence about 'the arrival of Blücher, to whom the victory is more to be attributed than to Wellington, and more credit due as a general'.[5] The perennial complaint that Wellington had fought with the forest of Soignies to his rear also rated a pencilled line.

Wellington failed to give credence to the absurd allegation that, before he went to Elba, Napoleon had been offered asylum in England by Castlereagh, who 'said that I should be very well treated there, and much better off than in Elba'. The statement that the equipping of the Waterloo campaign had been financed with money 'raised in London' also merited a disbelieving mark from Wellington, as did the declaration that the Princess of Wales had offered to visit Napoleon on Elba. In fact Caroline had every intention of visiting Napoleon, telling his wife Marie Louise at a dinner at the Hôtel d'Angleterre at Lausanne on 23 September 1814 that she was a warm admirer of his.[6] Her continental journeying between August 1814 and March 1815 took her to Rome and the first visit she paid there was to Lucien Bonaparte, but although she came within sight of Elba as she sailed from Civitavecchia to Livorno, she seems to have resisted the temptation to land while Napoleon was still resident there.

Wellington was more accurate in marking Napoleon's claim that he had 'commanded an army at twenty-two years of age', when in fact he had still been a lieutenant-colonel of volunteers at that age. (Napoleon was twenty-six on 26 October 1795 when he was given command of the Army of the Interior.) Slowly and methodically, therefore, Wellington was noting down all the parts of the Napoleonic myth whose truth he doubted.

Napoleon's assertion that he would have pardoned d'Enghien, who had offered him his services in return for his life, was marked in pencil, as was his statement that the pope had been well and fairly treated, and that Napoleon had plans for Paris to replace Rome as 'the centre of the Christian world'. Similarly, the remark that 'No force or compulsion' had been used to effect Ferdinand VII of Spain's abdication, and O'Meara's assertion that Wellington had 'narrowly escaped death by drowning at St Helena' merited marks, as did Napoleon's blaming of the Vendéans for denying him thirty thousand men at Waterloo, and the statement that Masséna had only lost in the Peninsula 'due to the bad state of his health'.

There were a number of other minor assertions made by Napoleon in the two volumes which Wellington deemed worthy of incredulous annotation, but overall he seems only to have marked the more outrageous and easily disprovable claims made by the ex-emperor. Wellington had already stated that Napoleon was an inveterate liar; this book could only have confirmed him in the opinion. Of course it is possible that O'Meara simply invented some of the misstatements he attributed to Napoleon, but as they so closely matched other remarks made to Gourgaud, Las Cases, Montholon and others on St Helena this is unlikely.

One result was that when General Comte Philippe-Paul de Ségur published his *Histoire de Napoléon et de la Grande Armée pendant l'année 1812*,

Wellington decided to go on to the offensive against the dead ex-emperor. Ségur, who had been a *général de brigade* during the Russian campaign, had dedicated his book to the veterans of the Grande Armée, and wrote in the preface of 'that prodigious genius and his gigantic feats, without which we should never have known the extent to which human energy, glory and misfortune may be carried'.[7] Wellington thought Ségur 'a great admirer of Napoleon and not a *faux frère*', yet Ségur was insufficiently admiring for some Bonapartists, and Gourgaud challenged the author to a duel over what he regarded as the book's unsympathetic tone towards Napoleon, wounding Ségur in the process.

Once he had read Ségur's book, Wellington set about researching Napoleon's 1812 campaign in painstaking detail, examining all the published information he could find on the subject. He intended to write a long study, but told Mrs Arbuthnot that he would not publish it, 'as a critique of that sort, with his name to it, would expose him to endless persecution and, even without his name, the author would soon be detected, as no other person could write such a criticism'.[8] Wellington had no intention of publishing and being damned. He nonetheless spent a great deal of time in 1825 researching and then writing a devastating fifty-three-page analysis of the 1812 Russian campaign, which, as Mrs Arbuthnot noted, 'even to my ignorant mind, has proved that Bonaparte committed the grossest faults'. The memorandum did appear as an appendix in the Reverend Gleig's *Life of Arthur, 1st Duke of Wellington* in 1862, and again in the third volume of the Duke's *Despatches, Correspondence and Memoranda*, edited by his son and published between 1867 and 1880.

Gleig said Wellington had set out 'to demonstrate that the true cause of Napoleon's failure was not the premature coming of the winter, but the false principle upon which he carried on war – over-taxing men and animals with forced marches, taking no proper care to establish either magazines or hospitals, and by long halts throwing away the advantages which those rapid marches were intended to secure'.[9] The memorandum was a pitiless analysis of these and many other errors that Napoleon had made in Russia, unmistakably laying bare the late emperor's personal responsibility for the disaster.

'Ségur's work has drawn the public's attention to the most extraordinary and stupendous transactions and events of modern times, and of which no times have produced a parallel,' Wellington began.[10] 'It is useless to consider what was the cause of the war between Napoleon and the Emperor of Russia. The ostensible causes of dispute were clearly removed. The diplomatists had agreed upon the principle of settling them all.' Instead Napoleon suddenly moved six hundred thousand men into Prussia with the 'real object' of destroying the tsar's power and influence.

It is clear, then, that there were no legitimate French interests involved in this war … there was an option, viz., for Napoleon to soften his policy … That policy was a system of insult and menace … The war was occasioned solely by the desire of [Napoleon] to fight a great battle, to gain a great victory, to occupy with his army one more great capital, and to subject to his rule the power of Russia.

Wellington was insistent that there was a 'total absence of principle in the examination of this great question of war and peace'. He believed that Napoleon had been contemplating his attack as early as his Austrian marriage in 1810. Yet, despite that, he utterly failed to create the optimum diplomatic and strategic environment for his invasion. Wellington stated that his memorandum, in dealing with Napoleon's diplomacy, would show 'how entirely the national policy of France was lost sight of by him when his own personal objects were in question'.

At Tilsit, hoping for a Russian marriage, Napoleon lost the opportunity of being reconciled with Turkey and he also consented to Russia's invasion of Finland, thereby 'depriving Sweden of all means of annoyance against Russia'. French policy had hitherto been to befriend those two potentially anti-Russian powers, yet Napoleon threw away both opportunities. Because of his personal dislike of Bernadotte, then Crown Prince of Sweden, Napoleon insulted his former marshal's adopted country by seizing Swedish Pomerania and the island of Rügen in order to enforce the Continental System. According to Wellington, Napoleon 'forgot the interests and ancient policy of France, and gratified his personal resentment against the Crown Prince'.

As a result of his antagonism towards Turkey and Sweden, Napoleon soon found that Britain befriended them both, and that during the 1812 campaign the tsar was able to withdraw troops from his north-western and southern borders for use against Napoleon's armies in Russia. 'There is no child who reads these histories who will not see', wrote Wellington, that Napoleon was hamstrung by his own incompetent and self-indulgent diplomacy. The indictment continued:

Great as the loss in the French armies was by war and famine, and the consequences of those irregularities which are inseparable from such a system as that of Napoleon … it must be obvious to all that the great destruction of the French army in Russia was to be attributed to the position of the Russian troops upon the Orcha and the Berezina in November 1812, the very troops thus brought into action in consequence of the political arrangements above referred to.

Furthermore, rather than encouraging the Poles and Lithuanians in their hopes of long-term independence from Russia, Napoleon 'was loose and cold in answer' to them, just when he most needed 'their goodwill and activity in supplying his armies'. In Wellington's view it was obvious that 'Napoleon, then, led the armies of Europe into Russia without any of the assistance the country could afford, whether of a military or of a civil or political nature, which common attention, or the ordinary policy of a statesman, would have placed at his disposal.'

Wellington believed that Napoleon was perfectly well aware of the enormous logistical problems that lay ahead in Russia, yet he consistently failed to make proper provision for such a huge army operating over such a vast area. A hospital at Wilna for six thousand men was set up 'without provisions, beds, covering, or even straw to lie upon, and even unprovided with medicine'. Those hospitals that did exist were for the wounded only; 'the sick shifted for themselves as they could'. Wellington noted that after the battle of Borodino, 'twenty thousand French wounded were left in the Abbaye of Kozoiskoi' with no troops deputed to look after them. The idea of 'plunder in order to supply the hospitals' caused Wellington to employ a rarely used exclamation mark. (Of course Wellington himself was forced to leave his own wounded behind after the battle of Talavera, where they had been abandoned by General de la Cuesta to the French.)

'The truth is that Napoleon learnt at Paris and Dresden', Wellington continued, 'that the Emperor of Russia had collected his army in the neighbourhood of Wilna. He conceived that he should surprise his enemy in that position and defeat him ... Forced marches were then to be undertaken, even from the Vistula, and were continued till the army reached the Dnieper ... nothing was thought of but the prospect of finding the enemy *en flagrant délit*, and destroying him at one blow.'

Wellington gave short shrift to Ségur's explanation that the loss of ten thousand horses and many men in the forced marches from the Niemen river had been due to rainstorms, snorting: 'Those who know what an army is well know that a storm of rain in the summer, whatever its violence and character, does not destroy the horses of an army.' Instead, Napoleon was personally guilty of forcing his horses to undergo 'hard work, forced marches, [with] no corn or dry fodder at the period at which the green corn is on the ground', thus rendering them 'incapable of bearing the hardship of the winter'. As for the men, Wellington went out of his way to argue that, because of conscription across society, French soldiers were 'upon the whole the best, the most orderly and obedient, and the most easily commanded and best regulated body of troops that ever existed. They were destroyed by their privations.' The French Revolution had introduced 'new systems of war, the objects and results of which were to render war as a resource instead of a burthen upon the country which unfortunately became the seat of its operations'. It meant that the state could mobilise the population.

According to Wellington's utterly *ad hominem* attack:

> Napoleon was educated in this system. He succeeded to the power it gave to the government, and carried its action to the greatest possible extent. The system of his tactics was founded upon forced marches. War, being the principal resource of his government, was to be carried on at the smallest possible expense of money to his treasury, but at the greatest possible expenditure of the lives of men, not only by the fire of the enemy, but by privations, fatigue and sickness. Till this Russian war he had never thought of supplying his armies with the necessaries requisite to enable such great bodies to keep the field. His object was to surprise his enemy by the rapidity of his marches, to fight a great battle, levy contributions, make peace, and return to Paris. But these objects were always attained at the expense of the utmost privations to his troops.

As a result, in Russia, what started off as a disciplined and formidable Grande Armée 'became at last a horde of *banditi*, all equally bad, and destroying itself by its irregularities'.

Wellington did not accept the explanation of the emperor's apologists that, as he put it, 'Napoleon complained that his orders were not obeyed, and that magazines of provisions for his army were not formed, upon the retreat, at the places at which he had ordered that they should be formed.' He admitted that that 'may be true', but argued that 'other generals at the head of armies' – doubtless meaning to include himself – showed their lieutenants the means by which the provisions were to be collected and then supplied the cash to buy them. Yet under Napoleon 'there was but one resource for collecting these magazines, that was, *la maraude*'. So, Wellington asked rhetorically, 'was money placed at their disposal to purchase these supplies in a country overrun by Jews, who, if money had been produced, would have procured provisions in exchange for it from any distance? No!'

Again and again Wellington returned to the personal attack, rather than including the French marshals or quartermasters in his indictment. 'If Napoleon entertained expectations that magazines would have been formed in such situations, it is not astonishing that he should have been disappointed on his retreat: it would have been astonishing if any officer had been able to collect a magazine under such circumstances.' Wellington was forced to admit that Napoleon had in fact created huge magazines at Smolensk and at Orcha on the Dnieper, but wrote that 'the army was at that time in such a state of disorganisation that those magazines were of little or no utility'.

The duke then entered into a minute analysis of Napoleon's personal movements, stating exactly how many days he had spent in Dresden, Thorn, Danzig, Königsberg, Gumbinnen and Kowno. He concluded that the use of forced marches, followed by long sojourns in towns, was entirely counter-productive, as the Russian army had not been caught by surprise, but they did leave Napoleon's troops and horses 'knocked up' and forced to 'leave behind all the equipments and stores of provisions which his foreknowledge of the difficulties of his enterprise had induced him to provide'.

There then followed a close analysis of the relative movements of the French and Russian armies, in which Wellington drew attention to Napoleon's many strategic errors. 'Neither Napoleon nor any other general ever had so fair an opportunity of carrying into execution his favourite measure,' he wrote of the situation near the Russian camp of Drissa, 'of placing his army on the communication of that of his enemy by cutting the army of the enemy in two. It would appear, however, that he was not aware of the advantage he had over his enemy.' It would have been fascinating to know how Napoleon would have rebutted these and the many other denunciations of his strategy levelled by his enemy.

On the escape of the Russian general Barclay de Tolly on 27 July 1812 towards Smolensk, where he managed to join up with General Bagration five days later, Wellington was scathing:

Napoleon might have attacked the Russian army on the 27th, in the afternoon, or he might have posted troops on their flank in such a manner that their movement must have been known to him as soon as it should be made. But this precaution was neglected; and the Russian army made a retreat so clean, and in such regular order, that some time elapsed before it was known by what route they had marched. Indeed this want of knowledge of the movements of their enemy from positions in their sight was more frequent in the armies commanded by Napoleon than in any other. It occurred again at Smolensk, once before and once after the battle of Borodino, and again in a very remarkable manner at the capture of Moscow.

He might have added that it also happened after the battle of Ligny three years later. It is hard to escape the conclusion that Wellington was attempting, despite all his well-documented remarks to the contrary in public, to portray Napoleon as essentially an incompetent commander, at least for posterity if not in his own lifetime.

'Napoleon must be supposed to have made up his mind as to what his object was in the war, and that this object was Moscow,' wrote Wellington with barely suppressed sarcasm. Yet the route taken, the time wasted and the way Napoleon had split his forces struck him as incomprehensible. Wellington went remorselessly over Napoleon's options and the exact positioning of every corps at each stage of the campaign. The amount of research required for the sheer factual side of the memorandum was impressive, especially considering the other calls on Wellington's time in 1825, and must bear witness to a personal motive behind its execution beyond a mere desire to add to the sum of human knowledge about the retreat from Moscow.

In his desire to fix almost the entire responsibility for the 1812 disaster upon Napoleon personally, Wellington was particularly keen to deny him any credit for anything that had gone according to plan. Of the route taken from Wilna via Minsk and thence on to the capture of Smolensk, 'which is greatly admired by all the writers upon the subject', Wellington put forward a revisionist analysis. Judging by 'the only tests of any military movements, its objects compared with its risks and difficulties...it will be found to have failed completely'. Wellington entirely refused to accept that Napoleon had done well to take Smolensk with hardly a shot fired, stating that it happened 'only because the Russian general had made no previous arrangement for occupying the place; and Barclay knew that if he left a garrison there unprovided it must fall into Napoleon's hands a few days sooner or later'.

Writing with over a decade's hindsight and utter certainty about counterfactuals – something he deprecated in other authors when they wrote on Waterloo – Wellington stated categorically that had he approached Smolensk differently, 'Napoleon would have cut off his enemy from his communication; would have obliged them to fight a battle to regain it; and in all probability Smolensk would have fallen into his hands without loss, and with its buildings entire.'

Of the operations of Ney and Davout at the Dnieper, Wellington wrote: 'Napoleon ought to have been on the ground himself to superintend and direct their movements.' He drew on his Peninsular experiences to criticise Napoleon for allowing his marshals too much independence, supposing that 'it may almost be believed that he was apprehensive of a refusal to obey an order', an accusation for which there seems to be little or no justification. He also blamed Napoleon for constantly failing to inform junior corps commanders that they had been placed under the command of senior ones. As a result of bad communications between Murat, Ney and Davout on the Dnieper, Wellington concluded, 'Napoleon's plan had again been defeated.'

'As usual, Napoleon delayed for seven days at Smolensk in uncertainty...whether he should proceed or not,' wrote the duke, never giving his antagonist any benefit of the doubt. The emperor who emerges from Wellington's account is a bumbling, procrastinating, heartless fool, far removed from the man Wellington continued to laud in public. 'A criticism upon a battle in which the critic was not present is not likely to meet with much confidence or attention,' wrote Wellington of Borodino, but doubtless with Waterloo also in mind, 'particularly when made upon the conduct of so consummate a captain on a field of battle as Napoleon was.' Yet that did not prevent him from commenting in detail on all of Napoleon's supposed errors during that battle. Davout's plan 'to force and turn the enemy's left by the old road from Smolensk to Mojaisk' might well have cut off the Russians' line of retreat, thought Wellington, but Napoleon failed to adopt it because 'he could not trust Murat, or decide between the conflicting pretensions of Ney and Davout'. As a result, Wellington believed, Borodino had only been a Pyrrhic victory, despite its having left the road to Moscow open to Napoleon.

'On the day Napoleon entered Moscow he ought to have made his arrangements to withdraw from that city,' thundered the duke. 'Moscow was not a military position,' he argued, but merely a political one. After the fire, 'the possession of the town lost its value...even in the way of provisions or military equipments'. Wellington believed that marauding French troops had set fire to the city in the 'search for plunder on the night of their arrival', but produced no evidence whatever to support this theory. Furthermore, 'The destruction of Moscow by fire apparently made no alteration in Napoleon's intention to remain in that city,' something that Wellington also found incredible.

He put it down to General Kutuzov's agreement to forward a letter to the tsar containing peace proposals, and suggested that 'the expectation of a favourable answer had tended to divert Napoleon's attention from his real situation'. Napoleon was thus guilty of wishful thinking as well as strategic ineptitude.

Of the various historical works on the retreat from Moscow, Wellington wrote:

> The habit of Napoleon has been to astonish and deceive mankind, and he had come at last to deceive himself. These works contain innumerable instances of this habit of his mind, but those which I am now about to discuss are the most remarkable and the most fatal to himself and his fortunes, and the most fortunate for the world that ever occurred.

He then went into great detail about the actual conduct of the retreat itself, again blaming the emperor personally:

> Napoleon would never believe, or act as if he believed, either that he was himself, with the body of troops under his immediate command, under the necessity of retreating from his position of Moscow, that any preparatory steps were necessary to enable him to perform that operation, or that the French corps destined to protect his flanks were not stronger than the Russian corps opposed to them. There is a curious instance in these works of the disposition of his mind to despise and depreciate his enemy, and to exaggerate the means at his own disposal.

Might there be a conscious or subconscious reference, in that final sentence, to Napoleon's remark about a 'sepoy general'?

Contending that 'If Napoleon could have taken a correct view of his position' he would have seen that after leaving Moscow on 19 October it was impossible to winter inside European Russia, Wellington suggested that he should have lifted the siege of Riga in September and thereby freed Macdonald's corps for operations in the field to give the French numerical superiority over the Russian field marshal Prince von Wittgenstein on the River Dwina. Yet this would have let the world realise that Napoleon's 'means of conquest' were 'not equal to the task of subduing the country', at least in a single season's campaigning, and Napoleon 'preferred to incur all risks, and to trust to all chances rather than to let out the secret'.

Wellington's contempt for Napoleon is clear from his comment on the orders the emperor gave Marshal Mortier on 20 October for the

Young Guard to stay in Moscow until the 23rd, and then blow up the Kremlin and retreat:

> It is impossible to advert to this fact without expressing the horror which it inspires. If Napoleon had destroyed a magazine or a work of utility to the Russian army or nation, or even a monument of art, or one to recall the memory of some glorious action by the Russian army or nation, the reader would not have been shocked as by the perusal of formal instructions to destroy the ancient palace of the Tsars, solely to mark the impotent desire of revenge because the Emperor of Russia, having declined to submit to insult, had afterwards refused to listen to insidious offers of peace.

These remarks shed fresh light on Wellington's opposition to the Prussians' plans to destroy the Pont d'Iéna and the Vendôme Column after Waterloo.

In the entire 24,000-word essay, Wellington was never more disdainful of Napoleon than over this intended vandalism of the Kremlin, but it was based on something of a misconception. Napoleon never ordered Mortier to blow up the Kremlin; indeed he specifically directed General Baston de la Riboisière, who was in command of the artillery left with Mortier in the Kremlin when the main army began its withdrawal, not to destroy the Palace, in case it was needed for defence should the Grande Armée be forced to return. Napoleon did, however, order the removal of tsarist coronation regalia, the destruction of the imperial Russian eagles from the Kremlin's turrets and the despoliation of the thirty-foot-high cross on the Ivan the Great tower, so Wellington's central point was still a valid one.

Wellington also derided Napoleon's choice of military formation during the retreat. Marching by two or three separate columns with rear guards on the roads, 'he might have saved his army at least from any military disaster; and time, of the greatest importance to him, would have been saved. Instead of adopting any of these modes of retreat he marched in one long column which extended the distance of two or three marches.' He also failed to render his army as light as possible by destroying all superfluous baggage and reducing the number of wheeled carriages, 'as however convenient to individuals they are the most inconvenient and burthensome to the army'.

Wellington entirely denied that the frost in Russia came prematurely in 1812, or that – as 'Gourgaud, who is Napoleon's apologist', argued – Napoleon was particularly unlucky with the weather.

Anyhow, 'in the midst of all the boasting' which Napoleon's 23rd and 24th bulletins to the Grande Armée contained, Wellington noticed that an early frost had indeed been foreseen. When the misfortunes of the army were attributed to the frost in the 29th bulletin on 3 December, Wellington wrote that 'Any other people in the world … would have been astonished,' considering what had been written about the frost in the bulletins of 9, 14 and 20 October. Wellington was equally sarcastic about Ségur's claim that the French horses had not been properly shod for the rough terrain they would encounter. 'Why were they not rough shod?' he asked. 'Is there never any frost in Russia? … Those who have followed a French army well know that their horses are always rough shod.'

As he built up to his peroration, Wellington used the same word – 'observations' – that Napoleon had used in his critique of the duke's performance at Waterloo. It is hard not to regard this entire exercise as at least in part his answer to Napoleon's original criticisms of his strategy in the 1815 campaign. As Wellington wrote:

> It will be seen from these observations that Napoleon was obliged to abandon all his projects one after the other, and to choose for his retreat the road least advantageous in his own opinion for the army, the most circuitous, not only positively but relatively, with that which he left in the power of his adversary; and this without attempting to gain a military advantage over his enemy, notwithstanding his own still existing superiority of numbers.

It was a heavy indictment, but one that has in its essentials been supported by historians. Through close reading of Napoleon's correspondence, Wellington built up a damning but overall accurate picture of the errors of 1812. He repeatedly showed all the options open to the emperor, and demonstrated that the one chosen was invariably wrong. Underlying it all was a heartfelt anger at Napoleon's lack of concern for the welfare of his troops.

Napoleon's refusal to alter his formations also struck Wellington as a grave tactical weakness. 'The retreat was continued in the same form, notwithstanding the military disasters and loss of time which had resulted from the use of it,' he noted. That this was a direct personal indictment, rather than a general criticism of the French High Command, is clear from the fact that Wellington mentioned Napoleon by name on no fewer than 136 occasions. Although Ney, Davout, Murat and many others were mentioned, occasionally favourably,

'Napoleon' – always given that name rather than 'Buonaparte' or even 'Bonaparte' – was held entirely responsible for the débâcle. (As the dictator who gave the order to invade, Napoleon was of course ultimately responsible for the war, unless one subscribes to Leo Tolstoy's weird view that it had been a spontaneous movement of peoples first eastwards and then westwards with no guiding hand or brain.)

That Wellington went to the enormous trouble of making himself such an expert on the minutiæ of the campaign is instructive about his changing relationship with Napoleon's posthumous memory. Napoleon had derided him on St Helena, attempted to belittle his victory at Waterloo and even left money to his would-be assassin. As a result Wellington privately revised the opinion he constantly gave of Napoleon in public, that he was the most gifted general of modern times. He believed that, diplomatically and militarily, Napoleon got everything wrong in Russia in 1812, and he set out to prove it with his characteristic eye for detail and a scorching prose style. The dish of vengeance was eaten as cold as the Beresina river in late November, but it was a private feast, intended only for family, friends and a few old colleagues. When Wellington went on a journey to Russia in 1826 to promote good relations with the new tsar, Nicholas I, he made notes of his memorandum for the Russian section of Sir Walter Scott's forthcoming biography of Napoleon, but overall he had no desire to provoke a public debate, or to seem churlish about his old enemy.

‍

In the course of writing his critique of the 1812 campaign in Russia, Wellington became, albeit via a divorce and at two removes, connected to Napoleon by marriage. Charles Carroll of Carrollton, Maryland, was the richest and last-surviving signatory of the Declaration of Independence. His daughter, a beauty much admired by George Washington, married a successful Baltimore merchant named Richard Caton, a 'tall, handsome man of fine presence and dignified carriage', and they had three daughters, called Marianne, Louisa and Elizabeth. The eldest daughter Marianne, who was as beautiful as her mother, also married a rich Baltimore merchant, named Robert Patterson, whose sister Elizabeth ('Betsy') had in 1803 married Napoleon's youngest brother Jérôme. They had a son, called Jérôme Bonaparte-Patterson. Napoleon annulled the marriage in 1806 and Betsy was obliged to live in Camberwell, while her ex-husband went on to become King of Westphalia and to marry Frederica Catherina of Württemberg.

(Napoleon once said that the Hereditary Prince of Württemberg was so fat because God had specifically designed him as an experiment to see how far human skin could stretch without breaking.)

In 1814 Robert and Marianne Patterson visited Europe, along with Marianne's two unmarried heiress sisters, Louisa and Elizabeth. They made an instant impression on London society, 'and were universally admired from the King downwards'.[11] A letter of introduction from Richard Caton to the Earl of Leicester, who was personally unknown to him, got them invited to Holkham Hall where they were 'entertained right royally'. In 1815 Marianne Patterson seems to have become yet another of Wellington's mistresses, somehow squeezed in during that very busy year for him. In 1817 her sister Louisa married Wellington's aide-de-camp Colonel Felton Harvey, who had lost an arm crossing the Douro and whom Wellington called 'one of my whipper-snappers'. Nine years after Harvey's death in 1819 Louisa married the Marquess of Carmarthen, who later succeeded to the dukedom of Leeds.

In 1820 Robert and Marianne Patterson returned to America, but within two years he was dead and his widow and her as yet unmarried sister Elizabeth came back to England. They stayed at Stratfield Saye, where Marianne met and fell for Wellington's eldest brother Richard, Marquess Wellesley, then lord-lieutenant of Ireland. Wellington was furious about the proposed match, denouncing his brother's profligacy as well as his 'jealous disposition', 'violent temper' and sexual licentiousness. (He had long disapproved of Wellesley's whoring, and in 1810 had suggested that his brother's career would prosper better were he castrated, although, with his own many mistresses and mistreatment of his at times suicidal wife, there was more than a whiff of hypocrisy to this.)

Sure enough, very soon after their wedding at Royal Lodge, Dublin, in 1825, Wellesley was being unfaithful to the new marchioness. She went to Wellington for consolation, and found it, and the duke refused his brother a place in his ministry when he became Prime Minister in 1828. When a few years later Marianne's younger sister Elizabeth married another peer, Lord Stafford, Wellington's friend Thomas Raikes wrote in his journal: 'It is a singular instance of three sisters, foreigners, and of a nation little known in our aristocratical circles, allying themselves to such distinguished families in England.'[12] To become a duchess, marchioness and baroness was not bad going for the three granddaughters of Charles Carroll, who started out in life, so recalled a snide Thomas Creevey, as 'a captain of an Indiaman in Liverpool'. It was the beginning of a long and generally mutually beneficial tradition of allying British birth with American cash, a process that was to produce, among many other distinguished people, Sir Winston Churchill.

Someone who greatly resented the Pattersons' social success was their sister-in-law Betsy Bonaparte-Patterson, who regaled the society of London, Paris and Geneva with catty remarks about her in-laws' social ambitions. 'The beautiful, gay, charming belle of Baltimore in 1803', wrote the historian of the long lawsuit in which she tried to legitimise her offspring under French law, 'became, ten years later, the unhappy divorcée, living alone or with her son in lodgings all over Europe, and going to parties every evening to avoid dying of boredom.'[13] She gleefully spread the scandal of Wellington's affair with his brother's future wife, spoke mockingly of the Catons' 'persevering endeavours and invincible courage' in finding eligible husbands for their daughters, and claimed that Marianne Patterson's lack of French had been 'a considerable advantage to her' in Parisian society, 'since it prevented her nonsense being heard'.[14]

Whatever it is about Baltimore that produces nearly-queens – a century later Wallis Simpson was also to hail from there – Betsy Bonaparte-Patterson returned to the city in old age, 'to become an embittered, avaricious old lady, yet still, until her death in 1879 at the age of 94, with the remains of that beauty which had made Jérôme love her more than any other of the many women in his life'. Her grandson, Charles-Joseph Bonaparte-Patterson, became attorney-general of the United States under Theodore Roosevelt.

⮑

When Sir Walter Scott's nine-volume *Life of Napoleon* was published in 1827, the Reverend G. R. Gleig wrote to say that 'it is a pity that the life of Bonaparte's conqueror should not accompany it', and was rewarded with Wellington's permission to write one.[15] Wellington was disappointed with Scott's work, describing parts of it as 'of no value' and little better than a novel. He had respected his fellow Tory ever since 1809 when Scott had championed his right to return to his Peninsular command, but in 1827 he complained of the Napoleon biography to Samuel Rogers that 'the tolerable part of it is what relates to his retreat from Moscow. I have thought much on that subject, and have made many inquiries concerning it. I gave him my papers. He used some, not all.' This might well have been due to Wellington's handwriting. Scott wrote that Wellington had given him 'a bundle of remarks on Bonaparte's Russian campaign', but, because they had been written in his carriage while on his 1826 mission to St Petersburg, 'it is furiously scrawled and the Russian names hard to distinguish'.

In 1827 Major-General Sir John Malcolm, the governor of Bombay, gave Wellington a letter dated 29 July 1796, in which the young 'M. de Buonaparte', commander of the Army of Italy, had requested his bookseller send him Rousseau's *Confessions*, several works on Corsica and two newly published memoirs.[16] Malcolm clearly assumed that Wellington would be interested in owning such Napoleonic memorabilia, and he was right.

There was a limit to his interest, however. In 1829, when Wellington was prime minister, a Mr Burke wrote to him to ask whether his son Joseph's theatre might be licensed, saying that his son had a 'claim upon Your Grace which is that he is the greatest likeness of your great opponent Napoleon Buonaparte whom he plays in a piece specially written for him'.[17] The reply was predictably frosty: 'Compliments. It is not part of the Duke's business to interfere with the licensing of theatres in London.'

France's pursuit of imperial glory in North Africa in 1830 struck Wellington as almost Bonapartist. Writing to his old friend the Marquess of Alava that May, he said that events in France were once again beginning to be of 'the greatest importance to the whole world', and he used the phrase he had employed five years earlier in his Russian treatise:

> It isn't important whether it's Napoleon's government, or the Directors', or Robespierre, or a prince from the house of Bourbon; whilst this government uses war as a resource, be it political or financial, and that in the country war isn't considered to be a disgrace, the world Powers without exception have to be on guard. Bonaparte's wars weren't revolutionary. They were wars of conquest; for the object of finance, or generally for reputation. Like they are going to do in Algiers. There is no lack of men in France, like Bonaparte, who could put everything into confusion.[18]

It was certainly not Napoleon's legal and administrative reform to which Wellington took exception. In a memorandum to Sir George Murray, the man responsible for administering justice on Mauritius, which had been captured from France in July 1810, Wellington wrote in August 1830 that the courts there should 'be formed upon an English principle, to administer justice according to the form and to the law of the Code Napoléon'.[19] In yet another permutation of his name, Wellington spelt the emperor's name in the French way, with an acute accent over the 'e'.

On many occasions during the 1830s, Wellington returned to the subject of Napoleon and the Waterloo campaign. 'Pooh,' he said to Croker in May 1831, 'he had no general preconceived plan of a campaign, as indeed he owned.' Speaking to Samuel Rogers a few months later about the Polish revolt then under way against Russia, he said it was only possible to campaign in Poland between June and February because rivers and roads became impassable during the thaw. 'Buonaparte began his campaign there in June, when he fought the battle that ended in the Peace of Tilsit. He was slow in Paris, but swift when he took the field.' Once again he reverted, that October, to his old mantra, telling Lord Mahon in October: 'Oh yes – there was nothing like him. He suited a French army so exactly! Depend upon it, at the head of a French army there was never anything like him. In short, I used to say of him that his presence made the difference of forty thousand men.'[20]

His low view of Napoleon's character had not improved since he had described him as a 'shabby fellow' because of the Cantillon bequest. In November 1831 he explained to Mahon how Napoleon used to boost his men's morale by calling out names from regiments he visited and pretending to remember the exploits of individuals concerned. 'I'll tell you how he managed it,' explained Wellington. Napoleon's aide-de-camp General Mouton – later Comte Lobau – drew up a list of prominent veterans beforehand for Napoleon to memorise. Napoleon would then pretend to recognise the soldiers concerned, and reminisce with them about the battles they had fought in. It never failed, but as Wellington complained: 'In all his works – I mean all he has ever written – you never find a thing related precisely as it happened. He seems to have had no clear or distinct recollection; scarcely once has he ever tripped into truth.'

To Lady Salisbury, who wanted to know whether Marlborough was a greater military genius than Napoleon, Wellington replied:

Why, I don't know – it is very difficult to tell…[Napoleon] had one prodigious advantage – he had no responsibility – he could do whatever he pleased; and no man has ever lost more armies than he did. Now with me the loss of every man told. I could not risk so much; I knew that if I ever lost five hundred men without the clearest necessity, I should be brought upon my knees to the bar of the House of the Commons.[21]

To the question of who was the greater general out of Napoleon or Marlborough, therefore, Wellington's considered answer seems to have been 'Wellington'.

Although Wellington was never brought to his knees in the Peninsular War it almost happened in 1832 when a pro-Reform mob stoned him on 18 June. Wellington had to be protected by Bow Street policemen, two Chelsea Pensioners and a magistrate called Ballantine from a mob which threw stones and shouted 'Bonaparte for ever!' on his way back home from a sitting for his bust in a studio near the Royal Mint in the East End. It was an unpleasant and potentially very dangerous situation, made all the more poignant and disgraceful for having taken place on Waterloo Day.

By the following year – the Reform Bill safely passed into law – Wellington had been restored to popularity. Showing Lady Salisbury and other guests around Apsley House in July 1833 he pointed out the paintings of the Duke of Marlborough, the Duke of Schomberg 'and a famous one by Lefèvre of Napoleon. It was observed to him that he would soon assemble all the celebrated generals of European history except the greatest: it is indeed much to be regretted that he does not seem likely to leave to his descendants any portrait of himself.'[22] This was the most absurd flattery; in fact Lord Gerald Wellesley – later the 7th duke – estimated that there were no fewer than 150 authentic portraits of the 1st duke in all, and many times that number of likenesses of him. 'Of all the Britons who have ever lived,' he wrote in his book *The Iconography of the First Duke of Wellington*, 'Arthur Wellesley 1st Duke of Wellington, has been the most portrayed.'

Although on the latter occasion Wellington does not seem to have demurred that he was the greatest European general, in a conversation with Mahon at Walmer on the 'Great Man' theory of History, Wellington denied that 'disturbed times bring forth able men'. When Mahon instanced France as an example of this thesis, Wellington disagreed: 'I think not. Bonaparte is a man apart: you must not put him into the common scale; he might have started up at any time. But, except him, the French Revolution has not produced very superior men.' (He counted Talleyrand as being of the *ancien régime*.)

The year 1833 also saw Wellington invent a yet more glorious role for himself in the Waterloo campaign, one in which he had personally ridden over to Blücher's headquarters the night before the battle in order to co-ordinate the next day's strategy with him. We can be absolutely certain that this never happened, but it was the story Wellington apparently told to Rt Hon. Henry Pierrepoint, the father of his daughter-in-law Lady Charles Wellesley, and also to Mr Justice Coltman of the Court of Common Pleas five years later at Stratfield Saye. According to the Reverend Charles Young, who was staying with Pierrepoint at the time, Wellington had claimed that:

> On the 17th [June 1815], early in the day, I had a horse shot under me. Few knew it, but it was so. Before ten o'clock I got on Copenhagen's back...I never drew bit, and he never had a morsel in his mouth, till 8pm, when Fitzroy Somerset came to tell me dinner was ready in the little neighbouring village – Waterloo...Somerset and I despatched a hasty meal; and as soon as we had done so, I sent off Somerset on an errand. This I did, I confess, on purpose that I might get him out of the way; for I knew that if he had had the slightest inkling of what I was up to, he would have done his best to dissuade me from my purpose, and want to accompany me.
>
> The fact was, I wanted to see Blücher, that I might learn from his own lips at what hour it was probable he would be able to join forces with us next day. Therefore the moment Fitzroy's back was turned, I ordered Copenhagen to be re-saddled, and told my man to get his own horse and accompany me to Wavre, where I had reason to believe old 'Forwards' was encamped. Now, Wavre, being some twelve miles from Waterloo, I was not a little disgusted, on getting there, to find that the old fellow's tent was two miles still further off.
>
> However, I saw him, got the information I wanted from him, and made the best of my way homewards. Bad, however, was the best; for, by Jove, it was so dark that I fell into a deepish dyke by the roadside; and if it had not been for the orderly's assistance, I doubt that I should ever have got out. Thank God, there was no harm done, either to horse or man![23]

Little in this tale rings true, yet the claim is also recorded by Lady Shelley who, shortly after meeting Wellington for the first time in 1815, wrote in her journal: 'On the day before the battle, the Duke rode Copenhagen to the Prussian headquarters, to ascertain whether he might depend upon old Blücher's co-operation.' If Wellington's recollections have been reported accurately by Pierrepoint, Coltman and Shelley it seems that he claimed an even greater personal role in the victory than the central one he already enjoyed. In fact an aide-de-camp had been sent to Blücher the evening before Waterloo, and had returned with the famous note promising Prussian assistance on the morrow. Wellington certainly never went to Blücher's headquarters personally that evening. It might have been that Pierrepoint, one of the original Regency dandies along with his friends Beau Brummel and Lords Alvanley and de Roos, had simply made the story up, or that the Reverend Young had misheard it, but that does not account for Coltman and Shelley. Could the duke have been simply exaggerating, showing off, or suffering from some kind of mild, old soldier's case of invented-memory syndrome?

In case anyone dared doubt his own contribution to Napoleon's defeat, Wellington told Raikes at Stratfield Saye in August 1833 that during the Peninsular War Portugal had been 'the basis on which the machinery was founded which finally overturned the world'.[24] Wellington was an essentially eighteenth-century figure who relished his own achievements, tended to talk them up, and did not indulge in false modesty; it was only the Victorians who tried to turn him in his old age into a paragon of self-effacement. Yet in his self-estimation, just as in his private life, he was always more a Regency figure than a Victorian. For example, of his own despatches, which began to appear in print in 1834 edited by Colonel Gurwood, Wellington said he was 'surprised to see them so good – they are as good as I could write now. They show the same attention to detail – to the pursuit of all the means, however small, that could promote success.'[25] (Old Whig habits died hard: one partisan asked Gurwood, 'When do you bring out another of your damned volumes?')

The publication of the despatches understandably prompted a certain amount of nostalgia in Wellington. In May 1834, when reminiscing at Apsley House to Mahon about the Waterloo campaign, he said that he thought Napoleon had been wrong in attacking him at all, as the four Allied armies marching into France – 'a country much exhausted by the last year's campaign' – before harvest-time 'would have been reduced to many straits for subsistence'. Had Napoleon stationed himself on the Meuse with three hundred thousand men, Wellington thought, 'He might have played again the same game which he had played so admirably the year before,' manoeuvring between each Allied army and leaving himself free to engage them separately. Yet that is largely what Napoleon had tried to do with Wellington and Blücher in June 1815, and he had failed – but only just.

Wellington much admired Napoleon's 1814 campaigns and thought that 'he ought to have taken the same line in 1815 and might have given us great trouble, and had many chances in his favour. Instead of this, by Waterloo he put an end to the war at once. But the fact is, he never in his life had patience for a defensive war.'[26] Wellington was just as keen as Napoleon to emphasise that he had been outnumbered at Waterloo. On 2 October he told Croker: 'I had less than sixty thousand, perhaps about fifty-six or fifty-eight thousand; Buonaparte had eighty thousand.'[27] These figures are just as wildly inaccurate as Napoleon's had been, and are a clear case of an old man remembering with advantages what deeds he had done.

Wellington was in boastful mood at Walmer Castle that day, claiming to have won the Napoleonic Wars virtually single-handedly, and saying that Salamanca had 'changed all the prospects of the war, and was even felt in Russia. Vitoria freed the Peninsula altogether, broke off the armistice at Dresden, and this led to Leipzig, and the deliverance of Europe; and Waterloo did more than any battle I know of, towards the true object of all battles, the peace of the world.' To describe a man who could make such statements as 'modest', as so many historians and biographers have done over the centuries, is to stretch the meaning of the adjective to breaking point.

When the painter Benjamin Robert Haydon wanted to portray Wellington on the field of Waterloo he found that the duke had given the cloak he had worn during the battle to his steward, Mugford, and 'God only knew where the hat was!' Haydon wondered whether this was 'simplicity, absence of vanity, or want of sentiment in the Duke', and contrasted it with his other hero, Napoleon, who 'dwelt on, often looked at, and left to his son, the coat he wore at Marengo and the sword of Austerlitz'. He finally put it down to the lack of poetry in the English character. Wellington was unsure about Haydon's request to paint a companion piece to his portrait of Napoleon on St Helena. He wrote to say that 'to paint the Emperor Napoleon on the rock at St Helena is a quite different thing from painting me on the field of the battle of Waterloo. The Emperor Napoleon did not consent to be painted. But I am supposed to consent; and, moreover, I on the field of the battle of Waterloo am not exactly in the situation in which Napoleon stood on the rock of St Helena.' Nonetheless, the dichotomy between Napoleon portrayed in defeat and Wellington in victory obviously failed to deter in the end, and Haydon was invited to stay at Walmer while sketching for his portrait, which today hangs in the Gallery at Apsley House.

SIXTEEN

The War for Clio's Ear
1836–1852

Man, and above all the historian, is full of vanity.
He gives fine scope to his imagination,
and tries to interest the reader at the expense of truth.

NAPOLEON

A t the end of 1835 Wellington wrote a long letter to John
Croker about Napoleon's deceit, which could almost stand as a
commentary upon the pencil lines he had made in O'Meara's
two volumes thirteen years earlier, and bears repetition at length:

Buonaparte's whole life, civil, political and military, was a fraud. There
was not a transaction, great or small, in which lying or fraud were not
introduced; but one must have a perfect recollection of facts, and must
be enabled to correct one's memory by reference to documents, in
order to be able to write of them with authority. Of flagrant lies, the
most important in the military branch of his life that I can now recollect are – first, the expedition from Egypt into Syria, which totally
failed, and yet on his return to Egypt was represented to the army there
as a victory; there were illuminations, &. The next was the battle of
Eylau. This he represented as a great victory. It is true that the Allied
army retired after the battle. So did Buonaparte. You will find the
details of the Syrian affair in [Louis-Antoine Fauvelet de] Bourrienne,
where you likewise find Buonaparte's lies about the defeat of the fleet.
  I should think that Spain would afford you instances of fraud in his
political schemes and negotiations…by which King Ferdinand was
coaxed into a departure from Madrid, and afterwards from one town to
another by a fresh lie, till he arrived at Bayonne, where he was seized as
a traitor towards the Government of his father. In the meantime St
Sebastian, Pampeluna, Figueras, Barcelona…were seized, each by some
military trick or fraud, and held by the French troops till deprived by us.

Buonaparte's foreign policy was force and menace, aided by fraud and corruption. If the fraud was discovered, force and menace succeeded; and in most cases the unfortunate victim did not dare to avow that he perceived the fraud. He tricked the King of Spain, Charles IV, by the concession of the kingdom of Etruria to his son-in-law. He afterwards forcibly deprived the said King in order to put in his brother-in-law. In short there is no end to the violence and fraud of his proceedings.[1]

It was a savage indictment of Napoleon's veracity, using the word 'fraud' no fewer than seven times, just as Wellington's Russian memorandum ten years earlier had been an attack on Napoleon's military strategy. Yet how valid were his criticisms? On the battle of Eylau, Wellington was right; although the French remained in possession of the field, they had lost around 25,000 men – one in three – compared to the Russians' 15,000. Over the battle of the Nile Wellington was also correct, but his interpretation of the capture of the Spanish fortresses was somewhat overdone. If the great walled cities of Spain surrendered to Marshal Junot without a fight, that can hardly be held against Napoleon. Furthermore, although the Spanish royal family were subjected to considerable hucksterism, there is plenty of evidence to suggest that they were perfectly willing to sit out the war in the comparative safety of their house arrest at the Château de Valençay. Ferdinand VII occupied himself with embroidery and cutting out paper patterns, never considered the possibility of escape, and occasionally wrote to Napoleon to congratulate him on his victories.

As the years passed Wellington proposed himself as Napoleon's military equal with increasing confidence. In February 1836 he told Lord Ellesmere that he had never lost a cannon in any battle of his career, whereas 'Napoleon lost guns in some of his greatest victories, certainly at Wagram.' This was also factually correct; Napoleon had lost twenty-one guns, twelve eagles and seven thousand prisoners in what was nonetheless overall a French victory. Equally, Wellington had never lost a single cannon at any engagement at which he was personally present, although of course neither had he ever commanded a conscript army of two hundred thousand men.

On 18 September 1836, Wellington wrote a memorandum slightly qualifying his theory that his great opponent had been worth forty thousand men on any battlefield, explaining that 'Napoleon was a *grand homme de guerre*, possibly the greatest that has ever appeared at the head of a French army', who had been hugely aided by the way in which the French Revolution had framed institutions 'for the purpose of forming and maintaining its armies with a view to conquest'. That evening, talking to Lady Salisbury after dinner at Hatfield House, Wellington claimed that he could 'distinctly see [the Prussians'] field of battle from the Quatre Bras, which was about eight miles off', and that 'Napoleon committed mistakes, just like other people. The great thing in military affairs is never to make a false step, or to go farther than you ought, especially when you are moving in parallel lines with such a man as Napoleon.'

It is highly doubtful that Wellington's first statement was literally true. Although it was possible for a telescope to cover the distance – at the battle of Bienvenida in April 1812 Generals Cotton and Le Marchant used theirs to spot French cavalry at Villagarcía and Llerena nine miles away, albeit from the top of a church tower – at Ligny the topography simply did not permit it. Wellington would have to have ridden far to the east to view the battle, and the road between Thyle at the eastern end of the Quatre Bras battlefield, and Marbais just north of the road on the western end of the Ligny battlefield, is always below the horizon. Ligny was fought at the foot of long gentle slopes running down to the Ligny brook, and with smoke and haze further restricting vision it is hard to escape the conclusion that, aged sixty-seven, Wellington was succumbing to the phenomenon by which 'old men forget'. It is certainly impossible to see Ligny village from anywhere but Brye or St Amand, and Wellington went nowhere near either of those villages during the battle of Quatre Bras.[2]

In citing Napoleon's mistake of 'not moving his forces by the great road from Mons to Brussels', and adding, 'It was my business to be prepared for all events,' not least by having fortified Mons, Wellington was making a virtue out of his incorrect initial judgment on 15 June 1815 that Napoleon would attack via that route. Three days later, when out riding on the Downs near Dover with his platonically close friend the Marchioness of Salisbury, he told an anecdote about the soldier Sir Thomas Stepney, an 8th baronet famed for his blunt speaking. As she recorded:

Once, at table, when Sir A. Wellesley and several other general officers were present, speaking of Napoleon, he turned to the Duke of York and said: 'I don't know as to Sir Arthur here, he knows something of the matter I dare say, but there is not one of you that would not run away before one of Napoleon's boots.'[3]

As so often, the story redounded to Wellington's credit.

Two months later, Wellington told Mahon that he 'did not think Napoleon's complaints well founded as to [St Helena's] being an arid and wretched spot – *ce rocher affreux* – as he called it. On the contrary, he thought the aspect very pleasing.' Admitting that Napoleon had had only the second-best house on the island, Wellington said (from the comfort of Stratfield Saye) that his opponent must have been 'very much worse lodged in his own headquarters a thousand times in his life'. It was of course hardly the point, as Napoleon was not on campaign on St Helena, and the quotation of Napoleon's description of the island as 'this frightful rock' shows that he was not unaware of the ex-emperor's complaints about his accommodation.

Wellington returned to the attack once more the following May, arguing that Napoleon had lost touch with reality in 1814, even though the duke had often highly praised those particular campaigns. As he told Lord Mahon:

> Nothing was too great or too small for his proboscis ... In his later days he would receive or admit no facts that were not agreeable to his pre-conceived ideas. Marmont assured me that at the close of the campaign of 1814, when forming their plans together, Napoleon said: 'Alors, Marmont viendra avec dix milles hommes' [Now, Marmont will come with ten thousand men]. Marmont interrupted him to say: 'Sire, je n'en ai que trois!' [Sire, I have only got three!]. The other nodded, and said I know; but soon afterwards again set out with 'Marmont avec ses dix milles hommes.' Again did Marmont declare that he had only three – again did Napoleon acquiesce; yet in a little while he once more began to point out and direct what Marmont would do with his ten thousand men ... Napoleon would not recede from his first idea.[4]

This image of Napoleon moving imaginary armies across maps is a powerful one, but Marmont had his own reasons for propagating it, as justifying in part his 'treachery' of 1814.

Wellington's complaint that nothing was too great or too small for Napoleon's proboscis, coming from a man known as 'Nosey' or 'that long-nosed bugger' who demanded total control over every aspect of his own army's existence, was somewhat hypocritical but it was nonetheless true. Napoleon had ordered regimental bands to play for his sick soldiers every day at noon in Cairo, he had reorganised the Parisian sewer system, and he had ensured that working men could walk in the Tuileries Gardens. Both men were masters of pointillist detail. (Wellington's nose has been preserved for posterity and can still be seen today on his descendant, the historian Dr Noel Malcolm.)

⌢

The many historians who criticise Wellington for not having sufficient-ly studied Napoleon's campaigns cannot have read Lady Salisbury's diaries at Hatfield House, where she records that on 30 August 1837, after dinner at Walmer Castle, 'the Duke was exceedingly amusing – talking over Napoleon's first campaign in Italy, the battle of Marengo, etc, etc'. On that occasion Wellington placed the blame for the Austrian defeat on their septuagenarian commander General Mélas, who 'went to bed in the middle of the day... supposing the battle won'.[5] As with Eylau, Wellington was not about to give Napoleon the credit for one of his greatest victories, but there can be no doubt that he had studied them.

Alluding to the subject of Waterloo later that month, Wellington came up with another criticism of Napoleon's strategy, telling Lady Salisbury that, as well as 'committing a great mistake' in trying to manoeuvre between himself and Blücher, the emperor had 'commit-ted another error in directing the march of a body of troops towards the English front on the day of the 16th'. This reference to the impo-tent manoeuvrings of d'Erlon's corps between Ligny and Quatre Bras was an explanation to which Napoleon himself, and all historians since, have rightly returned. Wellington was keen to make maximum capital from it, saying, 'I wonder what they would have said to me if I had done such a thing as that. But I have always avoided a false move. I preferred being too late in my movements to having to alter it.' It was an error Napoleon himself had already acknowledged, while (possibly justifiably) not accepting personal blame for it.

The idea that Wellington 'always avoided a false move' ignores his own initial orders on 15 June, after he had heard that Napoleon was south of Brussels, to move his army to the south-west *away* from the Prussians, rather than due south or south-east *towards* them. The underlying implication of Wellington's oral reminiscences tended to be that he had been omniscient during the Waterloo campaign, acquiring in full the victor's privilege of always having been right.

It is hard to ascertain whether Wellington was being laudatory or not when in October 1837, on the death of Napoleon's sister-in-law Queen Hortense, who had long denied intriguing for Napoleon's return from Elba, he wrote to Lord Mahon to say, 'you must never think it a proof that persons did not intrigue for Napoleon because he was angry with them: remember that Napoleon was not a personality, but a principle'. Wellington was, however, undoubtedly being laudatory when he told the courtier-soldier Sir John Le Couteur, having been asked whom he considered the greatest soldier of the age: 'In this age, in past ages, in <u>any</u> age, Napoleon.'[6] That he had defeated Napoleon of course added piquancy to the remark, which unfortunately cannot be dated with any degree of accuracy.

'Napoleon was right in many things,' Wellington said in April 1838 when assessing Soult's career, 'and especially in one thing – he forgave everything but want of success.' When Soult arrived in London to attend Queen Victoria's coronation later that year – where the crowd cheered him as loudly as they did Wellington – a dinner was given in his honour at Apsley House. Soult had had his marshal's baton restored in 1820 and had served as King Louis-Philippe's war minister from 1830 to 1834, and was to serve him again from 1840 to 1844. The dinner, held on Saturday, 28 July 1838 in the Gallery of Apsley House was a splendid affair, but, perhaps inevitably in that treasure house of Napoleonic trophies, Soult was faced with a great deal of evidence of his host's victories over Napoleonic France in general, if, tactfully enough, not over him in particular.

Lady Salisbury described the tangible sense of military triumph lent by the room as Wellington's forty-seven guests sat down to dinner:

On the table were two large porcelain vases given by the King of France, and two candelabras, by the City of London, but nothing <u>personal</u> to Soult. Of the silver plates some bore *Assaye* and some *Duque de Vitoria* upon them. But one could not help feeling, whatever care might be taken not to suggest such ideas, that it was a proud thing to witness Napoleon's great general sitting at his conqueror's table – especially <u>his</u> conqueror and of the master whom he served. Everything that surrounded us was a trophy, even the very room in which we were sitting, the pictures that adorned its walls, the splendid furniture, the magnificent plate, everything was the gift of a grateful nation in recompense of the triumph obtained by the victor over him who was now sitting at his table, and over the deadly and malignant foe to England whose instrument he was. There was a pleasure even in contemplating the figures of Victory that crowned the candelabras and seemed each to hold out her laurel wreath before Soult and his companions – before them, but above their reach, reserved for a greater than they.[7]

Perhaps conscious of this, Soult failed to appreciate the occasion and its surroundings, as he 'went away rather early' without even taking formal leave of Wellington, who in turn declined to attend a breakfast given in the marshal's honour the next morning.

Speaking of Napoleon's system of government to Benjamin Haydon in 1839, Wellington said it was all 'bullying and driving', but later that year he extended the accusation of bullying to Napoleon's battlefield tactics, in an illuminating monologue to Lord Ellesmere after dinner at Hatfield:

> Napoleon's system he believed to be very simple and effective, that of bullying with much noise and smoke, puzzling his cautious adversaries as to his point of attack, and massing under cover of light troops and guns his own people on one or two points. His cavalry he used with skill and effect in masses which moved forward, not fast, and occupied a position till the infantry could follow and secure it. 'He tried this', he said, 'with me at Waterloo, and when he had placed his men on the ground he probably concluded that, according to precedent, I should retire; but I moved up thirteen regiments of infantry, and destroyed or disorganized the cavalry before he could follow up the rush.'[8]

Once again Wellington was idealising what had happened. In fact he did not have thirteen infantry regiments to spare, let alone to 'move up'. The regiments had merely formed square where they were, and Ney had failed to 'follow up the rush' with infantry, as he ought to have done.

⌇

The disinterment of Napoleon's corpse from his grave on St Helena and reburial with enormous pomp and glory at Les Invalides in Paris was an event fraught with potential Anglo-French diplomatic difficulties. Adolphe Thiers, the president of the Council and minister of foreign affairs since March 1840, wrote to the British lord privy seal Lord Clarendon on 5 May to say that King Louis-Philippe 'm'autorise à demander au cabinet anglais la restitution des restes mortels de Napoléon'.[9] Thiers fully expected this to be refused, thereby adding yet another French grievance to a long list of them in that period of recurrent Middle Eastern crises. Instead, the British Cabinet chose to interpret *demander* as 'to ask' rather than anything that implied a demand or insistence.

The prime minister, Lord Melbourne, recommended acceptance, but added in a note to Clarendon: 'It would be well to inform the Duke...so do it as soon as possible, in order that he may hear it first in this manner.' Although there were twenty-one non-royal dukes in 1840, it was perfectly obvious which one Melbourne was referring to. Lady Clarendon wrote in her journal that when her husband visited Wellington, 'The Duke said that some day or other the French would be sure to make it a matter of triumph over England, but that, personally, "he did not care a two-penny damn about that!"' In fact he went further, and by December he was telling Lord Ellesmere that he was 'much pleased with a letter he had written to prevent some blockheads of our party from opposing our concession of Buonaparte's ashes'.[10] (At the time, 'ashes' could be a generic term for 'remains'. Napoleon was not cremated.)

When the French fell to debating the manner of Napoleon's interment in Paris, the *Courier Français* attacked what it called the 'cut-price' tomb proposed at Les Invalides, on the grounds that Wellington's victory had been commemorated by both a bridge and a statue, and that France must not be outdone.[11] Chateaubriand bravely opposed what was a very popular move in France, arguing that 'The translation of Napoleon's remains is an offence against fame. Napoleon's bones will not reproduce his genius; they will only teach his despotism to second-rate soldiers.' It was a prophecy amply fulfilled exactly a century later when, in 1940, Hitler was filmed contemplating Napoleon's marble sarcophagus for a Nazi propaganda film.

Bertrand, Gourgaud, Las Cases' son and Louis Marchand sailed to St Helena to bring back their master's body. One hopes they did not peruse the grave's visitors' book for 1836-7, which contained several cheery ditties along the lines of:

Alas, poor Bony!
Lies under some willows,
On an island very stormy,
Surrounded by billows.[12]

When the coffin was opened after nineteen years, the Abbé Coquereau, who sprinkled the holy water, saw that:

The whole body seemed to be covered with a light foam; it was as if we were looking at it through a diaphanous cloud. The head was unmistakable, a pillow raised it slightly; we could distinguish his broad forehead and his eyes, the sockets of which were outlined beneath the eyelids, still fringed with a few lashes; his cheeks were swollen; only his nose had suffered; his mouth, which was half-open, revealed three remarkably white teeth; on his chin the traces of his beard were perfectly clear; his two hands in particular seemed to belong to someone who still breathed, they were so fresh in tone and colouring... his nails had grown after death; they were long and white. One of his boots had come unsewn and showed four dull-white toes.[13]

The 'light foam' was adipocere, a greyish waxy substance produced by the decomposition of soft tissue in corpses exposed to moisture.

Someone else who was present, Charles Philpotts, an East India Company cadet returning from Benares on sick leave, also noted that the leather of Napoleon's boots 'had parted from the toes, exposing the feet'. Since the coffin had been partly broken in the process of being opened, 'one or two of us broke off portions and carried them away, no one forbidding'.[14] Philpotts gave his artefact to a young lady with whom he danced at a ball the following night.

Napoleon's remains were taken up the Seine and carried to Les Invalides in a snow-storm. It reminded some of the battle of Eylau, others of the crossing of the St Bernard Pass, and some less indulgent souls of the retreat from Moscow. Of his twenty-six marshals only Soult, Moncey, Oudinot and Grouchy were present to welcome Napoleon back to Paris, and it is doubtful that he would have approved of the presence of Oudinot and Moncey, who had stayed loyal to the Bourbons during the Hundred Days, or of Grouchy, who might just as well have done. Nearly one million Frenchmen and 150,000 soldiers lined the streets to watch the funeral procession. Under the dome of Les Invalides the musical programme was led by the mezzo-soprano Giuditta Grisi, the niece of Giuseppina Grassini.

Wellington was kept in close touch with events in Paris by Thomas Raikes, who described the ceremony to him in great detail the following day. 'Although there was an evident intention to give it a more triumphant than funereal air,' Raikes reported, 'it was really a serious and solemn sight.' As 'the gorgeous funeral car appeared, followed by the imperial eagles, veiled with crape', Raikes found himself thinking of:

The extraordinary career of the man, to whose tomb at St Helena this pilgrimage had been made; the countless multitudes assembled to hail

the corpse of one whose memory had for twenty-five years been pro-
scribed; the sudden silence; the torrent of heads that followed after, so
thick, so close that the earth seemed alive; altogether were of an effect
that created a nervous and extraordinary sensation of the mind.[15]

Wellington replied that he was 'very happy that this ceremony has
passed off so quietly. I cannot think it was so intended by those who
suggested it. It is fortunate that the Allied Governments had the good
sense to leave the affair entirely to the French themselves – to pass it
unnoticed.' Wellington suspected that Thiers had wanted to engineer
a diplomatic incident over it all, but then, fearing that because 'the
termination would not be quite so certain as its commencement', had
backed down from a confrontation. At Apsley House there is a litho-
graph of Jacques Guiad's picture, *The Funeral Cortège of Napoleon in the
Place de la Concorde, 15 December 1840*, the original of which is in the
Musée du Château de Versailles.[16]

꙳

September 1842 found Wellington writing another memorandum on a
Napoleonic theme, this time defending himself against the Prussian
general Karl von Clausewitz's criticisms of his strategy during the
Waterloo campaign. In it, he sought to emphasise that, while the
British army had been widely dispersed in 1815, with many men as far
away as North America,

> on the other hand, Buonaparte found an army in France completely
> organised, consisting of not less than 250,000 men, with cannon, and all
> that was required to render them efficient for the field ... Buonaparte
> had great advantages, whether for an offensive attack on the position of
> the Allies, or for the defence of his own, in the number, the position,
> and the strength of the fortresses on the north-eastern frontier of
> France. He might fix and organise his armies within these, out of sight,
> and almost without the knowledge, of the Allied generals, even to the
> last moment previous to an attack.

Wellington once again complained about his 1815 army, saying that
Clausewitz had forgotten about its inexperience, polyglot nature,
uncertain discipline and the doubtful military qualities of several of its
corps.

Furthermore, the initiative had entirely rested with Napoleon, whose intention was 'to create throughout Europe, and even in England, a moral impression against the war, and to shake the power of the then existing administration in England'. Yet Wellington would not go far down the counterfactual-history route. He considered it 'useless to speculate upon supposed military movements which were never made, and operations which never took place, or the objects of the several chiefs or generals opposed to each other'.

Wellington claimed that 'it was certainly true that he had known for some days of the augmentation of the enemy's force on the frontier and even of the arrival of Buonaparte at the army; but he did not deem it expedient to make any movement... till he should hear of the decided movement of the enemy'. Yet as late as 13 June Wellington had told Lord Lynedoch that he thought Napoleon was in Paris, and was not about to move northwards. Rather contradictorily, Wellington, employing the third person singular, admitted: 'It was perfectly true that the Duke of Wellington did not at first give credit to the reports of the intention of the enemy to attack by the valleys of the Sambre and the Meuse.' Yet when the attack came, he wrote, 'he was not unprepared to assist in resisting it', saying that his orders reached all parts of his army in six hours. He also pointed out that Soult's note to Grouchy written at 1 p.m. on the day of the battle of Waterloo, saying that Prussian cavalry had been perceived in the east, proved that Napoleon had no prior inkling of Blücher's impending arrival.

'Surely the details of the battle might have been left in the original official reports,' Wellington concluded. 'Historians and commentators were not necessary. The battle, possibly the most important military event in modern times, was attended by advantages sufficient for the glory of many such armies as the two great Allied armies engaged. The enemy never rallied; Buonaparte lost his empire for ever; not a shot was fired afterwards; and the peace of Europe and of the world was settled on the basis on which it rests at the moment.' It was undoubtedly a powerful argument, and Wellington ended his defence by indulging in precisely the 'what if?' history he had previously abjured:

> It might be a nice question for military discussion whether Buonaparte was right in endeavouring to force the position at Waterloo, or the Duke of Wellington right in thinking that, from the evening of the 16th, Buonaparte would have taken a wiser course if he had moved to his left, have reached the high road leading from Mons to Brussels, and have turned the right of the position of the Allies by Hal.[17]

In answer to his own question, Wellington stated that: 'It is obvious that the Duke was prepared to resist such a movement,' as indeed he was, having stationed such a large force at Hal, which sadly but necessarily saw no part of the fighting.

Wellington told Lord Mahon a fortnight after writing his memorandum that he wanted to lend it to his friend Lord Ellesmere to use in an attack on Clausewitz's 'erroneous statements' in an article in the leading Tory journal, the *Quarterly Review*. Although no such article appeared, the following year an essay was published in the *Review*'s October issue in defence of Wellington's strategy. 'We have been asked by an officer of high distinction to print, by way of a note or appendix to our recent article on the *Life of Blücher* and the campaign of Waterloo, a memorandum on the controversy about that campaign, which was drawn up ... by his friend Sir Francis Head,' announced the *Review*, adding that it would do so, out of 'Our respect for our correspondent and also for his friend'. Head was a regular contributor on military matters to the *Quarterly Review*. As a Royal Engineers officer who had been at Charleroi on 16 June and at Waterloo two days later, he was in a prime position to refute the allegations made by Clausewitz, and also by a Mr Alison who had argued in a recent review of a biography of Blücher that both the field marshal and Wellington had been 'surprised, outmanoeuvred, and out-generalled' by Napoleon.

There can be little doubt about the identity of the 'officer of high distinction', and in several important respects Sir Francis Head's memorandum was similar to the one that Wellington had written in his own defence the previous year. As Head put it: 'Not only was Napoleon's army so completely routed at Waterloo that it could not for a moment rally ... but Napoleon ... decided on abdicating his title of Emperor.' Head also suggested that Napoleon ought to have 'thrown his troops into the line of frontier fortresses in his position' and have 'pursued a more cautious plan of defensive operations', both views often expressed by Wellington.

Much of Head's memorandum is highly critical of Napoleon – 'no plan of operations would have proved more fatal to Napoleon than the hurried arrangements he adopted' – and frankly laudatory of the duke.[18] Head, a former lieutenant-governor of Upper Canada who had quelled a rising in 1835 and been rewarded with a baronetcy, wrote from the Athenæum, a club of which Wellington was a founder member. It is hard to escape the conclusion that Wellington placed at least one article favourable to himself and abusive of Napoleon into the foremost Tory intellectual publication of the day. His public stance of utter indifference to what writers said about the Waterloo campaign was subtly different from his private actions.

Usually, however, he would merely issue grand rebukes to would-be correspondents. When a citizen of Belfast wrote to ask whether he thought Napoleon had killed the Turkish prisoners at Jaffa, and whether any circumstances could justify such an action, the reply came: 'Field Marshal the Duke of Wellington presents his compliments to Mr H.; he has also received Mr H.'s letter, and begs leave to inform him that he is not the historian of the wars of the French republic in Egypt and Syria.'[19]

When in 1843 John Sainsbury's vast collection of Napoleana was opened to the public at the Egyptian Hall in Piccadilly, Wellington was among the hundred thousand people who visited it. Sainsbury had started to collect 'everything worth notice in a portable form relating to Napoleon' in the 1820s, and by the time of the exhibition two decades later the catalogue alone ran to seven hundred pages. The exhibition building, with its mock-Egyptian façade, had already put on a very successful show of Napoleonic artefacts in 1815–16, the centrepiece of which had been Napoleon's bullet-proof carriage, bought by Madame Tussaud's in 1843 for £168. The exhibition Wellington visited that year included bronzes, cameos, paintings, letters and a myriad of other Napoleonic bric-à-brac, and was intended to demonstrate the late emperor's 'wonderful character and uncommon genius and his general superiority over his species', not an object of which the exhibition's most illustrious visitor would have approved.[20]

In 1844 the American impresario Phineas T. Barnum hired much of the Egyptian Hall for the famous dwarf 'Colonel' Tom Thumb, an action which was indirectly to lead to the death of Benjamin Robert Haydon, who since painting Wellington and Napoleon had become morbidly obsessed with the duke and the emperor. When Haydon committed suicide on 22 June 1846, after the failure of his art exhibition in the Egyptian Hall – made all the worse for him by the huge crowds queuing up outside to meet Tom Thumb in the adjoining rooms – thoughts of Napoleon and Wellington were among the last to go through his brain before he tried to put a bullet through it.

Haydon had long thought of himself as a genius 'of the Napoleon species', a feeling merely encouraged in 1830 when he tried on Napoleon's hat and found that it fitted perfectly. His recurring dreams about the two antagonists had led him to suppose 'something grand in my destiny is coming on', but in the end his career spluttered out. After trying to shoot himself, but finding the bullet was deflected by his skull because the pistol was of too low a calibre, Haydon cut his throat, spattering his blood over the canvas of his never-to-be-finished painting *Alfred*. At the end of his 'Last Thoughts', a suicide note to his wife and daughter, who had heard the shot but thought it came from a nearby parade ground, the painter had written:

> Wellington never used evil, if the good was not certain; Napoleon had no such scruples and I fear the glitter of his genius rather dazzled me – but had I been encouraged, nothing but good would have come from me; because when encouraged I paid every body. God forgive me the evil for the sake of the good. Amen.[21]

∽

Wellington's thoughts were also turning to God at about this time. In November 1847 he wrote to his friend the heiress Angela Burdett-Coutts about a book he had recently read on Napoleon. In language unaccustomedly biblical in tone, he effectively presented himself as having been the instrument of God's Will at Waterloo. He had already stated that he believed that God had specifically protected him during the battle, but now he took the concept of divine intervention a stage further. In his letter, he complained:

> The author boasts of the fortune of Napoleon in having died quietly in his bed, after having been engaged through life in so many conquests, wars, revolutions, conquest of kingdoms, destruction of reigning dynasties! He did not, he could not do as he is a Frenchman, perceive and was not sensible that this particular fact and incident in the hero's life was to be attributed to the influence of a religion of peace and forgiveness, that of Christ, over modern civilization and manners. In ancient times, those of the Jews, in those of Greeks and Romans, a conqueror such as Napoleon would have been destroyed upon the scaffold by the executioner as soon as deprived of his power, as he was in his last great battle. But no! His treachery, his tyranny, his cruelty towards all were from that time forward forgiven. But no! He was banished and placed in a position in which, as long as he could be detained, the world might feel secure that he at least would not again disturb its tranquillity or endanger its security against the repetition of the same misfortunes. This was justifiable in a Christian sense.[22]

If Wellington did by then perceive Napoleon as some form of Anti-Christ, it did not prevent him from attending parties and dinners given by his son. Count Alexandre Walewski was the natural son of Napoleon and his favourite mistress, the Polish Countess Marie Walewska. He had been one of the little boys who had played at the Elysée Palace the night before Napoleon's second abdication. When Alexandre was born in 1810, Napoleon announced that 'The infant of Wagram will one day be king of Poland,' despite at the same time writing to Tsar Alexander offering Russia a free hand in that country in exchange for the hand in marriage of the tsar's sister, Grand Duchess Anna.

Greville records Alexandre Walewski as 'wonderfully handsome and agreeable, and soon...popular in London society' when he visited in 1831, especially when he later married Lady Caroline Montagu, the daughter of the 6th Earl of Sandwich. That Wellington socialised regularly with Walewski is clear from a letter he wrote to Croker in January 1845, saying: 'I know that gentleman perfectly, and have met him elsewhere: in London, at Hatfield, &, &. I knew his mother at Paris, and at Liège.'[23] That Wellington met Marie Walewska, Napoleon's faithful mistress who followed him to Elba (with her son) for a secret tryst, but who much to his chagrin married again in 1816 and was to die the following year, provides further evidence of the duke's interest in Napoleon's women.

The other young boy who had played at Napoleon's feet that night at the Elysée, as the crowd outside cried 'Vive l'Empereur!' and secret documents were being burned, was Prince Louis-Napoleon Bonaparte, son of Napoleon's brother Louis and Hortense de Beauharnais. In 1836 he tried to excite a revolt among the French garrison at Strasbourg, failed, and went into exile, initially to the United States. Two years later he was living at Carlton Terrace in London and was lionised by Whig society, with receptions being given for him by, as one might suspect, Lord Holland, the Duchess of Bedford and Earl Grey. Wellington was amused at first, writing in (somewhat premature) mockery: 'Would you believe it, this young man Louis-Napoleon will not have it said that he is not going to be Emperor of the French!'[24]

In August 1840 the Bonaparte pretender again tried to overthrow the Orleanist monarchy of King Louis-Philippe, and landed at Boulogne, but once again the coup proved abortive and he was captured, given a life sentence and imprisoned at Ham. Two days after the Boulogne fiasco, Wellington wrote to Thomas Raikes in Paris about the 'terrible event'. He was most apprehensive that the Whig prime minister Lord Melbourne and the foreign secretary Lord Palmerston might have held interviews with Louis-Napoleon shortly before he left on his expedition. 'This may be true; but, if I can answer for anything where I can know nothing, I should say that those ministers had never heard of his intentions.' As ever, Wellington was primarily concerned about Anglo-French relations. He was concerned about the French pamphleteers who were bruiting it about that the attempted coup had been covertly financed by the British Government, that Louis-Napoleon had met Queen Victoria, and that he was about to be recognised by Britain as emperor, none of which was remotely the case.[25]

When Louis-Napoleon did finally stage his successful *coup d'état* on 2 December 1851, Wellington was watching closely. 'Paris was still quiet last night!' he wrote to a correspondent Margaret Jones two days later. He had earlier assumed that 'there must be a fight!' but in fact Paris remained quiet. The following month he told Mrs Jones, a gifted conversationalist, hostess and something of a beauty who was sixty years his junior: 'I am not at my ease about Louis-Napoleon. He is going too fast. I see that his ministers have resigned on account of his last act – the plunder of the property of the Orleans family! This is a great mistake! The whole world will be against him on account of it.'[26]

The man Louis-Napoleon appointed as ambassador to London was none other than Count Walewski – 'the infant of Wagram' – some of whose dinners at the French embassy Wellington attended. When Wellington died peacefully in his armchair at Walmer Castle on 14 September 1852, aged eighty-three, his old opponent's nephew was only weeks away from declaring himself emperor. At 11 a.m. on Thursday, 2 December, a mere fortnight after Wellington's funeral, the prefect of the Seine, surrounded by the Paris municipal body at the Hôtel de Ville, proclaimed, among the revived cries of 'Vive l'Empereur!', that France was once again a Napoleonic empire. It was a day pregnant with symbolism – the anniversary both of Napoleon I's coronation in 1804 and of his victory at Austerlitz the following year. In his message to the Senate, the new emperor Napoleon III referred to 'the glorious reign of the head of my family' and his uncle's birthday, 15 August, was proclaimed a national holiday. Just as he had predicted on St Helena, thirty years after his death in 1821 Napoleon had had his posthumous vindication.

Wellington's last recorded comment about Napoleon, made to Croker at Folkestone only ten days before he died, was a very generous one. To the French poet-politician Alphonse de Lamartine's description of Napoleon's 'weakness, and even cowardice, towards the close of Waterloo', the duke strongly objected. 'Of course I could see nothing about it; but I can hardly believe it. I think that even with ordinary men a great interest would overcome personal fear.'[27] He went on to reiterate yet again the value to France of having Napoleon on a battlefield. They had been discussing Marshal Lannes' insistence on the importance of sang-froid during military engagements, and Wellington said that although he had never met Lannes:

> I have seen most of the other marshals, and I have no doubt that, as a general, Buonaparte was the best of them. When I met all the great Allied generals at Paris in 1814, they were so good as to compliment me on my successes in Spain. I told them that I quite agreed in the estimate that I had heard made, that the absence of Buonaparte was as good as forty thousand men. As I had never met Buonaparte, and as they had all been beaten by him in person, my allusion to that estimate was received as a compliment to them, and modesty on my part; but I really believe that it was true as to the continental armies. Yes, Buonaparte was certainly the best of them all, and his prestige worth forty thousand men.

Croker then said that it was 'easy to be best when one is master of them all, sovereign disburser of punishment and reward, and having no control to thwart, nor scruple to stop, and no responsibility to himself'. Wellington agreed that to be true, 'but I still don't think that any of them could, even in his circumstances, have done what he did'.[28] It was a fitting and final peroration to Wellington's estimations of Napoleon.

In the second battle Wellington fought against Napoleon, that of their funerals, the result was a draw. Napoleon's funeral had been a magnificent display, and, just as his nephew was about to ascend the French throne, the British were determined that Wellington's should be no less memorable. Historians have since seen Wellington's funeral as a self-conscious 'answer' to the entombment of Napoleon at Les Invalides twelve years earlier. Indeed, Professor James Stevens Curl has even stated of Wellington's 'severe and impressive sarcophagus' of Cornish porphyry that: 'This heroic tomb was obviously a riposte to Napoleon's recently completed mausoleum.'[29] Unfortunately, unlike

Napoleon's funeral which went smoothly, at Wellington's, held in the days before Britain perfected her talent for faultless pageantry, arrangements went awry.

At the lying-in-state in the Great Hall at the Royal Hospital in Chelsea – coincidentally in the very room where forty-four years earlier Wellington's career had nearly been buried by the Cintra Inquiry – two hundred thousand people filed past the bier between 11 November, when Queen Victoria arrived, and the 17th, when police estimated that 55,000 came. The crowds were not controlled properly and more than once people were injured when barriers were knocked down. Two women and one man were even suffocated to death in the crush.

On 18 November approximately one and a half million people watched the state funeral procession from Horse Guards to St Paul's Cathedral. 'On no public occasion has anything at all approaching it ever been manifested,' reported a black-bordered edition of *The Times* that morning. 'The streets have been blocked up with conveyances to an unprecedented extent, and the pavements so crowded with foot passengers that it was with the greatest difficulty people could get from point to point.' Even the Radical poet and Chartist political campaigner Thomas Cooper was deeply affected as he stretched his neck 'to get the last sight of the [funeral] car as it passed Piccadilly, till it was out of sight'. He felt that 'the great connecting link of our national life was broken; the great actor in the scenes of the Peninsula and Waterloo – the conqueror of Napoleon – and the chief name in our home political life for many years – had disappeared'.[30]

Whereas Napoleon's funeral car had been made of pine and papier mâché and had been destroyed afterwards, Wellington's was built to specifications approved by Prince Albert and was designed 'to preserve the military character suitable for the occasion, whilst retaining the effect of simplicity and grandeur. No tinsel or gimcrack work is to be used.' It was cast in solid bronze with six wheels supporting its length of twenty-four feet, width of eleven feet and its height of seventeen feet. It weighed an incredible ten tons and had to be pulled by twelve black horses harnessed three abreast.

Trophies, flags and arms were selected from the Tower of London armoury to emblazon it, and it carried the names of twenty-five of Wellington's victories, culminating in Waterloo. On the side of the funeral car – which is today preserved at Stratfield Saye – the trophies were surmounted by the strawberry leaves of the ducal coronet. Unfortunately its sheer weight meant that on reaching the Duke of

York's column in Pall Mall the car got stuck in several inches of mud, and members of the public had to help policemen and soldiers to dislodge it. At the end of the four-hour procession the mechanism for getting the coffin off it also stuck, so there was another hour's wait at St Paul's before it could be freed and carried into the cathedral. As *The Times* had to admit, this 'tended somewhat to impair the effect of the solemn ceremonial' and 'excited the anxiety of the spectators'.

In commending the duke for his victory over 'a despotic and arrogant enemy', *The Times'* obituary had stated that Wellington was 'without the slightest personal ostentation, with a simplicity of character utterly alien from display or egotism'. Yet, because he left no instructions, the Government – which took over the arrangements from the Wellesley family and therefore paid for everything – revelled in the opportunity for ostentation and display. Dickens called it 'such a palpably got up theatrical trick' and the Earl of Shaftesbury thought it 'a mere amusement', but it was undeniably magnificent and worthy of Britain's greatest soldier.

Count Walewski, despite being French ambassador to London, asked Napoleon III for permission not to attend the funeral of his natural father's conqueror. His cousin refused, saying 'that he wished to forget the past; that he had always reason to be grateful for the friendly terms in which the late Duke had spoken of him; and that he always desired to continue on the best terms with England'. When Walewski grumbled to the Russian ambassador Count Philipp von Brunnow about the humiliation of walking behind a catafalque emblazoned with the word 'Waterloo', he was told: 'If this ceremony were intended to bring the Duke to life again I can conceive your reluctance to appear at it; but as it is only to bury him, I don't see that you have anything to complain of.'[31]

Walewski attended, and was commended for doing so by the prime minister, the 14th Earl of Derby, who said that France had 'testified by their representative their respect and veneration of his memory. They regarded him as a foe worthy of their steel.' Over in the Commons the leader of the House, Benjamin Disraeli, gave what Charles Greville thought was a 'pompous' oration about Wellington, which later turned out to have been plagiarised from Thiers' 1830 panegyric on Napoleon's Marshal Gouvion St Cyr. Disraeli's excuse was that he had been 'much struck' by it at the time, had noted it down and came to believe that he had composed it, but Greville thought that 'the poor apology does not save him'.

To complement Count Walewski's presence in representing France,

Russia sent Prince Gorchakov, who had been present at Waterloo, and Prussia sent Count August von Nostitz, Blücher's dragoon aide-de-camp who had saved the field marshal after his charger had fallen on him after the battle of Ligny. Austria sent no one, in protest against the ill-treatment of General Haynau, who in 1850 had been roughed up by London draymen for his part in the brutal suppression of the nationalist revolts of 1848–9, when his flogging of women earned him the (hardly very imaginative) nickname of 'Hyena'.

After the interment at St Paul's, Garter King of Arms stood over the grave and read out a list of all of Wellington's titles and honours. For by the time of his death Wellington was, in the order that they were intoned,

> Most High, Mighty, and Most Noble Prince, Duke of Wellington, Marquess of Wellington, Marquess of Douro, Earl of Wellington, in Somerset, Viscount Wellington, of Talevera, Baron Douro, of Wellesley, Prince of Waterloo in the Netherlands, Duke of Ciudad Rodrigo in Spain, Duke of Brunoy in France [in fact a title Wellington had refused], Duke of Vitoria, Marquess of Torres Vedras, Count of Vimeiro in Portugal, a Grandee of the First Class in Spain, a Privy Councillor, Commander-in-Chief of the British Army, Colonel of the Grenadier Guards, Colonel of the Rifle Brigade, a Field Marshal of Great Britain, a Marshal of Russia, a Marshal of Austria, a Marshal of France, a Marshal of Prussia, a Marshal of Portugal, a Marshal of the Netherlands, a Knight of the Garter, a Knight of the Holy Ghost, a Knight of the Golden Fleece, a Knight Grand Cross of the Bath, a Knight Grand Cross of Hanover, a Knight of the Black Eagle, a Knight of the Tower and Sword, a Knight of St Fernando, a Knight of William of the Low Countries, a Knight of Charles III, a Knight of the Sword of Sweden, a Knight of St Andrew of Russia, a Knight of the Annunciato of Sardinia, a Knight of the Elephant of Denmark, a Knight of Maria Theresa, a Knight of St George of Russia, a Knight of the Crown of Rue of Saxony, a Knight of Fidelity of Baden, a Knight of Maximilian Joseph of Bavaria, a Knight of St Alexander Nevsky of Russia, a Knight of St Hermenegilda of Spain, a Knight of the Red Eagle of Brandenburgh, a Knight of St Januarius, a Knight of the Golden Lion of Hesse Cassel, a Knight of the Lion of Baden, a Knight of Merit of Wurtemburg, the Lord High Constable of England, the Constable of the Tower of London, Lord Warden of the Cinque

Ports, Lord-Lieutenant of Hampshire, Lord-Lieutenant of the Tower Hamlets, Ranger of St James' Park, Chancellor of the University of Oxford, Commissioner of the Royal Military College, Vice-President of the Scottish Naval and Military Academy, the Master of the Trinity House, a Governor of King's College, a Doctor of Laws, &.

Small wonder that his son Lord Douro had lamented: 'Think what it will be like when the Duke of Wellington is announced and only I appear.' It was not a bad collection of honours and titles for a man supposedly disdainful of such things who was furthermore, according to his obituarist, 'without the slightest personal ostentation' and entirely lacking in 'display and egotism'.

A year after the French *coup d'état*, the British Government wanted an exhibition of national solidarity, and by the mobilisation of a mass audience – special funeral trains were laid on from around the country to maximise the attendance – it was able to provide a fitting reply to Napoleon's funeral of 1840, with perhaps a slightly larger number of people attending the London obsequies than the Paris ones.[32] If honours in the battle of the funerals were about evenly divided, the great men were now about to engage upon their third and final battle – the struggle for primacy in their posthumous reputations.

CONCLUSION

*The only author who deserves to be read is he who never
endeavours to influence and direct the opinion of the reader.*

NAPOLEON

Any investigation into the relationship between Napoleon and
Wellington is bound to include a comparison of the two men.
'Napoleon and Wellington will be inseparably connected as long as
history is written,' wrote a British historian of the 1930s.

> They are as closely united as Hector and Achilles, Hannibal and Scipio,
> Pompey and Cæsar, and in another sphere, Disraeli and Gladstone.
> They had in common many of the attributes which combine to produce
> superlative military greatness, but an extreme dissimilarity of character
> made the exercise of their powers have very different consequences.
> Wellington may have been less gifted in scope and vision than
> Napoleon, but he was superior in character, which wins in the long run.[1]

This somewhat self-satisfied conclusion is the standard one that
British historians have adopted. Napoleon had genius, most readily
admit, but Wellington had fine, solid British common sense and hence
was ultimately victorious. For writers such as the Victorian moralist
Samuel Smiles the contrast was irresistible. 'Our own Wellington was
a far greater man,' he argued in his book *Self-Help* in 1859. 'Not less
resolute, firm and persistent, but much more self-denying, self-conscious and truly patriotic. Napoleon's aim was "glory"; Wellington's
watchword, like Nelson's, was "duty".' (Actually, Nelson was obsessed
with his own glory, and is linked with the concept of duty largely
because of his pre-Trafalgar signal.) Smiles even claimed that the word
'glory' 'does not once occur' in Wellington's despatches, which is
incorrect, but typical of an age that attempted to depict Wellington as
the paragon of the gentlemanly ideal.

Disraeli, who was no expert witness on the subject, recommended
the contemplation of Wellington's noble character in his Commons
panegyric. Creevey also lauded 'the uniform frankness and simplicity
of Wellington', failing to point out that frankness often tripped over

into downright rudeness. Nor did Wellington's sensitive musical and artistic tastes, and the enthusiastic display of his trophies, really make him the model of bluff soldierly 'simplicity' that the Victorians liked to project. He was a far more complex man than many of his panegyrists and would-be apologists allow, and his memory is not well served by the partisan generalisations of modern historians such as those who write: 'Wellington was honest, loyal, magnanimous, truthful, honourable and kindly; Napoleon was treacherous, disloyal, amoral, a cheat, liar and a bully – "fit for treasons, stratagems and spoils".'[2]

The denigration of Wellington by French writers is as ludicrous as his deification by some British writers. General Foy, who had been on the losing side to Wellington at Oporto, Busaco, Salamanca, Sorauren, the Bidaossa, Nivelle, the Nive, Orthez and Waterloo, and so should perhaps have known better, tried to argue in his 1827 memoirs that 'there were twenty officers... any one of whom would have commanded with as much, and perhaps with more ability and success than Wellington'. Foy could not have failed to know when he wrote it that this was simply untrue. In his editions of *Les Maximes de Napoléon Ier*, Honoré de Balzac stated: 'The soul of Napoleon passes before us. Wellington was an accident... France may say with pride that from the depths of his tomb Napoleon still combats England.'[3]

Victor Hugo, who described Napoleon as 'the mighty somnambulist of a vanished dream', agreed, and came up with a stupendously blasphemous reason for the outcome of Waterloo: 'To the question, was it possible for Napoleon to win this battle, our answer is No. Because of Wellington? Because of Blücher? No. Because of God... Napoleon had been impeached in heaven and his fate decreed; he was troublesome to God.' Chateaubriand took the somewhat unusual middle way of despising both men. 'An Irish Protestant,' he wrote in his *Memoirs*, 'a British general with no understanding of our history or our way of life, a man who saw nothing in the French year of 1793 but the English antecedent of 1649, was given the task of deciding our fate! Bonaparte's ambition has brought us to this sorry pass.'

Full-scale personality cults have grown up around both Napoleon and Wellington, which time and the tides of revisionist history have done nothing to diminish, and which many internet websites are today doing much to burnish. The process by which any witty or pertinent quotation gets attributed to the two men, whether they actually said it or not, means that both have benefited from a phenomenon that has similarly assisted the posthumous reputations of Winston Churchill, Oscar Wilde and George Bernard Shaw. Wellington, for example, did not suggest to Queen Victoria that 'Sparrow-hawks, Ma'am' should be used to expel the sparrows from the Great Exhibition's Crystal Palace, and the line 'Not tonight, Josephine' originated from W. G. Wills' play *The Royal Divorce*, written a full seven decades after Napoleon's death.[4]

Virtually anything will be believed of Napoleon, as the following distasteful extract from the Goncourt journals shows. On 25 October 1864, the publisher Georges Charpentier told the writer and diarist Edmond de Goncourt, that according to one of Napoleon's valets called Constant Wairy, 'Napoleon was in the habit of rolling his excrement into balls between his fingers: a habit which bears a curious and horrifying resemblance to similar cases, symptomatic of insanity, noted by Dr [Ulysse] Trélat.'

⏤

An historian has noticed that: 'The post-mortem contest of Napoleon and Wellington was given many meanings by those who used it. It typified the contest of order against revolution (or freedom against feudalism for the Napoleonists); of method against machines (or caution against genius); of modesty against ambition, and even of gentlemen against players.'[5] In the course of these polemical histories the contrasts between the two men are consistently emphasised, while their similarities − beyond a joint tendency to win battles − have been constantly downplayed because they failed to fit into the underlying messages the authors were hoping to promote. There is a Wellington-Napoleon High School in Missouri, and Ostend used to be protected by a Fort Wellington and a Fort Napoleon, but otherwise the two are always seen as polar opposites, in permanent contention.

It is asserted that Wellington understood and valued the contribution that naval warfare could make, describing the fleet in an 1808 Commons debate as 'the characteristic and constitutional force of Britain', while Napoleon is portrayed as a veritable land-lubber.[6] The fact that the Royal Navy completely dominated the seas during this period is under-emphasised in order to highlight this supposed difference. Wellington is praised for his unambiguous despatches, whereas Napoleon's 'meaning was sometimes as hard to unravel as his handwriting was difficult to decipher', a reasonable enough criticism.[7] In such a search for differences, one might as well add that Wellington acquired a taste for tea in India while Napoleon was enjoying coffee in Egypt.[8]

Wellington was fortunate in the assistance of his several brothers in the advancement of his career, whereas after the 1799 Brumaire coup

Napoleon's siblings only retarded his career, as King Joseph lost Spain, Louis had to be virtually deposed from the Dutch throne, and Jérôme failed to take Hougoumont. Wellington is credited with being as economical with men and material as Napoleon was prodigal. Yet Wellington opposed political reform, while Napoleon's civil and administrative reforms – admittedly undertaken partly out of a need to mobilise the country militarily – dragged France into the nineteenth century. Napoleon has been described as egomaniacal, mother-fixated, epileptic, introverted and so 'suppurating with psychosomatic symptoms, [he] might have been locked up in later times'. Wellington, on the other hand, has been generally portrayed as a simple soldier keen to get on in life.[9] The distortions and generalisations are manifest.

Here are some of the contrasts that writers have emphasised about the two men:

> The schemes of the French Emperor were more comprehensive, his genius more dazzling, and his imagination more vivid than Wellington's ... In the Waterloo campaign, while Napoleon made many mistakes, Wellington made none.[10] (Lord Roberts of Kandahar)
>
> Napoleon understood France and Frenchmen as Wellington never understood England and the English.[11] (Richard Aldington)
>
> For all his genius, for all his well-merited reputation as Britain's best commander after the Duke of Marlborough, Wellington was not on the same elevated plane as Napoleon. While Napoleon had dominated Europe both militarily and politically, the Duke conducted a mere sideshow in the Peninsula against a committee of quarrelsome French marshals.[12] (Andrew Uffindell)
>
> These two great men may be compared to the two purifying elements, fire and water. Napoleon the fire whose flames swept the earth. Wellington the water following steadily after to quench the flames, lest their purifying efficacy be turned to destructiveness. Even the battle portents of each represented fire and water, for the sun heralded Napoleon's triumphs, whilst a thunderstorm with torrential rains was the accepted symbol of a Wellington victory.[13] (Muriel Wellesley)
>
> Napoleon personified the fire, the dash, brilliance of the south. Wellington, an Irishman only in the place of his birth, certainly not in character, embodied the hardness, caution, sound sense and stubbornness of the Anglo-Saxon.[14] (J. Holland Rose)

I have never come across any example, in fiction or in reality, of someone mad enough to think he was the Duke of Wellington. In England, at least, wanting to be the Emperor was crazy, wanting to be the Duke was wholly understandable and even to be encouraged. (Iain Pears)[15]

It is undeniable that Napoleon has had a profound mental effect on people, and not only upon lunatics, or suicides like Benjamin Robert Haydon. Edmond de Goncourt recorded in his journal in 1865 that the literary critic Charles Augustin Sainte-Beuve, who was born in 1804, 'saw the first Emperor once: it was at Boulogne and he was urinating. It is, so to speak, in that position that he has judged all great men ever since.'

Despite all the attempts by both sets of apologists clearly to differentiate each man from the other, thereby bringing out aspects of each opponent's character in order to emphasise the obverse side in their hero, the two men had much more in common than either's supporters would care to admit. And, as Professor Lucien Henry pointed out in his edition of Napoleon's war maxims, 'Those who would libel Napoleon rob Wellington of half his glory,' an error Wellington himself went to strenuous lengths to avoid making, at least in public.

Both men enjoyed invincible self-belief, could occasionally be intolerably brusque and ruthless, and were interested in, but essentially repelled by, the other's character. Furthermore, each had a healthy respect for the abilities of the other, despite the subsequent distortions of historians. The military historian Sir John Keegan has spotted how Wellington succeeded 'between the ages of thirty and forty-five in banishing feeling from his personality. The desire to do so was deliberate and the effort by which he achieved it intellectual.' Perhaps the process had even begun at the age of twenty-four, when Wellington burned his violin in the Dublin grate and resolved to take himself and his career seriously. In 1959 the 7th Duke of Wellington wrote of his great ancestor: 'His reticence and aversion from displays of sentiment, his bursts of irritability at incompetence, his intolerance of human weakness like late rising or gambling, make his character as repulsive to some people as a love of publicity and lack of reticence to others.'[16]

In their *Realpolitik* use of religion – Wellington ordered his men to salute the Host when campaigning in the Catholic Peninsula, Napoleon persuaded Mecca to issue a proclamation making France an ally of Islam – they were similar (although Wellington would never have gone so far as Napoleon, whose minister for public worship, the sublimely named Comte Bigot, conveniently discovered a Saint Napoleon). In their use of nepotism – Napoleon married a friend of Barras,

Wellington found swift promotion under his brother the governor-general of India – they did not scruple, any more than did anyone else in that great century of jobbery and patronage. In their attitude to their legacies, both men affected to despise historians, yet as amateur military historians they were both interested in winning the approbation of History. In their unhappy marriages to women who were essentially unworthy of them, they were also more similar than either would have liked to admit. In their harshness towards subordinates – witness Wellington's sarcasm towards Uxbridge only hours before Napoleon's rudeness to Soult – both men exhibited the insolence of power.

As Keegan has pointed out, their minds worked along similar lines, for Napoleon:

> had unusual mathematical gifts, which imply strong analytic powers. Wellington was musical, and deeply interested in mechanics and astronomy, which are also mentally ordering. Neither man, however, had had formal university training, a deficiency Wellington always regretted. Given their quite unusual capacity to absorb and organize information, the suggestion presents itself that both may have in some way been exposed to the mnemonic 'theatre of memory' technique so influential in the Europe of revived classical learning.[17]

Above all in their complete concentration on success and victory, Napoleon and Wellington were not so utterly different people as the moralists, Victorians and partisans have tried to make out.

Wellington believed that Napoleon was 'A great man but also a great actor.'[18] Yet, in his long memorandum on Napoleon's Russian campaign, in his two written memoranda and in his many comments and occasional letters on Napoleon's strategy and tactics, he proved himself keen that his friends should think of him as the superior general. He could not publicly denigrate Napoleon's genius without concomitantly lessening his own achievements, but his comments before, during and after Waterloo all imply that he considered himself the more talented soldier in both strategy and tactics. It is thus inadvisable to take all Wellington's public statements about Napoleon at face value.

Similarly, British historians have regularly interpreted Napoleon's comments before Waterloo to prove that the emperor felt Wellington was a mere sepoy general. J. Holland Rose said Napoleon 'fought the battle against Wellington carelessly, assured that it was the affair of a *déjeuner*. He always despised the Duke.'[19] Elizabeth Longford wrote: 'Wellington did not make the mistake of despising his opponent.' Sir Arthur Bryant criticised Napoleon's 'overweening confidence and impatience'. Major-General John Strawson said Napoleon 'looked on Wellington as a man of passive character and did not see he was a man of patience'[20] (this despite Napoleon's remark commending Wellington's 'prudence' as superior to his own). Dr David Chandler unequivocally stated that Napoleon 'scorned Wellington as his enemy. He is a Corsican, and such foes tend to sneer at the opposition.'[21] Jac Weller wrote that 'Napoleon's lack of interest in his enemies is in contrast to Wellington's painstaking procedures.'[22] Literally dozens of other such generalisations about Napoleon's supposed over-confident contempt for Wellington could be quoted, and almost all cite as irrefutable evidence the remark Napoleon made to Soult at Le Caillou on the morning of the battle.[23]

Yet when Wellington was defeating Napoleon's marshals in the Peninsula, the emperor was perfectly willing to be thoroughly objective about his military qualities, at least off the record. Far from scorning or ignoring him, on Elba Napoleon squeezed people for information about Wellington's character and interests. Of course for propaganda purposes the public attack was kept up, but privately Napoleon was both curious and complimentary about Wellington. It was not until Waterloo – the only battle they ever fought against one another – that Napoleon began to concoct a series of 'observations' on Wellington's bad generalship to try to explain away his own defeat. His remarks at Le Caillou were simply intended to boost the morale of his seemingly defeatist generals, nothing more. What else could Napoleon have been expected to say only a matter of hours before the attack? The morning of a great battle is no time for objectivity.

Nor, of course, is exile after a great defeat. The list of people or factors that Napoleon explicitly blamed for what happened during the Waterloo campaign included Ney, Grouchy, Bourmont, the 'right flank', his restricted view of the battlefield, 'panic', 'darkness', the rain, his 'exhaustion', d'Erlon's actions both on 16 June and on the 18th, 'junior staff officers', treachery, the Vendée, Vandamme, Mortier, Drovot, Friant and Guyot. Of course there are several commanders on that list who did indeed deserve censure, and have received it from History, but the very length of the list implies that on St Helena Napoleon was thrashing around looking for scapegoats, as well as utterly refusing to commend Wellington for playing any part in the

Allied victory. Yet because Napoleon expressed contempt for Wellington in 1816 and thereafter, it does not necessarily mean that he genuinely felt it in June 1815.

Consider the long list of Napoleonic compliments about Wellington over the half-decade before the battle of Waterloo. In 1810 he had likened Wellington to himself, when he told the Comte de Chanteloup that there were only two commanders in Europe ruthless enough to retreat to Torres Vedras in the way Wellington had before Masséna. In 1812, returning from Moscow in his sleigh, he admitted to Caulaincourt that Wellington had made a 'reputation' for himself in the Peninsula. The following year in his reported conversation with Metternich, he specifically exempted Wellington from his generalisation that the Allies had no first-rate generals able to match him and his marshals.

In 1814, days after his tearful abdication at Fontainebleau, the ex-emperor 'passed high encomiums' on Wellington, telling Sir Neil Campbell that he was 'a man of vigour in warfare'. Soon after that, on Elba, he asked a series of British visitors about Wellington, openly praising his 'great merit'. Indeed at no stage do we have any authentic account of Napoleon privately disparaging Wellington's generalship, at least not before the Waterloo campaign itself. Even after the battle, on HMS *Bellerophon*, he was reported, via General Bertrand, as praising Wellington's 'prudence' as superior to his own. Of course Napoleon did not necessarily make that remark on board the ship; Bertrand had been grand marshal of the palace since 1813 and was with him on Elba. Yet, whenever it was that Napoleon said it, the record hardly shows a catalogue of contempt.

Indeed it is only really upon Napoleon's oft-repeated remark to Soult on the morning of the battle that the whole myth of Napoleonic contempt for Wellington at Waterloo rests, a comment that has been wrenched entirely out of context. Admittedly, soon afterwards, on St Helena, Napoleon laboured hard to present Wellington as a bad general upon whom Fortune had unaccountably smiled, but that was clearly in the interests of promoting his own myth, and might well not even have been his genuine view so much as one fuelled by resentment at the duke's perceived ill-treatment of him in the selection of the 'frightful rock' of St Helena for his prison.

The occasion on which Napoleon did explode with rage over Wellington, criticising his enemy's 'despicable' strategy at Waterloo, came immediately after he had been told that 'it is through Wellington that I am here; and I believe it'. His anger at Wellington's supposed involvement in the choice of prison-isle was the direct reason for his rant, for which he used his opponent's alleged bad strategy at Waterloo as ammunition. That Wellington had in fact saved Napoleon's life after Waterloo and had taken no part in picking St Helena are no more than two of the story's many minor ironies.

It is likely therefore that, in complete contradiction to the generally accepted historical record, Napoleon actually appreciated and even admired Wellington's talents as a military commander, but was for political and propaganda reasons prevented from expressing this publicly. Wellington, meanwhile, privately criticised Napoleon's actions in the 1812 Russian campaign, the 1814 French campaigns and the 1815 Waterloo campaigns, while all the time praising him publicly, and throughout his life repeating the familiar mantra that his presence on a battlefield was worth forty thousand men.

⤴

Historical exaggeration and invention is rife over the story of Waterloo. William Makepeace Thackeray satirised the way in which truth became war's first casualty when one of the characters in *Vanity Fair*, who actually spent the day of the battle in his hotel room in Brussels, over the following years told everyone that not only had he been present, but 'Napoleon would never have gone to St Helena at all but for him, Jos Sedley.' King George IV also convinced himself that he had served under the duke. (Riding on the Downs near Dover in 1836, Wellington told Lady Salisbury a story about the late king. 'His diet was beyond description,' said the duke, 'and after his death a bill of an apparently unreasonable amount was brought in by the apothecary at Windsor. The executors demurred to pay it but the man claimed it as a very moderate remuneration for the services for which he had been employed, such as scraping the King all over to remove the accumulated dirt.')

In one sense the battle of Waterloo was immaterial once Europe had finally adopted the policy of Collective Security, as happened in the treaty of Chaumont of 1814. Had Napoleon won Waterloo it would not, as he hoped, have taken the continent back to the days of 1800 or 1810. The Russians and Austrians were on their way with large armies, and all the Great Powers had solemnly resolved this time not to make any separate peace agreements with him. As one admirer has put it, Napoleon was doomed because 'he could not make a lasting peace. He could only dictate terms so severe that they incited a resumption of hostilities by former adversaries as soon as possible.'[24] Part of Napoleon's tragedy is that he knew this himself, for as he said when he was first consul in 1802: 'Between the old monarchies and a young republic the spirit of hostility must always exist. In the existing situation every treaty of peace means to me no more than a brief armistice: and I believe that while I fill my present office, my destiny is to be fighting almost continuously.' Indeed once he had stirred up the Iberian guerrilla war by his 1807 invasion, Napoleon was not even allowed a brief armistice.

With only Murat supporting him in 1815, something he neither wanted nor needed, Napoleon was finally cornered. (Murat attacked the Austrian army and lost the battle of Tolentino on 2 May, and was executed by firing squad on 13 October, the very day before Napoleon first caught sight of St Helena.) Triumph at Waterloo would therefore not have wrecked the Seventh Coalition in the same way that French victories had destroyed the previous six.[25] The days of rampaging across Europe defeating impermanent alliances were finally over, finished by the new era of Collective-Security-by-congress. Endeth the age, endeth the man.

In Napoleon, a man of superior intellect, undoubted military genius, great depths of knowledge, genuine artistic tastes and fine wit, History provides the ultimate proof that dictatorships cannot remain benevolent and absolute power does indeed corrupt absolutely. The (admittedly prosaic) moral of his career is that it is better to be perhaps incompetently governed by free and changeable institutions than to be well governed by those who cannot be removed constitutionally. Napoleon tells us much about the human condition; about what individuals, given genius and willpower, are capable of, what men and nations will endure if they have inspirational leadership, and what havoc hubris can wreak when untrammelled by representative institutions.

The law of unintended consequences could not be better served than by a revolution unleashed in the name of Reason, Logic and Enlightenment throwing up a Romantic self-proclaimed 'child of Destiny' who then fell prey to every Cæsarian fantasy, and even to Alexandrine dreams of Oriental conquest. When asked if he wanted the King of Rome one day to replace him, Napoleon declared: 'Replace me? I could not replace myself! I am the child of circumstance.'[26] Only once the political circumstances had altered and no longer permitted short-term peaces, was the 'snowball' – as Wellington described Napoleon – finally brought to a halt.

Might it have been better for the world if the Bastille had not fallen and Napoleon had reached the post of lieutenant-colonel of artillery, stationed in a variety of posts across Bourbon France? As Wellington's foremost biographer Elizabeth Longford wrote, the need for *la gloire* ruined the French palate for constitutional government, as Napoleon III, the Commune and Pétain thereafter discovered. An intact Bastille might not have served Britain so well, however, for, as Gneisenau rightly surmised as early as 1815, the Napoleonic Wars inestimably increased British power and prestige, a phenomenon that was massively exploited over the next ninety-nine years. Moreover, Russia was introduced to the western European sphere for the first time in her history. When Joseph Stalin was asked at Potsdam in East Germany in 1945 how it felt to stand on Frederick the Great's parade ground, he ominously answered that in 1814 Tsar Alexander I had ridden into Paris.

'There does not exist an epic', wrote an historian in 1860, 'the foundations of which are better suited for artistic treatment than the story of Wellington's struggle with Napoleon's power.'[27] Whereas in 1860 it was obvious that the British world view had triumphed over the Napoleonic, that is by no means still the case. When Canova was asked why the globe in the hand of Napoleon's statue at Apsley House had been made so small he answered: 'Ah, but you see, Napoleon's world did not include Great Britain.'[28] Today it does.

In one of his administrative rather than military phases, the first consul predicted that the Code Napoléon would be remembered long after his victories were forgotten. In the Prussian Rhenish provinces the Code lasted until 1900, and it still forms the basis of much of European jurisprudence today, a legal system that has already established its legislative primacy over British domestic law-making. As the authors of the 1993 edition of the legal textbook *French Administrative Law* point out: 'Napoleon may perhaps be thought of as the principal ... inspiration of the European Court [of Justice], which is itself buttressed by the principles of administrative law that his own institution, the Conseil d'Etat, has evolved during the last 190 years.'[29]

Napoleon's programme, of a politically united Europe controlled by a centralised (French-led) bureaucracy, of careers open to talent and of a written body of laws, has defeated Wellington's assumptions of British sovereign independence, class distinctions and the supremacy of English common law based upon established, sometimes ancient, precedent. 'I wished to found a European system, a European code of laws, a European judiciary,' wrote Napoleon on St Helena. 'There would be but one people in Europe.' There is some irony in the fact that Waterloo was fought a mere twelve miles from Brussels, the capital of today's European Union. For, although Wellington won the battle, it is Napoleon's dream that is coming true.

NOTES

Correspondance de Napoléon refers to the thirty-two volumes of Napoleon's letters edited by Henri Plon and J. Dumaire.

INTRODUCTION [pp. xxix–xxxii]

1 Hayman *Soult* 228–9
2 Robinson *Campaign* 608
3 Houssaye *Waterloo* 180, Cohen *Anecdotes* 241
4 Uffindell and Corum *Ligny* 171
5 ed. Jones *Marchand* 247
6 Saunders *Hundred* 195, Horricks *Ney* 229–30
7 ed. Haythornthwaite *Legacy* 281, Chandler *Campaigns* 1007, Forester 'Won' 17
8 Schom *Hundred* 276
9 Strawson *Duke* 285

CHAPTER 1: 'A Fine Time for an Enterprising Young Man': 1769–1799 [pp. 3–13]

1 Shorter *Napoleon* xxii
2 Young *Growth* 379–80, Kennedy *Waterloo* 28–9
3 Cust *History* 246, Nevill *Floreat* 125
4 ed. Hart-Davis *Lyttelton Hart-Davis Letters* III 77
5 ed. Stavordale *Further* 229
6 Elting *Swords* 710 n10
7 Thompson 'Unpredictable' 4–5
8 Stanhope *Notes* 167 26 September 1839
9 Aldington *Wellington* 22–33
10 Marshall-Cornwall *Napoleon* 23
11 Lord Salisbury *Saturday Review* XIX 533 6 May 1865
12 ed. Howard *Wellington Studies* 14
13 Strawson *Duke* 278, Fortescue *Army* IV 305
14 Sisman *Presumptuous* 38–41
15 Markham *Napoleon* 3
16 Metternich *Memoirs* I 277
17 Thrasher *Paoli* 238, Markham *Napoleon* 4

18 Shorter *Napoleon* xvi
19 Thrasher *Paoli* 238
20 ed. Wilson *Diary* 88 11 January 1817
21 Healey *Literary* 148–52, Sisman *Presumptuous* 52–5
22 Healey *Literary* appendix B
23 ed. Fletcher *Peninsular* 171 n7 and 160

CHAPTER 2: Apprenticeship at Arms: 1799–1805 [pp. 14–28]
 1 Fraser *Words* 36
 2 Rogers *Recollections* 219
 3 Butler *Brother* 331
 4 NAM 6807–391
 5 Markham *Bonapartes* 50
 6 WD I 166
 7 Butler *Brother* 166
 8 *Correspondance de Napoléon* XXIX 429
 9 ed. Lecestre *Lettres* I 144
10 Tulard *Myth* 300
11 James *Raj* 65
12 Aldington *Wellington* 78
13 Corbett *Wilks* 20
14 Valentia *Voyages* II 133–5
15 ed. Hanoteau *Caulaincourt* 445
16 WD V 57, V 78, V 84, X 557, De Grey *Characteristics* 97–127
17 WD XI 338
18 ed. Jennings *Croker* I ch. IX 339
19 Keegan *Mask* 142
20 Ellis *Napoleon* 209
21 O'Meara *Exile* I 401
22 Chandler *Wars* 238, McLynn *Napoleon* 279
23 Gash *Anecdotes* 16–17
24 *ibid*
25 ed. Fletcher *Peninsular* 158
26 *ibid* 159
27 Wellesley *Civil* 294
28 Woolf *Integration* 177
29 Stanhope *Notes* 10 4 November 1831
30 Keegan *Mask* 142
31 Markham *Napoleon* 52
32 ed. Strafford *Ellesmere* 100–1
33 ed. Jennings *Croker* I ch. XI 340

CHAPTER 3: A Near Miss: 1805–1808 [pp. 29–44]
 1 Blackburn *Island* 5
 2 Gourgaud *Journal* 66

3 Brookes *St Helena* 7

4 Ed. Strafford *Ellesmere* 143–4 November 1835

5 Ehrman *Pitt* III 808, Stanhope *Notes* IV 347

6 Aldington *Wellington* 96

7 Rogers *Recollections* 208

8 WSD V 420 May 1808

9 Letter from Andrew Uffindell 5 April 2000

10 Glover *Preparation* 4–5, Horne *Austerlitz* 241

11 Lachouque *Anatomy* 129

12 *Correspondance de Napoléon* XVII 434 9 August 1808

13 Oman *Heiress* 268

14 WD IV 38–9 and 47

15 Chandler *Wars* 185

16 Interview with the late Col. John Elting 20 February 2000

17 Paget *Peninsular* 12

18 Ellis *Empire* 71

19 Rudé *Revolutionary Europe* 268

20 Rose *Life* 171

21 ed. Partridge and Oliver *Battle Studies* 178

22 Glover *Cintra* 175

23 Elting *Swords* 163

24 Raikes *Journal* IV 312 9 October 1843

25 Schom *Napoleon* 470

26 Glover *Cintra* 137–9

27 Ziegler *Addington* 284–5

28 Thompson 'Unpredictable' 8

29 *Correspondance de Napoléon* XVIII 2–4

30 Esdaile *Spanish* 1

31 ed. Hanoteau *Memoirs* 446

32 Aldington *Wellington* 111

33 ed. Partridge and Oliver *Battle Studies* 268

34 Gleig *Wellington* 88–9

35 Chandler *Hundred* 58

36 Interview with Ian Fletcher 14–21 May 2000

37 Julian Humphreys' lecture at NAM 6 April 2000, Weller *Peninsula* 26 n2

38 Markham *Napoleon* 3, Forester 'Won' 18–21

39 Interview with Ian Fletcher 14–21 May 2000

40 Esdaile *Wars* 65–6

41 Keegan *Face* 160, Elting *Swords* 724 n8

42 Glover *Preparation* 262–3

43 Chandler *Campaigns* xxix

CHAPTER 4: To Lie Like a Bulletin: 1808–1809 [pp. 45–58]

1 Thompson *Rise* 241

2 *ibid*, Strawson *Duke* 294

3 Chandler *Campaigns* 620, Schom *Napoleon* 490
4 Glover *Preparation* 19, Gleig *Wellington* 114
5 *Correspondance de Napoléon* XVIII 237
6 Warre *Letters* 54
7 ed. Jennings *Croker* I ch. XI 354
8 *ibid* 355
9 ed. Strafford *Ellesmere* 168 24 January 1839
10 Chandler *Napoleon* 113
11 Schom *Napoleon* 490–1, Guérard *Napoleon* 115
12 McLynn *Napoleon* 409, Schom *Napoleon* 490–2, Cooper *Talleyrand* 186–9
13 ed. Bamford and Wellington *Arbuthnot* I 250 4 August 1823
14 ed. Burghclere *Friendship* 230–2
15 Macdonnell *Marshals* 151
16 Thompson *Rise* 296
17 ed. Strafford *Ellesmere* 144
18 Lanfrey *Napoleon* IV 174, Oman *Peninsular* II 297
19 Pears 'Gentleman' 223
20 Horne *Austerlitz* 270
21 *Correspondance de Napoléon* XIX 116–17
22 Paget *Peninsular* 96
23 Wellington and Steegman *Iconography* xv
24 *ibid*
25 Bainville *Napoleon* 293
26 Glover *Preparation* 5
27 *Correspondance de Napoléon* XIX 338
28 ed. Bingham *Selection* II 470–1
29 *ibid* 468–71
30 *ibid*
31 *ibid*
32 Thompson *Self-Revealed* 212–13
33 *Correspondance de Napoléon* 15700 XIX 387
34 *ibid* 15706 XIX 392
35 *ibid* 15716 XIX 400, ed. Bingham *Selection* II 468

CHAPTER 5: First Recognition: 1809–1810 [pp. 59–78]
1 Lean *Napoleonists passim*
2 Horne *Master* 63
3 Mitchell *Melbourne* 52
4 Hughes-Hallett *Immortal* 15–16
5 Oman *Heiress* 252
6 *Correspondance de Napoléon* 15832 XXIX 485
7 *ibid* XVIII 131
8 Gleig *Wellington* 714 and n
9 WD V 302
10 Paget *Peninsular* 138

11 James *Duke* 195, WP 1/286 p40

12 Salmon *Newspaper* 198 and n

13 Geer *Family* II 149

14 WD V 212–13

15 Tolstoy *War and Peace* bk 1, pt 2, ch. 10

16 *Correspondance de Napoléon* XIX 648–9

17 *ibid* XX 54

18 WD V 302

19 Horward *Iberia* 29, Madelin *Consulate* II 7

20 *Correspondance de Napoléon* 16031 XX 56–8, Horne *Austerlitz* 291

21 Longford *Sword* 176

22 ed. Fletcher *Peninsular* 65–92

23 Fournier *Napoleon* 124

24 ed. Rémusat *Memoirs* 528–9

25 McLynn *Napoleon* 450–1

26 Geer *Family* II 150

27 WD V 400

28 ed. Rousseau *D'Urban Journal* 81

29 Fournier *Napoleon* 125, ed. Haythornthwaite *Final* 103

30 Geer *Family* II 150

31 ed. Rousseau *D'Urban Journal* 91

32 WD V 556–9

33 ed. Maxwell *Creevey* II 128

34 WSD VI 515, James *Iron* 147

35 Markham *Napoleon* 1

36 WD VI 12

37 Macdonnell *Marshals* 187

38 Paget *Peninsular* 32, Rogers *Recollections* 201

39 Haythornthwaite *Who Was Who* 209–10

40 Paget believes Henriette Lebreton wore the uniform of the hussars, Haythornthwaite suspects dragoons, Chandler goes no further than cavalry officer. The great debate continues …

41 Lanfrey *Napoleon* IV 376

42 *Correspondance de Napoléon* XX 447

43 WD VI 240

44 *ibid* 266

45 *ibid* 269

46 French foreign office archives: England vol. 604 fol. 107

47 Coquelle *England* 255

48 Aldington *Wellington* 156

49 WSD VI 590

50 Lanfrey *Napoléon* IV 383

51 ed. Bingham *Selection* III 63, ed. Horward *Pelet* 329 n2

52 ed. Bingham *Selection* III 61

53 Paget *Peninsular* 104

54 ed. Howard *Wellington Studies* 31, Macdonnell *Marshals* 188
55 Schom *Napoleon* 489–90
56 ed. Picard and Tuetey, *Inédite* III 844, ed. Horward *Pelet* 259 n35
57 ed. Bingham *Selection* III
58 Schom *Hundred* 234, Pears 'Gentleman' 226, Grehan *Torres Vedras* 181
59 ed. Horward *Pelet* 323
60 *ibid* 377n
61 Rosebery *Napoleon* 194
62 Chaptal *Souvenirs* 304
63 HH Lady Salisbury's diary 136 6 August 1836

CHAPTER 6: Will He? Won't He?: 1810–1811 [pp. 79–97]
 1 Chandler *Campaigns* 747
 2 ed. Butler *Memoirs* II 147–8
 3 WD VII 65
 4 *Correspondance de Napoléon* XXI 398
 5 Holtman *Propaganda* 198, ed. Picard and Tuetey *Inédite* IV 7
 6 ed. Howard *Wellington Studies* I 28
 7 Gleig *Wellington* 164
 8 Aldington *Wellington* 156
 9 Lean *Napoleonists* 62–3
 10 WSD VII 117, Macdonnell *Marshals* 199
 11 Lanfrey *Napoleon* IV 407–9
 12 Macdonell *Marshals* 187 and 285, Rogers *Recollections* 201
 13 ed. Horward *Pelet* 147
 14 *Correspondance de Napoléon* XXII 172
 15 *ibid* 234
 16 WD VIII 235
 17 Interview with Ian Fletcher 14–21 May 2000
 18 WD VIII 300–1
 19 WSD VII 233
 20 *ibid* 244
 21 WD VIII 436
 22 *ibid* 482
 23 Rose *Personality* 250
 24 ed. Picard and Tuetey *Inédite* IV 847
 25 Esdaile *Spanish Army* 72–3, Paget *Peninsular* 40
 26 Wellington to Rebecque 31 December 1812
 27 Lyons *Legacy* 224
 28 Interview with Ian Fletcher 14–21 May 2000, Harvey *Collision* 153, Elting *Swords* 514–15
 29 ed. Griffith *History* 317, Geer *Family* I 344
 30 Paget *Peninsular* 158–9
 31 *ibid*, Glover *Wellington* 141
 32 Gleig *Wellington* 714

33 Christie *Wars* 312
34 Longford *Pillar* 79
35 Palmer *Russia* 113–14, Macdonnell *Marshals* 223
36 ed. Butler *Memoirs* II 276
37 Austin *1812* 266–7, Ludwig *Napoleon* 399
38 ed. Strafford *Ellesmere* 148
39 Stanhope *Notes* 61 18 September 1836
40 Ellis *Napoleon* 107
41 Gash *Liverpool* 83–4
42 Bainbridge *Romanticism* 127
43 Hansard XXI col. 1012, Brooks's Club Betting Book
44 ed. Hanoteau *Memoirs* 98
45 Werner *Laughed* 57
46 Palmer *Russia* 26
47 Madelin *Consulate* II 94
48 Rose *Personality* 251, Horne *Master* 218
49 Geer *Family* I 345
50 Stanhope *Notes* 102 16 October 1837
51 WD IX 530
52 WSD VII 475–6
53 ed. Hanoteau *Memoirs* 441–4
54 *ibid*
55 *ibid*
56 Harvey *Collision* 140

CHAPTER 7: Two Retreats, One Tragedy: 1812–1813 [pp. 98–112]

1 WD IX 370–1, interview with Ian Fletcher 14–21 May 2000
2 Aldington *Wellington* 176
3 *Correspondance de Napoléon* XXIV 387
4 WSD VII 494–5
5 WD IX 616
6 Woolf *Integration* 30
7 Chandler *Campaigns* 852–3
8 WSD VII 502
9 HH Lady Salisbury's diary 138 28 August 1836
10 Aldington *Wellington* 177
11 WD X 176, 230, and 436–7
12 Seward *Family* 143
13 Paget *Peninsular* 170–9
14 Londonderry *Narrative* 81 and 88, Fournier *Napoleon* 284
15 Buckland *Metternich* 525–6, Aldington *Wellington* 186
16 Glover *Preparation* 9, Buckland *Metternich* 525, ed. Jennings *Croker* I 336
17 ed. Jennings *Croker* II 235 2 October 1834
18 Lachouque *Anatomy* 303, WD X 567–8
19 Maclachan *Elba* 84–6

20 Broadley *Caricature* II 26
21 Glover *Preparation* 262, Brett-James *Europe* 28
22 Greville *George IV* 475–6
23 Thompson *Self-Revealed* 264
24 Aldington *Wellington* 190
25 WD XI 207
26 *ibid* 12 and X 614–15
27 WD X 614–15
28 NAM 6005–279
29 WD XI 272
30 Cronin *Napoleon* 438
31 Chandler *Napoleon* 148
32 Stanhope *Notes* 9 3 November 1831
33 Wellington *Chad* 6 26 August 1824
34 WD XI 299
35 Haythornthwaite *Who Was Who* 138–9
36 Dard *Talleyrand* 292–3
37 Bourrienne *Life* III 285
38 WD XI 303–7
39 Smith *Leipzig* 164
40 WD XI 413

CHAPTER 8: 'Napoleon Has Abdicated': 1813–1814 [pp. 113–122]
 1 WD XI 433–4
 2 *ibid* 435
 3 ed. Hart-Davis *Letters* V 171
 4 WD X 496, Paget *Peninsular* 56 n1
 5 Greville *George IV* I 71
 6 Stanhope *Notes* 6 31 October 1831
 7 Markham *Awakening* 121
 8 Paget *Peninsular* 53
 9 *Correspondance de Napoléon* 21353 XXVII 232
10 WD XI 617
11 ed. Tulard *Cambacérès* 1128–30
12 WD XI 617
13 Paget *Peninsular* 237, WD XI 642–3, Wellington *Chad* 7
14 Broughton *Recollections* I 189–90
15 Oman *Heiress* 282
16 Chandler *Campaigns* 1002, see McLynn *Napoleon* 595 for other theories
17 Markham *Awakening* 127
18 *ibid*, Bourrienne *Life* III 367
19 Morris *Napoleon* 302
20 Chandler *Wars* 156–8
21 Julian Humphreys' lecture at NAM 6 April 2000
22 Rogers *Recollections* 196

23 Letter from Andrew Uffindell 5 April 2000

24 *ibid*

25 Schom *Hundred* 235

26 Macdonell *Marshals* 185

27 Interview with Ian Fletcher 14–21 May 2000

28 ed. Fletcher *Peninsular* 151ff

29 Las Cases *Mémorial* II 134–5

30 Longford *Sword* 248–9

CHAPTER 9: Evenings on St Helena, Nights in Paris: 1814–1815 [pp. 123–137]

1 Mansel *Eagle* 113

2 ed. Howard *Wellington Studies* I 46

3 Dixon *Favourite* 175–6, WD XII 88–9

4 Bagot *Canning* I 63–4, Longford *Sword* 373

5 Seward *Family* 168

6 Gash *Anecdotes* 13, Gleig *Reminiscences* 141

7 Longford *Sword* 372

8 Abrantès *Autobiography* IV 479–81

9 *New Grove Dictionary of Music* 2nd edition (2001) 642

10 Aretz *Women* 143–53

11 Delaforce *Beau* 105, Lévy *Intime* 177

12 Kircheisen *Napoleon* 270, Castelot *Napoleon* 177

13 Masson *Fair* 104

14 Aretz *Women* 143–53

15 Masson *Fair* 98–109

16 Bruce *Josephine* 316–17

17 ed. Nicoullaud *De Boigne* I 138

18 ed. Granville *Correspondence* II 74

19 Masson *Fair* 108

20 ed. Granville *Correspondence* II 507, ed. Bourguinon *Marchand* 252

21 Pougin *Grassini* 54, Hibbert *Wellington* 162, Delaforce *Beau* 105n

22 ed. Nicoullaud *De Boigne* II 113

23 Cohen *Anecdotes* 259, Aretz *Women* 143–53

24 McLynn *Napoleon* 275

25 Masson *Fair* 118–22, Longford *Sword* 375, Delaforce *Beau* 74, Hibbert *Wellington* 162, Breton *Ladies* 109–19

26 Breton *Ladies* 119n

27 Delaforce *Beau* 74

28 ed. Hanoteau *Memoirs* 597

29 Delaforce *Beau* 108

30 Maclachlan *Elba* 300–2

31 *ibid* 317

32 Mansel *Louis XVIII* 214, Longford *Sword* 378

33 WD XII 192–3

34 Kerry *Napoleon* 94–5

35 Maclachlan *Elba* 332
36 HH Lady Salisbury's diary 143 15 September 1836
37 Markham *Awakening* 150, Maclachan *Elba* 326 and 341
38 Ebrington 'Conversation', Alger *Visitors* 297
39 Alger *Visitors* 319–24
40 *ibid*
41 Broughton *Reflections* I 194
42 *ibid* 184
43 WSD IX 553
44 Glover *Preparation* 10, Schom *Hundred* 246
45 Markham *Bonapartes* 157

CHAPTER 10: A Hundred-Day Dash for *La Gloire*: March–June 1815 [pp. 138–160]

1 WD XII 266–7
2 Rogers *Recollections* 207
3 HH Lady Salisbury's diary
4 Stanhope *Notes* 25 16 November 1831
5 ed. Weigall *Correspondence* 11
6 Hansard XXX col. 338
7 Lean *Napoleonists* 104
8 ed. Baldick *Goncourt* 7
9 ed. Bourguinon *Marchand* I 133, ed. Jones *Marchand* 213
10 WSD IX 609
11 *ibid* 622
12 Fraser *Words* 38
13 McErlean *Pozzo* 273
14 Haythornthwaite *Who Was Who* 268–9
15 McErlean *Pozzo* 273
16 ed. Maxwell *Creevey* II ch. X 215
17 WSD X 169
18 Chandler *Campaigns* 1015, Keegan *Face* 121
19 WD XII 372
20 *ibid* 378
21 Dumas *Memoirs* II 499, Chandler *Campaigns* 1017
22 Letter from Dr David Chandler 7 March 2000, Uffindell and Corum *Ligny* 26
23 Watson *Command* 229, Goodspeed *Bayonets* 169
24 Chandler *Campaigns* 1022
25 Chandler *Wars* 99
26 Uffindell and Corum *Ligny* 25
27 Markham *Napoleon* 221
28 Connolly *Blundering* 206, ed. Chalfont *Waterloo* 30, Uffindell and Corum *Ligny* 25

29 Horne *Austerlitz* 366, Chandler *Campaigns* 1020

30 Interview with Ian Fletcher 18 June 2000, Chandler *Campaigns* 1018, Horne *Austerlitz* 187, Keegan *Face* 122

31 Schom *Hundred* 251

32 Oman *Heiress* 282

33 Keegan *Mask* 132

34 WD XII 346

35 *ibid* 462, ed. Bingham *Selection* III 385n

36 Chandler *Campaigns* 1028, Schom *Hundred* 247–8

37 Ziethen, Dornberg and Müffling crop up, Siborne *Letters* 2

38 Malmesbury II 445–6

39 Gash *Anecdotes* 11

40 Lachouque *Anatomy* 478

41 Chandler *Campaigns* 1028–9

42 *ibid* 1039

43 Lyons *Legacy* 291, Houssaye *1815* 132–3, Ratcliffe *Grouchy* 14

44 ed. Strafford *Ellesmere* 101, ed. Fletcher *Peninsular* 151, Aldington *Wellington* 117

45 Kerry *Napoleon* 117, Houssaye *1815* 137 and 379

46 Kelly *Wavre* 83–4

47 Uffindell *Could Napoleon* 45, Chesney *Lectures* 254–5

48 James *Duke* 196

49 Guerrini *Paris* 3

50 Letter from Col. John Elting 14 March 2000, interview with David Marks 10 March 2000

51 Siborne *Letters* 2

52 For the debate over Grouchy's actions see Ratcliffe *Grouchy passim*, Uffindell *Fields* 271ff, Anonymous *Grouchy* 1–15, ed. Chandler *Marshals* 138–55, Korngold *Last* 14, Kennedy *Waterloo* 159, Uffindell and Corum *Ligny* 181 n10

53 Wootten *Waterloo* 3

54 Rose *Life* 484–5, I should like to thank Dr James Le Fanu for his help in explaining Napoleon's medical condition during the Waterloo campaign

55 Kerry *Napoleon* 125

56 Kemble *Immortal* 221–3

57 Howarth *Near* 54–8

58 Rose *Life* 485ff

CHAPTER 11: 'Thank God, I Have Met Him!': 18 June 1815 [pp. 163–181]

1 *Correspondance de Napoléon* 15933 XIX 666

2 For Napoleon on the morning of Waterloo see Houssaye *1815* 177–82, Oman *Studies* 97–108, Hamilton-Williams *Perspectives* 262–3, Uffindell and Corum *Ligny* 171, ed. Haythornthwaite *Legacy* 281, Hooper *Waterloo* 188–9, Chandler *Campaigns* 1066–7

3 Longford *Sword* 378

4 Cohen *Anecdotes* 240

5 Aldington *Wellington* 221

6 Keegan *Face* 138

7 Interview with Ian Fletcher 18 June 2000

8 Tarlé *Bonaparte* 387

9 Rogers *Recollections* 208–9

10 Chandler *Campaigns* 1070–1, Uffindell *Fields* 36–7, Rose *Life* 492–3

11 Lachouque *Anatomy* 482

12 Sir Charles Oman *Cambridge Modern History* X 633

13 Chandler *Wars* 161–2

14 Ropes *Campaign* 303 n33

15 Interview with Ian Fletcher 18 June 2000

16 ed. Fletcher *Peninsular* 152

17 Robinson *Campaign* 608

18 Kennedy *Waterloo* 164

19 Weller *Waterloo* 199, Uffindell *Could Napoleon* 46, Guedella *Hundred* 130, Uffindell and Corum *Ligny* 181

20 ed. Strafford *Ellesmere* 183 February 1847, Fraser 'Waterloo' 19

21 Glover *Commander* 200

22 Rose *Life* 492

23 Fraser *Words* 2–3, Oman *Heiress* 261

24 Elting *Swords* 264

25 Interview with Ian Fletcher 18 June 2000

26 ed. Strafford *Ellesmere* 179 6 May 1845

27 Keegan *Mask* 92

28 ed. Chalfont *Waterloo* 184

29 Rose *Napoleonic* 274–303

30 Girod de l'Ain *Vie* 107

31 Chandler *Wars* 138

32 Elting *Swords* 537

33 Robinson *Campaigns* 608, Fletcher *Galloping* 241, interview with Ian Fletcher 18 June 2000

34 Fletcher *Galloping* 237–66, Siborne *Letters* 3–12 for Uxbridge's account

35 Longford *Sword* 472

36 *Illustrated London News* 1 October 1892, Uffindell *Fields* 145

37 Siborne *Letters* 17

38 Glover *Commander* 136–7

39 Ropes *Campaign* 309

40 Chandler *Campaigns* 1085–6

41 Keegan *Mask* 155

42 Siborne *History* II 164

43 ed. Howard *Wellington Studies* 39, Uffindell and Corum *Ligny* 214–16

44 Cohen *Anecdotes* 251

45 ed. Maxwell *Creevey* ch. X 237

CHAPTER 12: Wellington Protects Napoleon (and His Own Reputation): June–July 1815 [pp. 182–198]

1 *The Times* 22 June 1815
2 Rogers *Recollections* 209
3 Siborne *Letters* 12, 18 and 20
4 *ibid* 18
5 *The Times* 22 June 1815
6 WSD X 507
7 ed. Jones *Marchand* 249
8 Sutherland *Walewska* 236
9 Gallagher *Davout* 315
10 Gleig *Wellington* 716
11 WSD X 583, Fleury *Memoirs* 210, WD XII 515, Lachouque *Last* 141–2
12 WD XII 507–8
13 Gronow *Reminiscences* 55
14 Müffling *Passages* 272–3
15 Lachouque *Last* 142
16 Müffling *Passages* 252–3
17 WD XII 516, Thiers *Consulat* XX 546
18 ed. Londonderry *Correspondence* 3rd series II 386, Müffling *Passages* 275
19 Martineau *Surrenders passim*
20 WSD X 625
21 Lachouque *Last* 140, Fleury *Memoirs* 349
22 Fleury *Memoirs* II 210
23 Gleig *Wellington* 331–3, Horricks *Ney* 249
24 Stanhope *Notes* 239 5 June 1840
25 WSD X 677
26 Mansel *Louis XVIII* 258
27 ed. Jennings *Croker* II ch. XVIII 236–40
28 Hansard XXX col. 988, Lean *Napoleonists* 106
29 Stanhope *Notes* 239 27 October 1838
30 Maitland *Narrative* 208
31 Semmel 'Past' 21 and 29
32 Edgecumbe *Shelley* I 105
33 WSD XI 47
34 *The Times* 24 July 1965
35 Young *St Helena* I 95
36 O'Meara *Exile* II 184
37 Montholon *Captivity* I 103
38 Maitland *Narrative* 222
39 Oman *Heiress* 261
40 Gourgaud *Journal* 66

CHAPTER 13: Shepherding the Scapegoats: 1815–1816 [pp. 199–225]

1 ed. Thompson 'St Helena' 544

2 Guedella *Hundred* 159–61

3 Guérard *Napoleon* 15

4 Bourrienne *Life* I 321

5 Markham *Napoleon* 27

6 Montholon *Captivity* IV 288, 161, 120 and 25

7 Chandler *Wars* 111

8 Las Cases *Mémorial* VII 275–7

9 Korngold *Last* 134

10 Edgecumbe *Shelley* II 144, ed. Maxwell *Creevey* ch. 12 288–9

11 Forsyth *Captivity* III 33–5

12 ed. Stavordale *Further* 217–18

13 Edgecumbe *Shelley* I 217

14 ed. Howard *Wellington Studies* 51

15 Lucas-Dubreton *July* 9, Stacton *Bonapartes* 177, Guerrini *Paris passim*, Eustace *Petre* 204, Honour 'Canova's', ed. Jennings *Croker* I 62, Hamilton-Williams *Fall* 278, Elting *Swords* 733 n7, Edgecumbe *Shelley* I 107

16 ed. Baldick *Goncourt* 3 December 1878, Guerrini *Paris passim*

17 ed. Rousset *Macdonald* 352

18 ed. Stavordale *Further* 226–7, Macdonnell *Marshals* 281

19 Longford *Pillar* 28–9

20 Oman *Heiress* 282

21 ed. Thompson 'St Helena' 548

22 *ibid* 546

23 Guerrini *Paris* appendix V

24 Gould *Trophy* 103

25 Ziegler *Dino* 129

26 Bagot *Canning* II 12, Mansel *Louis XVIII* 267

27 WD XII 643, Müffling *Passages* 262–3

28 Martineau *Last* 95, Méneval *Memoirs* I 179

29 Interview with Alicia Robinson

30 Kauffmann *Catalogue* 149–50

31 Interview with Alicia Robinson

32 Knowles *Gift* 4–5

33 Gourgaud *Journal* 37 and 40

34 Brookes *St Helena* 125

35 ed. Anglesey *Letters* 159

36 Gourgaud *Journal* 56–7

37 Las Cases *Mémorial* II pt 4 252–3

38 ed. Wilson *Diary* 28

39 Park *Captivity* 33, Kerry *Napoleon* 193, WSD XI 429, Gourgaud *Journal* 67, Meynell *Conversations* 7–8

40 Las Cases *Mémorial* II pt 4 328

41 *ibid* III pt 5 286–310

42 Forsyth *Captivity* 356–8, O'Meara *Exile* I 174

43 Las Cases *Mémorial* IV pt 7 221

CHAPTER 14: A Shrinking Colossus: 1817–1821 [pp. 226–243]

1 Meynell *Conversations* 45

2 ed. Wilson *Diary* 105 and 94

3 Gourgaud *Journal* 140

4 *ibid* 141

5 Meynell *Conversations* 51, ed. Wilson *Diary* 133

6 O'Meara *Exile* I 463

7 WSD XI 730, De Wertheimer *Reichstad* 238–41

8 O'Meara *Exile* II 95

9 *ibid* 229

10 Gourgaud *Journal* 287

11 Paget *Peninsular* 104–5, O'Meara *Exile* II 342

12 Gayot *Hamelin* 3, Gourgaud *Journal* 300–1

13 Broughton *Recollections* II 91, ed. Maxwell *Creevey* I 281, Wellington *Chad* 2

14 Longford *Pillar* 47–50

15 James *Duke* 27–8

16 Edgecumbe *Shelley* II 33

17 Horne *Austerlitz* 198

18 ed. Strafford *Ellesmere* 118

19 Greville *George IV* I 39

20 ed. Quennell *Letters* 101–2

21 ed. Bamford and Wellington *Arbuthnot* I 85

22 Las Cases *Mémorial* IV pt 8 314

23 Aldington *Wellington* 238, Korngold *Last* 400–1

24 ed. Bamford and Wellington *Arbuthnot* 104–5

25 Raikes *Journal* IV 309 9 October 1843, HH Lady Salisbury's diary 108 6 July 1833, Stanhope *Notes* 8–9 1 November 1831

26 McErlean *Pozzo* 279–80

27 Longford *Pillar* 77

28 ed. Bamford and Wellington *Arbuthnot* I 112

29 Stanhope *Notes* 232 25 April 1840, Palmer *Marie Louise* 217

30 Longford *Pillar* 78

31 Stirling *Bequest passim*, Antommarchi *Moments* II 90

32 ed. Bingham *Selection* III 427

33 O'Meara *Exile* II 241

34 Broughton *Recollections* I 314

35 ed. Jennings *Croker* I ch. XI 341

36 Stirling *Bequest* 91–5, my thanks to Roman Golicz for the information on Cantillon

CHAPTER 15: Remembering with Advantages: 1822–1835 [pp. 244–266]
1 O'Meara *Exile* I 17, Apsley House Library
2 *ibid* 176
3 *ibid* 215
4 *ibid* 312, 251 and 270
5 *ibid* 464–6 and 497
6 *ibid* II 32, 21 and I 497, Palmer *Marie Louise* 188
7 Ségur *Russia* viii
8 ed. Bamford and Wellington *Arbuthnot* II 3
9 Gleig *Reminiscences* 310
10 WDCM III 1–53, Gleig *Reminiscences* 344–409
11 Stirling *Coke* I 309, Butler *Brother* 497–8, Bagot *Canning* II 300
12 Butler *Brother* 513 and 496–8, Bagot *Canning* II 48, Raikes *Journal* II 384
13 Mitchell *Lawsuit* 179–80, ed. Maxwell *Creevey* I 279
14 Mitchell *Lawsuit* x, Bagot *Canning* II 63, Gallatin *Peace* 194, 263n, 222 and 665
15 WP 1/865/11
16 WP 1/893/1
17 WP 1/1020/17
18 WDCM VII 11
19 *ibid* 209
20 Stanhope *Notes* 6 31 October 1831
21 *ibid* 22 20 November 1831
22 Oman *Heiress* 82
23 Edgecumbe *Shelley* 97–8, Young *Young* 251–2
24 ed. Raikes *Correspondence* 62
25 Strawson *Duke* 271
26 Stanhope *Notes* 8
27 ed. Jennings *Croker* II 235
28 Hibbert *Wellington* 333–4, Semmel 'Past' 29

CHAPTER 16: The War for Clio's Ear: 1836–1852 [pp. 267–287]
1 ed. Jennings *Croker* II 285–6
2 My thanks to Ian Fletcher for pointing this out, Oman *Heiress* 212, Stanhope *Notes* 60 18 September 1836
3 HH Lady Salisbury's diary 150 21 September 1836
4 Stanhope *Notes* 73 28 May 1837
5 Oman *Heiress* 259
6 Stevens *Victorian* 99
7 HH Lady Salisbury's diary 236–7 28 July 1838
8 ed. Strafford *Notes* 98–9
9 Maxwell *Clarendon* I 202–4
10 ed. Strafford *ibid* 171
11 Martineau *Last* 91
12 NAM 6807–238

13 ed. Baldick *Memoirs* 315
14 NAM 8105–39
15 ed. Raikes *Correspondence* 203–10
16 Greenhalgh 'Funeral'
17 WSD XII 513ff
18 *Quarterly Review* October 1843 291–8
19 Aldington *Wellington* 334
20 Semmel 'Past' 12, 3 and 25
21 ed. Pope *Diary* V 538–9, Semmel 'Past' 237 n6
22 Wellington *Friends* 255
23 ed. Jennings *Croker* II 175
24 Geer *Napoleon III* 85
25 Jerrold *Napoleon III* 135
26 Wellington *Mrs Jones* 49
27 ed. Jennings *Croker* III 272–3
28 *ibid* 277
29 Curl *Death* 216, Pears 'Gentleman' 220
30 Garlick *Curtain* 115
31 Greville *Victoria* IV 7, Jerrold *Napoleon III* 440–1
32 *The Times* 19 November 1852, Wellington 'Funeral' 778ff, *RAOC Gazette* May 1960 459, Pears 'Gentleman' 219

CONCLUSION [pp. 288–298]
 1 Head *Napoleon* x
 2 Strawson *Duke* 17
 3 Chandler *Wars* 233
 4 Gash *Anecdotes passim*
 5 Pears 'Gentleman' 229
 6 Ehrman *Pitt* I 313
 7 Young *Growth* 153
 8 Watson *Command* 171
 9 William Doyle's review of Alan Schom's *Napoleon Bonaparte* and Frank McLynn's *Napoleon* in *Times Literary Supplement* 6 March 1998
10 Roberts *Rise* 188–90
11 Aldington *Wellington* 8
12 Uffindell and Corum *Ligny* 33
13 Wellesley *Civil* 297
14 Rose *Personality* 109–11
15 Pears 'Gentleman' 236 n54
16 ed. Howard *Wellington Studies* 8, Keegan *Mask* 162
17 Keegan *Mask* 139
18 Longford *Pillar* 414
19 Rose *Personality* 105
20 Strawson *Duke* 293, Longford *Sword* 488
21 Letter from Dr David Chandler 7 March 2000

22 Weller *Waterloo* xi
23 See Chapter 11 note 2
24 Conrad Black's review of David Chandler's *On the Napoleonic Wars* in *Daily Telegraph* 19 February 1994
25 Esdaile *Wars* 281
26 Longford *Pillar* 85
27 Hamley *Career* 1–8
28 Longford *Pillar* 51–2
29 ed. Brown and Bell *French* 270

SELECT BIBLIOGRAPHY

The bibliography on Napoleon and Wellington is notoriously extensive, and is said to comprise tens of thousands of monographs and articles. This therefore is merely a list of the archives, historical works and articles that I have consulted in researching this book, rather than any attempt at a comprehensive bibliography for the subject.

HH the Papers of the 2nd Marchioness of Salisbury at Hatfield House
NAM the Archives of the National Army Museum
PRO the Public Record Office at Kew
WD ed. Col. J. Gurwood, *The Dispatches of Field Marshal the Duke of Wellington during his various campaigns in India, Denmark, Portugal, Spain, the Low Countries and France from 1799 to 1818* 13 vols, 1834–39
WDCM ed. the 2nd Duke of Wellington, *Despatches, Correspondence and Memoranda of Field Marshal Arthur, Duke of Wellington* 8 vols, 1867–80
WP the Wellington Papers at Southampton University
WSD ed. the 2nd Duke of Wellington, *Supplementary Despatches and Memoranda of Field Marshal Arthur, Duke of Wellington KG* 15 vols, 1858–72

Place of publication is London unless otherwise indicated.

BOOKS

Aaronson, Theo, *The Golden Bees* 1964

Abrantès, Laura Saint-Martin Duchess d', *Autobiography and Recollections of Laura, Duchess of Abrantès* 4 vols, 1893

Aldington, Richard, *Wellington* 1946

Alger, John, *Napoleon's British Visitors and Captives* 1904

A Near Observer, *The Battle of Waterloo Containing a Series of Accounts published by Authority* 1816

Anglesey, Marquess of, *One-Leg: The Life and Letters of Henry William Paget, 1ˢᵗ Marquess of Anglesey* 1961

ed. Anglesey, Marquess of, *The Capel Letters 1814–1817* 1955

Anonymous, *The Principles of War Exhibited in the Practice of the Camp; and as Developed in a Series of General Orders of F.M. the Duke of Wellington* 1815

Anonymous, *Marshal Grouchy's Own Account of the Battle of Waterloo* (St Louis) 1915

Antommarchi, Dr, *Les Derniers Moments de Napoléon* 2 vols, 1898

Aretz, Gertrude, *Napoleon and his Women Friends* 1927

Ashton, John, *English Caricature and Satire on Napoleon I* 1884

Aubry, Octave, *St Helena* 1937

Austen-Leigh, Richard, *The Eton College Register 1753–1790* 1921

Austin, Paul Britten, *1812: The March on Moscow* 1993

ed. Bagot, Capt. Josceline, *George Canning and his Friends* 2 vols, 1909

Bainbridge, Simon, *Napoleon and English Romanticism* 1995

Bainville, Jacques, *Napoleon* 1932

ed. Baldick, Robert, *The Memoirs of Chateaubriand* 1961

——, *Pages from the Goncourt Journal* 1962

ed. Bamford, Francis and Wellington, 7th Duke of, *The Journals of Mrs Arbuthnot 1820–1832* 2 vols, 1950

Barnett, Correlli, *Bonaparte* 1978

Becke, Capt. A. F., *Napoleon and Waterloo* 2 vols, 1914

Bernard, J. F., *Talleyrand* 1973

Bertrand, General Henri-Gratien, *Napoleon at St Helena* 1953

Bingham, Capt D. A., *A Selection from the Letters and Despatches of the First Napoleon* 3 vols, 1884

Blackburn, Julia, *The Emperor's Lost Island* 1991

Bonaparte, Lucien, *Memoirs* 1836

Boswell, James, *An Account of Corsica* 1768

ed. Bourguinon, Jean, *Mémoires de Marchand* (Paris) 2 vols, 1952

Bourrienne, Louis-Antoine Fauvelet de, *The Life of Napoleon Bonaparte* 3 vols, 1885

Breton, Guy, *Napoleon and his Ladies* 1965

Brett-James, Anthony, *Life in Wellington's Army* 1972

——, *The Hundred Days* 1964

ed. Brett-James, Anthony, *Europe against Napoleon: The Leipzig Campaign 1813* 1970

——, *Wellington at War* 1961

Broadley, A. M., *Napoleon in Caricature 1795–1821* 2 vols, 1911

Brookes, Mabel, *St Helena Story* 1960

Broughton, Lord, *Recollections of a Long Life* 6 vols, 1911

ed. Brown, L. Neville and Bell, John S., *French Administrative Law* 1993

Bruce, Evangeline, *Napoleon and Josephine: An Improbable Marriage* 1995

Buckland, S. C. B., *Metternich and the British Government from 1809 to 1813* 1932

ed. Burghclere, Lady, *A Great Man's Friendship* 1927

ed. Butler, Arthur John, *The Memoirs of Baron de Marbot* 1988

Butler, Iris, *The Eldest Brother: The Marquis Wellesley 1760–1842* 1973

Byron, Lord, *Don Juan* 1815–22

——, *Childe Harold's Pilgrimage* 1816

Camon, Colonel Hubert, *La Guerre napoléonienne: les batailles* (Paris) 1910

Castelot, André, *Napoleon* 1967

Chair, Somerset de, *Napoleon on Napoleon* 1992

ed. Chalfont, Alun, *Waterloo: Battle of Three Armies* 1979

Chandler, David *The Campaigns of Napoleon* 1966

——, *Napoleon* 1973

——, *Waterloo: The Hundred Days* 1980

——, *On the Napoleonic Wars* 1994

ed. Chandler, David, *Napoleon's Marshals* 1987

Chaptal, Jean-Antoine, Comte de Chanteloup, *Mes souvenirs de Napoléon* 1893

Chesney, Col. Charles, *Waterloo Lectures* 1869

Christie, Ian R., *Wars and Revolutions: Britain 1760–1815* 1982

Cohen, Louis, *Napoleonic Anecdotes* 1925

Collins, Irene, *Napoleon and his Parliaments 1800–1815* 1919

Connolly, Owen, *Blundering to Glory: Napoleon's Military Campaigns* 1987

Cooper, Alfred Duff, *Talleyrand* 1942

Coquelle, P., *Napoleon and England 1803–1813* 1904

ed. Corbett, Julian S., *Colonel Wilks and Napoleon: Two Conversations Held at St Helena in 1816* 1901

Creston, Dormer, *In Search of Two Characters* 1945

Cronin, Vincent, *Napoleon* 1971

Curl, James Stevens, *The Victorian Celebration of Death* 2000

Cust, Lionel, *A History of Eton College* 1899

Dard, Émile, *Napoleon and Talleyrand* 1937
De Grey, Earl, *Characteristics of the Duke of Wellington* 1853
De Jonge, Alex, *Napoleon's Last Will and Testament* 1969
Delaforce, Patrick, *Wellington the Beau* 1990
De Wertheimer, Edward, *The Duke of Reichstadt* 1905
Dixon, Norman, *On the Psychology of Military Incompetence* 1976
Dixon, Sir Pierson, *Pauline, Napoleon's Favourite Sister* 1964
Duhamel, Jean, *The Fifty Days: Napoleon in England* 1969
Dumas, Count Mathieu, *Memoirs of his own Time* 2 vols, 1839
ed. Edgecumbe, Richard, *The Diary of Frances, Lady Shelley 1787–1873* 2 vols, 1912
Ehrman, John, *The Younger Pitt* 3 vols, 1969–96
Ellis, Geoffrey, *The Napoleonic Empire* 1991
——, *Napoleon* 1997
Elting, John R., *Swords around a Throne: Napoleon's Grande Armée* 1989
Epton, Nina, *Josephine: The Empress and her Children* 1975
Esdaile, Charles J., *The Duke of Wellington and the Command of the Spanish Army* 1990
——, *The Wars of Napoleon* 1995
Espisito, Vincent J. and Elting, John R., *A Military History and Atlas of the Napoleonic Wars* 1999
Eustace, John Chetwode, *A Letter from Paris to George Petre, Esq,* 1814
Faber, Gotthilf Theodor von, *Notices sur l'intérieur de la France* 1810
Fain, Agathon-Jean-François, Baron, *Memoirs of the Invasion of France and of the Last Six Months of the Reign of Napoleon* 1834
Fleischman, Théo, *Histoire de la ferme du Caillou* (Brussels) 1984
Fletcher, Ian, *In Hell before Daylight* 1984
——, *Fields of Fire: Battlefields of the Peninsular War* 1994
——, *Vittoria 1813* 1998
——, *Galloping at Everything* 1999
——, *Bloody Albuera* 2000
ed. Fletcher, Ian, *The Peninsular War* 1998
Fleury de Chaboulon, Eduard, *Memoirs of the Private Life, Return and Reign of Napoleon in 1815* vol. 1, 1820
Forsyth, William, *History of the Captivity of Napoleon on St Helena* 3 vols, 1853
Fortescue, B., *Napoleon's Heritage* 1934
Fortescue, John, *A History of the British Army* 4 vols, 1915
——, *Wellington* 1925
Fouché, Joseph *Mémoires* 1825
Fournier, August, *Napoleon I* 2 vols, 1911
Fox, Charles, *Napoleon Bonaparte and the Siege of Toulon* (Washington DC) 1902
Foy, Général Maximilien-Sebastien, Comte, *History of the War in the Peninsula* 2 vols, 1827
Fraser, Sir William, *Words on Wellington* 1892
Frémaux, Paul, *With Napoleon at St Helena* 1902

Gallagher, John G., *The Iron Marshal: A Biography of Louis N. Davout* 2000

ed. Gallatin, Count, *A Great Peace Maker: The Diary of James Gallatin* 1914

Garlick, Harry, *The Final Curtain: State Funerals and the Theatre of Power* (Amsterdam) 1999

Gash, Norman, *Lord Liverpool* 1984

——, *Wellington Anecdotes* 1992

ed. Gash, Norman, *Wellington: Studies in the Military and Political Career of the First Duke of Wellington* 1990

Gaskill, Howard, *James Macpherson: Poems of Ossian and Related Works* 1996

Gates, David, *The Napoleonic Wars 1803–1815* 1997

Gayot, André, *Fortunée Hamelin* 1900

Geer, Walter, *Napoleon the Third* 1921

——, *Napoleon and his Family* 3 vols, 1929

Geyl, Pieter, *Napoleon For and Against* 1957

Girod de l'Ain, Maurice, *Vie Militaire de Général Foy* (Paris) 1900

Gleig, Rev. G. R., *The Life of Arthur, 1ˢᵗ Duke of Wellington* 1862

——, *Personal Reminiscences of the 1ˢᵗ Duke of Wellington* 1904

Glover, Michael, *Britannia Sickens: Sir Arthur Wellesley and the Convention of Cintra* 1970

——, *The Peninsular War 1807–14* 1974

——, *Wellington as Military Commander* 1968

Glover, Richard, *Peninsular Preparation* 1963

Gneisenau, General Count, *The Life and Campaigns of F.-M. Prince Blücher* 1815

Goldsmith, Lewis, *The Secret History of the Cabinet of Bonaparte* 1810

Goodspeed, Donald, *Bayonets at St Cloud* 1965

Gould, C., *Trophy of Conquest: The Musée Napoléon and the Creation of the Louvre* 1965

Gourgaud, Général Baron Gaspard, *The St Helena Journal of General Baron Gourgaud 1815–1818* 1932

——, *The Campaign of 1815* 1818

ed. Granville, Castalia, Countess of, *Lord Granville Leveson Gower, 1ˢᵗ Earl of Granville, Private Correspondence* 2 vols, 1916

Grehan, John, *The Lines of Torres Vedras* 2000

Greville, Charles, *A Journal of the Reigns of King George IV and King William IV* 3 vols, 1875

——, *A Journal of the Reign of Queen Victoria* 5 vols, 1885

ed. Griffith, Paddy, *Wellington – Commander: The Iron Duke's Generalship* 1987

——, *A History of the Peninsular War* vol. IX, 1999

Griffiths, Arthur J., *The Wellington Memorial* 1897

Gronow, Captain, *Reminiscences and Recollections* 2 vols, 1892

Guedalla, Philip, *Napoleon and Palestine* 1925

——, *The Hundred Days* 1934

Guérard, Albert, *Reflections on the Napoleonic Legend* 1924

——, *Napoleon I* 1957

Guerrini, Maurice, *Napoleon in Paris* 1967

Hamilton, Jill, *Marengo* 2000
Hamilton-Williams, David, *Waterloo: New Perspectives* 1993
——, *The Fall of Napoleon* 1994
Hamley, E. B., *Wellington's Career: A Summary* 1860
ed. Hanoteau, J., *Memoirs of General de Caulaincourt, Duke of Vicenza* 1935
ed. Hart-Davis, Rupert, *The Lyttelton Hart-Davis Letters: correspondence of George Lyttelton and Rupert Hart-Davis* 5 vols 1979–88
Harvey, A. D., *Collision of Empires* 1992
Haydon, Benjamin Robert, *Correspondence and Table Talk* 2 vols 1876
Hayman, Sir Peter, *Soult: Napoleon's Much Maligned Marshal* 1990
Haythornthwaite, Philip J., *Napoleon's Military Machine* 1988
——, *The Napoleonic Source Book* 1990
——, *The Armies of Wellington* 1998
——, *Who Was Who in the Napoleonic Wars* 1998
ed. Haythornthwaite, Philip J., *Napoleon: The Final Verdict* 1996
Head, C. O., *Napoleon and Wellington* 1939
Healey, F. G., *The Literary Culture of Napoleon* 1959
Henry, Eugene L., *Napoléon's War Maxims* 1899
Herold, J. C., *The Age of Napoleon* 1963
——, *Bonaparte in Egypt* 1963
ed. Herrick, C. T., *The Letters of the Duke of Wellington to Miss J. 1834–1851* 1903
Hibbert, Christopher, *Wellington: A Personal History* 1997
Hinard, Damas, *Dictionnaire-Napoléon* (Paris) 1854
Hofschröer, Peter, *1815 – The Waterloo Campaign: The German Victory* 1999
ed. Holland, Henry, *Foreign Reminiscences by Henry Richard Lord Holland* 1850
Holtman, Robert B., *Napoleonic Propaganda* (Baton Rouge) 1950
Hooper, George, *Waterloo and the Downfall of the First Napoleon* 1890
Horne, Alistair, *Napoleon: Master of Europe 1805–1807* 1979
——, *How Far from Austerlitz?: Napoleon 1805–1815* 1996
Horricks, R., *Marshal Ney* 1982
Horward, Donald D., *Napoleon and Iberia: The Twin Sieges of Ciudad Rodrigo and Almeida 1810* 1994
ed. Horward, Donald D., *The French Campaign in Portugal 1810–1811: An Account by Jean Jacques Pelet* (Minneapolis) 1973
Houssaye, Henry, *1815 – Waterloo* 1900
ed. Howard, Michael, *Wellington Studies* 1959
Howarth, David, *A Near Run Thing: The Day of Waterloo* 1968
Hughes-Hallett, Penelope, *The Immortal Dinner* 2000
ed. Ilchester, Earl of, *The Spanish Journal of Elizabeth, Lady Holland* 1910
——, *Henry Fox, 1ˢᵗ Lord Holland, his Family and Relations* 2 vols, 1920
——, *The Journal of the Hon. Henry Edward Fox 1818–1839* 1923
James, Lawrence, *The Iron Duke* 1992
——, *Raj: The Making and Unmaking of British India* 1997
ed. Jennings, Louis J., *The Croker Papers* 3 vols, 1885

Jerrold, Blanchard, *The Life of Napoleon III* 4 vols, 1874

Jones, Proctor Patterson, *Napoleon: An Intimate Account of the Years of Supremacy 1800–1814* 2000

ed. Jones, Proctor Patterson, *In Napoleon's Shadow: Complete Memoirs of Louis-Joseph Marchand 1811–1821* 1998

Kauffmann, C. M., *Catalogue of Paintings in the Wellington Museum* 1982

Keegan, Sir John, *The Face of Battle* 1976

——, *The Mask of Command* 1987

Kelly, William Hyde, *The Battle of Wavre and Grouchy's Retreat* 1905

Kemble, James, *Napoleon Immortal* 1959

Kennedy, Sir James Shaw, *Notes on the Battle of Waterloo* 1865

Kerry, Earl of, *The First Napoleon: Some Unpublished Documents from the Bowood Papers* 1925

Kincaid, Captain John, *Random Shots of a Rifleman* 1835

Kircheisen, F. M., *Memoirs of Napoleon I* 1929

——, *Napoleon* 1931

Knowles, Sir Lees, *A Gift of Napoleon* 1921

Korngold, Ralph, *The Last Years of Napoleon* 1960

Kurtz, H., *The Trial of Marshal Ney* 1957

Lachouque, Henri, *The Anatomy of Glory: Napoleon and his Guard* 1961

——, *The Last Days of Napoleon's Empire* 1966

Lanfrey, P., *The History of Napoleon the First* 4 vols, 1886

Las Cases, Emmanuel, le Comte de, *Mémorial de Sainte Hélène: Journal of the Private Life and Conversations of the Emperor Napoleon at Saint Helena* 4 vols, 1823

Lean, Edward Tangye, *The Napoleonists* 1970

ed. Lecestre, Léon, *Lettres Inédites de Napoléon I* 2 vols, 1897

Lefebvre, Georges, *Napoleon* 2 vols, 1969

Lemoinne, Jean, *Wellington from a French Point of View* 1852

ed. Le Strange, Guy, *Correspondence of Princess Lieven and Earl Grey* 3 vols, 1890

Lévy, Arthur, *Napoléon intime* 1893

Liddell Hart, Basil H., *The Ghost of Napoleon* 1933

Londonderry, 3rd Marquess of, *Narrative of the War in Germany and France in 1813 and 1814* 13 vols, 1830

——, *Correspondence, Despatches and Other Papers of Viscount Londonderry* 12 vols, 1853

Longford, Elizabeth, *Wellington: Years of the Sword* 1969

——, *Wellington: Pillar of State* 1972

Lucas-Dubreton, J., *The Restoration and the July Monarchy* 1929

Ludwig, Emil, *Napoleon* 1927

Lyons, Martyn, *Napoleon Bonaparte and the Legacy of the French Revolution* 1994

Macbride, Mackenzie, *With Napoleon at Waterloo* 1911

Maccun, F. J., *The Contemporary English View of Napoleon* 1914

Macdonell, A. G., *Napoleon and his Marshals* 1996

Mackenzie, Norman, *The Escape from Elba* 1982

Maclachlan, Archibald Neil, *Napoleon at Fontainebleau and Elba* 1869

Madelin, Louis, *The Consulate and the Empire 1799–1815* 2 vols, 1936

Maitland, Capt. Frederick, *Narrative of the Surrender of Buonaparte and of his residence on board HMS Bellerophon* 1826

Malmesbury, Earl of, *A Series of Letters* 2 vols, 1870

Mansel, Philip, *Louis XVIII* 1981

——, *The Eagle in Splendour* 1987

Markham, Felix, *Napoleon and the Awakening of Europe* 1954

——, *Napoleon* 1963

——, *The Bonapartes* 1975

Marmont, Marshal, *Mémoires* 1856–7

Marshall-Cornwall, General Sir James, *Napoleon as Military Commander* 1967

Martineau, Gilbert, *Napoleon's St Helena* 1968

——, *Napoleon Surrenders* 1971

——, *Napoleon's Last Journey* 1976

Masson, Frédéric, *Napoleon and the Fair Sex* 1894

——, *Napoleon at St Helena* 1949

Maxwell, Sir Herbert, *Life of Wellington* 3 vols, 1899

——, *The 4th Earl of Clarendon* 2 vols, 1913

ed. Maxwell, Sir Herbert, *The Creevey Papers* 2 vols, 1904

McErlean, J. M. P., *Napoleon and Pozzo di Borgo in Corsica and After 1764–1821* 1996

McLynn, Frank, *Napoleon* 1998

Menéval, Baron Claude-François de, *Memoirs* 2 vols, 1894

Mercer, General Cavalié, *Journal of the Waterloo Campaign* 1969

ed. Metternich, Prince Richard, *Memoirs of Prince Metternich* 5 vols, 1881

Meynell, Henry, *Conversations with Napoleon at St Helena* 1911

Mitchell, Lieut.-Col. J., *The Fall of Napoleon* 3 vols, 1845

Mitchell, L. G., *Lord Melbourne 1779–1848* 1997

Mitchell, S., *A Family Lawsuit: The Story of Elizabeth Patterson and Jerome Bonaparte* (New York) 1958

Montholon, General Count Charles-Tristan de, *History of the Captivity of Napoleon at St Helena* 4 vols, 1846

Morris, W. O'C., *Napoleon* 1893

Morton, J. B., *Brumaire: The Rise of Bonaparte* 1948

Müffling, Baron von, *Passages from my Life* 1853

Myer, Valerie, *Harriette Wilson: Lady of Pleasure* 1999

Napier, W. F. P., *History of the War in the Peninsula* 6 vols, 1840

Napoleon, *The Correspondence of Napoleon Bonaparte with his brother Joseph* 2 vols, 1855

——, *Supper at Beaucaire* 1945

Neillands, Robin, *Wellington and Napoleon: Clash of Arms 1807–1815* 1994

Nevill, Ralph, *Floreat Etona* 1911

Nicolson, Nigel, *Napoleon: 1812* 1985

ed. Nicoullaud, Charles, *The Memoirs of the Comtesse de Boigne* 1907

ed. North, Jonathan, *The Napoleon Options* 2000

Nosworthy, Brent, *Battle Tactics of Napoleon and his Enemies* 1995

Oman, Carola, *The Gascoygne Heiress* 1968

Oman, Sir Charles, *A History of the Peninsular War* 3 vols, 1902

——, *Studies in the Napoleonic Wars* 1929

——, *Wellington's Army 1809–14* 1968

O'Meara, Dr Barry, *Napoleon in Exile* 2 vols, 1822

Ortzen, Len, *Imperial Venus: The Story of Pauline Bonaparte Borghese* 1974

Paget, Sir Julian, *Wellington's Peninsular War* 1990

Palmer, Alan, *Napoleon in Russia* 1967

——, *Napoleon and Marie Louise* 2001

Park, Julian, *Napoleon in Captivity: The Reports of Count Balmain 1816–1870* 1927

ed. Partridge, Richard and Oliver, Michael, *Battle Studies in the Peninsula* 1998

Pérès, J. B., *Comme quoi Napoléon n'a jamais existé* 1909

Pericoli, Ugo, *1815: The Armies at Waterloo* 1973

ed. Picard, Ernest and Tuetey, Louis, *Correspondance inédite de Napoléon 1ᵉʳ* 5 vols, 1913

ed. Plon, Henri and Dumaire, J., *Correspondance de Napoléon 1ᵉʳ* vols 17–32, 1865–70

ed. Pope, Willard Bissell, *The Diary of Benjamin Robert Haydon* 5 vols (Cambridge, Mass.) 1963

Pougin, Arthur, *Giuseppina Grassini* (Paris) 1920

ed. Quennell, Peter, *The Private Letters of Princess Lieven to Prince Metternich 1820–1826* 1937

ed. Raikes, Harriet, *Private Correspondence of Thomas Raikes with the Duke of Wellington and other Distinguished Contemporaries* 1861

Raikes, Thomas, *Portions of the Journal of Thomas Raikes* 4 vols, 1857

Ratcliffe, Bertram, *Marshal de Grouchy and the Guns of Waterloo* 1942

Reiche, General L. von, *Memoiren* (Leipzig) 1857

ed. Rémusat, Paul de, *Memoirs of Madame de Rémusat* 2 vols, 1880

Richardson, Hubert, *A Dictionary of Napoleon and his Times* 1920

Ridley, Jasper, *The Freemasons* 1999

Roberts, General Lord, *The Rise of Wellington* 1895

Robinson, C. W., *Wellington's Campaigns* 1907

Rogers, Samuel, *Recollections* 1859

Ropes, J. C., *The Campaign of Waterloo* 1892

Rose, J. Holland, *Napoleonic Studies* 1904

——, *The Personality of Napoleon* 1912

——, *The Life of Napoleon I* 1913

Rosebery, Earl of, *Napoleon: The Last Phase* 1900

ed. Rousseau, I. J., *The Peninsular Journal of Major-General Sir Benjamin D'Urban* 1930

ed. Rousset, Camille, *Recollections of Marshal Macdonald* 1892

Rudé, George, *Revolutionary Europe 1783–1815* 1967

Rush, Richard, *A Residence at the Court of London* 1833

Salmon, Lucy, *The Newspaper and the Historian* 1923

Saunders, Edith, *Napoleon and Mademoiselle George* 1958
——, *The Hundred Days* 1964
Schom, Alan, *One Hundred Days* 1993
——, *Napoleon Bonaparte* 1998
Scott, Sir Walter, *Paul's Letters to his Kinfolk* 1816
Ségur, General Count Philippe-Paul de, *History of the Expedition to Russia Undertaken by the Emperor Napoleon in the Year 1812* 2 vols, 1825
——, *An Aide-de-Camp of Napoleon* 1895
Seward, Desmond, *Napoleon's Family* 1986
——, *Napoleon and Hitler* 1988
——, *Metternich: The First European* 1991
Shorter, Clement, *Napoleon and his Defence* 1910
Siborne, Herbert, *Waterloo Letters* 1891
Siborne, William, *History of the War in France and Belgium* 2 vols, 1844
——, *The Waterloo Campaign* 1904
Sisman, Adam, *Boswell's Presumptuous Task* 2000
Smiles, Samuel, *Self-Help* 1859
Smith, Digby, *1813: Leipzig* 2000
Smith, E. A., *Wellington and the Arbuthnots* 1994
Stacton, David, *The Bonapartes* 1966
Stanhope, 5th Earl, *Notes of Conversations with the Duke of Wellington 1831–1851* 1888
ed. Stavordale, Lord, *Further Memoirs of the Whig Party 1807–1821* 1905
Stevens, Joan, *Victorian Voices* 1969
Stirling, A. M. W., *Coke of Norfolk and his Friends* 2 vols, 1908
Stirling, Monica, *A Pride of Lions: A Portrait of Napoleon's Mother* 1961
Stirling, William, *Napoleon's Bequest to Cantillon* 1858
Stockdale, John Joseph, *The Proceedings of the Enquiry into the Armistice and Convention of Cintra and into the Conduct of the Officers Concerned* 1809
ed. Strafford, Alice, Countess of, *Personal Reminiscences of the Duke of Wellington by Francis, 1ˢᵗ Earl of Ellesmere* 1904
Strawson, John, *The Duke and the Emperor* 1994
Sutherland, Christine, *Marie Walewska* 1986
Tarlé, Eugene, *Bonaparte* 1937
Tennyson, Alfred, Lord, *Ode on the Death of the Duke of Wellington* 1852
Thiers, L. A., *Histoire du Consulat et de l'Empire* vols XII, XVIII and XX, 1845
Thompson, J. M., *Napoleon Self-Revealed* 1934
——, *Napoleon Bonaparte: His Rise and Fall* 1952
ed. Thompson, J. M., *Napoleon's Letters* 1998
Thompson, Neville, *Wellington after Waterloo* 1986
——, *Earl Bathurst and the British Empire 1762–1834* 1999
Thrasher, Peter Adam, *Pasquale Paoli: An Enlightened Hero 1725–1807* 1970
Tolstoy, Leo, *War and Peace* 1869
Tone, John L., *The Fatal Knot: The Guerilla War in Navarre and the Defeat of Napoleon* (Chapel Hill) 1996

Tulard, Jean, *Napoleon: The Myth of the Saviour* 1984

ed. Tulard, Jean, *Cambacérès: lettres inédites à Napoléon 1802–1814* (Paris) 2 vols, 1973

Uffindell, Andrew and Corum, Michael, *The Eagle's Last Triumph: Napoleon's Victory at Ligny* 1994

Uffindell, Andrew, *On the Fields of Glory* 1996

Valentia, 9th Viscount, George Annesley, *Voyages and Travels to India, Ceylon, the Red Sea, Abyssinia and Egypt in the Years 1802–6* 4 vols, 1809

Ward, S. G. P., *Wellington's Headquarters* 1957

Warden, William, *Letters from St Helena* 1817

Warre, Sir William, *Letters from the Peninsula 1808–1812* 1909

Watersburg, Count Yorck von, *Napoleon as a General* 2 vols, 1902

Watson, S. J., *By Command of the Emperor: A Life of Marshal Berthier* 1988

Weider, Ben, *Napoleon: The Man Who Shaped Europe* 2000

Weider, Ben and Hapgood, David, *The Murder of Napoleon* 1983

ed. Weigall, Lady Rose, *The Letters of Lady Burghersh* 1893

——, *Correspondence of Lady Burghersh with the Duke of Wellington* 1903

Weiner, M., *The Parvenu Princesses* 1964

Weller, Jac, *Wellington in the Peninsula 1808–14* 1962

——, *Wellington at Waterloo* 1967

——, *Wellington in India* 1972

——, *On Wellington: The Duke and his Art of War* 2000

Wellesley, F. A., *The Diary and Correspondence of Henry Wellesley, First Lord Cowley 1790–1846* 1930

Wellesley, Muriel, *Wellington in Civil Life* 1939

Wellington, Evelyn, Duchess of, *A Descriptive and Historical Catalogue of Pictures and Sculpture at Apsley House, London* 2 vols, 1901

Wellington, 1st Duke of, *My Dear Mrs Jones* 1954

Wellington, 7th Duke of, *The Conversations of the 1ˢᵗ Duke of Wellington with George William Chad* 1956

——, *Wellington and his Friends* 1965

Wellington, 7th Duke of and Steegman, John, *The Iconography of the First Duke of Wellington* 1935

Werner, Jack, *We Laughed at Boney* 1943

Whately, R., *Historic Doubts Relative to Napoleon Bonaparte* 1849

ed. Wilson, Sir Arthur, *A Diary of St Helena: The Journal of Lady Malcolm 1816–17* 1899

Wilson, Harriette, *The Memoirs of Harriette Wilson* 2 vols, 1909

Woloch, Isser, *The New Regime* 1994

Woolf, Stuart, *Napoleon's Integration of Europe* 1991

ed. Woolgar, C. M., *Wellington Studies* 1996

Wootten, Geoffrey, *Waterloo 1815* 1992

Young, Julian Charles, *A Memoir of Charles Mayne Young* 2 vols, 1871

Young, Norwood, *The Growth of Napoleon* 1910

——, *Napoleon in Exile at St Helena* 1915

Ziegler, Philip, *The Duchess of Dino* 1962
——, *Addington* 1965

ARTICLES

Anon, 'Napoleon's Horse, Marengo' *Illustrated London News* 1 October 1892

Chandler, G. G., 'Napoleon's Battle System' *History Today* February 1965

Ebrington, Lord, 'A Conversation with Napoleon at Elba' *Macmillan's Magazine* December 1894

Esdaile, Charles, 'The Napoleonic Period: Some Thoughts on Recent Historiography' *European History Quarterly* vol. 23 (1993)

——, 'The Peninsular War: A Review of Recent Literature' *Historian* no. 64 Winter 1999

Forester, C. S., 'Could Napoleon have Won?' *History Today* January 1953

Fraser, Sir David, 'Wellington and the Waterloo Campaign' 7th Wellington Lecture, University of Southampton 1995

Glover, Michael, 'The Lavellette Affair, 1815' *History Today* November 1977

——, 'The Courtesies of War in Napoleonic Spain' *History Today* July 1978

Gray, D. S., 'An Audience of One: Sir Neil Campbell on Napoleon' *History Today* September 1974

Greenhalgh, Michael, 'The Funeral of the Duke of Wellington' *Apollo* September 1953

Haythornthwaite, Philip, 'That Unlucky War: Some Aspects of the French Experience in the Peninsula' in ed. Ian Fletcher, *The Peninsular War* 1998

Hill, Douglas, 'Chateaubriand and Napoleon' *History Today* December 1973

Hindmarsh, J. Thomas and Corso, Philip F., 'The Death of Napoleon Bonaparte: A Critical Review of the Cause' *Journal of the History of Medicine* vol. 53 July 1998

Honour, Hugh, 'Canova's Napoleon' *Apollo* September 1973

Horward, Donald D., 'Wellington as a Strategist 1808–14' in ed. Norman Gash, *Wellington: Studies in the Military and Political Career of the First Duke of Wellington* 1990

Hussey, John, 'Müffling, Gleig, Ziethen and the "Missing" Wellingtonian Records: The "Compromising" Documents Traced' *Journal of the Society for Army Historical Research* 77 no. 312 Winter 1999

Le May, G. H., 'A Conversation with Napoleon at St Helena' *History Today* November 1951 ed. Maxwell, Sir Herbert, 'More Light on St Helena' *Cornhill Magazine* February 1901

Oman, Sir Charles, 'The Hundred Days' *Cambridge Modern History* vol. IX 1906

Pears, Iain, 'The Gentleman and the Hero: Wellington and Napoleon in the Nineteenth Century' in ed. Roy Porter, *Myths of the English* 1992

Richardson, Joanna, 'Creevey and Greville: Two Diarists' *History Today* October 1973

Ridgeley, Paul, 'Wellington's Funeral' *The Waterloo Journal* vol. 21 no. 3 December 1999

Rowe, Michael, 'Between Empire and Home Town: Napoleonic Rule on the Rhine 1799–1814' *Historical Journal* vol. 42. no. 3 1999

Semmel, Stuart, 'Reading the Tangible Past: British Tourism, Collecting and Memory after Waterloo' *University of California Press Representations* Winter 2000

——, 'British Radicals and "Legitimacy": Napoleon in the Mirror of History' *Past and Present* no. 1999 167

ed. Thompson, C. W., 'Napoleon's Journey to St Helena' *Blackwood's Magazine* October 1896

Thompson, Neville, 'The Unpredictable Rise of the Duke of Wellington' *Historian* no. 64 Winter 1999

Tugan-Baranovsky, D. M., 'Napoleon as a Journalist' *Napoleonic Scholarship* vol. 1 no. 2 December 1998

Uffindell, Andrew, 'Could Napoleon Have Won?' British Army Review no. 118 April 1998

Webster, Sir Charles, 'Some Letters of the Duke of Wellington to his Brother William Wellesley-Pole' *Camden Miscellany* vol. 18 3rd series no. 79 1948

Wellington, 7th Duke of, 'The Great Duke's Funeral' *History Today* November 1952

INDEX